Theories of Race and Ethnicity

How have research agendas on race and ethnicity changed over the past two decades, and what new developments have emerged? *Theories of Race and Ethnicity* provides a comprehensive and cutting-edge collection of theoretically grounded and empirically informed chapters. It covers a range of key issues in race and ethnicity studies, such as genetics and race, post-race debates, racial eliminativism and the legacy of Barack Obama and mixed race identities. The contributions are by leading writers covering a range of perspectives employed in studying ethnicity and race, including critical race feminism, critical rationalism, psycho-analysis, performativity, whiteness studies and sexuality. Written in an authoritative yet accessible style, this volume is suitable for research-ers and advanced students, offering scholars a survey of the state of the art in the literature and students an overview of the field.

KARIM MURJI is based in the Department of Sociology at the Open University.

JOHN SOLOMOS is Professor of Sociology at the University of Warwick, where he is also head of department.

Theories of Race and Ethnicity

Contemporary Debates and Perspectives

Edited by

Karim Murji and John Solomos

CAMBRIDGE
UNIVERSITY PRESS

CAMBRIDGE
UNIVERSITY PRESS

University Printing House, Cambridge CB2 8BS, United Kingdom

Cambridge University Press is part of the University of Cambridge.

It furthers the University's mission by disseminating knowledge in the pursuit of
education, learning and research at the highest international levels of excellence.

www.cambridge.org
Information on this title: www.cambridge.org/9780521154260

First published 2015

A catalogue record for this publication is available from the British Library

ISBN 978-0-521-76373-8 Hardback
ISBN 978-0-521-15426-0 Paperback

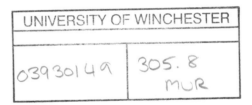

Contents

Part II: PERSPECTIVES

Notes on contributors

Editors

KARIM MURJI is based in the Department of Sociology at the Open University, United Kingdom, where he has contributed to a wide range of inter-disciplinary teaching in the social sciences. He has more than 80 publications in cultural and policy studies of ethnicity and racism and of criminology. He has edited two journal special issues, most recently, with Gargi Bhattacharyya, a special issue of *Ethnic and Racial Studies* on 'Race Critical Public Scholarship' (vol. 36, no. 9, 2013). With John Solomos, he is the editor of *Racialization: Studies in Theory and Practice* (2005). He is an editor of the journal *Sociology*.

JOHN SOLOMOS is professor and head of the Department of Sociology at the University of Warwick. He has researched and written widely on the history and contemporary forms of race and ethnic relations in Britain, theories of race and racism, the politics of race, equal opportunity policies, multiculturalism and social policy, race and football, and racist movements and ideas. His most recent book is *Transnational Families: Ethnicities, Identities and Social Capital* (with Harry Goulbourne, Tracey Reynolds and Elisabetta Zontini, 2010). He has also co-edited *The Sage Handbook of Race and Ethnic Studies* (with Patricia Hill Collins, 2010), *Race and Ethnicity in the 21st Century* (with Alice Bloch, 2010) and *Theories of Race and Racism: A Reader* (with Les Back, 2nd edn, 2009). He is joint editor with Martin Bulmer of the international journal *Ethnic and Racial Studies*.

Other contributors

MICHAEL BANTON is Professor Emeritus of Sociology at the University of Bristol. He taught social anthropology at the University of Edinburgh, 1954–65; political science at the Massachusetts Institute of Technology, 1962–63; and sociology at the University of Bristol, 1965–92. From 1986 to 2001, he was a member of the United Nations

Committee on the Elimination of Racial Discrimination (Chairman, 1996–98). His books include *The Coloured Quarter* (1955), *West African City* (1957), *The Policeman in the Community* (1964), *Race Relations* (1967), *The Idea of Race* (1977), *Racial and Ethnic Competition* (1983), *Racial Theories* (1987; 2nd edn, 1997), *International Action against Racial Discrimination* (1996), *Ethnic and Racial Consciousness* (1997) and *The International Politics of Race* (2002).

LEAH BASSEL is a New Blood Lecturer in Sociology at the University of Leicester. Her research interests include the political sociology of gender, migration, race and citizenship and intersectionality. She is the author of *Refugee Women: Beyond Gender versus Culture* (2012), and her work has also been published in journals, including *Politics and Gender, Ethnicities, Government and Opposition* and *French Politics*. She is an assistant editor of the journal *Citizenship Studies*.

EDUARDO BONILLA-SILVA is chair and professor of sociology at Duke University. His first article, 'Rethinking racism: toward a structural interpretation', appeared in the *American Sociological Review* in 1996 and challenged social analysts to abandon the prejudice problematic and anchor race analysis structurally. His books include *White Supremacy and Racism in the Post–Civil Rights Era* (2001), *White Out: The Continuing Significance of Racism* (2003), *Racism without Racists* (2003), *White Logic, White Methods: Racism and Methodology* (2008) and *The State of White Supremacy: Racism, Governance, and the United States* (2011). Recently, he has worked on the idea that racial stratification in the USA is becoming Latin America–like, on a critique of Obama and the post-racial logic that orients his politics and on a book tentatively titled *The Racial Grammar of Everyday Life in America*.

SIMON CLARKE is a founding member of the Centre for Psycho-Social Studies at the University of the West of England and consulting editor of *Psychoanalysis, Culture and Society*. He is the author of many publications, including *Social Theory, Psychoanalysis and Racism* (2003), *From Enlightenment to Risk: Social Theory and Contemporary Society* (2005), *Emotion, Politics and Society* (2006) and *White Identities: A Critical Sociological Approach* (2010). His current research interests focus on ethnic identity and emotional communities.

ÉRIC FASSIN is professor of sociology in the Department of Political Science and the Gender Studies programme at Paris 8 University (after 18 years at the École Normale Supérieure and 5 at New York University), affiliated with the research centre IRIS (CNRS/EHESS). His work focuses on contemporary sexual and racial politics in France and the United States and their intersections (in particular concerning immigration in Europe). He is frequently involved in French public debates on issues which his work addresses – from gay marriage and gender parity to the politics of immigration and race. He is the author of *Le sexe politique* (2009) and co-author (with the collective Cette France-là) of four volumes on French immigration policies (2008–12). He co-edited *De la question sociale à la question raciale?* (2006). His latest book is *Démocratie précaire. Chroniques de la déraison d'État* (2012). He is currently at work on *Actualité d'Aimé Césaire* and *The Empire of Sexual Democracy*.

CHARLES A. GALLAGHER is professor and chair of the Department of Sociology and Criminal Justice at La Salle University in Philadelphia, Pennsylvania, USA. His research focuses on social inequality, race relations and immigration, and he has published more than 50 articles, reviews and books on these topics. His scholarship examines the ways in which the media, state policy and popular culture construct, shape and disseminate ideas of race and social mobility. His most recent books include *Being Brown in Dixie: Race, Ethnicity and Latino Immigration in the New South* (with Cameron Lippard, 2011) and *Retheorizing Race and Whiteness in the 21st Century* (with France Winddance Twine, 2012). As a nationally recognised expert on race and social inequality, Professor Gallagher has given more than 50 talks on these topics around the United States and is a frequent media source for these topics, having appeared in the press, on television and in radio interviews more than 80 times. He is currently doing comparative research on whites' attitudes on immigration policy in the United Kingdom and the USA.

DAVID THEO GOLDBERG is director of the system-wide University of California Humanities Research Institute and executive director of the MacArthur–UCI Research Hub in Digital Media and Learning, the international centre coordinating all research for the MacArthur Foundation initiative in connected learning. He is a professor in comparative literature, in anthropology and in criminology, law and society at the University of California, Irvine. He has written extensively on digital media's impact on higher education, race and racism, law and society and critical theory. His recent books include *The Threat of Race* (2009) and *The Future of Thinking* (with Cathy Davidson, 2010).

MATTHEW W. HUGHEY earned his doctorate in sociology from the University of Virginia and is currently associate professor of sociology

at the University of Connecticut. A scholar of racial identity formation, racialised organisations and the intersection of race and the mass
media, Hughey has published an array of scholarly articles and several books, including *The White Savior Film: Content, Critics and Consumption* (2014), *White Bound: Nationalists, Antiracists and the Shared
Meanings of Race* (2012) and *The Obamas and a (Post) Racial America?*
(2011).

SANDRA SOO-JIN LEE is a medical anthropologist at the Center for
Biomedical Ethics and a faculty affiliate in the Science, Technology and
Society programme at Stanford University, whose research focuses on
the sociocultural dimensions and ethical issues of emerging genomic
technologies and their translation into biomedical practice. She is co-
editor of *Revisiting Race in a Genomic Age* (with Barbara A. Konig
and Sarah S. Richardson, 2008) and is currently writing a book that
examines modern American values in the context of the translation
of human genetic variation research. She is the recipient of several
National Institutes of Health grant awards, including for her current
project, 'Social networking and personal genomics: implications for
health research' (grant R01HG005086-01), which examines public
interpretation of personal genetic information and sharing practices.
She received her undergraduate degree in human biology from Stanford University and her doctorate in medical anthropology from the
University of California, Berkeley and San Francisco Joint Program.

VICTOR E. RAY is a doctoral candidate in sociology at Duke University
and an American Sociological Association Minority Fellow. His work
has appeared in a number of journals, including the *Journal of African
American Studies*, the *Journal of Marriage and Family* and *Contexts*.
His dissertation research, supported by the Ford Foundation and the
National Science Foundation, focuses on how race and gender shape
the transition to civilian life for veterans of the Iraq and Afghanistan
conflicts. Using qualitative interviews, he explores how the possible
mental health effects of life in a combat zone affect the daily lives of
veterans as they reintegrate into work and family.

MIRI SONG is professor of sociology at the University of Kent. Her research interests include race and racisms, ethnic identity, mixed race
and second-generation integration. She is currently working on a Lev-
erhulme Trust–funded project on the ways in which multiracial parents
identify and raise their children in Britain. She is the author of *Helping Out: Children's Labor in Ethnic Businesses* (1999), *Choosing Ethnic
Identity* (2003) and *Mixed Race Identities* (with Peter Aspinall, 2013).

BRETT ST LOUIS is senior lecturer in sociology at Goldsmiths, University of London. He is the author of *Rethinking Race, Politics and Poetics: C. L. R. James' Critique of Modernity* (2007). He is currently writing a book on racial eliminativism.

SHIRLEY ANNE TATE is associate professor in race and culture in the School of Sociology and Social Policy at the University of Leeds. Her research focuses particularly on the body, affect, work, 'race' performativity, 'mixed race' and post-coloniality. She has published widely in these areas in both the United Kingdom and Europe, and her books *Black Skins, Black Masks: Hybridity, Dialogism, Performativity* (2005) and *Black Beauty: Aesthetics, Stylization, Politics* (2009) take up these preoccupations.

ADRIEN K. WING is the Bessie Dutton Murray Distinguished Professor of Law at the University of Iowa College of Law, where she has taught since 1987. Author of more than 100 publications, she is the editor of *Critical Race Feminism* (2003) and *Global Critical Race Feminism: An International Reader* (2000). Her research focuses on the intersection of race/ethnicity and gender, specifically the legal rights of women of colour. Her regional interests include the Middle East, Africa and black America.

Preface

The process of developing and seeing an edited collection such as this one through to publication is inevitably longer than planned and sometimes tortuous. We started talking about the project initially when we felt that there was a need for more sustained discussion of the changing research agendas on race and ethnic relations that have emerged over the past two decades or so. As active participants in some of the debates, we had some understanding of key facets of these new agendas, but we saw a need for a collection of original chapters that explored key issues in more depth. It is with this overarching concern in mind that we started the process of bringing together the various contributions that make up this collection. As we talked, we felt that there were certain key areas of debate that have emerged over the past 20 years or more that we wanted to represent in this collection, and we have grouped these chapters in Part I. We also wanted to include a wide range of chapters that reflected developments within specific fields of scholarship; these are grouped together in Part II. We recognise that some themes and issues cannot be covered within the confines of a collection such as this one. This is partly why we have decided to include two substantive chapters by ourselves, as editors, which work both to provide the background to the issues that are covered in the book and to take a look forward at likely trends and developments in the future. We hope that the 15 chapters that make up this collection can help to encourage further debate and reflection at a time when questions about race and racism seem likely to continue to influence both political discourses and actions in civil society.

As editors, we are grateful to all the authors who have stuck with the project from the beginning. Without the hard work of the various authors, such a project would not be possible. We have also accumulated a number of debts for support, advice and intellectual stimulation during the time we have been working on this collection. In alphabetical order, we would like to say thank you to a number of people who have discussed this with us and encouraged us along the way: Claire Alexander, Les Back, Michael Banton, Gargi Bhattacharyya, Alice Bloch, Martin

Bulmer, Milena Chimienti, Patricia Hill Collins, Max Farrar, Paul Gilroy, Vicki Harman, Michael Keith, Marco Martiniello, Nasar Meer, Sarah Neal, Liza Schuster, Stephen Small, Satnam Virdee and Aaron Winter. We also thank the anonymous reviewers of the initial proposal and the manuscript for their suggestions and support for the book. We are also grateful to John Haslam and Carrie Parkinson from Cambridge University Press for their patience and understanding about the unavoidable delays such a project seems to involve.

KARIM MURJI
Open University

JOHN SOLOMOS
University of Warwick

1 Introduction: situating the present

Karim Murji and John Solomos

When we started a conversation about putting together an edited collection on *Theories of Race and Ethnicity*, we had in mind the need for a more up-to-date overview of the field of race and ethnic studies than the one provided in John Rex and David Mason's (1986) *Theories of Race and Ethnic Relations*. That volume had come out in the mid 1980s, after a period of passionate, and often conflictual, debate about the changing boundaries of the study of race and ethnicity. Rex's opening statement to his chapter provided a sense of this contestation. He wrote, 'The study of race relations, in common with other politically charged areas in the social sciences, seems beset with feuds and conflicts of a quite theological intensity' (Rex 1986: 64). The book set out to provide an overview of key theoretical lines of analysis in the field and to engage with some new and emergent perspectives. It contained 14 chapters covering the disciplines of sociology, social anthropology and social psychology as well as sociobiology. There were macro-level approaches to race and ethnicity drawing on class analysis, the study of plural societies and Weberian and Marxist perspectives, alongside micro-level approaches such as rational choice theory and symbolic interactionism. In other words, it combined and crossed over from traditional sociological perspectives to views from related social science disciplines; it ranged across biology and sociology, and it considered ethnicity and race in a variety of settings.

In hindsight, it is also worth recalling that the Rex and Mason volume came out at a relatively early stage in the emergence of race as a distinct field of scholarship and research within the contours of British sociology and that sociology led most other social science disciplines in engaging with race and ethnicity. While social anthropology focused mainly on the study of societies and communities in Africa and Asia, and social psychology was concerned with issues of prejudice, there had been relatively little research in this field before the 1960s. When the British Sociological Association held its 1969 annual conference on the theme of 'Race

Relations', it was more as a statement of intent than as an indication of the centrality of the study of race and racism within British sociology (Zubaida 1970a, 1972). There was a noticeable development of research on race issues during the 1970s and 1980s, particularly as a result of support from the Social Science Research Council (which was later renamed the Economic and Social Research Council, ESRC) (Banton, n.d.; ESRC 2007). Despite this expansion of research and a broadening of research agendas through the 1980s, publication of the Rex and Mason collection came at a time when scholars were searching for new conceptual tools to further our understanding of key facets of race relations in contemporary societies (Banton 1991; Brotz 1983).

The current volume inevitably shares a number of common elements with its predecessor, which should signal that, although there are considerable changes in social theorising and debates around race, some of the same questions and issues continue to recur. However, the context of scholarly work on race has, in many ways, been transformed in the time-lapse between the two books. By the time we started to think about our edited volume, well over two decades had passed since the publication of the Rex and Mason volume. In this period, new theoretical models emerged, often inflected by wide-ranging political and social mobilisations and changes in the world and civil society. Characterised initially by an engagement with Marxism and post-Marxism, such perspectives were also influenced by the wider cultural wars around feminism, cultural studies, post-structuralism, critical race theory and post-colonial theory (Back and Solomos 2009; Essed and Goldberg 2002; Goldberg and Solomos 2002). As a result, we have seen a rapid expansion of both theoretical and empirically focused research on race and ethnic relations; although this includes research that has a more global and comparative frame, there is still, however, a significant degree of methodological nationalism in studies of ethnicity and race.

We felt, therefore, that there was a need for a volume that would both reflect on the changing boundaries of race and ethnic studies and bring together in a single volume a diverse range of viewpoints and perspectives. It is with this overarching idea that we began work on this book. As, unfortunately, some contributors could not deliver their chapters according to our original plan, we had to make changes to the structure of the book; this has also led to some lacunae, which we have sought to fill by means of the introductory and concluding chapters that we have crafted as editors of the volume. Nevertheless, we hope that the end result provides an accessible resource for both scholars and students alike and engages with a range of audiences.

History and context

The study of race and ethnic relations has been part of the social sciences since the beginning of the twentieth century and the work of sociologists such as W. E. B. Du Bois, Robert Park and E. Franklin Frazier (Du Bois 1903; Frazier 1947, 1968; Park 1950). In the aftermath of these classic studies, in the period both before and after the Second World War, a number of approaches to the sociological study of race and ethnicity started to take shape. This is not the place to retrace that history or to evaluate the impact of these approaches, because our focus here is on the past four decades rather than on the historical background to the growth of this field of research. It is worth emphasising, however, that a wealth of research and theoretical reflection about race and ethnicity forms the background, to some extent, to the more recent controversies that are the concern of this chapter (Collins 2007; Stanfield 1993; Stanfield and Dennis 1993; Winant 2007). Yet it is also clear that, even in the American sociological tradition, the study of race, racism and ethnicity remained a relatively marginal sub-field of scholarship in sociology and anthropology and did not exercise much influence in other disciplines for a significant period of time.

It was only in the aftermath of the civil rights and black power movements in the 1950s and 1960s, and of the student unrest and race riots of the 1960s, that the study of race and racism became an important field of research in American sociology as well as in other disciplines (Blauner 2002; Bonilla-Silva 1997; Omi and Winant 1994). Its broad parameters have been shaped by the publication of both theoretical and empirical research, the work of key scholars and thinkers. Empirically, such research focused on issues of racial inequality, institutional racism and patterns of racialised discrimination. Initially framed by the neglect of race in debates about integration via the ethnic 'melting pot' debates (Glazer and Moynihan 1963), such work has developed to ask about the 'declining/continuing significance of race' (Wilson 2012) in the USA and, furthermore, to explore the contours of contemporary racisms (Bonilla-Silva 2001; Winant 2001). In Britain and other parts of Europe, the impact and consequences of post-war and post-colonial migration, as well as the ongoing and deepening struggles around unequal development and exploitation between the northern and southern hemispheres of the globe, provided important spurs to research on race and racism. Thus, it is now evident that the study of race and ethnic relations has become an established part of both the teaching and the scholarly culture of a number of disciplines in the social sciences and humanities.

A proliferation of books and specialised journals since the final decade of the twentieth century has been the basis on which we have seen the emergence of a growing number of undergraduate and post-graduate courses on race and ethnic relations. These transformations have been evident in the USA, through the growth of university departments of ethnic studies, African American studies and Asian studies, among others. But there has also been a noticeable expansion in research and scholarship in this field at a more global level, across a range of disciplines and in terms of both conceptual analysis and empirical research.

The study of race, racism and ethnic relations has been transformed quite markedly over the past three decades since the Rex and Mason volume. This is reflected in the wide range of approaches and empirical research studies that have helped to shape this field of academic and policy research. In this introductory chapter, we want to explore how new research agendas and debates have helped to transform this field of scholarship and research, which new perspectives have come to the fore in recent years and the impact of these transformations on the setting of research priorities. In exploring these issues, the chapter also explores the question of which key theoretical and empirical issues need to be addressed in developing both current and future research agendas. A particular theme that runs through the chapter is the need to rethink both the boundaries of this research field and how to make our research agendas relevant to current political and civil society debates.

Surveys of current scholarship and research have noted this expansion and also highlighted the diversity of conceptual perspectives that have come to the fore in recent years. We have seen intense debate in sociology and other disciplines about the role of race and ethnicity as categories of social analysis, the role of racism in contemporary politics and culture and the impact of migration processes and multiculture on national and social cohesion. Certainly, in the context of Britain and, in different ways, other European societies, questions about race, ethnicity and religious differences have become a recurring theme in both academic discourses and wider policy and political debates. It is in relation to this changing environment and political context that our chapter outlines some key points about theorisations of race and racism in contemporary social theory. This is an important issue to include in any analysis of theories of race and ethnic differences, because it seems evident that questions about race and ethnicity are inevitably part of political discourses as well as embedded in academic and scholarly research.

Changing theories, perspectives and debates

The study of ethnic and racial relations has seen many transformations in the period since the 1960s. From being a relatively small field of research and scholarship – with the possible exception of sociological analysis in the USA – there has been noticeable growth, as we noted earlier. The past three decades since the Rex and Mason (1986) volume have seen the development of a diverse range of research occurring across the globe on aspects of race and ethnic diversity. These changes in research agendas are in many ways not surprising, because these decades have witnessed intense social and political debate about race and ethnic issues in various parts of the globe. It is because of this changing geopolitical and social environment that we have seen strong arguments about the boundaries of what it is that we study when we research race and ethnicity in the contemporary environment. Thus, researching questions about race, ethnicity and racism inevitably draws scholars into questions about the nature of the social, cultural and economic realities that are being examined (Goldberg and Solomos 2002).

The role of racial and ethnic differences in British society has been a source of policy and scholarly debate since the 1960s, including landmark surveys of racial discrimination (Rose 1969) and the emergence of sociological attention to race and racism (Banton 1967; Rex 1970; Zubaida 1970b). In terms of public policy, this has been evident in the development of policies aimed at controlling immigration and promoting the social and cultural integration of racial and ethnic minorities, in anti-discrimination legislation aimed at tackling racism and in the promotion of a multicultural idea of Britain. This mixture of measures to integrate minorities while expanding legal controls over potential new migrants has been regarded as the 'liberal hour' in British politics (Rich 1990). These debates marked a growing political and scholarly awareness of Britain as an increasingly complex multicultural society; the intensity of public debates about issues such as immigration, race-relations policies and the changing boundaries of Britishness and national identity in the 1970s are captured in two landmark books, *Policing the Crisis* (Hall et al. 1978) and *The Empire Strikes Back* (Centre for Contemporary Cultural Studies 1982), along with Barker's (1981) analysis of 'the new racism'.

This is not to say that discussion and dispute about race and ethnicity can be seen simply as the product of recent developments and changes. Indeed, part of the expanding scope of ethnic and racial scholarship has been the opening up of historical research framed by Britain's role as a major global power and territorial empire over a number of centuries.

Issues of race and difference have, in this sense, been part of its national history and culture. Ongoing debates about transatlantic slavery, the role of William Wilberforce on the 200th anniversary of the abolition of slavery in Britain and the memorial to slaves in the city of Bristol, in addition to the reaction to 'foreigners' over the decades, attest to this (Rice 2003; Winder 2005). These issues are now part of a rich body of historical work which has analysed the ways in which ideas about race have taken shape in specific societal and political environments (Hall 2002; Panayi 2010). Although other analyses of the legacies of European and Western colonialism provide additional examples of racial formations in various contexts, there is a sense that much contemporary social science literature on race and racism remains somewhat national in focus. This has resulted in a lack of reflexivity about the historical background to the emergence of modern racism and a failure to come to terms with the transformations of racial ideologies and practices over time and space. Yet what is also evident is that, without a clear understanding of the historical context, it is unlikely that we shall be able to fully come to terms with the question of how racial ideas have emerged out of and become an integral part of specific societies and how they operate across national and international boundaries.

For the purposes of this chapter, however, the primary focus is on the contemporary period, specifically on how questions about race and ethnic relations have been discussed within academic discourses and beyond. The study of race, racism and ethnicity has become a core theme in the British sociological tradition in the period since the 1980s. The work of key scholars such as Michael Banton and John Rex helped to establish the study of race and ethnicity within British sociology during the 1960s and 1970s (Banton 2001; Small and Solomos 2006). The expansion of scholarly research and debate which followed brought the study of race from the margins to nearer to the centre of sociological concerns in the United Kingdom. Such work was often influenced by radical and Marxist forms of sociological theory and shaped by the political and social transformations that marked the global economic crisis of the 1970s, and the ways in which race, migration and crime were often linked in popular and political racist discourses (Hall et al. 1978; Miles and Phizacklea 1984). Events such as the urban riots of the 1980s (Benyon and Solomos 1987; Keith 1993); new patterns of migration and minority formation, including the emergence of 'new ethnicities' (Cohen 1999; Hall 1988); and new racist movements and public tensions about religious and cultural diversity and multiculturalism, initially after the Rushdie affair in 1989 and, more intensely, since 9/11 and 7/7 (Lentin and Titley 2011; Modood 2005; Rattansi 2007), have all been significant in influencing new scholarship and public debate around the politics of difference, Islamophobia and changing patterns of ethnic and racial identification and racism in Britain. While reflections on the relationship between race and religion, owing to the controversies around Islam, have become significant, there has also been continued and renewed interest in the understanding of contemporary anti-Semitism. This has taken it from the preserve of historians and scholars of the Holocaust and more into the social sciences. Although still focused on the Holocaust, Bauman's (1989) book is a significant marker, whereas more recent deliberations examine the linkages between anti-Semitism and anti-racism, which Fine and Cousin (2012) argue have become lost, and the use of the concept of racialisation as a framework for locating anti-Semitism and Islamophobia (Meer 2013).

This period has also seen the emergence of an array of other perspectives and debates. A prominent one, particularly in the USA, is the advent of critical race theory (CRT) and its development via critical race feminism (Razack et al. 2010). Critical race theory, with its roots in legal studies, marks another way in which the field of race and ethnicity studies has become more multidisciplinary and, to some extent, inter-disciplinary. It has been taken up in sociology and other parts of the social sciences, mainly in relation to education and sport (Hylton et al. 2011; Taylor et al. 2009). Whiteness and white domination are both foci of CRT, and in that sense, CRT shares common ground with the emergence of whiteness studies in the wake of key works by Roediger (1991), Frankenberg (1993) and Jacobson (1998). However, both the idea of a field of 'whiteness studies' and the content and direction of some of what is studied in various approaches to whiteness have come under critique by scholars who argue that they have tended to become a diversion from addressing racism in its historical and situated forms (Garner 2007; Ware and Back 2002).

The other significant theme of recent times is around the idea that we have entered, or should enter, a post-race era, which, in the USA, is linked to the culture of black celebrities (Cashmore 2012) and particularly to the first presidential victory of Barack Obama in 2008 (although Ward 2011 notes a decline in post-racial rhetoric in the period which followed). Yet the meaning of the term *post-race* era is a slippery one, as Brett St Louis analyses in Chapter 7, and of much longer provenance than the past decade, not least in intellectual circles. The appeal to or claim for the post-racial combines political, ontological and biological–scientific dimensions and crosses over sociological and philosophical arguments; it includes agendas that we would regard as progressive as well as ones that are reactionary. As this suggests, *post-race* operates as something of a portmanteau term, and we hope that the chapters and debates in this volume help to clarify some aspects of it. A common method of responding to post-race claims is to regard them as an error that can or will be corrected by an insistence on the 'facts' of race – its continuing significance in shaping social worlds; the deeper analytical task, though, is to understand its (re)emergence affectively and ideologically, as Hesse (2011) suggests.

As the arguments around post-race indicate, one way of seeking to make sense of these diverse phenomena and strains of debate is to be clear about what is subsumed under terms such as *race* and *racism*. A key question that has shaped contemporary discussions is the following: How has the category of race come to play such an important role in shaping contemporary social relations? This is not to say that there is any concord about how best to answer this question. On the contrary, scholars and researchers show little sign of agreeing about what it is that we mean when we use notions such as race, racism, ethnicity and related social categories (Winant 2006). Many of the questions raised in these debates take us to the following: Is race a suitable social category? Is ethnicity preferable? What do we mean when we talk of racism as shaping the structure of particular societies? What role have race and ethnicity played in different historical contexts? Is it possible to speak of racism in the singular, or do we need to refer to racisms in the plural? Are we in a post-racial age? These questions are at the heart of many of the theoretical and conceptual arguments that dominate current debates. Yet what is interesting about much of the literature about race and racism is the absence of commonly agreed conceptual tools or even a common framework about the general parameters of race and racism as fields of study.

Ethnicity and *race* are terms often used in conjunction or in parallel to refer to social groups which differ in terms of physical attributes which are accorded social significance in the case of race or in terms of language, culture or place of origin – or common membership of a descent group without distinguishing physical characteristics in the case of ethnicity. However, despite many linkages, there is also something of a divergence between them, with conceptual and political discussions about ethnicity drawing on a different heritage and set of theories (Fenton 2003). Nonetheless, a core issue in ethnicity debates – the division between 'primordialist' and 'constructivist' approaches – corresponds loosely to arguments about essentialism and anti-essentialism around race. Significantly, though, there is no equivalent term to *racism* in relation to ethnicity. Perhaps ethnic conflict is analogous, but despite genocidal 'ethnic cleansing' in Europe and Africa in the past two decades, ethnic conflict remains more a descriptive term of certain consequences of patterns of migration and political mobilisations around ethnicity – as in the USA and, to a lesser extent, Canada. Racism as a concept is much more closely tied to the concept of race and is a reminder that, where members of society make distinctions between different racial groups, at least some members of that society are likely to behave in ways which give rise to racism as a behavioural and ideational consequence of making racial distinctions in the first place. Unfortunately, the opposite does not hold. A society or a nation which denied or did not formally acknowledge the existence of different racial groups would not necessarily thus rid itself of racism. Indeed, recent discussions on racial and ethnic classification in censuses, surveys and administrative records show that the identification of members of a society in terms of their racial, ethnic or national origin may be a prerequisite to taking action to counteract racism.

The growth in scholarship and research has, if anything, not only highlighted a certain lack of consensus but also led to sustained debate about the very language that scholars use in talking about race and racism. This lack of agreement, on one hand, makes the field of ethnic and racial studies dynamic and wide-ranging; on the other hand, it also makes it one in which there are overlapping and contradictory understandings of what scholars mean when they discuss race and racism. Over the past decade or so, the shifting boundaries of race and ethnicity as categories of social analysis have become ever more evident. In particular, a plethora of studies have provided new perspectives on difference, identities, subjectivities and power relations. In this environment, ideas about race, racism and ethnicity have become the subject of sustained debate and controversy. The role of racial and ethnic categorisation in the construction of social and political identities has been highlighted in a number of recent conflicts in countries such as Rwanda and those of the former Yugoslav Republic. Yet it is paradoxically the case that there is still much confusion about what we mean by such notions, as evidenced by the range of terminological debates that have tended to dominate much discussion in recent years. A number of questions remain to be analysed: What factors explain the mobilising power of ideas about race and ethnicity in the contemporary environment? What countervalues and ideas can be developed to undermine the appeal of racist ideas and movements? Is it possible for communities which are socially defined by differences of race, ethnicity, religion or other signifiers to live together in societies which are able to ensure equality, justice and civilised tolerance? In turn, consideration of these questions has thrown up further questions about the persistence of race and racism and a diverse set of proposals and arguments about the best ways of addressing these issues.

Part of the complexity of analysing the historical impact of racism is that it is often intertwined with other social phenomena and, indeed, can only be fully understood if we are able to see how it works in specific social settings. An interesting example of this process can be found in the ways in which modern racial and nationalist ideologies rely on a complex variety of images of race, sexuality and nationhood (Mosse 1995; Stoler 2002). Such themes and images often emphasise questions about identity, in relation to both majority and minority communities. Because race and ethnicity are, intrinsically, forms of collective social identity, the subject of identity has been at the heart of both historical and contemporary discussions about these issues. This has become an important theme in contemporary European discussions about migrant, Muslim and refugee communities and other groups that are seen as somehow not fully part of a 'European' identity or, more widely, as not conforming to 'Western' liberal values.

The preoccupation with identity can be taken as one outcome of concerns about where ethnic and racial minorities in societies such as our own actually belong and about their placement by racist ideologies outside the borders of 'the West'. At a basic level, after all, identity is about belonging, about what we have in common with some people and what differentiates us from others. Identity confers a sense of personal location and provides a stable core of one's individuality; but it is also about one's social relationships and complex involvement with others and, in the modern world, these have become even more complex and confusing. Each of us lives with a variety of potentially contradictory identities, which battle within us for allegiance: as men or women, black or white, straight or gay, able-bodied or disabled. The list is potentially infinite and so, therefore, are our possible belongings. Which of them we focus on, bring to the fore and identify with depends on a host of factors, and feminist, intersectional and queer theorising has done much to engage with these issues (Collins 1990, 2006). At the centre, however, are the values which we share or wish to share with others.

So identity is not simply imposed. It is also chosen, and actively used, albeit within particular social contexts and constraints. Against dominant representations of others, there is resistance. Within structures of dominance, there is agency. Analysing resistance and agency repoliticises relations between collectivities and draws attention to the central constituting factor of power in social relations. But it is possible to overemphasise resistance, to endorse others through validating the lives of the colonised and the exploited. Valorising resistance may also have the unintended effect of belittling the enormous costs exacted in situations of unequal power, exclusion and discrimination. While political legitimacy, gaining access or a hearing, may depend on being able to call up a constituency and authorise representations through appeals to authenticity, it provides the basis for policing the boundaries of authenticity wherein some insiders may find themselves excluded because they are not authentic enough.

For example, stressing race and ethnic differences can obscure the experiences and interests that women may share as women. We therefore need to ask: Who is constructing the categories and defining the boundaries? Who is resisting these constructions and definitions? What are the consequences being written into or out of particular categories? What happens when subordinate groups seek to mobilise along boundaries drawn for the purposes of domination? What happens to individuals whose multiple identities may be fragmented and segmented by category politics? One of the problems with some discussions of identity politics is that the dilemmas and questions outlined earlier are not adequately addressed. This is largely because some arguments are underpinned by the presumption that there is a close connection between a person's identity and his or her politics and that there can be no politics until the subject has excavated or laid claim to his or her identity. Inherent in such positions is the failure to understand the way in which identity grows out of and is transformed by action and struggle, and there are complex forms of subjectivity formation and action.

This is one of the dangers of the preoccupation of exactly who is covered by specific racial and ethnic categories in contemporary British and European societies. By way of example, the usage of the term *black* to cover a variety of diverse communities has been rejected by scholars in favour of other categories such as *Asian, Muslim* or *African Caribbean*. Yet others, particularly in the USA, have sought to argue for a notion of black, or people of colour, grounded in racial particularity. The danger of these approaches is that, on one hand, there is no more than a strategy of simple inversion wherein the old, bad, black, essentialist subject is replaced by a new, good, ethnic or cultural essentialist subject, and, on the other, that changes in and the decomposition of racial identities and politics are neglected in favour of an insistence on the 'changing same' of race.

Rethinking the field: beyond 'white sociology' and the West

The field of race and ethnic studies may be standing at a crucial crossroads regarding its theoretical development. As noted in various chapters in this volume, race and ethnicity have routinely been approached using theoretical frameworks initially grounded in traditional disciplines and, more recently, through insights gained from inter-disciplinary scholarship. This pressure to subsume the study of race and ethnicity under other categories has meant that scholars within the field of race and ethnic studies have had to be mindful of continuing to create the conditions which would ensure the integrity of the field.

One response to this challenge to define the field as an independent area of inquiry has been to wed it closely with actual social phenomena that cannot be understood in the absence of racial and ethnic analyses. Correspondingly, because the field of race and ethnic studies occupies the political space that encourages the empirical study of important social issues as well as policy solutions to social problems, it provides an important grounding in producing empirical work in the field. Clearly this has been important for developing more effective social policies and in shedding light on social problems that have accompanied the trajectory of racism itself.

Yet it might serve the field well to supplement this emphasis on empirical work with greater attention to defining the theoretical contours of the field. In brief, the shift from the institutional perspectives that accompanied the dominance of Marxist social theory to the post-structuralist perspectives that characterised later twentieth-century academic circles raised important questions concerning the theoretical future of the field of race and ethnic studies. Prior to the 1980s, the traditional theoretical frameworks that loosely marked the boundaries of the field were grounded in institutional analyses drawn from the political and social sciences. These are reflected in the coverage provided in the Rex and Mason (1986) volume. As a result, the field did reflect the social issues and social policy concerns that stemmed from processes of desegregation and decolonisation in the USA, Africa and Europe. However, Rex and Mason's book, for all its wider coverage, overlooked the important and emergent perspectives from the cultural turn in the social sciences and the rise of cultural studies as an alternative – or sometimes an addition – to sociology.

The emergence of critical theoretical perspectives – challenging in particular both conventional Marxist and Weberian approaches, as well as the sociology of race relations itself – is only partially evident in Rex and Mason (1986). A key intellectual influence on these critical perspectives drew upon currents of neo-Marxist thought (Solomos 1986). Although there had been some degree of interest in Marxist approaches to the study of race from the 1960s onward (Gabriel and Ben-Tovim 1978; Wright 1978), the main spur to a Marxist analytics frame and the study of race and racism was linked to scholars such as Robert Miles and Annie Phizacklea. Focusing on migration and labour relations, they emphasised the role of class in shaping the ideological and political impact of race in modern capitalist societies (Miles 1982, 1989; Miles and Phizacklea 1979; Phizacklea and Miles 1980). In studies such as *Racism and Migrant Labour*, Miles (1982) made a significant critique of the sociology of race relations itself, arguing that race was essentially an ideological construct produced by the social and class relations of capitalist society. He saw the race relations problematic of scholars such as Banton and Rex as taking for granted the utility of race as a sociological category. From Miles's perspective, race functions as an ideological effect, a mask which hides real economic relationships based on class and structural forms of inequality. This line of analysis drew much of its inspiration from a rethinking of the contributions of classic Marxist scholarship on race and racism. This included the contributions of scholars such as Oliver C. Cox. Yet, it was also influenced in a number of ways by Miles's critical engagement with the work of Michael Banton (see Ashe and McGeever 2011).

Another influential strand of radical thinking on race and racism emerged largely through the work of the Race and Politics Group of the Centre for Contemporary Cultural Studies (CCCS) at the University of Birmingham (Amos et al. 1982; Centre for Contemporary Cultural Studies 1982; Gray et al. 2007). This work was crucially influenced by cultural sociologists such as Stuart Hall, who had supervised some of the doctoral research work at the CCCS. The main publication was *The Empire Strikes Back: Race and Racism in 70s Britain*, which came out in 1982 and led to intense argument and criticism from a range of sources, including John Rex and Jock Young (Rex 1983; Young 1983) as well as an extraordinary 'recanted' review of the book by Lee Bridges (1983). Those battles reveal the strength of the debates at the time.

Much of the emphasis in *The Empire Strikes Back* was on the complex ways in which race and racism were shaping British political culture and social relations. A recurrent theme throughout was the argument for a more critical engagement with the complex processes by which race is constructed as a social and political relation. But, somewhat in contrast to Miles, it also emphasised that the race concept is not simply confined as a process of regulation operated by the state but that the meaning of race as a social construction is contested and fought over. In this sense, it viewed race as an open political construction where the political meaning of terms like *black* are struggled over. Collective identities spoken through race, community and locality are, for all their spontaneity, powerful means through which to coordinate action and create solidarity. In some ways, these shared Rex's concern with the role of race in shaping social action, although, of course, key parts of

the CCCS book rejected his sociological framework as being at best ill-founded and at worst politically spurious. The sociology of race relations stood accused of being implicitly conservative and unable to articulate the theorisation of racism with the nature of a class-divided society characterised by deep-seated and structural inequalities in power. On the other hand, the sociologists of race and ethnic relations were also criticised for letting their theoretical imaginations be coloured by an implicit Eurocentrism.

In exploring these issues, *The Empire Strikes Back* acted as a catalyst to a politicisation of debates about the role of race relations research. In a sense, the political struggles that were occurring within black communities from the 1960s and the urban riots of the 1980s were being echoed in the context of the production of knowledge about racism. This is reflected in books which were among the first efforts to outline a black feminist perspective within the British context (Carby 1982, 1999). *The Empire Strikes Back* also marked a wider argument about and against the white sociology of race (as distinct from the sociology of whiteness, which emerged later) which had originated in the USA in the 1960s. In *The Death of White Sociology*, Joyce Ladner (1973: xx) called for a black sociology as a counter to the mainstream, white liberal sociology that had, 'in the main, upheld the status quo'. Robert Staples (1976) castigated white racist sociology from the classical period through to the pro-segregationist arguments of early-twentieth-century U.S. sociologists. Billingsley (1988) attacked social science research on the family for either ignoring black families or for producing distorted and pathological views of them when they were included. White social science, he argued, was unable to correct its distortions and stereotypes of black families. The works of John Stanfield (2011a, 2011b) have continued this tradition. Edward Said's influential work on Orientalism was a further spur to critiques of race scholarship, particularly on the understandings of Asian cultures (Sharma et al. 1996). While the interventions of Miles and scholars from the CCCS tradition did much to give voice to a growing body of critical scholarship on race and racism, in hindsight, one of the limitations of this expansion of critical perspectives was that it remained largely, though not wholly, conceptual and theoretically focused. Important qualitative accounts of specific facets of racialised social relations from the 1990s onward have appeared (Alexander 1996, 2000; Back 1996; Keith 1993). Alongside these, a wide range of empirical studies of race and racism have emerged; we point here to just a few examples from the United Kingdom on racist crimes, urban communities, youth cultures and mixed identities (Bowling 1998; Hesse et al. 1992; Nayak 2003; Tizard and Phoenix 1993).

The groundbreaking work of philosopher Michel Foucault and the growth of post-structuralist social theoretical frameworks from the 1980s onward raised entirely new questions about the relationship between power, knowledge and culture (Macey 2004; Stoler 1995). Although post-structuralist social theory argues against grand theories – and this would include efforts to construct broad theories of race, ethnicity and racism – three features of post-structuralist social theory have been especially important for racial theory. For one, post-structuralist analyses highlight language, discourse and representation as central to relations of racial domination and subordination. Through discourse analyses, scholars working in this tradition have expanded this approach to race and ethnicity to diverse topics such as elite discourse and imperialism. Post-structuralist frameworks also suggest more robust analyses of racial and ethnic identity formation. They explore such issues as the ways in which more fluid racial categories foster more dynamic bi- or multiracial identities; the effects of social context on how racial identity is perceived and performed; identities and social institutions, especially families; and the performativity of racial identities in social settings. This is currently a major preoccupation of the field. A third and more abstract formulation is concerned with biopolitics and biopower – the power over life itself that increasingly comes under the purview of the state through technologies to govern fertility, mortality and populations which has been explored in many ways from Ann Stoler's (1995, 2002) work to more recent reappraisals (Brah 2005).

Another significant development in and for the field of race and ethnic studies in the twenty-first century lies in deepening its understanding of a host of topics by using intersectional frameworks. Intersectional analyses of the material foundations of race, ethnicity and racism tend to be situated in one of two locations. On one hand, the most comprehensive and long-standing intersectional approach to links between race and class, particularly questions of political economy, comes from Marxist social theory, versions of which are evident from Carter and Virdee (2008) and Kyriakides and Torres (2012). Materialist analyses also emphasise the centrality of state power in producing racially and ethnically unequal outcomes across the world and between the global north and south, particularly under neoliberal hegemony (Goldberg 2008). Given the significance of globalisation for race and ethnicity, we think that continuing to investigate these intersections is worthwhile. On the other hand, the challenges from feminism to conventional and somewhat static approaches to race and class have profoundly altered the terrain by raising questions about gender, identity, subjectivity and the limits of race and class analyses (Brah 1996; Brah and Phoenix 2004; Carby 1982; Collins 1990;

Davis 1982; hooks 1981; Mirza 1997; Yuval-Davis 2012). While not always drawing on the term *intersectionality*, theories of the body advanced within post-structuralism and, subsequently, within feminist and queer theory constitute a further location for developing a materialist analysis of race, ethnicity and racism. This work argued that bodies did not contain sexuality or gender but rather that sexuality and gender are socially constructed categories inscribed upon the body. Judith Butler's (1990) discussion of performativity reintroduces and updates social constructionist approaches to sexuality and gender. Building on her theoretical approach, scholars of race and ethnicity drew upon these categories to decentre race as a biological category to unpack its social construction. For example, post-structuralist analyses of the body which investigate how race and ethnicity operate can provide provocative windows into how one might use the body itself as the basis for social analysis.

These ways of rethinking the theoretical foundations of the field engage with what may be one fundamental theoretical question of the field itself. Developing a better understanding of race and ethnicity may not only tell us much about how these concepts operate across different settings but might also advance theories of racism. If we approach racism as a system of power and make racism the object of theoretical analysis, where might the field go? How might we better understand this social phenomenon? And, as part of that, the scholarly field itself comes under renewed scrutiny. The arena of race and ethnic studies primarily reflects its origins in explaining patterns of nineteenth- and twentieth-century racial formations, especially within U.S. and European societies. Initially, the field was mainly composed of white male academics who studied non-white populations, primarily through the lens of their own theoretical and methodological concerns. Such scholars may have incorporated knowledge produced by non-white populations, generally refracted through the concerns of dominant social theories. Over time, scholars of colour certainly entered the field, such that it is no longer white and does have a heterogeneous community of researchers, especially in the USA. Though this heterogeneity is a welcome development, the globalising scope of research on ethnic and racial formations raises further and deeper questions. Does the field itself exist as yet another example of a Western imperialism imposed on the remainder of the world, as Bourdieu and Wacquant (1999) provocatively argued, or do core questions exist that transcend the specificity of Western history? Does the field of race and ethnic studies remain viable solely as a Western preoccupation? Critiques of colonial and Eurocentric perspectives are part of what makes the field dynamic and, perhaps, unstable at the same time. Equally, while challenging the field, the emergence of decolonial approaches (e.g., see

Bhambra 2014; Gutiérrez Rodríguez et al. 2010) also marks the need for critical and rigorous analyses of what is taken for granted about 'our' knowledge, as modes of knowledge production about race and racism evolve in a number of directions in terms of theoretical perspectives and empirical research agendas. At the same time, it has also become an established field of research in various social science disciplines – sociology, politics, social geography – as well as in philosophical, cultural, literary and historical approaches in the humanities.

The rich diversity of approaches and themes makes it challenging to capture the entirety of the field, and we doubt that any single volume can now do so. In this collection, we have set out to explore various perspectives and topics which provide readers with a guide to key debates and perspectives that frame ethnic and racial studies in the contemporary period and for the future. The various chapters that make up this edited collection do not speak with one voice. As we have indicated, there *is* no single voice or perspective on many of the core and continuing debates and battles within and across the field. Indeed, one of our key aims in compiling this book has been to bring together scholars to provide a range of views from a diversity of theoretical perspectives. These are not exhaustive, nor do or can they stand still. It is important in the coming period that the perspectives we have set out in this volume do not remain static and unchanging. Indeed, given the importance of context and the continuing and changing formations of racialised ideas and inequalities across the world, any viewpoints that fail to take account of significant changes will probably become irrelevant.

We have organised this collection in two parts though, inevitably, there are some overlaps between them. Part I is focused on some key debates that provide an overview of contemporary configurations of race and racism. They range from the impact of genomics on thinking about what race is (Lee), to U.S. debates about a post-racial society in which racism is overlooked or denied through 'colour-blind' thinking (Gallagher). The changing contours of race are also evident in those chapters which discuss the emergence and significance of mixed-race identities (Bonilla-Silva [with Ray]; Song); the links between migration, race and politics (Bassel); and the principles and praxis of racial eliminativism (St Louis). Part II moves the analysis a step further by bringing together seven chapters that focus on a range of explanatory approaches to the study of race and racism. Here we have brought together perspectives on and from critical rationalism (Banton), performativity (Tate) and psychoanalytical perspectives on racial identities and racism (Clarke); critical whiteness studies (Hughey) and its intersections with sexualities (Fassin); and critical race feminism (Wing). The final chapter in this section takes us back to the methods and conceptions which we use in the study of race and racism (Goldberg). While we have employed some chronology to make sense of developments in and of the field of race and ethnicity studies, we hope that readers will also see that chronology provides only a limited guide; some contemporary disputes are not that different from the questions that the founders of social science research into race and ethnicity set out and struggled to resolve. Thus, in the closing chapter, we return to one of these – what race is and is not, and how it is studied and understood.

REFERENCES

Alexander, C. E. (1996). *The Art of Being Black: The Creation of Black British Youth Identities*. Oxford: Clarendon Press.
(2000). *The Asian Gang: Ethnicity, Identity, Masculinity*. Oxford: Berg.
Amos, V., Gilroy, P. and Lawrence, E. (1982). White sociology, black struggle. In D. Robbins, ed., *Rethinking Social Inequality*. Aldershot: Gower, pp. 15–42.
Ashe, S. D. and McGeever, B. F. (2011). Marxism, racism and the construction of 'race' as a social and political relation: an interview with Professor Robert Miles. *Ethnic and Racial Studies*, 34(12), 2009–26.
Back, L. (1996). *New Ethnicities and Urban Culture: Racisms and Multiculture in Young Lives*. London: UCL Press.
Back, L. and Solomos, J., eds. (2009). *Theories of Race and Racism: A Reader*, 2nd edn. London: Routledge.
Banton, M. (1967). *Race Relations*. New York: Basic Books.
(1991). The race relations problematic. *British Journal of Sociology*, 42(1), 115–30.
(2001). Progress in ethnic and racial studies. *Ethnic and Racial Studies*, 24(2), 173–94.
(n.d.). The management of social science research: reflections on the SSRC Research Unit on Ethnic Relations, 1970–78. Unpublished manuscript.
Barker, M. (1981). *New Racism: Conservatives and the Ideology of the Tribe*. London: Junction Books.
Bauman, Z. (1989). *Modernity and the Holocaust*. Cambridge: Polity.
Benyon, J. and Solomos, J., eds. (1987). *The Roots of Urban Unrest*. Oxford: Pergamon Press.
Bhambra, G. K. (2014). A sociological dilemma: race, segregation, and US sociology. *Current Sociology*, 62(4), 471–92.
Billingsley, A. (1988). *Black Families in White America*. New York: Touchstone.
Blauner, R. (2002). *Racial Oppression in America*, 2nd edn. New York: Harper and Row.
Bonilla-Silva, E. (1997). Rethinking racism: toward a structural interpretation. *American Sociological Review*, 62(3), 465–80.
(2001). *White Supremacy and Racism in the Post–Civil Rights Era*. Boulder, CO: Lynne Rienner.

Bourdieu, P. and Wacquant, L. J. D. (1999). On the cunning of imperialist reason. *Theory, Culture and Society*, 16(1), 41–58.

Bowling, B. (1998). *Violent Racism: Victimization, Policing and Social Context*. Oxford: Clarendon Press.

Brah, A. (1996). *Cartographies of Diaspora: Contesting Identities*. London: Routledge.

(2005). Ambivalent documents/fugitive pieces: author, text, subject, and racializations. In K. Murji and J. Solomos, eds, *Racialization: Studies in Theory and Practice*. Oxford: Oxford University Press, pp. 69–86.

Brah, A. and Phoenix, A. (2004). Ain't I a woman? Revisiting intersectionality. *International Journal of Women's Studies*, 5(3), 75–86.

Bridges, L. (1983). Review: *The Empire Strikes Back: Race and Racism in 70s Britain. Race and Class*, 25(1), 99.

Brotz, H. (1983). Radical sociology and the study of race relations. *New Community*, 10(3), 508–12.

Butler, J. (1990). *Gender Trouble: Feminism and the Subversion of Identity*. London: Routledge.

Carby, H. V. (1982). White woman listen! Black feminism and the boundaries of sisterhood. In *The Empire Strikes Back: Race and Racism in 70s Britain*. London: Hutchinson, pp. 212–35.

(1999). *Cultures in Babylon: Black Britain and African America*. London: Verso.

Carter, B. and Virdee, S. (2008). Racism and the sociological imagination. *British Journal of Sociology*, 59(4), 661–79.

Cashmore, E. (2012). *Beyond Black: Celebrity and Race in Obama's America*. London: Bloomsbury Academic.

Centre for Contemporary Cultural Studies. (1982). *The Empire Strikes Back: Race and Racism in 70s Britain*. London: Hutchinson.

Cohen, P., ed. (1999). *New Ethnicities, Old Racisms?* London: Zed Books.

Collins, P. H. (1990). *Black Feminist Thought: Knowledge, Consciousness and the Politics of Empowerment*. London: HarperCollins.

(2006). *From Black Power to Hip Hop: Racism, Nationalism, and Feminism*. Philadelphia: Temple University Press.

(2007). Pushing the boundaries or business as usual? Race, class, and gender studies and sociological inquiry. In C. J. Calhoun, ed., *Sociology in America: A History*. Chicago: University of Chicago Press, pp. 572–604.

Davis, A. Y. (1982). *Women, Race and Class*. London: Women's Press.

Du Bois, W. E. B. (1903). *The Souls of Black Folk*. New York: Bantam Classic.

ESRC. (2007). *SSRC/ESRC: The First Forty Years*. Swindon: Economic and Social Research Council.

Essed, P. and Goldberg, D. T., eds. (2002). *Race Critical Theories: Text and Context*. Oxford: Blackwell.

Fenton, S. (2003). *Ethnicity*. Cambridge: Polity.

Fine, R. and Cousin, G. (2012). A common cause: reconnecting the study of racism and antisemitism. *European Societies*, 14(2), 166–85.

Frankenberg, R. (1993). *The Social Construction of Whiteness*. London: Routledge.

Frazier, E. F. (1947). Sociological theory and race relations. *American Sociological Review*, 12(3), 265–71.

(1968). *E. Franklin Frazier on Race Relations*. Chicago: University of Chicago Press.

Gabriel, J. and Ben-Tovim, G. (1978). Marxism and the concept of racism. *Economy and Society*, 7(2), 119–54.

Garner, S. (2007). *Whiteness: An Introduction*. London: Routledge.

Glazer, N. and Moynihan, D. P. (1963). *Beyond the Melting Pot: The Negroes, Puerto Ricans, Jews, Italians, and Irish of New York City*. Cambridge, MA: MIT Press.

Goldberg, D. (2008). *The Threat of Race*. London: Blackwell.

Goldberg, D. T. and Solomos, J., eds. (2002). *A Companion to Racial and Ethnic Studies*. Oxford: Blackwell.

Gray, A., Campbell, J., Erickson, M., Hanson, S. and Wood, H., eds. (2007). *Centre for Contemporary Cultural Studies Selected Working Papers*, 2 vols. London: Routledge.

Gutiérrez Rodríguez, E., Boatca, M. and Costa, S., eds. (2010). *Decolonizing European Sociology: Transdisciplinary Approaches*. Aldershot: Ashgate.

Hall, C. (2002). *Civilising Subjects: Metropole and Colony in the English Imagination, 1830–1867*. Cambridge: Polity.

Hall, S. (1988). New ethnicities. In K. Mercer, ed., *Black Film/British Cinema*. London: Institute of Contemporary Arts, pp. 27–30.

Hall, S., Critcher, C., Jefferson, T., Clarke, J. and Roberts, B. (1978). *Policing the Crisis: Mugging, the State and Law and Order*. Basingstoke: Macmillan.

Hesse, B. (2011). Self-fulfilling prophecy: the postracial horizon. *South Atlantic Quarterly*, 110(1), 155–78.

Hesse, B., Rai, D. K., Bennett, C. and McGilchrist, P. (1992). *Beneath the Surface: Racial Harassment*. Aldershot: Avebury.

hooks, b. (1981). *Ain't I a Woman? Black Women and Feminism*. Cambridge, MA: South End Press.

Hylton, K., Pilkington, A., Warmington, P. and Housee, S., eds. (2011). *Atlantic Crossings: International Dialogues on Critical Race Theory*. Birmingham: C-SAP.

Jacobson, M. F. (1998). *Whiteness of a Different Colour: European Immigrants and the Alchemy of Race*. Cambridge, MA: Harvard University Press.

Keith, M. (1993). *Race, Riots and Policing: Lore and Disorder in Multi-Racist Society*. London: UCL Press.

Kyriakides, C. and Torres, R. D. (2012). *Race Defaced: Paradigms of Pessimism, Politics of Possibility*. Stanford: Stanford University Press.

Ladner, J. A., ed. (1973). *The Death of White Sociology*. New York: Vintage Books.

Lentin, A. and Titley, G. (2011). *The Crises of Multiculturalism: Racism in a Neoliberal Age*. London: Zed Books.

Macey, D. (2004). *Michel Foucault*. London: Reaktion.

Meer, N. (2013). Racialization and religion: race, culture and difference in the study of antisemitism and Islamophobia. *Ethnic and Racial Studies*, 36(3), 385–98.

Miles, R. (1982). *Racism and Migrant Labour*. London: Routledge/Kegan Paul. (1989). *Racism*. London: Routledge.

Miles, R. and Phizacklea, A., eds. (1979). *Racism and Political Action in Britain*. London: Routledge/Kegan Paul.

(1984). *White Man's Country: Racism in British Politics*. London: Pluto Press.

Mirza, H. S. (1997). *Black British Feminism: A Reader*. London: Routledge.

Modood, T. (2005). *Multicultural Politics: Racism, Ethnicity, and Muslims in Britain*. Minneapolis: University of Minnesota Press.

Mosse, G. L. (1995). Racism and nationalism. *Nations and Nationalism*, 1(2), 163–74.

Nayak, A. (2003). *Race, Place and Globalization: Youth Cultures in a Changing World*. Oxford: Berg.

Omi, M. and Winant, H. (1994). *Racial Formation in the United States*, 2nd edn. London: Routledge.

Panayi, P. (2010). *An Immigration History of Britain: Multicultural Racism since 1800*. London: Longman.

Park, R. E. (1950). *Race and Culture: Essays in the Sociology of Contemporary Man*. New York: Free Press.

Phizacklea, A. and Miles, R. (1980). *Labour and Racism*. London: Routledge/ Kegan Paul.

Rattansi, A. (2007). *Racism: A Very Short Introduction*. Oxford: Oxford University Press.

Razack, S., Smith, M. and Thobani, S., eds. (2010). *States of Race: Critical Race Feminism for the 21st Century*. Toronto: Between the Lines.

Rex, J. (1970). *Race Relations in Sociological Theory*. London: Weidenfeld and Nicolson.

(1983). Doctors of the revolution. *New Society*, 13(January), 67–68.

(1986). The role of class analysis in the study of race relations: a Weberian perspective. In J. Rex and D. Mason, eds, *Theories of Race and Ethnic Relations*, pp. 64–83.

Rex, J. and Mason, D., eds. (1986). *Theories of Race and Ethnic Relations*. Cambridge: Cambridge University Press.

Rice, A. (2003). *Radical Narratives of the Black Atlantic*. London: Continuum.

Rich, P. B. (1990). *Race and Empire in British Politics*. Cambridge: Cambridge University Press.

Roediger, D. R. (1991). *The Wages of Whiteness: Race and the Making of the American Working Class*. New York: Verso.

Rose, E. J. B. (1969). *Colour and Citizenship: A Report on British Race Relations*. Oxford: Oxford University Press.

Sharma, S., Hutnyk, J. and Sharma, A. (1996). *Dis-Orienting Rhythms: The Politics of the New Asian Dance Music*. London: Zed Books.

Small, S. and Solomos, J. (2006). Race, immigration and politics in Britain: changing policy agendas and conceptual paradigms 1940s–2000s. *International Journal of Comparative Sociology*, 47(3–4), 235–57.

Solomos, J. (1986). Varieties of Marxist conceptions of 'race', class and the state: a critical analysis. In J. Rex and D. Mason, eds, *Theories of Race and Ethnic Relations*, pp. 84–109.

Stanfield, J. H., ed. (1993). *A History of Race Relations Research: First-Generation Recollections*. Newbury Park, CA: Sage.

Stanfield, J. H. (2011a). *Black Reflective Sociology: Epistemology, Theory, and Methodology*. Walnut Creek, CA: Left Coast Press.

(2011b). *Historical Foundations of Black Reflective Sociology*. Walnut Creek, CA: Left Coast Press.

Stanfield, J. H. and Dennis, R. M., eds. (1993). *Race and Ethnicity in Research Methods*. Newbury Park, CA: Sage.

Staples, R. (1976). *Introduction to Black Sociology*. New York: McGraw-Hill.

Stoler, A. L. (1995). *Race and the Education of Desire: Foucault's History of Sexuality and the Colonial Order of Things*. Durham, NC: Duke University Press.

(2002). *Carnal Knowledge and Imperial Power: Race and the Intimate in Colonial Rule*. Berkeley: University of California Press.

Taylor, E., Gillborn, D. and Ladson-Billings, G. (2009). *Foundations of Critical Race Theory in Education*. New York: Routledge.

Tizard, B. and Phoenix, A. (1993). *Black, White, or Mixed Race? Race and Racism in the Lives of Young People of Mixed Parentage*. London: Routledge.

Ward, B. (2011). 'I want my country back, I want my dream back': Barack Obama and the appeal of postracial fictions. In D. McGuire and J. Dittmer, eds, *Freedom Rights: New Perspectives on the Civil Rights Movement*. Lexington: University of Kentucky Press, pp. 329–64.

Ware, V. and Back, L. (2002). *Out of Whiteness: Color, Politics and Culture*. Chicago: University of Chicago Press.

Wilson, W. J. (2012). *The Declining Significance of Race: Blacks and Changing American Institutions*, 3rd edn. Chicago: University of Chicago Press.

Winant, H. (2001). *The World Is a Ghetto: Race and Democracy since World War II*. New York: Basic Books.

(2006). Race and racism: towards a global future. *Ethnic and Racial Studies*, 29(5), 986–1003.

(2007). The dark side of the force: one hundred years of the sociology of race. In C. Calhoun, ed., *Sociology in America: A History*. Chicago: University of Chicago Press, pp. 535–71.

Winder, R. (2005). *Bloody Foreigners: The Story of Immigration to Britain*. London: Abacus.

Wright, E. O. (1978). Race, class, and income inequality. *American Journal of Sociology*, 83(6), 1368–97.

Young, J. (1983). Striking back against the empire. *Critical Social Policy*, 3(8), 129–40.

Yuval-Davis, N. (2012). *The Politics of Belonging: Intersectional Contestations*. London: Sage.

Zubaida, S. (1970a). Introduction. In S. Zubaida, ed., *Race and Racialism*, pp. 1–16.

ed. (1970b). *Race and Racialism*. London: Tavistock.

(1972). Sociologists and race relations. In *Proceedings of a Seminar: Problems and Prospects of Socio-Legal Research*. Oxford: Nuffield College.

Part I

Debates

Introduction to Part I

In the introduction to this volume, we pointed out that the past few decades have seen important transformations in research agendas on questions about race, racism and ethnicity. In Part I of the collection, we bring together chapters that explore key facets of these debates. This begins in Chapter 2, through Sandra Soo-Jin Lee's overview of key aspects of debates about the contemporary meanings attached to the category of race within scientific discourses. Lee's critical discussion focuses on the impact of research into the human genome on our understandings of ideas about race. Her suggestive analysis helpfully guides us through the ways in which scientific debates about the human genome are likely to impact on both scholarly and popular discourses of race as a social category. Her analysis highlights the importance of contemporary scientific research agendas in the analysis of race as a social category.

The question of the changing dynamics of contemporary racial norms is also at the core of Chapter 3, by Charles Gallagher. Locating his analysis within the broader transformations of debates about race in American society, Gallagher argues that a discourse of 'colour-blind egalitarianism' has become the dominant racial norm in narratives about race in the USA. In situating both the historical and contemporary reasons for this process, he also seeks to argue that such a framing of race in American society can be seen as limiting the potential for a critical understanding of the racialised inequalities that remain an integral component of its social, economic and cultural relations in the present.

An important undercurrent in contemporary debates about race in American society, particularly in the aftermath of the election of Barack Obama, is that about the trend toward the emergence of the 'post-racial'. This is a theme touched upon by Gallagher, and it is the main focus of Chapter 4, by Eduardo Bonilla-Silva (with Victor E. Ray). Their account is framed around the notion that, far from racism disappearing in 'post-racial' America, it can be seen as taking on new forms. A key concern running through the chapter is the argument that, in the aftermath of the civil rights period, we have seen the emergence of new racialised inequalities that continue to frame the experiences of racial minorities. Bonilla-Silva and Ray also focus on the limitations of accounts that see the election of Obama as a turning point in the politics of race in American society.

Chapter 5, by Miri Song, addresses the question of 'mixed race' as a socially constructed category, an issue that has attracted much attention in a number of different social contexts, including the USA, contemporary European societies and Brazil, for example. Song argues that, in recent debates about this issue, we have seen a kind of normalisation of mixedness that has helped to shape policy as well as political discourses. She also explores some of the connections between ideas about 'mixed race' and 'post-race'.

This is followed by Chapter 6, by Leah Bassel, which considers the ways in which identity and activism are understood to connect when identities are multiple and serve both as a site of challenge and as a resource. Bassel's account draws on the work of French philosopher Jacques Rancière and the feminist sociologist Patricia Hill Collins to highlight both commonalities and differences in their approach to the analysis of political identities. Bassel also uses her research on undocumented migrant women in France to explore the complexities of what is understood as politics in the processes of mobilisation, resistance and identity formation.

The concluding chapter in this part of the book is by Brett St Louis and focuses on a critical account of post-racial problematics. St Louis investigates, in particular, how ideas such as 'post-race' and 'racial eliminativism' can be located within an uneven history of anti-race thinking across the human, social and life sciences that often attempts to reject racial categories and concepts. His analysis links up to some of the themes that are taken up in the chapters in Part II of this collection.

2 Race and the science of difference in the age of genomics

Sandra Soo-Jin Lee

> After all, I believe one of the great truths to emerge from this triumphant expedition inside the human genome is that in genetic terms all human beings, regardless of race, are more than 99.9 percent the same. What that means is that modern science has confirmed what we first learned from ancient faiths. The most important fact of life on this earth is our common humanity.
> — *New York Times*, 27 June 2000

The beginning of the second millennium coincided with the highly celebrated completion of the draft of the human genome. In conclusion of the race to identify the entire genetic sequence of a representative human genome in 2000, President Clinton, flanked by then director of the National Human Genome Research Institute, Francis Collins, and Craig Venter, then president of Celera Genomics, took the opportunity to reject any assertion of a genetic basis for race. In the epigraph, President Clinton recites a position that becomes the 99.9 per cent mantra among leading researchers in genomics and the general media on lessons learned from the completion of the Human Genome Project (HGP): race does not exist in our genes – we are all the same. Given this unequivocal chorus on race and genetics, it is surprising that more than a decade of developments in human genetics and biomedicine have resulted in a dogged focus on the search for population differences at the molecular level. Although the scientific community has repeatedly affirmed that the vast majority of the human genome is synonymous among human beings, scientists continue to emphasize that the key to understanding the genetic basis for common, complex diseases and variability in drug response lies in the minutiae of genetic differences among groups. Inspecting the incongruity of the mantra of sameness and the increasing salience of racial and ethnic identification of research populations is useful in identifying how concepts of race are operationalized and, in particular, how 'technologies of racialization' that highlight, demarcate and exact difference from the human body – phenotypical characteristics such as skin tone, eye shape and blood type – are increasingly supplanted by molecular signatures. The recent surge in human genetics research through the development

26

of high-throughput technologies and the deciphering of the genomic alphabet into meaningful categories of risk is the latest to be deployed in 'race making', where the color line is inscribed beyond the surface of the skin.

Racial thinking occurs when ideas about race become the dominant explanatory model for understanding phenomena in the world. The power of race is best understood as an organizing framework in answering complex questions about group differences. Indeed, one may argue that, by merely invoking taxonomies of race, as is implicitly done in much of biomedical research, race is operationalized as a research variable and already configured as a manifestation of the question posed. As such, it may be most useful to recast *race* as a verb, rather than a noun, as in *racing* or *racializing*. By emphasizing the 'work' of race, social analysis demands a focus on the processes that co-construct group differences into that which seems tangible and commonplace. Sociologists Michael Omi and Howard Winant (1994), in their landmark book *Racial Formation in the United States*, explain how racial formation occurs through the social, economic and political forces that determine the content and importance of racial categories. They argue that race is a 'central axis' of social relations, which cannot be further reduced. By approaching race as the culmination of both collective action and individual practices, skin color, genetic sequences, differences in test scores and other social indices are emerging as the artifacts of a racializing process rather than inherent, predetermined qualities of primordial conceptions of race. This is not to deny that differences between and among human groups exist. Clearly they do. However, how these are interpreted and imbued with meaning reveals the ideologies of difference that are critical in determining how the perception of difference manifests itself in human experience and is rendered significant.

For years, scholars and scientists from across the disciplinary spectrum have argued over how to define and approach issues relevant to what has been recognized as race. Often accepted as a given, consensus on the specific definition of race is illusive. Attempts to define this concept are, at the same time, too limited and too expansive to adequately reflect the power of race on individual lives and group identity. This is nowhere more true than in the USA, whose history has been shaped by struggles over how groups of individuals are defined and how to reveal the assumptions that go into making these designations. A robust literature on the study of race relations reveals how prevailing ideas, values and attitudes on race and the interpretation of population differences are inflected in our politics, economics and national consciousness. Relatively little, however, has investigated how racial thinking also impacts on the practice of our science. The imprimatur of objectivity in science occludes from view an infrastructure that is built on assumptions and stock knowledge of how and why populations differ from one another. Our fascination with these questions of group difference continues to drive our science for answers. A critical question is not only how, but why?

Human genetic variation research and the focus on populations

Two years after the announcement of the completion of the HGP in December 2003, the popular science magazine *Scientific American* published a cover story asking the provocative question, 'Does Race Exist?' A seemingly simple question in light of the HGP, the query was oddly facile, given the robust scientific literature that had challenged the notion that race could be excavated from human genes. Nonetheless, the question addressed a fundamental concern for an American public, given the long and tortured history of race relations in the USA and the continuing struggle over social equity. The bold query and the teaser answer 'Genetic Results May Surprise You' reflect basic assumptions about stock ideas of group difference and the explanatory power of 'the gene' in addressing what can and cannot be identified as difference within human species. Underlying these is an assertion that the variation that exists can, in powerful ways, be explained by identifying, inspecting and extrapolating from what we understand as race. As an enduring explanatory framework, it seems hardly worthy of headline news. What *is* newsworthy is the assertion that the test of whether race is 'real' lies somewhere hidden in the human genome, and herein lies the source of discomfort. The return to genetics in the context of race seems anachronistic in a twenty-first-century America that heralds itself as 'color-blind' (Bonilla-Silva 2006). Could it be that the early-twentieth-century forays into eugenics that served as the rationale for state-sanctioned violence both in the USA and abroad dissipated so quickly from public memory? Could it be that, a mere century later, genetics again has become the authority over whether race is real? The fact that *Scientific American* and other journals ask the question again in the midst of significant developments in genetic technology must be taken seriously, as genomics continues to develop and become integrated into social practice and institutions.

In 1996 the American Association of Physical Anthropologists (1996: 569) issued a statement that included the following assertion: 'Pure races, in the sense of genetically homogenous populations, do not exist in the human species today, nor is there any evidence that they have ever existed in the past.' Although it acknowledges that differences between individuals exist, the statement emphasizes that those differences are the result of hereditary factors and the effects of natural and social environments. The statement stresses that genetic differences between populations result from the effect of the history of human migration and reproduction and consist of a gradient of varying frequencies of all inherited traits, including those which are environmentally malleable.

The last few decades have ushered in a new era of genetic technologies which have fuelled a shift from the science of human *genetics* to human *genomics*, a shift which reflects the escalating pace of research attempting to probe the human genome for links to disease, drug response, ancestry and other human traits. The rapid decrease in the sequencing patterns of genetic differences among genomes – the full sets of human genes found in the nucleus of each cell – involves finding the patterns of the four nucleotide 'letters' A (adenine), C (cytosine), T (thymine) and G (guanine), the building blocks that combine in pairs to create the rungs of the archetypal double helix famously identified by James Watson and Francis Crick in 1953. The exact combinations of these base pairs among the millions that make up human DNA differ between individuals and contribute to the 'unique' characteristics we attribute to each person. These base-pair differences are identified as single nucleotide polymorphisms, or SNPs (pronounced *snips*), which are rare and estimated to occur in less than 1 per cent of the total genome. SNP variation occurs when a single nucleotide, such as an A, replaces one of the other three nucleotide bases – C, G or T. SNPs are believed to be associated with individual differences in susceptibility to disease; environmental insults such as bacteria, viruses, toxins and chemicals; and drugs and other therapies (Weiss 1995). The shift from genetics and genomics is, then, a function of scale, with the former focused on single genes, whereas genomics addresses all genes and their inter-relationships to identify their combined influence on the growth and development of the organism.

Patterns within the genome vary across a species, depending on the history of mating within that species. The patterns or genetic frequencies of human populations have been affected by *mutation, migration, natural selection* and *random genetic drift* to varying extents. These forces have resulted in the current genetic variation that exists among human populations. Genetic differences between global populations do not map neatly onto the racial categories that have emerged through sociohistorical processes. Instead, race, suggesting discrete group boundaries, serves as a poor proxy for the continuum of human genetic variation, as evidenced by the work of Richard Lewontin (1982) and others (Cavalli-Sforza et al. 1994).

Nonetheless, populations continue to be important units of analysis in genomic research. The completion of the HGP has resulted in new and well-funded areas of scientific inquiry in medicine that strive toward a central goal of identifying the genetic and environmental causes of human disease and translating these findings into clinical products and approaches. Recent advances, such as high-throughput genomic sequencing technology, have increased the efficiency of large-scale rapid genotyping and ushered in a new era of genetic epidemiological research of complex diseases such as cancer, diabetes, vascular disease and some forms of mental illness. In identifying patterns of such differences, populations are of special interest. Although every population has all possible genotypes, populations may differ in regard to the frequencies of individual genotypes.

To create a genetic test that will screen for a disease in which the disease-causing gene has been identified, scientists collect blood samples from a group of individuals affected by the disease and analyze their DNA for SNP patterns. Next, researchers compare those patterns to others obtained by analyzing the DNA from a group of individuals not affected by the disease. This type of comparison, which is referred to as a genetic association study, can detect differences between the SNP patterns of the two groups, indicating which pattern is the most likely to be associated with the disease-causing gene. Identifying SNP profiles is of particular interest in drug development, where the efficacy of a drug that interacts with a gene target may depend on enriching a study population for a particular set of alleles. As part of that effort, scientists have called for increased funding for the DNA sampling of racial minority populations. The collection of DNA samples has resulted in a proliferation of data sets and biobanks that are organized by racial and ethnic taxonomies.

Racial categorization and the taxonomy of difference in biomedicine

Since its genesis in the sixteenth century, the concept of 'race' and whether it suggests a biological 'kind' have been focal points of debate (Zack 2001). Controversy over the use of the term has emerged in regard to the values that have been attached to groups identified by race and the characteristics that have been attributed to radicalized populations. While social scientists have argued that race emerges through a historically grounded context and is best understood as fluid and reactive to historical and political conditions, genetics and the search for differences revisit notions of 'race' as embedded in the physical body. Treated as material reality, race is recast as a natural kind, while, at the same time, researchers engage the Aristotelian notion of 'kinds' as those entities that are understood by their 'essences'. As such, 'kinds' are believed to have their own intrinsic reality, apart from the particular circumstances in which they are discovered. Philosopher Naomi Zack (2001: 54) addresses this apparent paradox and writes, 'Again, the genes for traits deemed racial are scientifically real but, there is no racial aspect of these genes which is scientifically real. And yet, on a folk level the prevailing assumption is that race itself is physically real.' Race becomes embedded in the body through a slippage whereby traits and conditions that travel with race become understood as artifacts of race itself.

More recently in the twentieth century, scholars have challenged the validity of assertions of biological differences between populations that were linked to race. Scientific research has consistently revealed that more genetic variation exists within than between populations (Lewontin 1982). Despite this finding, race has become increasingly salient in understanding disparities in the health status of population groups and continues to be an important factor in both biomedical research and clinical medicine. This is particularly true as public health goals of mitigating and ultimately eliminating health disparities among populations are identified and funded by national governments.

A central dilemma facing researchers in genetic epidemiology and biomedicine is the variability in racial and ethnic categories. As a social category, race comes into being within a particular sociocultural context and, as a result, has changed over time – as illustrated by the history of U.S. Census racial and ethnic categories (Lee et al. 2001). Since the inception of the term *race* in scientific discourse, its definition has been a moving target, and this has contributed to confusion about its meaning and implications for biomedical research and clinical care. In his detailed study of racial classification and the impact of the National Revitalization Act of 1991, sociologist Steven Epstein (2008) describes the requirement that all federally funded researchers in the USA identify their study participants by racial and ethnic categories; this has entrenched conceptions of race into health research. Following the governmental categories used in the U.S. Census, research participants may be identified using five race categories: American Indian or Alaska Native, Asian, Black or African American, Native Hawaiian or Other Pacific Islander, and White. Respondents to federal data collection activities must be offered the option of selecting one or more racial designations. Hispanics or Latinos, who current standards define as an ethnic group, can be of any race. Although the intention of the legislative requirement was to enable researchers and policy makers to study the impact and influence of race in research, Epstein suggests that, by superimposing categories in biomedicine, identity politics and governmental administration in an effort toward 'categorical alignment', other modes of identity (such as behavioral traits, social class) and social and environmental factors are obscured.

Although the use of census categories has been heavily criticized, there remains a lack of agreement on how to approach the characterization of group identity. In a manner that often remains implicit, biomedical researchers and clinicians use a potpourri of surrogate concepts, including skin color, hair type, national origin and citizenship, to signal group differences (Sankar et al. 2007). This situation is further complicated by the common practice of relying on self-reported identity, which may be based on factors that have little to do with the specific research question addressed by researchers. As Tutton et al. (2010) suggest, there are two visions for ascribing identity – one which emphasizes self-report and, for population geneticists, the use of genotypic identification. The development of ancestry informative markers, or AIMs (Fujimura and Rajagapolan 2011; Sankar 2010), in assigning genetic ancestry to individuals reflects the shifting landscape described by Tutton and his colleagues. Attempts to use other terms, such as *ethnicity*, offer little intervention on these practices. As St Louis (this volume) points out, ethnicity all too often resembles conventional categories of race, falls similarly into functioning as a proxy for biological differences and is used interchangeably or synonymously with race (Risch et al. 2002). In a context of whole genome sequencing and the increasing use of genetic markers to determine ancestry, the tension over self-identity and the scientific call for increased standardization put the question of who is the expert on his or her own identity in stark relief. Easy solutions and standardized approaches are illusive, as the question of individual and population identity will always depend on the scientific question being asked and for what purpose.

Scientific racism and eugenics: cautionary tales

In considering the implications of human genetics research for race, it is prudent to keep in mind the lessons learned from the history of scientific racism in medicine. In the United States and abroad, scientific racism has resulted in the exploitation of racially identified populations in the name of scientific and medical progress. Although science has often been portrayed as 'value-free', scientific theories are borne from a social landscape of values and beliefs and have too often been used to support beliefs in the inferiority of radicalized populations, resulting in discriminatory policies. Historically, race has been exercised as a biological taxonomy by which humans were categorized according to phenotypical differences such as skin color, facial features and specific behavioral traits. Despite general rejection of such definitions, current scientific research is at times compromised by a priori assumptions that build on notions of race as biology.

The term *eugenics*, which was coined by Francis Galton early in the twentieth century, has been incorporated into various state-sponsored programs around the world (Galton 1987), the most notorious of which was guided by the German program of *Rassenhygiene*, or 'racial hygiene', which ultimately led to the Holocaust. In the early 1900s, the eugenics program was promoted through scientific organizations such as the Society for Racial Hygiene and the Kaiser Wilhelm Institute for Anthropology, Human Genetics and Eugenics. Later, when incorporated into Nazi ideology after the rise of Adolph Hitler, the racial hygiene program led to a broad spectrum of egregious scientific experimentation and the eventual extermination of millions of Jews, Gypsies, homosexuals and other individuals deemed undesirable by the Third Reich (Weigmann 2001).

During that period of state-sponsored racism, other nations, such as Great Britain, Norway and France, were adopting their own brands of eugenics policies. Eugenics gave scientific authority to social fears and lent respectability to racial doctrines. Powered by the prestige of science, it was coupled with the modernization of national projects that promoted claims of social order as objective statements grounded in the laws of nature (Dikötter 1998). Unfortunately, history provides several examples of how the marriage of scientific racism and national political agendas has led to the unfair treatment of socially and politically vulnerable racial minorities. In South America, for example, eugenics policies have been the key to a national revival in which indigenous concerns over racially diverse and socially disparate societies have led to race-based initiatives to regulate human reproduction. Brazil and Argentina have experienced the use of science in the name of forging 'superior and cosmic national races' (Stepan 1996).

Perhaps the longest single study involving the exploitation of human subjects in medical research was the Tuskegee Syphilis Study conducted by the U.S. Public Health Service. The Tuskegee Study of Untreated Syphilis in the Negro Male began in 1932 and did not end until 1972. The study involved the recruitment of more than 300 black men afflicted by syphilis, who were told by researchers that they were being treated for 'bad blood', a local term used to describe several ailments, including syphilis, anemia and fatigue (Jones 1981). These men did not receive proper treatment even after penicillin became available as an effective therapy in 1943. In exchange for taking part in the study, the men received free medical examinations, free meals and burial insurance. The Tuskegee Syphilis Study generated public outcry that led the assistant secretary for health and scientific affairs to appoint an Ad Hoc Advisory Panel, which concluded that the study was 'ethically unjustified' (Brandt 1985). It is a 'powerful metaphor that has come to symbolize racism in medicine' (Gamble 1997) and a cautionary tale about the vulnerability of racial minorities in biomedical research.

Against this historical landscape, the rapid development of genomic technologies deserves special scrutiny. The iconic power of the gene has contributed to anticipation for the potential of genetic research to dramatically improve biomedical prevention and treatment of disease. The promise of 'personalized medicine' has fuelled the large-scale funding of efforts to identify genetic mutations associated with disease. In the absence of cost-effective ubiquitous genotyping technology, researchers have tended to favor population-based sampling. Current strategies of using racially identified populations in the mapping of genetic markers, however, should be viewed with due consideration of the potential social and ethical implications of such research. Of particular concern is how to ensure democratic participation and social equity among historically marginalized populations in the scientific enterprise.

Population-based DNA sampling and the identification of racial minorities in research on human genetic variation have broadened the debate over ethical participation and, in particular, informed consent. At issue is the responsibility of researchers and clinicians to prevent *future* harm associated with knowledge that links race, disease and genes and the need for the participation of research populations in the scientific process. Harm from race-based genetic research may extend beyond the individuals at risk of a particular disease if targeted genetic testing implicates socially identifiable groups. Increasing attention to the ethical implications of research on human genetic variation has resulted in a shift of emphasis from individuals to 'groups'. The question of who should 'consent' to genomic research demands a discussion of who are the potential victims of research-related harm (Kass and Sugarman 1996). Although the current informed consent process focuses on individual participants in scientific studies, risks stemming from population-based research may affect those who are not direct participants but who are implicated by their identification with a particular group (Faden and Beauchamp 1986; Wilcox et al. 1999).

Acknowledgment of such harms has fuelled a growing debate over whether individuals alone are sufficient to consent to research participation or whether others who subscribe to or are ascribed membership in a racial group should also participate in this process as potential victims of research (Greely 2001). Several scholars and policy makers have advocated 'community consultation', arguing that internal review boards should implement new mechanisms that supplement individual consent with group permission (Clayton 1995; Foster and Sharp 2000; Weijer 1999). Others have countered that giving groups the moral authority to bestow informed consent is conceptually flawed and logistically confusing (Juengst 1998). In dispute are the assumptions that there is a singular, self-evident social body that represents a particular individual human subject, that this social body has the moral authority to 'speak' for all the members of a particular group and that consultation with that social body absolves researchers of any responsibility for prospective harm.

The perils of genetic reductionism

Genetic reductionism reflects the power of integrated theories of knowledge production that begin with faith in one particular approach to the scientific endeavor. A reductionist perspective relies on a 'unity of knowledge' that suggests an opposition between culture and science and that privileges genes as a fundamental basis for human behavior. In this framework, culture is understood as mechanistic. Just as ethnicity is often relegated to a static list of attributes associated with particular groups, culture has been relegated to mental or cognitive constructs that are unchanging and essentializing. In the reductionist model of knowledge production, culture is subsumed within a genetic epistemology. Reductionist science leads to a particular approach to health research and a particular, similarly decontextualized, approach to ethnic or cultural identity.

Despite the mantra of sameness, the link between race, genetics and disease has particular salience in the development of the calculus of risk in biomedicine. Policies that require racial and ethnic categorization inevitably lead to correlations that may prematurely be interpreted as causal. The conflation of correlation with causation in medical research presents particular risks that any racial or ethnic identifiers used in human genetic variation research will come to be reified as biological constructs, fostering genetic essentialism. This essentialism could obscure the fluid nature of the 'boundaries' between groups and the common genetic variation within all groups.

One example is sickle-cell anemia, an autosomal recessive disease that is caused by a point mutation in the hemoglobin beta gene *HBB*. It is a condition that has been racialized as a 'black disease' in the United States. However, closer scrutiny reveals that the incidence of sickle-cell anemia is associated with zones of high malaria incidence, because carriers of that gene have some degree of protection against malaria. The condition is the result of human migration and the interaction of genes with the environment. Its emergence as a racial disease is an artifact of U.S. history. If the source of slaves to the Americas had been Mediterranean regions, where the incidence of the disease is also appreciably high, rather than from Africa, sickle-cell anemia might have become known as a southern European disease. Historian Keith Wailoo (2000) provides a richly detailed account of the politicization of sickle-cell anemia in the USA in his book *Dying in the City of Blues*, which powerfully demonstrates the reification of race.

Alternatives to a reductionist understanding of ethnic or racialized identity do offer a different approach to health research. Recent work in the social sciences on race and ethnicity has emphasized notions of 'situational ethnicity', in which identity is dependent on the specific contexts in which individuals find themselves. In addition, the concept of 'plastic ethnicity' highlights individual and group agency as opposed to structural inscriptions of identity. Gillborn (1995: 19) writes, 'Thus, while race and ethnicity continue to be of critical importance, their precise form and interaction with other variables is uncertain, open to change – it is a *plastic ethnicity*' (emphasis original). It is the view that how ethnicity is deployed is highly politicized and changes depending on the social frame – it is never stable across political domains and social interfaces. Again, in Gillborn's view, 'it is a multi-faceted, malleable ethnicity that may at once give meaning to a person's life, just as it is open to manipulation and abuse – it is about power' (20). As such, plastic ethnicity is useful in suggesting a continual recalibration of self-agency in defining who and what one is and the structural constraints that determine how one is perceived.

The significance of such theories for health is an understanding that racial and ethnic identities – including health-related beliefs – take on different qualities and cannot be treated as stable entities even within an individual life course. We possess 'multiple identities'; a person's gender, religion, nationality or age may take on lesser or greater importance at different times and in different places, contributing to a number of cultural identities. Reductionist research that locates ethnic identity in genetic variation confounds the notion of malleable identity. The implication of such research is that self-identity may be supplanted by the genetically based identification of individuals and groups. The result of such a shift in which identity is no longer a product of self-definition but rather is ascribed by science has serious implications for how human identity will be conceived. Critical to this shift in identity politics is the explanatory power of genetic discourse in its 'appearance and allure of specificity' in classifying individual identity. To incorporate these alternative frameworks of group difference, dialogue between social scientists and scientists will be crucial.

To return to Omi and Winant (1994), it is useful to retain a framework of engaging race that emphasizes what the sociologists identify as the process of 'making race' – *racialization* – to signify the extension of racial meaning to a previously racially unclassified relationship, social practice or group. Racialization is an ideological process that can only be fully understood within the specific historical context in which it unfolds. St Louis (this volume) argues for racial eliminativism that combines 'epistemological scrutiny, ethical critique and political prescription', which identifies race as an erroneous and pernicious social category. Strategies which build on the suggestion that race is not real in the sense of being an object of empirical inquiry are challenging in the context of human genetic variation research, where close scrutiny of genetic ancestry, for example, assumes difference at the continental level, recapitulating the age-old prism of race. Race work results in the ascribing of gene segments as Asian, African and European, where race is operationalized as a research variable.

The prevailing assumptions and values associated with identifying population differences are informed by a racial ideology which may result in a reawakening of an era of racial biology. A challenge for those who have inherited the 'new genetics' will be to vanquish the continuing paradox of reciting a 'mantra of sameness', yet all the while searching for meaningful differences. There are dire costs for chronic ambivalence over the issues of race and justice in science – we only need to look to history as our proof. Social scientists and humanists can contribute to and catalyze a conversation on the meaning of difference in the context of the emerging genomic sciences.[1] To underestimate the power of science to define our social agenda is to lose an opportunity to determine our future course.

REFERENCES

American Association of Physical Anthropologists. (1996). Statement of biological aspects of race. *American Journal of Physical Anthropology*, 101, 569–70.
Bonilla-Silva, E. (2006). *Racism without Racists: Color-Blind Racism and the Persistence of Racial Inequality in the United States*. Lanham, MD: Rowman and Littlefield.

[1] Several edited volumes have provided useful contributions to discourse on race and genetics since the completion of the HGP. These include Koenig et al. (2008), Wailoo et al. (2012) and Whitmarsh and Jones (2010).

Brandt, A. (1985). Racism and research: the case of the Tuskegee Syphilis Study. In J. Walzer Leavitt and R. L. Numbers, eds, *Sickness and Health in America: Readings in the History of Medicine and Public Health*. Madison: University of Wisconsin Press, pp. 331–46.

Cavalli-Sforza, L. L., Menozzi, P. and Piazza, A. (1994). *The History and Geography of Human Genes*. Princeton, NJ: Princeton University Press.

Clayton, E. W. (1995). Why the use of anonymous samples for research matters. *Journal of Law, Medicine, and Ethics*, 23(4), 375–77.

Dikötter, F. (1998). Race culture: recent perspectives on the history of eugenics. *American Historical Review*, 103(2), 467–78.

Epstein, S. (2008). *Inclusion: The Politics of Difference in Medical Research*. Chicago: University of Chicago Press.

Faden, R. and Beauchamp, T. (1986). *A History and Theory of Informed Consent*. New York: Oxford University Press.

Foster, M. and Sharp, R. (2000). Genetic research and cultural specific risks: one size does not fit all. *Trends in Genetics*, 16(2), 93–95.

Fujimura, J. and Rajagapolan, R. (2011). Different differences: the use of 'genetic ancestry' versus race in biomedical human genetic research. *Social Studies of Science*, 41(1), 5–30.

Galton, F. (1987). Eugenics: its definition, scope, and aims. *American Journal of Sociology*, 10(1), 1–25.

Gamble, V. (1997). Under the shadow of Tuskegee: African Americans and health care. *American Journal of Public Health*, 87(11), 1773–78.

Gillborn, D. (1995). Racism, identity and modernity: pluralism, moral antiracism and plastic ethnicity. *International Studies in Sociology of Education*, 5(1), 3–23.

Greely, H. (2001). Human genomics research: new challenges for research ethics. *Perspectives in Biology and Medicine*, 44(2), 221–29.

Jones, J. H. (1981). *Bad Blood: The Tuskegee Syphilis Experiment*. London: Free Press.

Juengst, E. (1998). Groups as gatekeepers to genetic research: conceptually confusing, morally hazardous and practically useless. *Kennedy Institute of Ethics Journal*, 8(2), 183–200.

Kass, N. and Sugarman, J. (1996). Are research subjects adequately protected? *Kennedy Institute of Ethics Journal*, 6(3), 271–82.

Koenig, B., Lee, S. S.-J. and Richardson, S. (2008). *Revisiting Race in a Genomic Age*. New Brunswick, NJ: Rutgers University Press.

Lee, S. S.-J., Mountain, J. and Koenig, B. (2001). The meaning of 'race' in the new genomics: implications for health disparities research. *Yale Journal of Health Policy, Law and Ethics*, 1, 33–75.

Lewontin, R. C. (1982). *Human Diversity*. New York: Scientific American.

Omi, M. and Winant, H. (1994). *Racial Formation in the United States*, 2nd edn. London: Routledge.

Risch, N., Burchard, E., Ziv, E. and Tang, H. (2002). Categorization of humans in biomedical research: genes, race and disease. *Genome Biology*, 3(7), 1–12.

Sankar, P. (2010). Forensic DNA phenotyping: reinforcing race in law enforcement. In I. Whitmarsh and D. Jones, eds, *What's the Use of Race?*, pp. 49–62.

Sankar, P., Cho, M. K. and Mountain, J. (2007). Race and ethnicity in genetic research. *American Journal of Medical Genetics*, 9(143A), 961–70.

Stepan, N. L. (1996). *The Hour of Eugenics: Race, Gender, and Nation in Latin America*. Ithaca, NY: Cornell University Press.

Tutton, R., Smart, A., Ashcroft, R., Martin, P. and Ellison, G. T. H. (2010). From self-identity to genotype: the past, present, and future of ethnic categories in postgenomic science. In I. Whitmarsh and D. Jones, eds, *What's the Use of Race?*, pp. 125–46.

Wailoo, K. (2000). *Dying in the City of the Blues: Sickle Cell Anemia and the Politics of Race and Health*. Raleigh: University of North Carolina Press.

Wailoo, N., Nelson, A. and Lee, C. (2012). *Genetics and the Unsettled Past*. New Brunswick, NJ: Rutgers University Press.

Weigmann, K. (2001). In the name of science. *EMBO Reports*, 21(101), 871–75.

Weijer, C. (1999). Protecting communities in research: philosophical and pragmatic challenges. *Cambridge Quarterly of Health Care Ethics*, 8(4), 501–13.

Weiss, K. (1995). *Genetic Variation and Human Disease*. Cambridge: Cambridge University Press.

Whitmarsh, I. and Jones, D., eds. (2010). *What's the Use of Race?* Cambridge, MA: MIT Press.

Wilcox, A. J., Taylor, J. A. and Sharp, R. R. (1999). Genetic determinism and the overprotection of human subjects. *Nature Genetics*, 21(4), 362.

Zack, N. (2001). Race and philosophical meaning. In B. Boxhill, ed., *Race and Racism*. Oxford: Oxford University Press, pp. 43–57.

3   Color-blind egalitarianism as the new racial norm

Charles A. Gallagher

Profound changes are currently taking place in the United States in terms of how race, race relations and perceptions of social mobility are defined, perceived and understood. It is now the case that a majority of white Americans subscribe to a color-blind narrative of society where institutional racism has been eliminated and the American Creed of 'racial equality for all' has been achieved. The perception held by a majority of whites is that skin color is no longer the basis for discriminatory treatment, nor does race play a role in shaping socioeconomic mobility. White Americans can now point to President Barack Obama, the first black president of the United States, as proof that the goals of the civil rights movement of the 1960s have been achieved (Ludwig 2004). As many whites now see it, the United States has shifted from a country where race was the means by which all socioeconomic resources were allocated to a meritocractic country. This perspective, which I define as color-blind egalitarianism, is the tendency to claim that racial equality is now the norm, while simultaneously ignoring or discounting the real and ongoing ways in which institutional racism continues to disadvantage racial minorities. Color-blind egalitarianism reflects the fact that most whites, as expressed in national polling data, now view race as a benign social marker that has little or no bearing on an individual's or group's educational, economic or occupational mobility. This 'leveled playing field' perspective of society held by most whites is now the common-sense understanding of race relations, even though an extensive body of research documents how and in what ways institutional racism and racial discrimination continue to shape the life chances of racial minorities. In this chapter, I examine how color-blind racial egalitarianism came to dominate the narrative of race in the United States and the implications which this perspective holds for both race relations and the challenges which scholars face when they attempt to examine race-based social inequalities.

From race and racism to color-blindness

The black–white racial dichotomy, once the singular and dominant theoretical model for understanding the dynamics of race relations in the United States, has been supplanted by competing narratives of why racial inequality persists and how the meanings of racial categories shift over time. Theoretical models that include the cultural and political implications of racial hybridity (Brunsma 2006; Dalmage 2000; Gallagher 2006), neoliberal accounts of continued racial inequality (Bobo 2001; Bonilla-Silva 2003) and continua based on black and non-black hierarchies (Bonilla-Silva 2003, 2004; Gallagher 2006; Gans 1999; Yancey 2003) now provide a more nuanced and realistic depiction of contemporary racial identity construction and race relations.

Distinct from and emerging alongside these theories of racial inequality is an account of race that reflects a new understanding about race relations and the role and status of what it currently means to be white in the United States. What has emerged in the media and politics and has been articulated in popular culture is a narrative of race relations grounded in the perception that the United States is now a color-blind nation. The rise of a color-blind perspective reflects the belief that the universal enforcement of civil rights in the 1960s and the rising socioeconomic status of racial minorities that accompanied the dismantling of discrimination in the labor market reflected the end of institutional racism. Parallel to this account of upward mobility for racial minorities was the eradication of white privilege. Indeed, in many political and cultural corners, it is argued that there has been a reversal of racial fortunes, where whites have lost out socioeconomically to racial minorities because government programs, as a U.S. senator recently put it, 'favor anyone who does not happen to be white' (Webb 2010).

Existing models of race relations that focus on the centrality of white privilege, white supremacy or the institutions that reproduce racial inequality have at their theoretical core an assumption that whites acknowledge and understand structural accounts of racial inequality but consciously support the existing social hierarchy because these social arrangements privilege whites (Bobo 2001; Bonilla-Silva 2003). Race scholars assert that whites know that their whiteness is a privileged and privileging racial category and are aware of institutional racism but discount the social factors responsible for racial inequality because the denial of race-based inequality serves their collective material interests (Bobo 2001; Wellman 1993). This explanation of acknowledged white privilege, while still applicable to parts of the white population, is, however, incomplete. It is now the case that a sizable part of the white population no longer believes that institutional racism or the legacy of slavery and Jim Crow accounts for racial disparities between whites and blacks. President Obama, television and sports celebrities and other high-profile black and Latino luminaries further cement the notion that the glass ceiling of institutional racism has been shattered. While the rich and famous are exceptions among any racial or ethnic groups, black and brown celebrity figures come to represent the norm of what is possible rather than the exceptions that they are. Given the success stories of non-white celebrities in the media, color-blind egalitarianism provides whites with a way of seeing race-based inequalities as a function of non-racial factors.

The core belief that undergirds color-blind egalitarianism is the conviction that white privilege is a prerogative of the past. This framework creates mutually exclusive categories for understanding racial equality; it is simply not possible to espouse a philosophy of color-blindness and also acknowledge that society is organized in ways which continue to benefit whites. Color-blindness is no longer an abstract description of how society should be or a vaulted political ideal but a concrete, systematic way of seeing, organizing and processing information about other racial groups that ultimately serves to erase white privilege. Alternately, this perspective also discounts or simply ignores the extent to which institutional racism continues to block the socioeconomic mobility of racial minorities. In the media and many political circles, racial equality is taken at face value, a cultural given at a time when every quality-of-life indicator – from rates of infant mortality, incarceration and home foreclosure to poverty – disproportionately affects racial minorities.

What if embracing a color-blind view of society is not an evasive maneuver through which to maintain privilege, as many race theorists suggest, but is now simply regarded as the way things are? What if color-blindness has evolved into a social fact that is part of society's collective consciousness? It is my contention that, for many whites, that time is now. We have arrived at the point where a large part of the dominant group has truly come to believe that individuals are now judged by the content of their character and not by the color of their skin. A number of social forces have converged that have pushed color-blind egalitarianism from an abstract cultural ideal to a social fact that is now normative. Demographic trends, changes in how later-generation whites self-identify in terms of their ethnicity, an ideology of neoliberalism and the framing of whites as a cultural and numerical minority group have allowed a color-blind description of race relations to gain cultural traction, becoming the dominant cultural narrative of U.S. race relations. In this chapter, I draw on survey evidence and the media's depiction of race to demonstrate that the shift to a color-blindness perspective is now the 'new normal'. In the face of continued and growing racial inequality and the resegregation of parts of American society, the implications of a color-blind perspective have enormous and dire implications for social policies that have historically attempted to ameliorate race-based inequality.

Media-mediated color-blindness

Two instances are illustrative of how race is currently being reframed in the media and interpreted by a sizable segment of the white population. The first is summed up in the cultural analysis offered by the mainstream press when the USA elected its first black president. The day after Barack Obama was elected president of the United States, the *New York Times* declared 'OBAMA WINS! RACIAL BARRIER *FALLS* IN DECISIVE VICTORY' (Nagourney 2009). The *Boston Globe* had this to say about this historic event: 'Beyond the policies, Obama's election will stand forever amid the great milestones of America's racial history, the *end* of a torturous progression from emancipation, to the civil rights movement, to the election of the first black president' (Canellos 2008). After the election, the *Wall Street Journal*'s (2008) editorial board asserted that: 'While Mr. Obama lost among white voters...his success is due in part to the fact that he also *muted* any politics of racial grievance. One promise of his victory is that perhaps we can put to rest the myth of racism as a barrier to achievement in this splendid country. Mr. Obama has a special obligation to help do so.'

The 'racism as myth' theme was repeated by conservative commentators Abigail and Stephan Thernstrom, who remarked that 'the myth of racist white voters was destroyed by this year's presidential election' (Thernstrom and Thernstrom 2008). Left unsaid in their analysis was that a majority of whites (53 per cent) voted for John McCain, the white presidential candidate. Immediately after Obama was elected, *Washington Post* columnist Richard Cohen explained that 'it is not just that Obama is post-racial; so is the nation he is generationally primed to lead' (Cohen 2008).

These newspaper accounts made their point exceptionally clearly – racism is not, and presumably has not for some time, been an obstacle to upward mobility, unequal treatment or a 'barrier to achievement'. According to these mainstream media accounts, the election of President Barack Obama to the White House has exposed the idea that institutional racism continues to infect our country for what it is – a set of archaic beliefs held by those who refuse to acknowledge that our nation's ideological mandate that all men and women are created equal has been achieved. Racism is, as these commentators noted, a myth – a false collective belief no longer grounded in empirical fact. That white voters were instrumental in electing a black man to the White House is undeniable proof that color-blindness has become America's new racial norm. Those individuals who do sift, read and divine racial inequality from census reports, housing audits and objective empirical research are increasingly viewed as clinging to an antiquated worldview or inserting race into the analysis of social situations when race was merely an incidental factor.

A second example, also revolving around a black man and the symbolic meaning of race, mobility and color-blindness, involved a high-status professor who unwittingly became a Rorschach test for the meaning of race in the United States. As an academic who studies race, I had been invited on a radio talk show to discuss the controversy surrounding the arrest of Harvard University Professor Henry Louis Gates Jr. A white Cambridge, Massachusetts, police officer responded to a call that a black man was attempting to break into a house. When police arrived, Professor Gates, an older black man, was thought to be the perpetrator and was arrested for attempting to burgle what turned out to be his own home.

The CBS radio affiliate which had me on the air to discuss the role that race played in the arrest of Professor Gates is a sports and political venue that carries conservative talk show hosts like Glenn Beck, Rush Limbaugh, and Sean Hannity. In terms of the demographic profile of those who tune in to this talk radio station, it is safe to say that the typical listener is white and mostly male. When the call-in lines were opened for discussion, what became immediately clear was that most callers had no interest in discussing whether Professor Gates's race had played any role in the way the situation unfolded or, more generally, if racial minorities are subject to different treatment by the police relative to whites. What most callers made absolutely clear was that it was preposterous to assert, in this day and age, that race played any role in what happened to Professor Gates. It was simply outrageous for this rich, successful, Harvard professor to cry racism when the White House was now home to a black family and racial minorities occupy positions of power at every societal level in American society. As was raised a number of times during the call-in period, Barack Obama's election as president was proof to these callers that we are now a post-race, post–civil rights, color-blind society. The fact that blacks are treated, on average, more harshly than whites within the context of our system of criminal justice was an extraneous point. This incident snowballed into a major 'race' event when President Obama commented that the Cambridge police acted 'stupidly' in Professor Gates's arrest. The president was harshly criticized by callers for racializing a situation that had nothing to do with race. The fault, as these callers let it be known, was that this pampered 'elite' refused to follow simple police instructions and, as a result, was arrested.

Within the framework of color-blind race relations, it was President Obama who was being racist because acknowledging racism – that is, the act of pointing out racist actions – is a form of racism itself as, in a color-blind society, institutional racism no longer exists. Adherents of color-blindness will readily admit that there are individual manifestations of racism but that these singular acts of hate are carried out by fringe elements of the population, individual outliers who are unrepresentative of America's new consensus on race.

A comment sent in to me on a blog that followed a newspaper interview I did on the Gates affair clarifies the new racial logic of color-blindness. The blogger wrote that

this whole whiney baby bull about racism is getting really old . . . get the hell over it . . . The race card is played out, no one feels bad for you anymore, GET OVER IT.

Many of these callers and bloggers believe it was racist to claim that racism was a motivating factor in this event because, as they see it, race is no longer an obstacle to mobility or the basis for differential treatment. Fox's Glenn Beck's comment on the Gates affair illustrates the defensive rhetoric of color-blindness where the messenger is attacked for pointing out that race still matters. Beck said, 'This president has exposed himself as a guy over and over and over again who has a deep-seated hatred for white people . . . This guy is, I believe, a racist.'

The color-blind framework follows this line of reasoning: 'If we were still a society where race shaped life chances we would not have a Barack Obama in the White House, a Henry Louis Gates Jr. at Harvard, or a Latina and black man serving on the Supreme Court. How can racial animus still motivate American society when 43 per cent of the eligible white electorate voted for a black president? How can racism be systemic when a 2009 Gallup poll tells us that seven of the top twenty most-admired people chosen by Americans were black? Are we not beyond color when the third, fourth and fifth most-admired women in the United States are African-American females?' (Jones 2009: 1–2).

Embracing color-blind egalitarianism as a way of understanding racial hierarchy allows individuals to inhabit a skin color but to view race as not conferring any relative social privilege or disadvantage. Within this perspective, there is no such thing as white privilege. Within this binary, color-blindness and white privilege are mutually exclusive categories because you cannot simultaneously believe that racial equality is the new norm and acknowledge that being white affords a host of social and economic privileges. There simply cannot be white privilege in a post-race, color-blind America.

Many race scholars argue that the reason why whites deny the existence of institutional racism is because they get tangible benefits out of buying into a color-blind belief system (Bobo 2001; Wellman 1993). Much of the scholarship on white racial attitudes starts with the assumption that whites are fully aware of the structural disparities that exist between whites and racial minorities and, despite this knowledge, embrace a color-blind view of society that erases or minimizes institutional racism. The dominant line of thinking among researchers is that whites fully understand that the system is rigged in their favor yet choose to do nothing about it because the status quo serves their interests.

While some part of the white population may actively understand the privileges they enjoy and do nothing to alter these arrangements, there is evidence that how racial privilege is now understood is much more complicated. For many whites, the denial of white privilege and the embracing of color-blindness is not a slick, knowing dodge or an evasive, calculating maneuver to maintain racial dominance and the established racial pecking order. For much of white America, color-blindness rests on the deeply and widely held false belief that the socioeconomic playing field is now level and failures and successes reflect individual efforts, not race-based structural barriers.

Survey trends: pointing toward color-blindness

Recent trends in racial attitudes suggest that a sizable portion of the white population have arrived at a tipping point where perceptions of equality have pushed aside structural explanations of racial disparities between groups. Nationally representative survey data on racial attitudes paint a picture where equity, equality and the perceived absence of discrimination are now the everyday commonsense understanding of race relations for many white Americans.

A Gallup poll in 2007 found that 71 per cent of white Americans were satisfied with the way in which society treats blacks (Jones 2007). Close to half of white Americans, 43 per cent, said that racial discrimination toward blacks was not serious or not serious at all. More than half of all whites (55 per cent) believe that racism is not widespread, though 42 per cent of whites do believe racism against whites to be widespread in the USA (Jones 2007, 2008). A 2010 *New York Times* poll found that close to half, 48 per cent, of whites agreed with the statement that 'Discrimination against whites has become as big a problem as discrimination against blacks and other minorities' (Blow 2010). This number jumps to 58 per cent among whites between the ages of 18 and 24 (Jones 2012).

A majority of whites, 71 per cent, believe that African Americans have 'more' or 'about the same opportunities in life' as whites. An ABC poll found that 76 per cent of whites believed blacks have achieved or will soon achieve 'racial equality' in the USA. This same poll found that, in 1996, a majority of whites – 52 per cent – saw racism as a 'large societal problem'. By 2009, that number had dropped to 22 per cent (ABC News 2009). Gallup tells us that 8 in 10 whites believe that there is no difference in educational opportunities between blacks and whites. Opinion polls tell us that a majority of white Americans believe that 'all or most' of the goals of the civil rights movement have been accomplished and that a majority of whites, 54 per cent, believe the country 'has done enough to give blacks equal rights with whites' (Jones 2008: 2–3). A 2010 *New York Times* poll found that 60 per cent of all Americans believe blacks and whites have an equal chance of getting ahead in today's society (Connelly 2010). A survey by Pew Research Center (2005) found that 63 per cent of whites believe that 'Blacks who can't get ahead in this country are responsible for their own condition.'

If we connect the dots on these surveys, what emerges is a picture of society from which the racial barriers of our past are absent. By some measures, whites believe that they, like racial minorities, are victims of discrimination because of their race. Of course, this view of a color-blind nation begs the question: From an empirical perspective, how color-blind are we? If a sizable part of the population believes that the playing field has been leveled, is it the case that equality of opportunity and equality of results are one and the same? If we examine just a few areas that are indicative of mobility and relative racial equality, it becomes exceptionally difficult to square perceptions of racial equity with the real world. A large and robust body of research points to a number of areas where there has been significant backsliding in terms of the relative fortune and mobility of whites relative to racial minorities. The wealth gap between blacks and whites has grown over the last two decades, with whites on average being five times wealthier than African Americans. In the decades under study, average white wealth went from $22,000 to $100,000, while average black household wealth went from $2,000 to $5,000 (Shapiro 2010). In 2009, the median net worth of white households was $113,149; for black households, it was $5,677 (Pew Research Center 2011). In the early 1980s, high-income blacks had accumulated more assets than middle-income whites – this is no longer the case. The inter-generational transfer of wealth to children and grandchildren is simply not possible when groups are shut out from occupations, pensions and the type of housing that produce wealth assets over time.

State schools are more segregated today than they were in 1970, and these hypersegregated institutions, which serve a largely poor population, have exceptionally high dropout rates (Orfield 2009). Tied closely to segregated schools is the extent to which neighborhoods remain segregated. The wealthiest blacks live in communities that are more segregated than the poorest Latino and Asian neighborhoods. According to U.S. Department of Housing and Urban Development data, Hispanics and blacks continue to face discrimination in the housing and rental markets. Whites are more likely to be shown housing in white neighborhoods than equally qualified black home buyers. Matching studies found that geographic steering was on the rise, suggesting that 'whites and blacks are increasingly likely to be recommended and shown homes in different neighborhoods' (Taylor et al. 2002: 1). Reverse redlining and predatory sub-prime lending in minority neighborhoods have devastated many of these communities. In 2009, in New York City, blacks and Latinos were nine times as likely as whites to be stopped by the police, although they were no more likely to be arrested (Baker 2010). The jobless rate for blacks is 16.5 per cent, almost twice the rate for whites. Access to health care, long-term unemployment, college graduation rates and infant mortality are trends which all point in one direction – enormous race-based disparities remain a central and seemingly intractable facet of who we are as a nation. On one hand, there is the belief by many that the 'race problem' has been addressed, and on the other, an abundance of data show that every quality-of-life measure indicates persistent and, in some cases, growing racial disparities between whites and racial minorities. It is premature at best and reckless at worst to suggest, as many in the media have, that we are now color-blind or that institutional racism is a myth.

While racial and ethnic stereotypes are still present in the media, the degrading racist imagery that was a ubiquitous mainstay of most television programming history has been replaced by a multiracial approach to entertainment. America's racial 'presentation of self' in the mass media is overwhelmingly depicted as an integrated, multiracial environment where individuals consume products in a post-race, color-blind world. Advertisements routinely depict whites, blacks, Asians and Latinos gathering together to shop, eat, work and interact in spaces where race is meaningless. In this carefully manufactured racial utopia, television commercials depict actors of different races inhabiting race-neutral environments where social integration is the norm. In the last two decades, white America has been utterly saturated with images of middle- and upper-middle-class couples from across the racial spectrum living a life quite similar to its own. Watching television depictions of well-off, successful black, brown and Asian Americans has the effect of convincing white Americans that racial minorities share the same socioeconomic opportunities. The non-white success stories in situation comedies, reality programs and television dramas, much like the day-to-day experiences of most whites, convey a message that society is now free of institutional racism or discrimination. The ease with which individuals dance, date, love and marry across the color line in the media is further evidence that race has been defanged of its institutional powers. It is simply unremarkable in 2014 that the USA has a black president, Disney's first black cartoon princess or the most ethnically and racially diverse executive cabinet in the government's history. With such an overwhelming number of examples of mobility for racial minorities, particularly in the area of sports and entertainment, the conclusion is clear: the racist structures of the past that prevented racial minorities from advancing socially, politically and economically are gone.

From ethnicity to race

There has been a shift by many academics toward treating race and ethnicity as similar conceptual categories. Sociologists tend to view ethnicity as a set of cultural characteristics (language, religion) that a group shares, whereas race is understood to be socially selected and privileged phenotypical traits (skin color, facial features) that have been used to create and maintain social hierarchies. The cultural blurring of the distinctions between the 'soft' and 'hard' boundaries of ethnicity and race has allowed color-blind egalitarianism to gain a foothold in our collective imagination. Berkeley historian David Hollinger, among others, has claimed that we are now a post-ethnic society where 'ethnoracial categories central to identity politics would be more a matter of choice than ascription' (Hollinger 2008: 1033). For example, in such a 'post-ethnic' society, President Obama could just as easily celebrate his multiracial upbringing in Hawaii or his white, midwestern identity as he could his black, East African ancestry. Most importantly, according to this model, those around him in Kansas or Kenya, white or black, would see him as an accepted and undifferentiated member of that community.

The blurring of distinctions between race and ethnicity most certainly explains the experiences of whites whose European ancestors are now several generations removed from their immigrant experiences. Most young whites today have undergone such extensive generational and spatial ethnic assimilation and a convergence of cultural experiences that the option to engage in those activities or embrace the traditions which forge and give shape to an ethnic identity no longer exists. The psychological and political functions which ethnicity may have served at one time for earlier waves of white immigrants have, in large part, been lost or are now instrumentally obsolete. Ethnic identity, however, still gets 'used' by later-generation whites to evoke stories of immigrant relatives who overcame adversity by engaging in the thrift and hard work that made upward mobility and the achieving of the American Dream possible. These accounts validate many whites' beliefs that, if past generations could climb the social and occupational ladder in an environment brutally hostile to white ethnic newcomers with no government intervention, why is it that non-whites, particularly blacks, have been unable to mirror their grandfathers' mobility path? Within this perspective, where white ethnicity is reconstructed as the social equivalent of being black, Latino or Asian, whites are able to maintain the fiction that every group, regardless of color, has been equally victimized by racial and ethnic prejudice.

We can see the conflation of race and ethnicity and its lineage to a philosophy of socioeconomic bootstrapping in a recent 2010 survey on political ideology. Whites were given the following statement: 'Irish, Italians and Jewish and many other minorities overcame prejudice and worked their way up. Blacks should do the same without special favors.' The survey found that 70 per cent of whites agreed with this statement, whereas a white majority, 58 per cent, disagreed with the statement 'Generations of slavery and discrimination have created conditions that make it difficult for blacks to work their way out of the lower class' (Parker 2010). In the former survey statement, the past and present social, political and economic conditions of blacks are equated with those of white ethnics. The real discrimination to which white ethnics were temporarily subjected upon arrival in the United States becomes analogous to and indistinguishable from three centuries of slavery, Jim Crow, legal segregation and state-sanctioned 'benign neglect'. The survey responses suggest that, in 2010, blacks should have attained the same inter-generational mobility and socioeconomic parity as white immigrants because the barriers to mobility were gone. Equating the historical and contemporary experiences of white ethnics and blacks places the color-blind perspective, with its explicit message of equal opportunity, as being normative, while ignoring existing racial hierarchies and centuries of institutional racism which privilege one racial group over another.

Color-blindness as political ideology

The ascendancy of color-blind egalitarianism also reflects a political narrative that has been a constant theme of neoconservatives over the last several decades. Political writers suggest that 'if you tell the same story five times, it's true.' It has been the sheer repetition of this color-blind message from politicians and neoconservative writers and the depiction of a post-race integrated world manufactured and disseminated by Hollywood that has made the color-blind perspective part of our collective consciousness. More than 30 years ago, liberal sociologist William Julius Wilson's (1978) book titled *The Declining Significance of Race* was used as the mantra of right-wing and neoconservative pundits who announced that the end of racism had arrived. Conservative critic Dinesh D'Souza (1995) announced that the end of racism had arrived, appropriately enough, in his book titled *The End of Racism*. Embedded in this end-of-racism philosophy is a neoliberal account that reflects a belief in the non-discriminatory, rational logic of the market where merit and not arbitrary factors like race or gender defines social outcomes. Given the lack of structural obstacles like discrimination or racism, success – like failure – is an individual choice. One is free to choose where one would like to be on the socioeconomic ladder: president of the USA, a partner in a law firm, cleaning out the law partner's trash can or incarceration. Placement in the post-race economic pecking order reflects investments in human capital and individual agency, not the outcomes of racist social structures. Shelby Steele, a black conservative commentator at the Hoover Institute, sums up the neoliberal color-blind perspective perfectly, noting that racism 'no longer remotely accounts for the difficulties in black America' (Scott 2008).

President Obama mastered the ability to maneuver around or simply avoid issues that would require him to explicitly discuss institutional racism. In so doing, he was viewed by many Americans as a politician, who happened to be black, who had transcended race politics. President Obama used the theme of racial transcendence as early as 2004, when he famously said, 'There is not a liberal America and a conservative America – there is the United States of America. There is not a black America and a white America and Latino America and Asian America – there's the United States of America' (Obama 2004). This 'from many, one' philosophy set the stage for a campaign that would be defined by the media, rightfully or not, as post-race. The post-race aphorism that followed Obama's election further cemented the color-blind egalitarian perspective.

What has become painfully obvious is that the 'declining significance of race' narrative does not reflect a continued reduction in racial inequality but now refers to our inability to candidly talk about the role which race continues to play in how resources are allocated and how society remains stratified by race. Pointing out that institutional racism remains one of our nation's social ills has become the third rail of politics; touch the rail at your own peril. President Obama learned the dangers of going off script and candidly and honestly talking about race by suggesting that racial bias by the police may have been a factor in the arrest of a black man. The Gates affair resulted in a public reconciliation (aka the beer summit) that included the president, Professor Gates, the arresting officer and Vice President Joe Biden. The implicit message concerning a color-blind race narrative was clear; within the public discourse, any suggestion that institutional racism is the motivation for discriminatory behavior should be discounted, downplayed or ignored. The end result is color-blind egalitarianism, which has resulted in a chilling effect on public dialogue about the root causes of racial inequality.

Minority or majority: who's on first?

Changes in the demographic makeup of the country and shifting definitions of racial categories have resulted in some confusion as to which racial group now constitutes a numerical majority and which individuals should be included in which ethnic and racial groups. In March 2010, the press once again ran the story 'WHITES IN U.S. A MINORITY BY 2050' (Spillius 2010). This demographic projection has been in the news cycle for more than a decade, but what seems to get lost on most Americans is the qualifier that this projection is almost a half-century away in 2050. This projection is also extremely deceptive because it uses a rather limited and narrow definition of who should or can be included in the white category. Almost 30 million Latinos, or 62 per cent of this population, define themselves as 'white only' in the U.S. Census. The Latino population more than doubled, from 22 million in 1990 to 47 million in 2010. Latinos now make up 15 per cent of the U.S. population, making them more numerous than the black population and the largest minority in the USA (U.S. Census Bureau 2006). If Latinos who define themselves as white are added to the non-Hispanic population as defined by the U.S. Census, whites account for nearly 80 per cent of the U.S. population. If we use predictions of the growth of the Latino population and predict ahead to 2050, those who define themselves as white would still constitute about 75 per cent of the U.S. population. Whites are the overwhelming numerical majority in the USA and will remain so for some time.

Many race scholars argue that what is supplanting the black–white model is a racial hierarchy better characterized as 'black and non-black.' The 'non-black category' includes whites; middle-class, mixed or light-skinned Asians and Latinos; and newly arrived white immigrants from Eastern Europe (Gallagher 2010; Gans 1999). In many ways, this model looks like the racial hierarchy that exists throughout Latin America, where light skin and European features are a form of social and cultural capital. It is now the case that there is simply no shortage of well-placed, highly visible, successful, light-skinned assimilated Latinos who can be pointed to as examples that the color line has been erased. The ideal of color-blindness is reinforced as this rather narrow sub-population of the Latino community is held up as an example of this erasure, even though much of the Latino community finds itself in the same difficult socioeconomic situation as African Americans.

The implications of color-blind egalitarianism

A convergence of factors has shifted the idea of color-blindness as an abstract legal principle or cultural goal to one viewed by many whites as a social fact whose time has arrived. A sizable portion of white America has reached what they believe is the truthful conclusion that whites and racial minorities have achieved socioeconomic parity. The implications for embracing a color-blind egalitarian perspective when race-based inequality remains a glaring social issue are many. Young Americans have been subject to an endless loop of color-blind imagery on television, in popular culture and in the press. If a color-blind view of racial inequality is taken at face value, which polling data suggest is now the case, raising the question of racial inequality is bound to be met with resistance or denial because many believe such inequality no longer exists. With color-blindness as the accepted racial frame, any race-conscious remedies by the government will be construed as discrimination toward whites, who will see themselves as the targets and victims of reverse racism.

I have witnessed such pushback, almost exclusively from my white students, when discussing racial inequality in the university classroom. In what appears very similar to the newspaper sound bites which I discussed earlier in this chapter, students challenge any talk of institutional racism with the 'What about Obama?' retort, which implies that we are beyond race because there is a black man in the White House. This is a fair question from 18-year-old college students, many of whom were raised in almost exclusively white, middle-class suburbs. But we must realize that, for many whites of all ages, the 'What about Obama?' knee-jerk response is now the default answer about the nature of racial equality in the USA. How the topic of racial inequality and institutional racism is currently being reframed by the media and political elites around a narrative of color-blind egalitarianism reflects how systems of racial oppression can maintain white privilege simply by redefining institutionally based racial stratification out of existence. Color-blind egalitarianism as a perspective and ideological conviction will mean that any substantive discussion of racial justice in the United States, and the programs required to ameliorate these inequalities, will be met with resistance, shock or, most probably, disgust by the growing population of whites who truly believe that we are a color-blind society.

REFERENCES

ABC News. (2009). How big a problem is racism in our society today? www.pollingreport.com/race2.htm.

Baker, A. (2010). Minorities frisked more but arrested as same rate. *New York Times*, 13 May, A1.

Blow, C. (2010). Let's rescue the race debate. *New York Times*, 19 November, A19.

Bobo, L. (2001). Racial attitudes and relations at the close of the twentieth century. In N. Smelser, W. J. Wilson and F. Mitchell, eds, *America Becoming: Racial Trends and Their Consequences*. Washington, DC: National Academy Press, pp. 262–99.

Bonilla-Silva, E. (2003). *Racism without Racists: Color-Blind Racism and the Persistence of Racial Inequality in the United States*. New York: Rowman and Littlefield.

(2004). From bi-racial to tri-racial. *Ethnic and Racial Studies*, 27(6), 931–50.

Brunsma, D., ed. (2006). *Mixed Messages: Multiracial Identities in the 'Colour-Blind' Era*. Boulder, CO: Lynne Rienner.

Canellos, P. (2008). Shift in tone will bring a watershed for the nation. *Boston Globe*, 5 November, A1.

Cohen, R. (2008). The election that LBJ won. *Washington Post*, 4 November, A16.

Connelly, M. (2010). Poll finds tea party backers wealthier and more educated. *New York Times*, 15 April, A1.

Dalmage, H. (2000). *Tripping the Color Line: Black–White Multiracial Families in a Racially Divided World*. New Brunswick, NJ: Rutgers University Press.

D'Souza, D. (1995). *The End of Racism: Principles for a Multiracial Society*. New York: Free Press.

Gallagher, C. A. (2006). Color blindness: an obstacle to racial justice? In D. Brunsma, ed., *Mixed Messages: Multiracial Identities in the 'Colour-Blind' Era*. pp. 103–16.

(2010). In-between racial status, mobility and the promise of assimilation: Irish, Italians yesterday, Latinos and Asians today. In K. Korgen, ed.,

Multiracial Americans and Social Class: The Influence of Social Class on Racial Identity. New York: Routledge, pp. 10–21.

Gans, H. (1999). The possibility of a new racial hierarchy in the twenty-first-century United States. In M. Lamont, ed., *The Cultural Territories of Race: Black and White Boundaries*. Chicago: University of Chicago Press, pp. 371–90.

Hollinger, D. (2008). Obama, the instability of color lines, and the promise of a post-ethnic future. *Callaloo*, 31(4), 1033–37.

Jones, J. (2007). Only 4 in 10 Americans satisfied with treatment of immigrants. *Gallup*, 15 August, 1–14.

(2008). Majority of Americans say racism against blacks widespread. *Gallup*, 4 August, 1–6.

(2009). Clinton edges Palin out as most admired woman. *Gallup*, 30 December, 1–7.

(2012). *A Generation in Transition: Findings from the 2012 Millennial Values Survey*. Washington, DC: Public Religion Research Institute.

Ludwig, J. (2004). Has the Civil Rights Movement overcome? *Gallup*, 8 June, 1–4.

Nagourney, A. (2009). A year after dousing, Republicans hope rekindled. *New York Times*, 4 November, A1.

Orfield, G. (2009). *Reviving the Goal of an Integrated Society: A 21st Century Challenge*. Los Angeles: University of California Los Angeles, The Civil Rights Project.

Parker, C. (2010). *Multi-State Survey on Race Politics*. Washington, DC: University of Washington, WISER Institute. http://depts.washington.edu/uwiser/mssrp_table.pdf.

Pew Research Center. (2005). The black and white of public opinion. 31 October, 1–8.

(2011). Wealth gap rises to record highs between whites, black and Hispanics. 26 July, 1–37.

Scott, J. (2008). What politicians say when they talk about race. *New York Times*, 23 March. www.nytimes.com/2008/03/23/weekinreview/23scott.html?ref=jannyscott.

Shapiro, T. (2010). *The Racial Wealth Gap Increases Fourfold*. Waltham, MA: Brandeis University, Institute on Assets and Social Policy.

Spillius, A. (2010). Whites in the US minority by 2050, study finds. *Phoenix Star*, 13 March, A16.

Taylor, M. A., Ross, S. L., Galster, G. and Yinger, J. (2002). *Discrimination in Metropolitan Housing Markets*. Washington, DC: Urban Institute.

Thernstrom, A. and Thernstrom, S. (2008). Racial gerrymandering is unnecessary. *Wall Street Journal*, 11 November, A15.

Turner, M. (2002). *Discrimination in Metropolitan Housing Markets*. Washington, DC: The Urban Institute.

U.S. Census Bureau. (2006). Hispanic population in the U.S. www.census.gov/population/www/socdemo/hispanic/files/Internet_Hispanic_in_US.pdf.

Wall Street Journal. (2008). Editorial. November 5, A22.

Webb, J. (2010). Diversity and the myth of white privilege. *Wall Street Journal*, 22 July.

Wellman, D. (1993). *Portraits of White Racism*, 2nd edn. Cambridge: Cambridge University Press.

Wilson, W. J. (1978). *The Declining Significance of Race: Blacks and Changing American Institutions*. Chicago: University of Chicago Press.

Yancey, G. (2003). *Who Is White? Latinos, Asians, and the New Black/Nonblack Divide*. Boulder, CO: Lynne Reinner.

4   Getting over the Obama hope hangover: the new racism in 'post-racial' America

Eduardo Bonilla-Silva (with Victor E. Ray)

As Obama's presidency enters its second term, it is more than time to get over the Obama-induced hangover and realize that his real 'audacity' has been to carry out a centre-right political agenda while doing absolutely nothing on the race front. In this chapter, I provide a much-needed aspirin to help readers regain their critical faculties, understand how and why a black man like Obama was elected and assess the likely repercussions of having this black man heading the American political machine.

In previous work (Bonilla-Silva 2010; Bonilla-Silva and Ray 2009), I have suggested that the claim that Obama's election is clear and convincing evidence of racism's declining significance in the country is based on a flawed conceptualization of the nature of racism in general as well as of its specific articulation in the post–civil rights era. Theoretically, I contend that racism is, more than anything else, systemic or institutionalized (Bonilla-Silva 1997), hence the crux of the matter (with or without a black president) is assessing whether we have practices, mechanisms, traditions and institutions in place that produce and reproduce racial privilege. Traditional racism, and the practices associated with it, have changed and become covert, subtle and seemingly non-racial. These new racial practices are the central cogs behind modern-day racial domination in America.

In this chapter, I revisit and update some of my earlier arguments with the goal of providing an adequate explanation of the Obama phenomenon. First, because the conceptual waters on racism in the USA are still polluted by the 'prejudice paradigm' (Bonilla-Silva 1997), I begin with a review of the problems associated with conceptualizing racism as prejudice and offer my own structural interpretation. Second, I address the emergence of the 'new racism' and provide a very short review of some of the 'racial practices' responsible for continued minority disadvantage. Third, I explain Obama's ascendancy to the presidency as part and parcel of this 'new racism'. Finally, revisiting a series of arguments I made during the first election, I argue that Obama's candidacy and the surrounding hype were directly connected to his adoption of the hegemonic color-blind racial discourse. In contrast to those who see Obama's election as a progressive development in American history, I claim, more than anything else, that it is a manifestation of nearly 40 years of transformation of the prevailing racial order.

We have a black president, so . . . what is racism?

Drinking impairs thinking, and far too many Americans drank Obama's post-racial Kool-Aid (Bonilla-Silva 2010), leading to lethargic analyses and commentary on the state of racial affairs. Drunk on the Obama brew, pundits and academics alike saw the long-prophesied 'end of racism' (D'Souza 1995) or at least its declining significance (Wilson 1978). Many whites construed Obama as their 'best black friend' because, in the words of now Vice President Biden, 'he [is] the first mainstream African-American who is articulate and bright and clean and a nice-looking guy' and he is 'a storybook, man' (Wheaton 2007). Through their imaginary connection to this 'exceptional' black man, they absolved themselves of the 'sin' of racism – a religious interpretation of racial matters facilitated by Obama's Philadelphia 'race speech'. For most blacks and minority folks, Obama is the Joshua in charge of completing the mission which Dr King began – again, an image facilitated by Obama's posture in speeches where he hinted that he was Joshua-like (Obama 2007). This peculiar moment has ushered in a new nationalism that has drastically reduced the space for a critical analysis, in communities of color, of anything Obama related. In conjunction with this blinding nationalism, across the political spectrum, media commentators have focused on Obama's 'post-racial' appeal, lauding his avoidance of anything that is explicitly racial or race related. For the right, Obama's rise is just more evidence that blacks should stop complaining. In fact, McCain lost no time in making this point in his concession speech, implying that blacks who viewed racial injustice as a barrier to advancement did not value their citizenship (McCain 2008). On the left, this trend has been especially pronounced in the work of some black commentators, such as media celebrity Melissa Harris-Perry (2009), who compared Obama's accommodationist politics to Dr King's civil rights maneuvering and has forcefully argued that Obama should not be held to a 'race' agenda.[1]

---

[1] This stance is extremely problematic, as generally, in a democracy, voters hold elected officials to whatever agenda they value. And it is more problematic given that labor unions, gays and lesbians and, increasingly, Latinos are pressuring the Obama administration, trying to make him deliver on promises he made to them during the campaign. But one

Beyond media commentators, academics have gone so far as to claim that Obama's election has the potential to transform race relations because of the increased 'intergroup contact' presented by his ubiquitous media presence (Dovidio et al. 2011). Some social psychologists have made sweeping claims about Obama's election – arguing, for instance, that Obama's speeches provided black children with a positive role model, thus helping to raise their test scores (Marx et al. 2009).[2] The drunken jubilation spread to radical black authors such as Cornel West and Manning Marable, who, although doubtful at times (particularly West), ended up supporting Obama uncritically, despite his position on issues such as the War in Afghanistan and his timid stand on race. West hoped that Obama would be a 'progressive Lincoln' (West 2008), whereas Marable went so far as to claim, 'If there is any hope for meaningful change inside the U.S. electoral system in the future, it lies with progressive leaders like Barack Obama' (Marable 2008). At this point, it is clear that Obama's presidency is less than progressive and that former staunch supporters such as West have dropped their allegiance.

One reason why Americans have not been able to interpret properly the Obama phenomenon is because they are still stuck in an outdated and limited conceptual understanding of 'racism'. Mainstream social analysts, as well as most Americans, regard racism as a matter of prejudice, that is, as individual-level animosity or hatred toward people of color (blacks in particular). Accordingly, racism is identified in things such as Archie Bunker–type rhetoric, Klan rallies or overt racial behavior like hanging a noose from a tree (Jones 2007). In harmony with the commonsense view of racism, the election of a black man as president is seen as prima facie evidence that race is no longer a central social force in the country – in a 'racist' country, a black man would never have been elected president. In contrast, things such as 'white flight' from neighborhoods experiencing integration, the slow but consistent 'resegregation' of schools in America (Orfield and Lee 2007) and the existence of historically white colleges and universities are not considered and – in some quarters – not even classified as racial events.

---

thing helps Obama on this front. Blacks did not make any formal demands on him, unlike these other constituencies. They just hoped for him to win and expected him to deliver based on brotherly love. The record so far shows that, as in relationships, love is never enough (see Harris-Perry 2009).

[2] This argument is bogus, as researchers on the subject of self-esteem find that black children have slightly higher levels than their white counterparts. The issue is that having self-esteem is not enough to be successful if one faces a restricted 'opportunity structure'. For a meta-analyses of 265 studies on self-esteem among children, see Gray-Little and Hafdahl (2000).

Because of the prevailing conceptualization of racism, analysts have not been able to effectively explain how race *matters* in post–civil rights America. Instead, their racism-as-prejudice lenses lead them to rely on the language of 'discrimination'[3] when documenting the massive structural inequalities in job opportunities, housing and credit markets (Pager and Shepherd 2008) that pervade American society. The problem here is twofold. First, because most of the behaviors and practices associated with contemporary racial inequality are institutionalized, normative and seemingly non-racial, they are not adequately studied (and understood) by these analysts. Second, because racial inequality has not decreased significantly, but traditional prejudice has declined precipitously since the 1970s (Bobo 2001; Schuman et al. 1997), most analysts explain the current racial situation by 'blaming the victims' in one way or another. Some explain contemporary inequality as the product of minorities' 'culture of poverty' (Mead 1997; Wilson 2010), some as owing to a mismatch between opportunities and the location of the black and minority masses (Wilson 1987). Others see residential segregation as the fulcrum but claim that blacks and Latinos suffer from the 'culture of segregation' (Massey and Denton 1993); yet others attribute it to minorities' intellectual (Murray and Herrnstein 1994) or moral deficiencies. Accordingly, well before Obama's election, the white masses already believed that America was 'beyond race' and that minorities' standing was their own fault.

My main arguments against this interpretation of racism are that it (1) reduces the phenomenon to a matter of ideas (or ideology) blinding analysts about its material foundation, (2) assumes that racism is immutable (racism in slavery is like racism today) and (3) unnecessarily focuses analysts' attention on the active behavior of 'racists' and their overt practices (see Bonilla-Silva 2001, Chapter 2). My alternative theory to the study of racism is the *racialized social system* framework (Bonilla-Silva 1997). Here I provide just a bare-bones outline of this approach.

First, once populations are 'racialized' (Omi and Winant 1994) in any society, a system of racial domination emerges that provides material benefits (social, economic, political and psychological) to all those labeled as 'white' and 'honorary whites' (Bonilla-Silva 2009a) and disadvantages to those labeled 'black', 'Indian', 'Oriental' or any other non-white social category. This is the *material* foundation of what we call 'racism', as actors racialized as whites and non-whites develop systemic interests: the

---

[3] My colleagues and I have suggested replacing the notion of discrimination, which is intrinsically connected to the prejudice paradigm and unnecessarily focuses attention on the intentions and malice of actors, with that of *racial practices*. By racial practices, we refer to behaviors, styles, cultural affectations, traditions and organizational procedures which help to maintain white rule.

former's lie in defending the racial order and the latter's in challenging it. But the expression of and consciousness about these interests, as in the case of class or gender interests, need not be direct and clear-cut; hence, in many societies, the non-white masses are, in a 'race-in-itself' state, sharing a common position and status without that leading them to fight *collectively* to change the racial order of things (Lewis 2004; Twine 1998).

Second, the maintenance of racial order does not depend on 'racist' actors beating down subordinated racial groups. Although terror and violence are always part of the business of ruling (see Jung et al. 2011; Rodriguez 2011), domination in modern-day racial regimes tends to be hegemonic, routinized and experienced by the oppressed as 'this is the way things are'; contemporary regimes depend *more* on normative, everyday forms of domination than on spectacular ones to maintain social control.[4] Accordingly, the reproduction of domination is not necessarily based on 'prejudiced' actors and their 'racism' but on a series of practices at multiple levels that guarantee *systemic* privilege for whites.

Third, the series of practices responsible for systemic privilege forms the *racial structure*, that is, a set of practices, behaviors, traditions and culture that reproduces racial domination. Thus, the main task for analysts of 'racism' in any society is not to separate the 'racists' and the tolerant people in a clinical way but to identify the various mechanisms responsible for the maintenance of racial inequality.

On the basis of this theorization, I have divided U.S. racial history into three broad periods in regard to the black–white dynamic:[5] slavery, Jim Crow and the 'new racism' regimes. Most readers are familiar with the dynamics and components of the first two periods, hence, in what follows, I examine the 'new racism' regime that crystallized in America in the late 1960s to early 1970s.

The 'new racism'

Although Jim Crow has not died completely, racial domination is no longer solely accomplished through poll taxes, White Citizen Councils and the strict and brutal enforcement of racial segregation in schools,

---

[4] This is one reason why I am working on a project dealing with the idea that there is a 'racial grammar' that forms the deep structure of what one can say, see and even feel on race-related matters. Hence, racial domination is already present in everyday interactions (see Bonilla-Silva 2009b).

[5] I acknowledge that, if the point of entry were Indian–white or Mexican–white relations, and for many reasons this might actually be a better road, the historical examination would be different. This is important, but, given the purpose of this chapter (engaging critically with the Obama phenomenon), I follow the traditional story line of race in America.

neighborhoods and other realms of life. Instead, a 'new racism' has emerged which is characterized by (1) the *covert* nature of racial discourse and racial practices, (2) the avoidance of racial terminology and the ever-growing claim by whites that they experience 'reverse racism', (3) the elaboration of a racial agenda over political matters that eschews direct racial references, (4) the invisibility of most mechanisms to reproduce racial inequality and, finally, (5) the rearticulation of some racial practices characteristic of the Jim Crow period of race relations.

This new racial regime came about as the result of various social forces and events that converged in the post–World War II era: the civil rights struggles of the 1950s and 1960s; the contradiction between an America selling democracy abroad and one giving hell to minorities at home, which forced the government to engage more seriously in the business of racial fairness; the black migration from the South that made Jim Crow less effective as a strategy of social control; and the change of heart of so-called enlightened representatives of capital who realized that they had to retool the racial aspects of the social order to maintain an adequate 'business climate' (for a detailed discussion, see Bonilla-Silva 2001). The most visible positive consequences of this process are well known: the slow and incomplete school desegregation that followed the 1954 *Brown v. Board of Education* Supreme Court decision; the enactment of the Civil Rights Act of 1964, the Voting Rights Act of 1965 and the Housing Rights Act of 1968; and the haphazard political process that brought affirmative action to life.

Unfortunately, alongside these meaningful changes, whites developed very negative interpretations of what was transpiring in the nation. The concerns they expressed in the early 1970s about these changes (Caditz 1976) gelled into a two-headed beast in the 1980s. The first head of the monster was whites' belief that the changes brought about by the tumultuous 1960s represented the end of racism in America. Therefore, because they believed that racism had ended, they began to regard complaints about discrimination by people of color as baseless and as a product of their racial 'hypersensitivity'. The second head of the beast was that a substantial segment of the white population understood the changes not just as evidence of the end of racism but also as the beginning of a period of 'reverse discrimination'. Hence, this was the ideological context that helped to cement the 'new racism'. Compared to Jim Crow, this new system may seem genteel, but it is a formidable way of preserving systemic advantages for whites and keeping people of color at bay. Indeed, as Charles Gallagher shows in this volume, color-blindness is the 'new normal' for whites, allowing them to mobilize against any policy-based attempts to ameliorate racial inequality.

The new racism regime also created profound changes among communities of color. Following the 'one-drop' rule (Davis 1991) that anchored the black–white racial system in the USA, there began a shift from a 'biracial' order to a 'triracial' one. Elsewhere, I have thoroughly described the contours of this shift (Bonilla-Silva 2004). For the sake of this argument, it is important to note that a category of 'honorary white' allowed some mixed-race blacks, along with other marginalized racial groups, a degree of mobility. This mobility has reinforced the color-blind ideology asserting that race is no longer a major detriment to minority advancement and that it has some advocates among the black middle class. Furthermore, as I outline later, a new style of minority politician has emerged whose symbolic presence as a black figurehead replaces any concrete program for black advancement.

Racial inequality today is not the product of 'impersonal market forces' (Wilson 1978, 1987), nor is it due to the presumed cultural, moral, ethical, intellectual or family 'deficiencies' of people of color, as conservative commentators such as Charles Murray (1984) in *Losing Ground*, Murray and Herrnstein (1994) in *The Bell Curve: Intelligence and Class Structure in American Life*, Abigail and Stephan Thernstrom (1997) in *America in Black and White* and many others have argued. Contemporary racial inequality is due to the 'continuing significance' of racial discrimination (Feagin 1991). And this 'discrimination', which some have labeled as 'smiling discrimination' (Brooks 1990), affects almost every aspect of the lives of people of color. It affects them in hospitals (Blanchard and Lurie 2004; Penner et al. 2009), in restaurants (Rusche and Brewster 2008), when trying to buy cars (Ayres 2001) or hail a cab (Kovaleski and Chan 2003) and when driving (Meehan and Ponder 2002), flying (Harris 2001) or doing almost anything in America. Indeed, 'living while black [or brown]' is quite hard and affects the health (physical and mental) of people of color tremendously, as they seem to always be in 'fight or flight' mode.[6]

'I was drunk, but now I see': Obama and the future of race in America

In this chapter, I have explained why Obama, his policies and his election to the highest office in the nation cannot be interpreted as a sign of

---

[6] Professor William A. Smith has worked tirelessly to demonstrate that racism produces the syndrome which he calls 'racial battle fatigue'. The constant thinking, preparing, expecting and being concerned about the potential for racial discrimination create an almost constant state of 'fight or flight' in people of color, with deleterious health consequences (see Smith et al. 2007).

race having declined in significance. My overall claim has been that the Obama phenomenon was the product of 40 years of racial transition from Jim Crow to the regime I have labeled the 'new racism'. As such, instead of signifying the 'end of racism', Obama's election as president may help to bring to the fore a more powerful type of racial domination: a Latin America–like or 'multiracial white supremacy' regime (Bonilla-Silva 2009a; Rodriguez 2008). In Obama's America, which I have labeled in my writings 'Obamerica',[7] the space for talking about race matters is dwindling, as whites have gained the upper hand symbolically. Although little has changed in the fundamentals of the racial order, having a black man 'in charge' gives the impression of monumental change and allows whites to tell those who research, write, talk and organize against racial inequality that they must be crazy. Whites can now say, 'How can racism be important in a country that just elected a black man as its president?' and add, 'By the way, I voted for Obama, so I cannot be a racist' (racial ideologies are always work-in-progress, thus the '*I voted for Obama, so . . .* ' may join the list of semantic moves I listed in *Racism without Racists*; Bonilla-Silva 2006). Evidence already points to this, as some whites who supported Obama are using their votes as proof that race no longer matters (Knowles et al. 2009).

During his presidency, Obama has studiously avoided any direct talk on race matters. Throughout his first term, Obama always tried to avoid seeming *too* black (for instance, press aides apparently refused to put the Obamas on BET for the first six months of his presidency; see Kantor 2012). Such careful dancing around reminding the electorate of his blackness has also limited Obama's responses to racist events, sometimes farcically (as in the infamous 'beer summit' with Skip Gates and the man who arrested him in his home). But this also has important ramifications for Obama's policy, as I show later in this chapter. Indeed, political scientist Daniel Gillion has found that, in the first half of Obama's term, the president has said less about race than *any* president since 1961 (cited in Coates 2012).

President Obama's 'race lite' stand was vital during the campaign and remains so. He has avoided any serious discussion on race and, when forced to talk about it, has remained frustratingly vague. For instance, in a 2008 interview with ABC's George Stephanopoulos, he took seemingly all sides on affirmative action. He talked about the importance of *how* affirmative action is carried out, mentioned that race still matters, said

---

[7] I used this term to refer to the fact that his campaign made him into a rock star–like leader and that, despite protestations to the contrary, his campaign was a typical political one that cannot be considered social movement–like.

that his daughters will probably not need affirmative action and hinted at a class-based program.[8] In a comment on Obama's performance in the interview, Peter S. Canellos (2008) observed in the *Boston Globe* that Obama rarely deals with the substance of the policies but focuses on the values, a tactic that seems to go down well with his supporters.

This tactic is dangerous given that blacks have *fared worse* economically under Obama. In the month before the 2012 election, according to data from the Bureau of Labor Statistics (2012), the overall unemployment rate was at 7.9 per cent. Whereas whites' unemployment was at 6.6 per cent, Latinos experienced higher unemployment (11 per cent), and blacks were more than twice as likely to be unemployed (14.3 per cent). According to the same source, more than one-third (34.9 per cent) of uninstitutionalized black men aged between 16 and 19 years are unemployed.

This growing racial disparity is also starkly visible in statistics on poverty. Although the media and Wall Street reported an early recovery from the recession, in 2010, the U.S. Census reported that the poverty rate had increased to 15.1 per cent, a 52-year high. Whereas 12.8 per cent of whites were poor, 27.6 per cent of blacks and 25.3 per cent of Latinos were poor in 2011, a respective increase of 3.6 and 4.2 per cent in only three years (U.S. Census Bureau 2012). Black average income decreased to $32,229 in 2011, a loss of $6,000 or *18 per cent of income* from 2008. Although whites' incomes also decreased by a significant amount, they still earned $20,000 more than blacks, on average (U.S. Census Bureau 2012).

These statistics are frightening indicators of the worsening economic well-being of blacks, but even they do not tell the true extent of the story – as we have seen, the racial wealth disparity can be even more important than income differences (Oliver and Shapiro 1995). Perhaps the most sobering is the doubling of the wealth gap between blacks and whites in only the four years between 2005 and 2009. Where the gap used to be 10 to 1, whites now possess 20 times the wealth of blacks and 18 times that of Latinos (Kochhar et al. 2011). Much of this huge jump in wealth disparity comes from the racialized effects of the housing market crash. The Center for Responsible Lending (2011) reported that, by the end of the crash, almost one-quarter of black home owners would lose their homes owing to foreclosure, although whites experienced more foreclosures. Several major banks (Wells Fargo, Bank of America, Sun Trust) have already agreed to settlements as a penalty for their targeting

---

[8] Since taking office, Obama's administration has defended affirmative action to achieve increased diversity but not to remedy past (or current) racial injustices.

of black and Latino customers and communities for sub-prime mortgages and higher rates (Savage 2012), but it is not clear whether these racially biased practices will ever be stopped – the Obama administration has done little to stop them.

Significantly (and provocatively), I contend that the American racial and class order may work best in 'blackface', making it harder for those working for social justice. In the 'new day in America' (Will.i.am. 2009), a black man is in charge of defending empire, selling neoliberalism to Third World countries and defending the notion that race is no longer the big obstacle it was in the past. Racialized capitalist domination in America and 'empire' (Hardt and Negri 2000), I predict, will be reproduced from now on in a 'multicultural' way.

The racial moment we are living and the post-racial common sense that it has brought forth have not been challenged by most progressive activists and academicians alike, in part because they drank of the hope liquor and also because they tend to filter race matters through the sterile prejudice paradigm. This led some to believe that Obama could not be elected because of the 'Bradley effect'[9] (whites saying to pollsters that they would vote for a black candidate and then not doing so on election day) or that he would be elected because whites were no longer voting based on race.

For those who believe that racism forms a structure, the task before us is both identifying the racial practices that help to reproduce racial domination and working politically to organize a social movement for racial justice. Accordingly, if Americans truly want Obama's campaign slogan – 'Change we can believe in' – to become a reality, they must develop the organizations and the strategies to mobilize the people to produce it. The more Americans continue to buy into mainstream politics, as they did in 2008, the less likely it is that they will be able to effect the social change the nation needs. On this the words of Adolph Reed (2007: 15) ring as true today as when he wrote them:

It's a mistake to focus so much on the election cycle; we didn't vote ourselves into this mess, and we're not going to vote ourselves out of it. Electoral politics is an arena for consolidating majorities that have been created on the plane of social movement organizing. It's not an alternative or a shortcut to building those movements, and building them takes time and concerted effort.

---

[9] This was the position of my colleague and friend Professor Joe R. Feagin, even though he subscribes to an institutionalist view on racism. See his comments on the election in *Contexts* magazine at http://contexts.org/articles/fall-2008/the-social-significance-of-barack-obama/.

Second, in the process of building these social movements, we must develop *individual* and *collective* practices to resist class, race and gender domination. These resistance experiences are the political school for those who truly aspire to live in an Ameri*k*a without the *k*, in an America where real substantive democracy has emerged. Far too many of the young (and the not-so-young) Americans who participated in Obama's campaign have not experienced the deep political experience of working *with* real people and *for* real causes in social movements. Thus, my call is for liberals, progressives, leftists and people of consciousness to move away from mainstream Democratic Party politics and engage in social movement–type work for health care reform, in anti-racist groups and campaigns, in pro-labor and feminist organizations and in all sorts of anti-systemic political work.[10] These experiences will immunize them against what passes as 'politics' and 'political participation' in this country and open their eyes and minds forever.[11]

Third, liberals and progressives must radicalize the spaces they inhabit no matter where and no matter what. They have become too passive and, for fear of creating controversy, avoid saying or doing much where they work or live (this problem afflicted – or, perhaps, *facilitated* – the Obama campaign, as those who participated were not encouraged to study the issues at hand deeply). The not entirely self-imposed silence of the left has reduced the space for contestation in the public square. Although it is true that the 'public square' in America is tilted to the centre-right and that the media is not free, as it is owned by corporations, it is also true that progressives have retreated, further reducing their already limited corner in the square.

Fourth, there is a desperate need for critiques of President Obama from the left. On this, paraphrasing the lyrics of a song by Michael Jackson, 'It don't matter if [our president is] black or white.'[12] We must not stop

---

[10] The Republican Party overreached in the budget battles of 2011, and their attempt to end 'collective bargaining' produced the largest mobilization of workers in decades.

[11] Although I am today a 'successful' professor of sociology at a 'major' university, my political roots go back to my work with pro-independence groups, with groups defending the rights of squatters and with the student movement that led to a major strike in the University of Puerto Rico in 1981. Later, while a graduate student at the University of Wisconsin, I participated in campaigns against the American intervention in Central America and for divestment in South Africa; subsequently, I was active in the creation and development of a group called the Minority Coalition, which demanded diversity at Wisconsin and produced some reforms in the late 1980s.

[12] Michael Jackson's song 'Black or White' appeared on his 1991 album *Dangerous*. I cited this point in speeches in 2008, before Jackson's tragic death in June 2009.

debate, critique and dissent just because the president of the United States is black, white, Latino or Asian. Only by organizing movements to oppose and challenge many of the policies President Obama is enacting will we be able to change his political trajectory and the content of his policies. Unfortunately, far too many people on the American left have avoided any public engagement on Obama – whites because they think that, if they criticize him, they will be called 'racist' and many people of color because, even though Obama is not 'all that', they still think his victory has at least symbolic value.[13] Any true progressive, regardless of his or her race or gender, should never cease to have a deep engagement in political matters. And if, through this engagement, one concludes that a minority politician or a woman of any racial background does not represent the best interest of the people, one must say so loudly and clearly, regardless of the consequences (do we remember the debate around the Clarence Thomas confirmation hearings?).[14] Not engaging in critique is not only a sign of cowardice and accommodationism but is also self-defeating. By not criticizing President Obama's policies and actions now, we are digging our own graves, as it will be even harder to do so in the future.

Finally, the pressure I suggest we should put on the Obama administration to 'do the right thing' can and should be done in *creative* ways. The progressive community has become somewhat ossified and has not kept up with the times. I have preached the need to *think* and *act* beyond the traditional repertoire of the politics and tactics of the left and the civil rights movement before, and I repeat my claims (see Bonilla-Silva 2006, 'Postscript'). We need new ways of *doing* politics, organizing and working

---

[13] I addressed this claim about the symbolic value of his election in two ways. First, I argued that the symbolic value of Obama for people of color was different to that for whites. Whereas, for people of color, he is their Joshua, for whites, he is a symbol of post-racial America. Second, for those who kept saying that now 'little kids' will be able to believe they can be anything they want to be, I pointed out that (1) minority children exhibit higher levels of self-esteem than white children and (2) having the symbol without the 'opportunity structure' could create all sorts of dislocation in minority children, as they can now be blamed if they do not achieve all they presumably can. On black children and their self-esteem, see the work of Gray-Little and Hafdahl (2000).

[14] The NAACP, the largest civil rights group in the nation, deliberated for too long on this case and, when it issued its opposition to the nomination of Clarence Thomas to the Supreme Court, it was too late to make an impact. Although Thomas's record was clearly that of a conservative man who opposed almost *all* legislation and jurisprudence of interest to the association, the group hesitated for only one reason: Thomas was a black man, and many members thought that this fact alone would make him see the light once in the Court. More than 20 years later, the folly of this thinking is crystal clear, as Thomas has been one of the most conservative members of the Court and has voted against all issues of interest to the NAACP.

with people to help them see what is truly going on in the world in which they live. Some of the strategies of the past (marches, sit-ins, political rallies, etc.) may still be part of our tool kit, but progressives need to listen to those of the younger generation who can help them to think political praxis anew. Accordingly, 'yes we can' use humor, as Michael Moore and others have shown, as an effective political weapon; 'yes we can' be post-modern in style and, on occasion, do truly 'wacky' things (wouldn't it be great to do an all-white post-racial rally lampooning Obama's race views?); and 'yes we can' dare to talk once again about the revolution and the significance of Malcolm X for racial and social change in *our* America (these are things and names that few dare to mention these days). It is time that the American left recovers from the political depression it has been in since Reagan was elected president in 1980. It is time for the left to take a strong political dosage of Prozac and end the vote-for-whomever-the-Democrats-nominate-for-president political option it has exercised since 1980 – voting for the proverbial 'lesser of two evils' always keeps evil in power.

If we do these things, we can recover from this drunken moment where things seem upside down. But if we wait until the next election and limit our political engagement to electoral politics, which has become the political praxis of far too many progressives, history is likely to, as Marx wrote, repeat itself 'the first time as tragedy, the second as farce'. The tragedy in this moment is that the first person of color elected to the highest office in the nation is a post-racial, accommodationist, so-called 'pragmatic' and 'non-ideological' man without connections to any social movement. The farce is that Obama won in 2012 because his Republican opponents were viewed as inept and racist Tea Party lovers (few Republicans dared to break ranks with the extreme right in their party), who helped to reify the post-racial narrative of the Obama moment. The color-blind racism typical of those who hold power in America has been normalized, making it more difficult than ever to challenge it. At this moment in history, I am 'pes/optimistic' about the racial prospects of the USA. Will we recover from the hangover and see what is happening in our America, or will we continue, drunk with hope, believing – like Pangloss – that Obamerica is 'the best of all possible worlds'? Only time, and what we do as potential agents of change, will tell.

REFERENCES

Ayres, I. (2001). *Pervasive Prejudice? Unconventional Evidence of Race and Gender Discrimination*. Chicago: University of Chicago Press.

Blanchard, J. and Lurie, N. (2004). R-E-S-P-C-T: patient reports of disrespect in the health care setting and its impact on care. *Journal of Family Practice*, 53(9), 721–30.

Bobo, L. (2001). Racial attitudes and relations at the close of the twentieth century. In N. J. Smelser, W. J. Wilson and F. Mitchell, eds, *America Becoming: Racial Trends and Their Consequences, vol. 1*. Washington, DC: National Academy Press, pp. 264–301.

Bonilla-Silva, E. (1997). Rethinking racism: towards a structural interpretation. *American Sociological Review*, 62(3), 465–80.

(2001). *White Supremacy and Racism in the Post-Civil-Rights Era*. Boulder, CO: Lynne Rienner.

(2004). From bi-racial to tri-racial: towards a new system of racial stratification in the U.S. *Ethnic and Racial Studies*, 27(6), 931–50.

(2006). *Racism without Racists*, 2nd edn. Oxford: Rowman and Littlefield.

(2009a). The invisible weight of whiteness: the racial grammar of everyday life in America. *Ethnic and Racial Studies*, 32(5), 173–94.

(2009b). Are the Americas 'sick with racism' or is it a problem at the poles? A reply to Christina A. Sue. *Ethnic and Racial Studies*, 32(6), 1071–82.

(2010). *Racism without Racists*, 3rd edn. Oxford: Rowman and Littlefield.

Bonilla-Silva, E. and Ray, V. (2009). When whites love a black leader: race matters in Obamerica. *Journal of African American Studies*, 13(2), 176–83.

Brooks, R. L. (1990). *Rethinking the American Race Problem*. Berkeley: University of California Press.

Bureau of Labor Statistics. (2012). Labor force statistics from the Current Population Survey. www.bls.gov/web/empsit/cpseea15.pdf on 11/5/12.

Caditz, J. (1976). *White Liberals in Transition*. New York: Spectrum Press.

Canellos, P. (2008). Shift in tone will bring a watershed for the nation. *Boston Globe*, 5 November, A1.

Center for Responsible Lending. (2011). Lost ground, 2011: disparities in mortgage lending and foreclosures. www.responsiblelending.org/mortgage-lending/policy-legislation/regulators/facing-the-foreclosure-crisis.html.

Coates, T. (2012). Fear of a black president. *The Atlantic*, September. www.theatlantic.com/magazine/archive/2012/09/fear-of-a-black-president/309064/.

Davis, J. F. (1991). *Who Is Black? One Nation's Definition*. University Park: Penn State University Press.

Dovidio, J. F., Gaertner, S. L., Saguy, T. and Hehman, E. (2011). Obama's potential to transform the racial attitudes of white Americans. In G. Parks and M. Hughey, eds, *The Obamas and (Post) Racial America?* New York: Oxford University Press, pp. 245–62.

D'Souza, D. (1995). *The End of Racism*. New York: Free Press Paperbacks.

Feagin, J. R. (1991). The continuing significance of race: antiblack discrimination in public places. *American Sociological Review*, 56(1), 101–16.

Gray-Little, B. and Hafdahl, A. R. (2000). Factors influencing racial comparisons of self-esteem: a quantitative review. *Psychological Bulletin*, 126(1), 26–54.

Hardt, M. and Negri, A. (2000). *Empire*. Cambridge, MA: Harvard University Press.

Harris, C. (2001). *Flying While Black: A Whistleblower's Story*. Los Angeles, CA: Milligan Books.

Harris-Perry, M. (2009). Don't hold Obama to a race agenda. *CNN Politics*. www.cnn.com/2009/POLITICS/06/05/lacewell.race.agenda/.

Jones, R. G. (2007). Thousands protest arrests of 6 blacks in Jena, La. *New York Times*, 21 September. www.nytimes.com/2007/09/21/us/21cnd-jena.html?_r=1&scp=3&sq=jena%206&st=cse.

Jung, M., Costa, V.-J. and Bonilla-Silva, E. (2011). *The State of White Supremacy: Racism, Governance, and the United States*. Palo Alto, CA: Stanford University Press.

Kantor, J. (2012). For president, a complex calculus of race and politics. *New York Times*, 23 October. www.nytimes.com/2012/10/21/us/politics/for-president-obama-a-complex-calculus-of-race-and-politics.html?pagewanted=2&_r=1&smid=fb-share.

Knowles, E. D., Lowery, B. S. and Schaumberg, R. L. (2009). Anti-egalitarians for Obama? Groups-dominance motivation and the Obama vote. *Journal of Experimental Social Psychology*, 45(4), 965–69.

Kochhar, R., Fry, R. and Taylor, P. (2011). Wealth gaps rise to record highs between whites, blacks and Hispanics. Pew Research Center. http://pewresearch.org/pubs/2069/housing-bubble-subprime-mortgages-hispanics-blacks-household-wealth-disparity.

Kovaleski, S. and Chan, S. (2003). D.C. cabs still bypass minorities, study finds; city crackdown called sporadic, inadequate. *Washington Post*. www.highbeam.com/doc/1P2-313833.html.

Lewis, A. E. (2004). What group? Studying whites and whiteness in the era of colour-blindness. *Sociological Theory*, 22(4), 623–46.

Marable, M. (2008). Barack Obama's problem – and ours. *Free Press*. www.freepress.org/columns/display/4/2008/1629.

Marx, D. M., Ko, J. S. and Ray, F. (2009). The 'Obama effect': how a salient role model reduces race based performance differences. *Journal of Experimental Social Psychology*, 45(4), 953–56.

Massey, D. S. and Denton, N. A. (1993). *American Apartheid: Segregation and the Making of the Underclass*. Cambridge, MA: Harvard University Press.

McCain, J. (2008). John McCain's concession speech. *New York Times*. http://elections.nytimes.com/2008/results/president/speeches/mccain-concession-speech.html?scp=1&sq=McCain's%20Concession%20speech&st=cse.

Mead, L. (1997). Welfare employment. In L. Mead, ed., *The New Paternalism: Supervisory Approaches to Poverty*. Washington, DC: The Brookings Institution, pp. 39–88.

Meehan A. and Ponder, M. (2002). Race and place: the ecology of racial profiling African American motorists. *Justice Quarterly*, 19(3), 399–430.

Murray, C. (1984). *Losing Ground*. New York: Basic Books.

Murray, C. and Herrnstein, R. (1994). *The Bell Curve: Intelligence and Class Structure in American Life*. New York: The Free Press.

Obama, B. (2007). Obama's Selma speech. *Chicago Sun Times*, 5 March. http://blogs.suntimes.com/sweet/2007/03/obamas_selma_speech_text_as_de.html.

Oliver, M. and Shapiro, T. M. (1995). *Black Wealth, White Wealth*. New York: Routledge.

Omi, M. and Winant, H. (1994). *Racial Formation in the United States: From the 1960s to the 1990s*. New York: Routledge.

Orfield, G. and Lee, C. (2007). *Historic Reversals, Accelerating Resegregation, and the Need for New Integration Strategies*. Los Angeles: University of California Los Angeles.

Pager, D. and Shepherd, H. (2008). The sociology of discrimination: racial discrimination in employment, housing, credit, and consumer markets. *Annual Review of Sociology*, 34, 181–209.

Penner, L. A., Dovidio, J. F., West, T. V., et al. (2009). Aversive racism and medical interactions with black patients: a field study. *Journal of Experimental Social Psychology*, 46(2), 436–40.

Reed, A. (2007). Sitting this one out. *The Progressive*. www.progressive.org/mag_reed1107.

Rodriguez, D. (2008). Inaugurating multiculturalist white supremacy. http://colourlines.com/archives/2008/11/the_dreadful_genuis_of_the_oba.html.

  (2011). The black presidential non-slave: genocide and the present tens of racial slavery. In J. Go, ed., *Rethinking Obama, Political Power and Social Theory*, vol. 22. Bingley, UK: Emerald Group, pp. 17–50.

Rusche, S. E. and Brewster, Z. W. (2008). 'Because they tip for shit!': the social psychology of everyday racism in restaurants. *Sociology Compass*, 2(6), 2008–29.

Savage, C. (2012). Wells Fargo will settle mortgage bias charges. *New York Times*, 12 July. www.nytimes.com/2012/07/13/business/wells-fargo-to-settle-mortgage-discrimination-charges.html.

Schuman, H., Steeh, C., Bobo, L. and Krysan, M. (1997). *Racial Attitudes in America: Trends and Interpretations*. Cambridge, MA: Harvard University Press.

Smith, W. A., Allen, W. R. and Danley, L. (2007). 'Assume the position . . . you fit the description': psychosocial experiences and racial battle fatigue among African American male college students. *American Behavioral Scientist*, 51(4), 551–78.

Thernstrom, S. and Thernstrom, A. (1997). *America in Black and White: One Nation, Indivisible; Race in Modern America*. New York: Simon and Schuster.

Twine, F. W. (1998). *Racism in a Racial Democracy: The Maintenance of White Supremacy in Brazil*. New Brunswick, NJ: Rutgers University Press.

U.S. Census Bureau. (2012). Income, poverty, and health insurance coverage in the United States: 2011. www.census.gov/prod/2012pubs/p60-243.pdf.

West, C. (2008). 'I hope he is a progressive Lincoln, I aspire to be the Frederick Douglass to put pressure on him'. *Democracy Now*, 19 November. www.democracynow.org/2008/11/19/cornel_west_on_the_election_of.

Wheaton, S. (2007). Biden says he's in . . . again. *New York Times Caucus Blog*, 31 January. http://thecaucus.blogs.nytimes.com/2007/01/31/biden-says-hes-inagain/?scp=1&sq=Biden%20mainstream%20articulate%20clean&st=cse.

Will.i.am. (2009). America's song. www.eonline.com/uberblog/b79734_download_williams_new_anthem_americas.htm.

Wilson, W. J. (1978). *The Declining Significance of Race: Blacks and Changing American Institutions*. Chicago: University of Chicago Press.

    (1987). *The Truly Disadvantaged: The Inner City, the Underclass and Public Policy*. Chicago: University of Chicago Press.

    (2010). Why both social structure and culture matter in a holistic analysis of inner-city poverty. *Annals of the American Academy of Political and Social Science*, 629(1), 200–19.

5   Does a recognition of mixed race move us toward post-race?

Miri Song

Back in 1997, the *Guardian G2* headline proclaimed, 'BEIGE BRITAIN: A NEW RACE IS GROWING UP. IT'S NOT BLACK, IT'S NOT WHITE AND IT'S NOT YET OFFICIALLY RECOGNISED. WELCOME TO THE MIXED-RACE FUTURE' (Younge 1997). More than 15 years later, there is growing evidence not only that mixed people are officially recognised (e.g., in terms of census categories and in many other manifestations of officialdom) but also that mixed people (and especially celebrities) often feature prominently in various forms of media and popular culture. Inevitably, the election of the current U.S. president, Barack Obama, has also generated huge amounts of debate about what his rise to power signals in terms of contemporary attitudes and social mores concerning race and 'mixed race'. Contemporary multiethnic Britain is now steeped in images and references to mixing and 'cultures of conviviality' (Back 1996; Gilroy 2004; Solomos and Back 1996).

Despite this relative 'normalisation' of mixedness, in a contemporary context in which cultural hybridity and 'superdiversity' are increasingly evident in multiethnic metropolitan contexts, societal anxieties about mixing and the transgression of racial boundaries remain and are manifest in various policy debates. For instance, in a speech from 2006, Trevor Phillips, the head of the new Equality and Human Rights Commission, talked about mixed people being potentially disadvantaged and vulnerable to 'identity stripping', as a result of them growing up 'marooned between [disparate] communities'.

Whether of a seemingly positive or negative bent, mixed people are still subject to discourses and characterisations in which they are essentialised and lumped together – regardless of their specific ethnic background, social class, region, gender or family type. All too often, popular discussions and debates about mixed individuals and relationships (in their various forms) reduce to simplistic normative discussions about whether the growth of mixed people and relationships bodes ill or well for society.

This chapter explores the social and political implications of the recognition of mixed people in Britain. Does their recognition enable us to progress toward a post-race scenario, or does it actually reinscribe race and racial difference? I first provide a brief overview of the growth of mixed people in Britain, followed by a discussion of how they have been depicted and written about in the past as well as in more recent years. Next, I examine the question of how to characterise the so-called mixed population, and what disparate types of mixed people may share in common. Lastly, I explore some of the concerns raised about the recognition of mixed people as a specific group – for both academic theorising and in terms of social justice.

As I argue throughout this chapter, the growth and recognition of mixed people have engendered a new round of controversial debates about the continuing salience (or not) of race as well as discussions about how academics and policy makers should write about, and theorise, the experiences of so-called mixed people. As there is no consensus about the terms one should use, I use the terms *mixed race*, *mixed* and *multiracial* throughout the chapter. I also dispense with scare quotes around these terms.

The growth of mixed people in Britain

Demographers have identified mixed people as one of the fastest-growing of all ethnic groups, estimating that, by 2020, the ethnic group will have grown by more than 80 per cent compared with 2001 (Bradford 2006). Such predictions are based upon significant rates of inter-marriage in Britain (Muttarak and Heath 2010; Song 2009). In an analysis of the Labour Force Survey, nearly half of black Caribbean men (and about one-third of black Caribbean women) *in a relationship* were partnered (married or cohabiting) with someone of a different ethnic group, whereas 39 per cent of Chinese women in relationships had a partner from a different ethnic group (Platt 2009).[1]

For the first time, the growth in mixed people was officially recognised by the inclusion of a 'mixed' group category in the 2001 England and Wales Census, in which around 677,000 people (about 1.2 per cent of the population) were identified as mixed – almost certainly a significant

---

[1] Platt's (2009: 13) analysis of the Labour Force Survey notes that 'inter-ethnic partnerships are defined as those where one partner regards themselves as belonging to a different one of the 15 ethnic group categories to that claimed by the other partner'. Given the wide range of 15 ethnic groups (such as mixed white and Asian, black African, white Other, and Other Asian, to name only a few), inter-ethnic unions were not necessarily ones involving a white partner, though many of them probably do. Note, too, that only one-third of black Caribbean women and just over half of black Caribbean men are married or cohabiting (Platt 2009).

undercount.[2] A more recent analysis of the UK Household Longitudinal Survey has found that the true number of mixed people (in terms of actual ethnic origins) is actually closer to twice this number (Easton 2011). One possible reason for this discrepancy is that, whereas the census aims to capture how respondents self-identify, such identifications may not always correspond with the actual ethnic origins of that person (Berthoud 1998). For instance, someone who has mixed origins (e.g., Indian and white) may identify only as Indian or only as white. Individuals in the 2001 Census were asked 'What is your ethnic group?' and were able to choose a mixed category (with the following sub-categories):

- 'mixed'
- white and black Caribbean
- white and Asian
- white and black African
- any other mixed background (please describe)

The provision of the four sub-categories explicitly acknowledges the diversity of the so-called mixed population (Aspinall 2003).[3] Yet very little is known about different types of mixed individual, as most research to date has focused upon black–white individuals in Britain (see Barn and Harman 2006; Ifekwunigwe 1999; Olumide 2002; Tizard and Phoenix 1993; Twine 2004; Wilson 1987). In comparison with the USA, where both quantitative and qualitative studies of 'multiracial' people have constituted a virtual academic industry in the last several decades, academic research on mixed people in Britain has not kept up with the demographic reality (and diversity) of 'mixedness' in many urban, and even less urban, parts of Britain (see Caballero et al. 2008).

New directions in the study of mixed-race people

An opposition to, and fear of, racial mixture has been a constitutive element in the development of modern thought and most branches of

---

[2] In many households, it is likely that, given the young age profile of many mixed children, a parent (and not his or her child) would have filled in the census survey. Thus an undercount of mixed children is a possibility if a parent identified a child in relation to only one ethnicity or race.

[3] The differential sizes of these mixed groups are notable: those with either black Caribbean or black African (and white) heritage constitute almost 48 per cent of the total mixed population, whereas almost 29 per cent are Asian and white. Many of the Chinese–white (and other East Asian–white individuals), and individuals with two disparate non-white parents, ticked the 'Any other mixed background' box. One commonly shared characteristic across the four sub-categories is their youth: over 17 per cent were children aged younger than 5, and almost half (47.5 per cent) of the mixed population were children aged younger than 15 (Owen 2007).

the sciences (Parker and Song 2001). In the late nineteenth and early twentieth centuries, the emergence of mixed-race children adumbrated the ominous process of genetic deterioration of the nation and of the human race itself (Parker and Song 2001: 3). Perhaps the best known example of such preoccupation with racial mixture is the so-called one-drop rule of hypodescent, in which any known non-white ancestor in the USA rendered that individual 'black' (Davis 1991).

Historically, multiracial people were pathologised as occupying a marginal location, in which they did not belong in any one racial group (e.g., see Stonequist 1937). The image of the tortured mulatto, who was characterised by not only a physical disharmony but also psychological instability, was widely propagated, especially (though not exclusively) in the USA. And despite the post-war reaction against Nazism evident in the 1950 UNESCO declaration, in which race (and thus 'mixed race') was to be regarded as a social myth, societal concerns and fascination with racial mixture did not die out.

Contemporary studies of mixed people have tried to map out not only their demographic growth but also the diversity of their experiences. The growth of so-called mixed people and relationships today refutes the idea that there exist exclusive, natural races among people in multi-ethnic societies around the world (Parker and Song 2001). Increasingly, research (both in the USA and in Britain) has debunked depictions of mixed people as fragmented, marginal and necessarily confused (King and DaCosta 1996; Root 1996; Spickard 1989). Arguing against what is perceived to be an essentialist, rigid and now rather dated view of the dynamics surrounding racial identification, a large (and diverse) body of research has found that multiracial people can adopt a variety of identifications, including a mixed or 'border' identification, which refutes the primacy of one race over another, and can think reflexively about race (see Ali 2003; Barn and Harman 2006; Mahtani 2002; Rockquemore and Brunsma 2002; Root 1996; Tizard and Phoenix 1993).

This growing attention to the experiences of mixed people has also enabled many scholars to point to the socially constructed and historically changeable ways in which racial boundaries and classifications were arbitrarily drawn and enforced (see DaCosta 2007; Nobles 2000; Roth 2010).

There is an interesting paradox in the recognition of mixed people. While the very existence of so-called mixed people undermines the idea that all human beings can be neatly classified into a pre-existing set of categories, which are putatively revealing of significant differences among people, the recognition of mixed people has entailed a continuing reliance upon the language and concept of 'race', even if it is framed in a critical fashion. Furthermore, before social movements, such as the multiracial movement in the USA, demanded the recognition of multiracial status, much academic and political thinking and stances adhered to a neat binary of white and non-white, whereby mixed people (if even explicitly made visible) were usually regarded as one part of the ethnic minority population (despite de facto variations in how disparate types of mixed people may have fared 'in reality').

An exploration of what it means to recognise a mixed-race category is timely, not only in demographic terms, but also because theorising around 'difference' more generally has not abated and has been articulated in various ways on both sides of the Atlantic. For example, Alexander (2002) has discussed the disparate ways in which Asian and black Britons are seen to embody difference, as illustrated in academic writings which tend to depict them in terms of polarised stereotypical problematics. In the last several decades, attention to the often unspoken privileges of whiteness, especially in contexts in which overt forms of racism are less easily detected and/or proven, has been a key insight of 'critical race theory' (see Delgado and Stefancic 2001 for examples in the USA and Hylton et al. 2011 for a U.K. perspective). Critical race theory has importantly addressed the difficulties of getting past racial thinking (see also Goldberg 2008). As aptly put by Hylton et al. (2011: 14), 'CRT pragmatics accept the constructed "falsehood" of "race", and yet the lived reality of "race" in an oft-pronounced post-racial world cannot be denied.' Recent studies of mixed race have also spawned 'critical mixed-race studies' (see the *Journal of Critical Mixed Race Studies* edited by Daniel, Dariotis and Kina), which entails a critical analysis of the institutionalisation of practices, policies and ideologies based upon dominant understandings of 'race'.

Such critical approaches coincide with a major 'turn' toward post-race thinking in Britain. A number of scholars in Britain have generated controversial discussions about the need to transcend race and racial thinking (e.g., see Ali 2003). There has also been ongoing debate about the appropriate use of racial terminology. And as John Solomos (1998: 53) has argued, discussions of identity politics do not sufficiently address the following key questions: 'Who is constructing the categories and defining the boundaries? Who is resisting these constructions and definitions? What are the consequences being written into or out of particular categories?'

In the remainder of this chapter, I wish to pose the following questions: First, given the official recognition of mixed people, how should such people be characterised, and in what way(s) can they be said to share any commonalities and/or interests? Second, what are the social and political implications of this growing recognition and institutionalisation of mixedness? Does the recognition of mixed people enable us to progress toward a post-race scenario, or might it actually reinscribe race and racial difference? In so doing, I draw upon discussions from both the USA and Britain.

Who are the mixed-race group?

There is growing evidence that mixed people (and people in mixed families) are demanding public recognition of being mixed, as indicated in the provision of a 'mixed' category in the England and Wales Census and in discourses about ethnic and racial difference. As illustrated by their visibility in popular culture and in 'serious' discussions of change in contemporary society, mixed people are achieving a degree of recognition as part of the British population and not just as an outlier group.

In recent years, a number of public figures and commentators in Britain have advocated the recognition of a mixed experience, as distinct from those of both white and monoracial minority people. As Yasmin Alibhai-Brown (2001: 124) observes in her book *Mixed Feelings*, 'it is foolish to generalise about mixed race families or to impose strong but false categories on them . . . What is new however is that we now have a critical mass of young Britons who see themselves as mixed-race and who wish to challenge many of the assumptions that have been made about them for four centuries.'

Unlike the 'multiracial movement' in the USA, which has been active for some decades, there is no such organised 'movement' in Britain. Although there is no *one* multiracial movement as such in the USA, various multiracial organisations have sponsored educational forums for the public, organised petitions, lobbied for changes in racial classification and provided support for mixed families and individuals (DaCosta 2007; Daniel and Castañeda-Liles 2006: 141). But, as with some parents of mixed children in the USA who campaigned to have the mixed status of their children officially recognised in schools (and the U.S. Census), parents of mixed children in Britain are also beginning to demonstrate an awareness of specific concerns and needs as members of mixed families (see Okitikpi 2005; Olumide 2002; Twine 2004).

Some mixed people are themselves asserting a mixed identity – though this is articulated in many diverse ways. The emergence of various grassroots organisations for multiracial people in Britain suggests an embryonic, yet real, growth of a mixed consciousness – at least for a sector of the mixed population. For instance, while acknowledging the diversity of multiracial individuals, the Mix-d website (www.mix-d.org) calls on a wide range of 'mix-d' people to add their voices and experiences to

societal understandings of mixedness. Gill Olumide, an academic, and one of the trustees of People in Harmony (PIH; www.pih.org.uk/aims.html), acknowledges the diversity of 'the' mixed group in Britain but also suggests, cautiously, that, whether offline or online, organisations such as PIH reveal a real need on the part of mixed people to engage with one another, seek advice or simply share stories and experiences, as individuals, partners and parents. Intermix (www.intermix.org.uk) also emphasises an inclusive conceptualisation of mixed experiences and counters the negative societal assumptions held about mixed people and their families. The question of whether mixed people in Britain feel some sense of commonality with each other is still an empirically open question.

Some analysts, such as Mengel (2001), claim that a 'third space' is occupied by all multiracial people. In such a space, being mixed per se constitutes an experimental link between people, and this link differs from the linkages between mixed people and monoracial individuals who share a common ancestry. However, there is by no means a consensus about whether mixed people comprise a coherent group on the basis of their mixedness per se. Michael Thornton (1996), among others, has criticised the celebratory suggestion that mixed people constitute a coherent group of their own. A genuine and meaningful multiracial identity must be based on more than the common denominator of being mixed (Song 2003).

Given the official recognition of mixed people, what does a 'mixed' category mean for society and for the state? While practitioners and analysts acknowledge the growth of mixed people, there is no agreement about how such people should be regarded or categorised. In what contexts should mixed people be differentiated from other minority groups in terms of their needs and experiences (and thus require specific interventions and representation)? Can mixed people be said to constitute a coherent group, in the way that specific ethnic minority groups, such as Black Caribbeans in the United Kingdom, or Asian Americans in the USA, do?

In terms of ethnic monitoring, some analysts, such as Richard Berthoud (1998: 62), have argued against the legitimacy of a 'mixed' category:

Mixed is not an ethnic origin it its own right. In particular, it seems unlikely that people of mixed black and white heritage would have much in common with those of mixed Indian white heritage. A single mixed category would therefore be both unpopular with the people concerned, and meaningless to analysts.

One impediment to organising and mobilising around mixedness, and to a meaningful sense of being part of a broader mixed group, is the sheer diversity of so-called mixed people. Leaving aside the potentially variable experiences of mixedness associated with disparate types of mixed people (see Song 2010a, 2010b) – such as African Caribbean–white English, Chinese–white English, Pakistani–white English or 'minority mixed' people who may be Indian–Chinese or Portuguese–Pakistani – mixed people's experiences will vary considerably according to gender (see Tate in this volume), class background, physical appearance and the specific localities they inhabit – whether it be metropolitan London or a completely white town or village in the West Country.

Even mixed individuals with the same ethnic mixed background can have quite disparate lives and experiences, which cannot be boiled down to broad commonalities on the basis of shared mixed-race backgrounds (see also Rockquemore and Brunsma 2002). Furthermore, individual mixed siblings within families may encounter very different experiences and treatment by the wider society (Song 2010b). Among other factors, feeling a sense of connection with other mixed people (or not) is likely to be influenced by the relative centrality of an individual's own ethnic or racial identification. Although there is a nascent awareness of a broad, mixed identity in Britain, there is no basis (at this point) for claiming that mixed people manifest a sense of shared experience and status.

Moreover, should mixed people be regarded as a disadvantaged minority group? Do they suffer racism? Such questions are now being explored in studies in the USA, where the multiracial category does not denote a protected class under the law (Daniel and Castañeda-Liles 2006). In their survey of attitudes toward multiracial people in the USA, Campbell and Troyer (2007) found that about half of the monoracial minorities and most of the white respondents they surveyed opposed the inclusion of multiracial people in anti-discrimination policies in the USA. Though this survey did not differentiate between disparate types of multiracial people, this finding suggests that most Americans do not believe that multiracial people actually experience racism or forms of racial disadvantage – despite the fact that the authors found that the multiracial people in their survey reported similar levels of discrimination to other monoracial minorities.

In Britain, discussions about how mixed children (especially black–white children in care) should be regarded and treated are illustrative of debates concerning the status of mixed-race people (vis-à-vis monoracial minority people) and the appropriate degree of race consciousness informing various social policies. Policy makers and social workers have disagreed about how to categorise and treat black–white children – as mixed, or as black (Barn and Harman 2006). Opponents of a mixed category for such children argue that it propagates a view of a society which obscures the very real racism which these children will encounter as *black* children. For instance, the British Agencies for Adoption and Fostering has argued that black–white children should be seen and treated as black so that they may develop a healthy identity (Prevatt Goldstein 1999) – an argument which is contested in findings by Tizard and Phoenix's (1993) study of adolescent black–white individuals in London. Yet Laura Smith (2006), a mixed writer for *The Guardian*, advocates for the societal and governmental recognition of mixed people, as distinct from other types of minority people. According to Smith, specific forms of social disadvantage experienced by mixed children can be overlooked, and she argues that mixed children are not generally considered to be minority individuals in the way that black or Asian children are.

It is clearly very difficult to formulate policies about the ways in which mixed people may be racially or socioeconomically disadvantaged, as their racial status (as with monoracial minority people) is so intertwined with their other attributes, including their class background and physical appearance (Rondilla and Spickard 2007). For instance, because policy concerns about children in care (in Britain) tend to centre heavily upon the experiences of black and white children, it is increasingly necessary for policies to be targeted at specific sectors of the mixed-race population.

The social and political implications of a mixed-race category

What are the social and political implications of officially recognising mixed people? In this section, I discuss two related concerns: (1) the effects of recognising mixed people for social divisiveness and the further denigration of monoracial (especially black) people and (2) how the recognition of a mixed category may be employed in arguments about a colour-blind society and thus undermine continuing efforts toward racial justice.

Social divisiveness and the further denigration of black people

First, a number of analysts have argued that the recognition of mixed people is divisive for 'communities of colour' and that it reinforces racial hierarchies in which whiteness and blackness constitute the two poles. The legitimation of a mixed group can be divisive for ethnic minority people by differentiating between 'monoracial' and 'mixed' (or 'multiracial') people – when it could be argued that monoracial and mixed people may share many common interests and experiences.

The recognition of mixed people as a separate category within a racially stratified society will, according to some, result in the further denigration of black and other minority people (see Bonilla-Silva 2004 regarding the emerging 'triracial' system in the USA, in which most multiracial people would occupy the middle, 'honorary whites' strata, between 'whites' on top and 'collective black' on the bottom). In fact, various analysts in the USA (e.g., Lee and Bean 2004; Twine and Gallagher 2008; Yancey 2006) have argued that the growth of such non-black mixed people (such as Asian–white and Latino–white individuals) may effectively expand the boundaries of whiteness (see also Cashmore 2008). Such mixed people are said to be able to claim membership as white people, so that all *non-black* mixed people will automatically enjoy the benefits of inclusion within the 'white' fold. Given the historically specific ways in which non-black mixed people in the USA have been incorporated into whiteness, 'there exists a space for non-black immigrants and their children to position themselves as "white"' (Twine and Gallagher 2008: 14).[4]

Moreover, analysts in the USA suggest that some mixed individuals may wish to disassociate themselves from a stigmatised minority population. In the shadow of the former apartheid regime in South Africa, or the racial hierarchy which reigned most flagrantly in America's Deep South, such a concern is understandable, and not without historical basis. F. James Davis (1991) has argued that the recognition of black–white individuals as mixed, as opposed to black, would encourage lighter-skinned part-black people to 'leave' the black community for the white, resulting in not only significant political losses for the black community but also a potential (re)stigmatisation of being solely black.

Therefore, the creation of a mixed category is said to provide yet another essentialist intermediate category of difference which reifies

---

[4] I would question the view that the growth of non-black mixed people inevitably signals their inclusion in the white category. This argument is premised upon the assumption that non-black mixed people (such as part-Asian and part-Latino individuals) possess an ability to exercise a range of ethnic options (Song 2003; Waters 1990) as well as the assumption that such mixed people *wish to be seen* as white. Though such a generalisation is debatable, even in the USA, the evidence in Britain would not suggest such a clear-cut scenario (see Song 2010a). The implication that non-black mixed people possess an unfettered array of ethnic options, including that of being white, is not consistently tenable, given (1) the variation in physical appearance among mixed people and (2) persistent attributions about the foreignness and otherness of many physically ambiguous mixed people. Therefore, the suggestion that non-black mixed people possess the ability (and wish) to enter into the white mainstream is unfounded, as some mixed people are simply not seen as white by the wider society; nor would they necessarily wish to be seen as white, despite its concomitant privileges. Furthermore, this line of argument also tends to regard inter-marriage with whites as totally unproblematic and as signalling the effective erasure of ethnic and racial boundaries and ties (Song 2009).

existing racial categories. Rainier Spencer (2006) argues that the whole multiracial movement in the USA just ends up vilifying black people and reinforcing, not undermining, racial boundaries: 'The assertion of a multiracial class as the product of mixture between whites and Afro-Americans creates the theoretical space for whiteness to maintain its mythical purity and for blackness to retain its essentially impure quality' (87).

George Yancey (2006) concurs and argues that the emergence of more and more black–white Americans, and the possibility of choosing a 'mixed' identity (as opposed to black), may worsen the status of monoracial black people as well as endanger a commitment to racial justice, based upon his belief that people who are part-white (including white–black people) will not be as concerned with, or committed to, issues of racial justice as monoracial minorities have been in the past.

To a lesser extent, however, there was some debate about categories for the 2001 British Census, and the question of if, and how, the census should account for the existence of mixed people in Britain. As in the USA, this debate centred primarily upon a black–white mixture. However, in addition to concerns about enumeration and social divisiveness, some British commentators also questioned whether mixed people would actually be recognised as such by the wider society. Bernie Grant, the late Labour MP for Tottenham, argued, 'Society sees mixed-race people as black, and they are treated as black. They are never accepted as White, so they have no choice' (quoted in Younge 1997). Interestingly, even though Britain never *legally* adopted the one-drop rule of hypodescent, in which anyone with a known black ancestor in the USA was considered to be black, some analysts, including Grant, appeared to support this rule. While there would be no clear consensus on the issue now, in 2014, it is almost certainly the case that there is more societal awareness and recognition of mixedness than there was when Grant made his remarks – though his observations about part-black people being seen as black continue to hold for many black–white individuals in Britain, as discussed by Shirley Anne Tate in this volume.

Countering claims about a colour-blind society

Some analysts have also claimed that recognition of a mixed category and identity feeds insidious claims that we are now occupying a colour-blind society, in which racial difference should not be recognised at all. Such uses of a colour-blind rhetoric have been at the heart of a neoconservative agenda in which race monitoring would be abolished altogether (Bonilla-Silva 2003).

The purported danger of recognising and celebrating mixedness has been written about in a variety of ways. According to various analysts, the growing recognition of mixedness is regarded, simplistically, and opportunistically, as evidence of the demise of racism and the social barriers which have particularly marked relations between white and black Americans (Bonilla-Silva 2003; Gallagher 2006).

One key way in which a mixed category can be used to bolster conservative agendas is that recognising an official 'multiracial' group which is separate from other minority groups, such as African Americans, would significantly reduce the enumeration of African Americans. Historically, especially with the operation of the one-drop rule of hypodescent, part-black people were regarded and counted as black. Thus, the NAACP, along with some multiracial organisations themselves, opposed the single multiracial category for the 2000 U.S. Census on the grounds that it could dilute the collective power of people of colour. In the end, this concern about the reduced enumeration of minority populations, which was the basis of some intense lobbying in the USA, was instrumental in the U.S. Census Bureau's decision to employ a 'tick-all-that-apply' approach (multiple tick boxes) for the U.S. 2000 Census, as opposed to the provision of a single 'mixed-race' box – as in the British (England and Wales) 2001 Census (DaCosta 2007).

In his discussion of Tiger Woods and the celebration and commodification of his mixedness, Ellis Cashmore (2008: 622–23) argues, 'Woods is both an exemplar of a new racial order and a reminder that the past is exactly that – the past... Woods, or more correctly, the media portrayal or visible representation of Woods, is a discursive product for managing difference.' Cashmore argues that the media frenzy regarding the success of mixed celebrities like Woods effectively downplays the reality of racial inequality and injustice still rampant in the USA. But he goes further by criticising not only Woods but also other mixed or black celebrities, be it Whoopi Goldberg or Oprah Winfrey, who seem to wish to transcend racial thinking. It is difficult to miss the tokenistic portrayal of mixed people as exemplars of a less racially burdened and divided society.

Whereas some criticisms are levelled at specific celebrities, other analysts point to how support for a mixed identity can involve an uncritical celebration of race transcendence, even by some multiracial organisations. According to Daniel and Castañeda-Liles (2006: 141),

That said, many of the organizations and individuals involved in the multiracial movement have failed to mount political initiatives that address the issue of lingering structural inequality... Their advocacy, informed by an uncritical acceptance of the dominant ideology of colour blindness, reflects a naïve egalitarianism that views all forms of race consciousness as detrimental to societal progress, thus ignoring the context of sustained racial inequality that requires the collection of racial data and race-based policy.

There is no necessary and ineluctable link between recognising the existence of a mixed identity and social experience and automatic support for the ideology of colour-blindness (or a denial of persistent forms of racism). However, the existence of mixed people who either refuse to be racially assigned to a minority or white category (and who may refuse to legitimate any racial categorisation) or who may question the salience of race in every social encounter and institution has led some analysts to question the commitment of mixed people and organisations to the pursuit of racial justice.

Such a stark assessment of the U.S. landscape does not neatly apply to the situation in Britain; although a black–white duality has been at the centre of discussions around mixedness, the social distance posited between white and minority groups in Britain is much more uneven, interspersed with spaces and modes in which meaningful connections are forged (Alexander 1996; Back 1996).

It is notable that political concerns about the introduction of a mixed category have centred primarily (though not exclusively) upon the effects of such a category for black people, as opposed to other minority groups. One reason why this may be the case is that the black–white mixture is historically emblematic of ideas concerning racial transgression and boundary blurring (see Stonequist 1937); the social distance posited between black and white people is still regarded, especially in the USA, as most significant (Lee and Bean 2004). Nevertheless, given the very substantial rates of inter-racial partnering for other ethnic minority groups (both in Britain and in the USA), wider discussions about what the recognition of *mixed race* portends must address the wide array of mixed people and experiences, not just the black–white dualism; this would also mean conceiving of 'mixture' which does not involve whiteness (see Song 2010a; Thornton 1996). But, in doing so, it is imperative that we do not lose sight of the considerable diversity to be found within specific types of mixed populations, whether they be, for example, South Asian–white or black Caribbean–white, or the various ways in which so-called mixed people are part of wider white and non-white networks and communities.

Conclusion

In Britain, the growth of mixed people and families has raised numerous questions about the ability of state policies and official taxonomies of ethnic and racial categorisation to capture (and measure) their identifications and lived experiences. Does the category 'mixed' actually aid us in capturing this complexity and diversity? What does this term mean for those who are mixed? The answer, so far, is that it can mean very different things. With the growth in superdiversity in metropolitan areas of Britain (Vertovec 2007), multiethnic states greatly capture increased diversity both in relation to myriad migrant groups and through 'mixture'.

The emergence of a mixed consciousness and/or organisations should be regarded as evidence of both a collective (albeit nascent and not necessarily unified or homogenous) identification as mixed and a form of political mobilisation around specific interests – though the identification of such interests has not yet gone beyond claims for recognition. This emergent awareness and mobilisation cannot simply be trivialised as a manifestation of media excess. However, assertions of mixedness can be very diverse in meanings and expression, and there is little evidence (thus far in Britain) that most mixed people believe that they necessarily have much in common with other people, on the basis of their mixedness per se.

How do we reconcile the demand for recognition by mixed people, without losing sight of the very real commonalities of experiences and interests, both material and cultural, in relation to other ethnic minority groups? Yet one more banner for identity politics, especially following in the wake of the narrower redefinition of 'black' in the British context (see Modood 1996), perhaps should give us pause. Do and should mixed people have the right to assert a distinctive status and identity, and is it akin to the rights of other 'subaltern' groups who have gone down this route in the last several decades? Britain must consider a variety of ways in which to recognise the desire of mixed people to identify as such, but this need not take the form of a mixed tick box as such. In addition to multiticking (the route taken in the USA), we may need to consider a reconceptualisation of ethnic and racial groups (and categories) as more inherently diverse and inclusive of mixed people.

This question of rights is a political and social one, but it cannot be wholly divorced from the fact that the intent and outcomes of racial classification systems must be carefully scrutinised and can be both ambiguous and unpredictable (see Skinner 2011 regarding the use of racialised DNA data). The creation and recognition of ever more finely graded ethnic and racial categories per se is neither automatically retrograde nor unproblematically emancipatory. But, as argued by a number of analysts, the introduction of new ethnic and racial categories and systems may not actually change or undermine the logic of racism.

Reductive arguments which claim that the growth and recognition of mixed people are either a 'good' or a 'bad' phenomenon must be resisted.

The creation of a mixed category may help to officially legitimate the existence of people who wish to be known as mixed. And, although its introduction may be an important step in recognising the diversity and complexity surrounding both demographic change and ethnic and racial identification, it may also be a means of lumping together individuals who are not 'purely' of any one heritage (Berthoud 1998).

Furthermore, the introduction of a mixed category may unintentionally engender outcomes which are at odds with traditional, anti-racist initiatives (such as the civil rights movement in the USA). Support for the idea of transcending race and racial thinking can, therefore, result in bolstering a conservative colour-blind agenda. Certainly, a facile and naïve claim that mixedness per se signals the death of racial inequality, or the demise of negative racial ideologies, especially on the back of the Obama presidency, is absurd. But, at the same time, some analysts (especially in the USA) seem to bristle at the thought of conceding that *any* social and political change may be underfoot – change which may, in certain respects and in specific contexts, signal the blurring of boundaries (and the lessening of social distance) between white and non-white (including black) people, at least in certain ways.

What some critics of (the proponents of) a mixed status fail to acknowledge is that the aims, meanings and experiences of those who back a mixed status may be much more varied, ambivalent and critical than is usually characterised (DaCosta 2007; Daniel and Castañeda-Liles 2006). For instance, some proponents of a mixed status reject the essentialist trappings of race, but they support a political recognition of mixed people to identify and mobilise on the basis of their shared interests and/or experiences (DaCosta 2007; Root 1996). An insistence upon the recognition of a different type of family and social experience (by some mixed people or people in mixed families) need not be automatically interpreted as a sinister attempt to distance oneself from a 'black' or other non-white category and an attempt to capitalise upon whiteness. In fact, some sectors of the multiracial movement in the USA have made a point of working with wider movements concerning racial justice.

Do the recognition of and mobilisation around a mixed status necessarily reinscribe 'race' and spurious understandings of racial difference? The very use of terms such as *mixed race* is said by some to be problematic as it implicitly legitimises the existence of 'pure races' (see Banton's chapter in this volume; Rattansi 2007). Paul Gilroy (2000: 250) puts the challenge ahead of us well: 'The main problem we face in making sense of these and more recent developments is that lack of a means of describing, let alone theorizing, inter-mixture, fusion and syncretism without suggesting the existence of anterior "uncontaminated" purities.'

To the extent that mixed organisations and individuals understand their mixedness as derived from the idea of the existence of two or more (socially constructed) distinct 'races' of people, an assertion of mixedness cannot help but reify this notion of racial difference. Ironically, an organised multiracial movement may end up putting the spotlight back on the idea of race, and the notion of distinct racial categories and differences, rather than on what they may have in common with other people, on the basis of shared concerns about racial injustice, social disadvantage, locally specific concerns and so on. The maintenance of race consciousness is necessary if more equal outcomes are a key societal goal; whether such a race consciousness can accommodate the recognition of a mixed category is yet unknown.

Rather than asking whether we should (and can) be post-race, it would be more realistic, for now, to ask to what degree our interactions and conflicts with one another as individuals, groups and societies are *less racialised* than they have been in the past (Rattansi 2007) – or racialised in ways in which 'race' intersects inextricably with many other key attributes, such as gender, class, religion and region (see Anthias and Yuval-Davis 1992). We still need a language with which to discuss both asserted and attributed forms of difference and disadvantage. In fact, the very critics who chastise others for using the terms *race* or *mixed race* are unable to marshal language which is entirely untainted with racial inflections (as in Gilroy's quote). The simple replacement of one seemingly less problematic term for another does not take us any further in our attempts to understand how and why human beings continue to demarcate, identify and attribute forms of ethnic and racial difference onto ourselves and others.

Although it is important that scholars remain alert to the ways in which masked power relations still operate in multiethnic societies (which are putatively, but not actually, colour-blind), and reject overly optimistic claims about the demise of racial barriers and discourses, an insistence that gradual changes in societal relations signal a sinister continuation of white privilege is simply too reductive, especially in Britain. There is evidence that, in Britain, being mixed (including black and white) is increasingly ordinary in cosmopolitan contexts marked by superdiversity, such as in London (Gilroy 2004; Vertovec 2007). And such growing ordinariness is not confined to the social worlds of the mixed elite. In metropolitan contexts in Britain, the growth of mixed people (and of inter-racial relationships) cannot be read, neatly, as the cooptation of mixed people into a wannabe-white status.

A number of studies show that, in Britain, mixed people (e.g., see Ali 2003; Song 2010a; Tizard and Phoenix 1993) are quite *varied* in how they think about their mixedness. Race is also going to be of differential levels of salience across mixed people. In Britain, it appears that, at least in large, metropolitan settings, an inclusive and increasingly race-neutral nationality, as British, is a central part of the experiences of many younger multiracial Britons today. Increasingly, it will be difficult to talk intelligently about monoracial and mixed minority groups, because there is now so much internal diversity within specific groups, whether they be black, Asian, mixed or white. Although mixed people have gained official recognition, at least in particular ways, what will be politically contested in the coming years are the terms of this recognition, including debates about what, if anything, mixed people's interest may be (Gallagher 2006). Because there is growing evidence of mixed persons' highly diverse experiences, analysts and policy makers need to be careful when making assumptions about what being mixed means.

One obvious limitation of the existing debate is that it is still largely framed in relation to the black–white binary. Nevertheless, future debates and policy making must contend with the growing diversity around disparate kinds of mixed experience and need to avoid generalisations which tend to polarise the assumed experiences and options between part-black and non-black mixed people.

REFERENCES

Alexander, C. (1996). *The Art of Being Black*. Oxford: Clarendon Press.
  (2002). Beyond black: rethinking the colour/culture divide. *Ethnic and Racial Studies*, 25(4), 552–71.
Ali, S. (2003). *Mixed-Race, Post-Race: Gender, New Ethnicities and Cultural Practices*. Oxford: Berg.
Alibhai-Brown, Y. (2001). *Mixed Feelings: The Complex Lives of Mixed-Race Britons*. London: The Women's Press.
Anthias, F. and Yuval-Davis, N. (1992). *Racialised Boundaries*. London: Routledge.
Aspinall, P. (2003). The conceptualisation and categorisation of mixed race/ethnicity in Britain and North America. *International Journal of Intercultural Relations*, 27(3), 269–96.
Back, L. (1996). *New Ethnicities and Urban Culture*. London: UCL Press.
Barn, R. and Harman, V. (2006). A contested identity: an exploration of the competing social and political discourse concerning the identification and positioning of young people of inter-racial parentage. *British Journal of Social Work*, 36(8), 1309–24.
Berthoud, R. (1998). Defining ethnic groups: origin or identity? *Patterns of Prejudice*, 32(2), 53–67.
Bonilla-Silva, E. (2003). *Racism without Racists*. Lanham, MD: Lynne Rienner.
  (2004). From bi-racial to tri-racial: towards a new system of racial stratification in the USA. *Ethnic and Racial Studies*, 27(6), 931–50.

Bradford, B. (2006). *Who Are the 'Mixed' Ethnic Groups?* London: Office for National Statistics.

Caballero, C., Edwards, R. and Smith, D. (2008). Cultures of mixing: understanding partnerships across ethnicity. *21st Century Society*, 3(1), 49–63.

Campbell, M. E. and Troyer, L. (2007). The implications of racial misclassification by observers. *American Sociological Review*, 72(5), 750–65.

Cashmore, E. (2008). Tiger Woods and the new racial order. *Current Sociology*, 56(4), 621–34.

DaCosta, K. (2007). *Making Multiracials*. Stanford, CA: Stanford University Press.

Daniel, R. and Castañeda-Liles, J. M. (2006). Race, multi-raciality and the neo-conservative agenda. In D. Brunsma, ed., *Mixed Messages: Multi-Racial Identities in the 'Color-Blind' Era*. Boulder, CO: Lynne Rienner, pp. 125–46.

Davis, F. (1991). *Who Is Black?* University Park: Pennsylvania State University Press.

Delgado, R. and Stefancic, J. (2001). *Critical Race Theory: An Introduction*. New York: New York University Press.

Easton, M. (2011). Britain: more mixed than we thought. *BBC Online*. www.bbc.co.uk/news/uk-15164970?print1/4true.

Gallagher, C. (2006). Colour blindness: an obstacle to racial justice? In D. Brunsma, ed., *Mixed Messages: Multi-Racial Identities in the 'Color-Blind' Era*. Boulder, CO: Lynne Rienner, pp. 103–16.

Gilroy, P. (2004). *After Empire*. London: Routledge.

Goldberg, D. (2008). *The Threat of Race*. London: Blackwell.

Hylton, K., Pilkington, A., Warmington, P. and Housee, S., eds. (2011). *Atlantic Crossings: International Dialogues on Critical Race Theory*. Birmingham: University of Birmingham, C-SAP.

Ifekwunigwe, J. (1999). *Scattered Belongings*. London: Routledge.

King, R. and DaCosta, K. (1996). Changing face, changing race: the remaking of race in the Japanese American and African American communities. In M. Root, ed., *The Multiracial Experience*, pp. 227–45.

Lee, J. and Bean, F. (2004). America's changing colour line. *Annual Review of Sociology*, 30, 221–42.

Mahtani, M. (2002). What's in a name? Exploring the employment of 'mixed race' as an identification. *Ethnicities*, 2(4), 469–90.

Mengel, L. (2001). Triples. In D. Parker and M. Song, eds, *Rethinking 'Mixed Race'*. London: Pluto Press, pp. 99–116.

Modood, T. (1996). The changing context of 'race' in Britain. *Patterns of Prejudice*, 30(1), 3–13.

Muttarak, R. and Heath, A. (2010). Who intermarries in Britain? Explaining ethnic diversity in intermarriage pattern. *British Journal of Sociology*, 61(2), 275–305.

Nobles, M. (2000). *Citizenship*. Stanford, CA: Stanford University Press.

Okitikpi, T. (2005). Identity and identification: how mixed parentage children adapt to a binary world. In T. Okitikpi, ed., *Working with Children of Mixed Parentage*. Lyme Regis, UK: Russell House, pp. 76–92.

Olumide, G. (2002). *Raiding the Gene Pool*. London: Pluto Press.

Owen, C. (2007). Statistics: the mixed category in Census 2001. In J. Sims, ed., *Mixed Heritage: Identity, Policy, Practice*. London: Runnymede Trust, pp. 1–5.

Parker, D. and Song, M. (2001). Introduction. In D. Parker and M. Song, eds, *Rethinking 'Mixed Race'*. London: Pluto Press, pp. 1–22.

Platt, L. (2009). *Ethnicity and Family: Relationships within and between Ethnic Groups: An Analysis Using the Labour Force Survey*. Colchester, UK: University of Essex, ISER.

Prevatt Goldstein, B. (1999). Black, with a white parent, a positive and achievable identity. *British Journal of Social Work*, 29(2), 285–301.

Rattansi, A. (2007). *Racism*. Oxford: Oxford University Press.

Rockquemore, K. and Brunsma, D. (2002). *Beyond Black*. Thousand Oaks, CA: Sage.

Rondilla, J. and Spickard, P. (2007). *Is Lighter Better? Skin-Tone Discrimination among Asian Americans*. Lanham, MD: Rowman and Littlefield.

Root, M., ed. (1996). *The Multiracial Experience*. Thousand Oaks, CA: Sage.

Roth, W. (2010). Racial mismatch: the divergence between form and function in data for monitoring racial discrimination in Hispanics. *Social Science Quarterly*, 91(5), 1288–311.

Skinner, D. (2011). How might critical race theory allow us to rethink racial categorisation? In K. Hylton et al., eds, *Atlantic Crossings*, pp. 115–31.

Smith, L. (2006). Finding voice. *The Guardian*. www.guardian.co.uk/news/blog/2006/sep/13/ findingvoice 1.

Solomos, J. (1998). Beyond racism and multiculturalism. *Patterns of Prejudice*, 32(4), 45–62.

Solomos, J. and Back, L. (1996). *Racism and Society*. Basingstoke, UK: Macmillan.

Song, M. (2003). *Choosing Ethnic Identity*. Cambridge: Polity Press.
    (2009). Is intermarriage a good indicator of integration? *Journal of Ethnic and Migration Studies*, 35(2), 331–48.
    (2010a). Is there a mixed-race group in Britain? *Critical Social Policy*, 30(3), 337–58.
    (2010b). Does 'race' matter? A study of mixed race siblings' identifications. *Sociological Review*, 58(2), 265–85.

Spencer, R. (2006). *Challenging Multiracial Identity*. Boulder, CO: Lynne Rienner.

Spickard, P. (1989). *Mixed Blood*. Madison: University of Wisconsin.

Stonequist, E. (1937). *Marginal Man*. New York: Russell and Russell.

Thornton, M. (1996). Hidden agendas, identity theories, and multiracial people. In M. Root, ed., *The Multiracial Experience*, pp. 101–21.

Tizard, B. and Phoenix, A. (1993). *Black, White or Mixed Race?* London: Routledge.

Twine, F. W. (2004). A white side of black Britain: the concept of racial literacy. *Ethnic and Racial Studies*, 27(6), 878–907.

Twine, F. W. and Gallagher, C. (2008). The future of whiteness. *Ethnic and Racial Studies*, 31(1), 4–24.

Vertovec, S. (2007). Super-diversity and its implications. *Ethnic and Racial Studies*, 30(6), 1024–54.

Waters, M. (1990). *Ethnic Options*. Berkeley: University of California Press.

Wilson, A. (1987). *Mixed Race Children*. London: Allen and Unwin.

Yancey, G. (2006). Racial justice in a black, non/black society. In D. Brunsma, ed., *Mixed Messages: Multi-Racial Identities in the 'Color-Blind' Era*. Boulder, CO: Lynne Rienner, pp. 49–62.

Younge, G. (1997). Beige Britain. *Guardian G2*, 22 May.

Leah Bassel

> When I was arrested after the police had invaded Saint-Bernard, two
> events seemed significant to me.
>   The first is the way I was stripped by policewomen in front of my
> daughter. It was obvious that their aim was to humiliate me, to break
> me. So I stripped amid sarcastic comments and questionable jokes.
> 'She's not being that clever anymore, the spokeswoman,' or 'You're
> not supposed to wear a bra inside out' (a man wouldn't have thought
> of that). But the nature of the mocking, the sarcastic comments and
> the gibes also said much about the state of mind of the police: 'Aha!
> the spokeswoman doesn't have her mobile phone anymore.' The mobile
> phone had become the symbol of the modernity to which, as a foreigner,
> as an African, as a black woman, as a Negro, I had no right: 'They've
> hardly come down from the trees, and they already have mobiles in their
> hands.'
>   The second one was that I was immediately taken to court, even
> though I had a perfectly valid leave to stay. It was obviously another
> attempt to break the symbol represented by an African woman chosen
> to be the spokeswoman of her comrades in struggle. And for this, they
> were prepared to commit many illegalities: they did not themselves
> respect the laws which they praised so much.
>   During that whole period, we had many identities to reestablish.
>   – Madjiguène Cissé, *The Sans-Papiers*

The woman who spoke these words, Madjiguène Cissé, became the symbol of the struggle of the *sans papiers* – literally migrants 'without papers' –
for regularisation and for justice in France in the 1990s. In this chapter, I
consider the role of racial identity in the political mobilisation of undocumented women in France, the *sans papieres* – the term *papieres*, with an -*es*,
is the feminine version of *papiers* – when, as we see in Cissé's words, identities are multiple and serve both as a site of challenge and as a resource.
I consider two understandings of the role of race in migration politics.
In one, interruption of and extraction from existing identities and hierarchies are essential to becoming a political subject and are expressed
in the thought of French philosopher Jacques Rancière. In the other,

mobilisation occurs *within* an interlocking matrix of oppression, constituted by race, gender and other identities, as proposed by Patricia Hill Collins.

The *sans papiers* movement in France became widely known when, in 1996, undocumented African women, children and men occupied the churches of St Amboise and St Bernard in Paris and were violently evicted after taking sanctuary for several months. Press coverage of African women and children dragged from the sanctuary of the church by unpopular CRS (French police) and the support of French celebrities for the *sans papiers* led to popular outcry and awareness of the movement (Lloyd 2003). Their protest spread within and beyond France with church occupations, demonstrations and hunger strikes, and *sans papiers* collectives continue to mobilise to this day. The role of women in this movement, though central, has been less visible, and in recent years, scholars have highlighted the unique contribution of leaders such as Cissé as well as of women who continue to work in the trenches of these movements (Freedman and Tarr 2000; Lloyd 1997; Raissiguier 2010). This work has created new spaces for these women's voices and stories, but the way in which this action can be theorised and, in turn, the ways in which the mobilisation challenges existing theoretical accounts are less developed. To this end, this chapter explores the two contrasting approaches of Rancière and Hill Collins to develop this movement's unique contribution to understanding the role of race in migration politics and, in turn, to consider the light these theoretical approaches shed on race and migrant mobilisation.

This chapter first explores the compelling vision a Rancièrian politics of rupture and interruption suggests in *sans papieres* activism, in which racial categorisations and identities are transcended. I recognise that a Rancièrian politics can help us to appreciate the world-disclosing potential of this action. Rancière helps us to understand the way in which undocumented migrants act politically as equal-speaking subjects in spaces and places where they were hitherto non-existent. In his view, race and other identities must be transcended to reinvent politics rather than reproducing the categories that are the tools of oppression and control in an unequal social world. However, this lens excludes the actual friction between racial, gender and other identities and social locations that Patricia Hill Collins's intersectionality reveals and that *sans papieres* seek to reestablish, as Cissé describes. I argue that the mobilisation of these undocumented migrant women challenges the Rancièrian account of the links between race and migration politics. While it offers an account of the great possibility of disrupting and expanding the contours of French society, Hill Collins's intersectionality provides a richer and more convincing account of how the mobilisation unfolded in practice and of the role of race.

Second, I explore *sans papieres* activism through the lens of Hill Collins's concept of 'intersectionality'. The frictions between race and gender identity that intersectionality draws into focus led to women in this movement acting both as racialised undocumented migrants and as women combatting gender oppression. The latter was the 'struggle within the struggle' in which women sought gender equality within the movement. *Sans papieres* women were simultaneously situated within these interlocking hierarchies. Rather than acting *as if* they transcended this racial and gendered social order and its categorisations, it was by acting *as* both women and racialised migrants that they created the everyday building blocks and solidarity that formed the backbone of the movement. A focus on the intersection of race and gender reveals the ways in which identities served as a political resource. It also makes visible this 'struggle within the struggle' that took place through everyday action, solidarities and coalitions as well as spectacular moments of rupture.

Rupture: what we might learn from Rancière

The democratic politics of those who are not recognised as existing, speaking subjects is central to Rancière's work.[1] Here I consider his insistence on the capacity of the excluded to break with the identities that are assigned to them and thereby to enact a radical understanding of equality. Rancière argues for a politics which takes place in a space 'outside' of social – including race – hierarchies, created by the struggles of actors to be recognised as speaking subjects when they aim to occupy spaces in which they 'do not exist' and therefore do not count.

The order of 'police' – which Rancière uses in a broad sense to refer to the way society is organised, bodies are arranged and 'ways of doing, ways of being, ways of saying' are allocated (Chambers 2010: 63) – determines who is visible and intelligible, and who counts. It 'distributes the sensible' (Rancière 2006). It comprises what we conventionally think of as politics and the technocratic nature of law and policy making that reinforces the 'statist and government functioning' we live in that is contrary to democracy and, instead, is the rule of oligarchy (Chambers 2010: 67).

Racial categories are part of police logic, a return to a primordial hatred of the Other (Rancière 1998a: 92) that comes 'from above', emanating from the state with the support of the intelligentsia. As Ann Stoler

---

[1] This summary of Rancière's thought draws on Bassel (2012).

(2011: 131) notes, Rancière has persistently directed his 'analytics of subversion' to speak out against state racism in France. For example, in autumn 2010, he spoke at an event that I attended denouncing the expulsion of Roma from France. He characterised the expulsion as an act of today's racism that is 'primarily a logic of the state and not a popular passion'. He reminded us, the audience, that, 15 years earlier, he had used the term 'cold racism' to refer to the process through which 'the universal logic of the rational state' is opposed to popular passions 'to give the state's racist policies a certificate of antiracism'. Universality is invoked to achieve the opposite objective:

The establishment of a discretionary state power that decides who belongs and who doesn't belong to the class of those who have the right to be here; the power, in short, to confer and remove identities. That power has its correlate: the power to oblige individuals to be identifiable at all times, to keep themselves in a space of full visibility before the state. (Rancière 2010)

Rancière speaks against the French Republican universalistic tradition. However, he is nonetheless strongly anchored within it (Deranty 2003: 146), for instance, denying the need to address post-colonial studies and subjects in a 2008 interview because there was no post-colonial studies in France (cited in Stoler 2011: 131). Racism is quite clearly a matter of concern, but race is problematic as a political category because the return to 'identity' categories signifies the breakdown of what he calls *heterology*, the way in which the meaningful fabric of the sensible is disturbed (Rancière 2006: 63) and manifests the fear of the other (Rancière 1998a: 92). The return to identity categories heralds new forms of racism and fear of the other – instead, identification has to be 'impossible' (not universal in the French Republican sense) to be properly political and to avoid participating in dominant police projects of racism, including the racism 'from above' of the French Republic. We now explore the nature of this 'impossible' identification further.

The police order seeks consensus whereby it is presupposed that every part of a population can be incorporated into a political order and taken into account. Because what is intelligible and visible has been determined in advance, the established framework of perception cannot be confronted with the 'inadmissible'. Thus 'consensus reduces politics to the police' (Rancière 2006: 83).

It is the 'police order' that 'distributes the sensible':

The police is thus first an order of bodies that defines the allocation of ways of doing, ways of being, and ways of saying, and sees that those bodies are assigned by name to a particular place and task; it is an order of the visible and the sayable that sees that a particular activity is visible and another is not, that this speech is understood as discourse and another as noise. (Rancière 1998b: 29)

The police order, then, does not clumsily constitute subjects by interpellating them with a shout, as Louis Althusser (1977) proposed (see also Bassel 2008) – instead it orders space and circulation within it, determining who can exist and be perceived within its confines:

Police intervention in public spaces does not consist primarily in the interpellation of demonstrators, but in the breaking up of demonstrations. The police is not that law interpellating individuals (as in Althusser's 'Hey, you there!') . . . It is, first of all, a reminder of the obviousness of what there is, or rather, of what there isn't: 'Move along! There is nothing to see here!' The police says that there is nothing to see on a road, that there is nothing to do but move along. It asserts that the space of circulating is nothing other than the space of circulation. (Rancière 2001)

There is space for *equal* political subjects in the perpetual conflict of the police order with politics. Instead of interpellation, *subjectivation*: political subjects are created through resistance to this contingent ordering and distribution of the sensible through the assertion of a radical equality between all speaking subjects. So 'politics, in contrast, consists in transforming this space of "moving along" into a space for the appearance of the subject: i.e., the people, the workers, the citizens: It consists in refiguring the space, of what there is to do there, what is to be seen or named therein' (Rancière 2001).

Politics involves the exposure of the contingency of the police order to reconfigure social space and demand the admissibility of the hitherto 'non-existent' subject. Unlike under a deliberative democratic vision, subjects do not pre-exist whom are recognised by all as valid speakers. Instead, the fight is to appear as a valid speaker and to make the situation of speech visible (Deranty 2003: 147), to claim a 'part' by those 'without a part' in the counting of the police order. In this break with the existing order, subjectivation takes place. Political subjects are created through extracting themselves from the dominant categories of identification and classification (Rancière 2006: 92), including racial categories. In the act of becoming visible and audible, a possibility opens up – 'new' subjects are recognised as speaking.

This does not mean abolishing the police order altogether. For Rancière, the police is always a condition of possibility for politics – it is by acting as equals within a particular configuration of social inequality that subjectivisation occurs, the police order is transformed and its racial and other categorisations are transcended. Though Rancière certainly recognises the very real effects of assigned identities, for him the solution does not lie in exploring these predetermined categories, which return to the violence of the police logic which 'distributes the sensible' and 'does not leave the space for a litigious meeting between the classes' (Cohen 2004: 100).[2] This police logic must be confounded.

Impossible identification: acting 'as if'

But who can be the agent of this transformation, in Rancière's view? The criteria are strict for what it means to act as a political subject, rather than operating within the 'police order' and the racial and other identities it assigns. A political subject must be 'between two or more identities . . . defined sociologically as both dominated and democratically as equal. This contradictory nature is what makes it possible as a political subject . . . the political subject can, or even must, claim an identity it does not have as an ontological subject' (Deranty 2003: 146).

Rancière describes this positioning as '*entre-deux*', literally 'between-two'. A process of subjectivation is a process of 'dis-identification' or 'de-classification'. It is a

crossing of identities that relies on a crossing of names: names that connect the name of a group or a class to the name of that which is un-counted [*hors-compte*], that connects a being to a non-being or a being-that-will-come . . . it always holds an impossible identification, an identification that can only be incarnated by those who articulate it. (Rancière 1998a: 88)[3]

For example, he explains that his generation could act as political subjects in the interval between two identities they could not assume: they could not identify with the Algerians who were beaten to death and thrown in the Seine by the French police in 1961, but they could question their identification with the 'French people' in whose name they had been killed (88). This process of subjectivation may have found its 'true' name in another impossible identification in the 1968 slogan 'We are all German Jews.' Of course we are not. Instead, what Rancière asks is 'What is the result?' (*Qu'est-ce qui en resulte?*) when the only political universal, equality, is demonstrated by linking the logic of either–or, 'Are we or are we not?,' to the 'paratactic' logic of 'We are *and* we are not this.'[4]

---

[2] 'Ne laisse pas de place à une rencontre (litigieuse) entre les classes' (Cohen 2004) and, below, 'les lieux et valeurs à disposition d'un acteur libre d'en jouer à sa guise'.

[3] 'Un croisement d'identités reposant sur un croisement de noms: des noms qui lient le nom d'un groupe ou d'une classe au nom de ce qui est hors-compte, qui lient un être à un non-être ou à un être-a-venir . . . il comporte toujours une identification impossible, une identification qui ne peut être incarnée par ceux ou celles qui l'énoncent' (Rancière 1998a: 88).

[4] 'Nous le sommes et nous ne le sommes pas' (Rancière 1998a: 89).

Subjectivation, therefore, is never the simple affirmation of an identity but instead the rejection of identities imposed by the police order, and it is about '*misnomers* which articulate a fault [*faille*] and demonstrate a wrong' (Rancière 1998a: 89).[5]

Furthermore, it is a demonstration addressed to an other, even if refused. It therefore creates a 'common place' (*lieu commun*), though this is not a space of dialogue or in which a deliberative consensus is sought. 'There is no consensus, no communication without damage . . . But there is a common polemic space to address a wrong and for the demonstration of equality' (Rancière 1998a: 89–90).[6] Therefore, the site of subjectivation, of acting politically, is in the *interval* between identities, not in assuming a different identity or in the conflict between two identities. This political possibility evaporates and new forms of racism are ushered in when the racial identity categories of the police order are used. Where once we were all German Jews, using the 'improper' names of impossible identification, we are now 'proper' and good, as Europeans and xenophobes (Rancière 1998a: 92). We see 'immigrants' where once there were 'proletarians' – and there are too many of them!

Reading *sans papiers* activism through this lens can provide an exciting vision of this kind of 'impossible' identification. In Bonnie Honig's reading of Rancière, foreignness is double-edged: a site of instrumentalisation and exclusion but also of new forms of political action. She draws our attention to the counterimage of the foreigner as a 'democratic taker', who *takes* in the sense of 'demanding, or better yet, simply enacting the distribution of those powers, rights, and privileges that define a community and order it hierarchically' (Honig 2001: 9). As Honig explains, this takes place through what Rancière calls the 'staging of a non-existent right' (100), where the immigrant is not a national but insists nonetheless on exercising national citizen rights. Foreigners undertake 'a form of activity that "shifts a body from the place assigned to it or changes a place's destination. It makes visible what had no business being seen; it makes heard as a discourse what was once only heard as noise"' (Rancière, as cited in Honig 2001: 100–101). This is a

story of illegitimate demands made by people with no standing to make them, a story of people so far outside the circle of 'who counts' that they cannot make claims within the existing frames of claim-making. They make room for

---

[5] 'Misnomers qui articulent une faille et manifeste un tort' (Rancière 1998a: 89).

[6] 'Il n'y a pas de consensus, pas de communication sans dommage . . . Mais il y a un lieu commun polémique pour le traitement du tort et la démonstration de l'égalité' (Rancière 1998a: 89–90).

themselves by staging nonexistent rights, and by way of such stagings, sometimes, new rights, powers, and visions come into being. (Honig 2001: 101)

The democratic taker has the potential to stretch the boundaries of citizenship, 'modeling transgressive forms of agency and possessing potentially inaugural powers' (Honig 2001: 8). Drawing on a Rancièrian politics, we can understand the way in which undocumented migrants act politically by demanding to be treated as equal speaking subjects in spaces and places where they were hitherto non-existent. This action has trans-formative potential through the radical assertion of equality at the interval between identities, *entre-deux*, claiming an identity that does not corre-spond to assigned social position(s) and breaking with the social order.

Rancière's 'only political universal' – the equality of any speaking sub-ject with any other speaking subject – is not the work (*œuvre*) of an enacted identity (*identité en acte*) or the demonstration of the specific val-ues of a group, in this case racialised undocumented migrants. Instead, it is the product of the process of impossible identification: acting 'as if' one has rights one does not have, or between two definitions of citizen-ship. The difference is between acting 'as' what one is (mis)recognised as being and acting 'as if' one is something impossible, that exceeds the existing framework of identification which belongs to the police order. This difference grounds the radical possibility of reinventing politics.

Under this kind of reading, the *sans papiers* make a broader questioning and transformation of citizenship possible (McNevin 2006: 147). Anne McNevin sees this questioning in Cissé's own account of the movement:

We can see the results today . . . Little by little masses of people have understood that our struggle was raising questions which go beyond the regularization of the Sans-Papiers. New questions have gradually emerged: 'Do you agree to live in a France where fundamental human rights are trampled on? Do you agree to live in a France where democratic liberties are not respected?' (Cissé 1997: 40)

Thus, for McNevin, this struggle can be connected to 'new spatial config-urations of political belonging' and set in the context of 'a global political economy and the transnational practices of a colonial and neoliberal state'. In the spaces of the city, through new practices of and resistances to exclusion, 'a new common sense is being shaped about who belongs and who does not, about the shape and limits of community, about the legitimacy of claims made with reference to new types of borders' (McNevin 2006: 146).

A Rancièrian reading offers us the radical possibility of stepping outside of the inequalities of the social order to challenge it through the demand by hitherto non-existing subjects, the *sans papiers*, that their speech be equal to that of any other.

Rancièrian exclusions

Although this reading is compelling, I would like to suggest that the challenge made by the women involved in the movement, the *sans papieres*, was in fact more profound than it allows. Though exciting, this reading may exclude too much and deny vital forms of mobilisation and contestation, with the sharp rejection of race as a political category in migration politics and the refusal to connect race politics to other identity categories, particularly gender, which serves as both a political resource and a site of struggle.

For Rancière, claims must be universal to count as politics; otherwise, they are 'identitarian', 'interest group' or 'lobby' activities within the police order and are disqualified (Cingolani, in Nordmann 2006: 207). The latter are the root of the political impasse between universality and identity because they naturalise the arbitrary: 'It is the principle of the police to present itself as the actualisation of the community, to transform the law of government into natural laws of society' (Rancière 1998a: 85).[7] While equality is always 'put into action' (*mise en œuvre*) in the name of a category to whom equality is denied, it is not the 'manifestation of the essence or attributes of the category in question' (Rancière 1998a: 85).[8] Equality exists through action; it is a universal

which must be presupposed, verified and demonstrated in each case . . . universality does not lie in concepts [humanity and rights] . . . It resides in the process of argument which demonstrates their consequences, which says what results from the fact that the factory worker is a citizen, the Black a human being etc. The logical schema of social protest can be summarised as follows: Do we belong, or not, to a certain category – citizens, humans etc. – and what is the result? Political universality is not in *man* or *citizen*. It is in the 'What is the result?', in the discursive and practical move to action. (Rancière 1998a: 86)[9]

---

[7] 'C'est le principe de la police que de se présenter comme l'actualisation du propre de la communauté, de transformer les règles du gouvernement en lois naturelles de la société' (Rancière 1998a: 85).

[8] 'Manifestation du propre ou des attributs de la catégorie en question' (Rancière 1998a: 85).

[9] 'Qui doit être présupposé, vérifié et démontré en chaque cas . . . l'universalité ne réside pas dans les concepts [l'humanité et ses droits] . . . Elle réside dans le processus argumentatif qui démontre leurs conséquences, qui dit ce qui résulte du fait que l'ouvrier est citoyen, le noir un être humain etc. Le schéma logique de la protestation sociale en générale peut se résumer ainsi: Est-ce que nous appartenons ou non à telle catégorie – citoyens, hommes, etc. – et qu'est-ce qui en résulte? L'universalité politique n'est pas dans homme ou dans

Rancière is, therefore, exacting as to what counts as acting politically. *Entre-deux*, the intervals between identities, are the only site of political subjectivation properly understood and would not encompass claims grounded on experience of multiple forms of oppression, claims *within* matrices of oppression, which we explore in Patricia Hill Collins's thought (Hill Collins 2000). Rancière refuses a sociology which resolves the determining force of *habitus* by multiplying 'the places and values available to an actor, who is free to use them as they see fit'. In other words, he is 'antisociological' in that 'politics cannot be based on the social hierarchy. Politics is the theoretical and practical assertion of absolute equality and it must radically break with the social order' (Deranty 2003: 152). Subjects, therefore, are constituted through action that breaks from the established order.

The alternative is an understanding of the role of race in migration politics, where political challenge comes from the friction *between* race and gender identities – which the work of Hill Collins on intersectionality draws into focus. The challenges the movement presents are arguably more fundamental than Rancièrian rupture allows for, and under a Hill Collins–inspired reading, race and migration politics are situated within a social hierarchy and connected to other identities rather than beyond them. This makes the 'struggle within the struggle' visible: the ways in which women contested their status not only as racialised migrants but also as women experiencing multiple forms of gender oppression.

Intersections: Patricia Hill Collins and black feminist thought

In *Black Feminist Thought* – her account of political subjectivity – Patricia Hill Collins (2000) places black women's ideas and experiences at the centre of analysis. Black women occupy an 'outsider-within' status as a result of their unique history at the intersection of mutually constructing systems of oppression (race, class, gender, sexuality and nation), which generates a black feminist standpoint (Hill Collins 1986). She and other scholars of intersectionality[10] have drawn our attention to the simultaneous and interacting effects of these systems of oppression as categories of difference and have advanced a powerful critique of mutually exclusive categories such as 'woman' or 'black' which serve to mask the

---

citoyen. Elle est dans le « Qu'est-ce qui en résulte ? », dans sa mise en œuvre discursive et pratique' (Rancière 1998a: 86).

[10] See hooks (1981, 1984), Combahee River Collective (1986), Crenshaw (1991), Hancock (2007), Jordan-Zachery (2007) and Yuval-Davis (2006a, 2006b).

intersecting and interacting relations of domination and inequality that structure the lives of minority women and men. Hill Collins's project is to empower African American women within the context of social injustice sustained by intersecting oppressions (Hill Collins 2000: 22). These self-defined standpoints stimulate resistance, and 'identity is not the goal but rather the point of departure in the process of self-definition' (Hill Collins 2000: 114). Black women are agents of knowledge because they are the people authorised to discuss a theoretical knowledge based on their own experience, which provides a window into related processes for other groups with whom coalitions can be built.

'Grounding their authority in their ability to speak self-defined voices as knowledge creators, African-American women have carved out a modest authority emanating from a Black feminist standpoint' (Hill Collins 2000: 58). The development of black feminist thought 'itself represents a hard-fought struggle to name oneself, to claim an identity that more accurately reflects Black women's lives and subjectivities' (64). Four criteria characterise an epistemology employed by African Americans: (1) the use of dialogue in assessing knowledge claims, (2) the centrality of personal expressiveness, (3) the ethic of personal accountability and (4) concrete experiences as criteria of meaning (Hill Collins 2000: 251–71).

Identification is difficult but not 'impossible' in Rancière's sense. The struggle is to act 'as' a black woman and be recognised and taken seriously politically as such. As political actors, black women are firmly located at the meeting point of multiple systems of oppression, not in the interval between them. This location produces particular group vantage points that arise from the specific historical location that a marginalised group has struggled to name and articulate.

'Intersectionality' refers to particular forms of intersecting oppression that cannot be reduced to one fundamental type within a *matrix of domination* in which intersecting oppressions are organised socially (Hill Collins 2000: 18). Intersecting systems of domination can be analysed according to their organisation in four distinct yet inter-related domains of power: structural (laws, interlocking large-scale institutions), which organises oppression; disciplinary (bureaucracy, administration), which manages it; hegemonic (ideology, culture, consciousness), which justifies it; and inter-personal (level of everyday social interaction), which influences everyday life and individual consciousness (Hill Collins 2000: 277–90).

Identity as a political resource

Resistance begins with self-definition. In contrast to rupturing with the existing social hierarchy, 'the act of insisting on Black female self-definition validates Black women's power as human subjects' (Hill Collins 1986: S17) and thereby questions some of the basic ideas used to control dominated groups in general. Defining and valuing 'a self-defined standpoint in the face of images that foster a self-definition as the objectified "other" is an important way of resisting the dehumanization essential to systems of domination' (S18) and to reject internalised domination. Black women, who occupy an 'outsider-within' position, will have a clearer view of oppression (S19).

For Cissé, identity provides both knowledge of oppression and the political resources to combat it, not just as a *sans papiers* but also as an African woman and as a Senegalese:

The Senegalese women don't only have a tradition of struggle; they also have a tradition of self-organization. It is in some way linked to our education: as women, we are used to managing on our own from a very early age. Because back home, it is the woman who is in charge of the home, who is in charge of the compound. Little girls from the age of eight look after their younger brothers, go to market, cook. And they have a very important role in forging links with the other families in the compound. (Cissé 1997: 42)

She also points to the Soninke origin of many of the West African *sans papiers* involved in the movement: 'It is often said that the Soninké "are a travelling people". They are a great people who come together in the Empire of Mali and who were scattered across five or six different countries: that might also explain why they always feel the need to go beyond national borders' (Cissé 1997: 38). Furthermore, colonial legacies attract West Africans to France: 'Of course, as soon as there is any question of leaving our country, most of the time in order to find work, it's natural that we turn to France. It's the country we know, the one whose language we have learned, whose culture we have integrated a little' (Cissé 1997: 38).

Hill Collins recognises these connections between identity, knowledge and action and views identity as a political resource, which is inadmissible to Rancière. Identity, in her view, is where knowledge and strength come from. She argues that black women can 'trust their own personal and cultural biographies as significant sources of knowledge' (Hill Collins 1986: S29), a compelling and potentially empowering vision. Her definition of political action is, therefore, much more inclusive than Rancière's: 'People who view themselves as fully human, as subjects, become activists, no matter how limited the sphere of their activism may be. By returning subjectivity to Black women, Black feminists return activism as well' (Hill Collins 1986: S24). There is a dialectical relationship between oppression, consciousness and activism.

Therefore, to understand 'what makes an action political or not, or indeed what disinclines individuals to behave in a political manner in the first place', it is essential to engage with individuals' own understandings and interpretations of self and world (McNay 2010: 512). This is a capacity of embodied subjects (McNay 2010) that is historically rooted rather than springing up as a Rancièrian miracle (Nordmann 2006).[11] Constraint, too, is deeply embodied. For Cissé, this was a particularly harsh experience: she was stripped, her undergarments ridiculed and her African female body opposed to the use of reason and technology – the mobile phone. Her account of her experience suggests the ways in which individuals' understandings of self and the world are deeply rooted in social locations and bodies (McNay 2010).

Cissé also describes Senegalese women's resistance to colonialism and their mobilisation for fair elections since 1960 (Cissé 1999: 136). Though undoubtedly shaped by neoliberal configurations of space, as Cissé herself notes when describing the effect of structural adjustment on Malian and Senegalese women in the 1990s, *sans papieres*' actions are also shaped by a legacy of resistance that springs out of specific identities as 'Senegalese'. It is difficult to make direct comparisons with the influence of the legacy of African American women's resistance to slavery that Hill Collins explores, but the similarity lies in the ways in which memory and preserved identity can shape activism. When these forms of 'identity'-based knowledge are excluded, a political resource that was vital to the *sans papieres*' struggle is neglected.

The 'struggle within the struggle'

Hill Collins's intersectionality also reveals possibilities for activism within multiple structures of domination, such as the private decision to maintain self-definitions in the face of objectifying definitions as 'other' (Hill Collins 1986: S23–S24) and in everyday behaviour and roles. Under a Rancièrian reading, only a narrow spectrum of action becomes visible, and spectacular decisions and moments of rupture from racial categorisations are privileged (Deranty 2003), rendering a vital range of human activity invisible (Bassel and Lloyd 2011). In contrast, attending to the intersection of race and gender makes the 'struggle within the struggle' visible and highlights its political importance.

---

[11] Rancière is also deeply committed to recognising the political knowledge of the oppressed and their capacity to know their own circumstances. 'It is the oppressed who are intelligent and it is from their intelligence that the weapons of freedom are born' (Rancière 1974: 40). 'Opposition to the bourgeoisie begins with the refusal of its first axiom, that is, "the idea that help for the oppressed is necessary"' (Rancière 1974: 42). However, this knowledge comes from the interval *between* identities, outside of the social hierarchy, not from the friction between them.

The *sans papieres* undertook the kind of hard, everyday political work within multiple structures of domination that we see, drawing on Hill Collins, throughout their movement. A Rancièrian reading focuses on the ways in which *sans papiers* are challenging their racialised non-status and expanding citizenship as Honig's 'democratic takers' who occupy churches and are dragged out by police. But reading their action through Hill Collins's lens, we can see, in fact, multiple dimensions to this struggle. Challenging the boundaries of French citizenship was not the only fight; this singular focus obscures the challenges and dynamism at the intersections, in the friction between race and gender identities. In the movement, there was another revolution as well, in which 'women affirmed their need for emancipation' (Cissé and Quiminal 2000: 343). Husbands 'discovered that their wives were intelligent, that they could keep up an argument, and that made them scared. There was a kind of rebellion where we had to defend these women against their husbands who didn't want them to be there' (Freedman and Tarr 2000: 33).

Cissé further explains:

> It was even a little revolution. I would say, without exaggerating, because struggle is one of the best places to learn, what we learned in four years, we practically wouldn't have learned in 10 years, 20 years, for sure. Women affirmed their need for emancipation. That's how it happened, there was even friction between couples. There were men who found that their wives were exaggerating by going to a demonstration 'and leaving me with the baby, what is this all about etc?'. But there was a transformation in the traditional African couple to the extent that journalists who would come to see us were surprised to see the men doing the cooking. . . 'But in Africa it is women who cook!', I say to them, 'But we are not in Africa!'. Women felt that need to be free, to choose their activities, and they said it, and imposed it. Men also had to change their ways. We even found men who encouraged their wives to take literacy courses, because we also organised literacy courses within the group, always with a majority of women, especially students, and other friends, teachers etc who came regularly and taught courses to the women. Men even accepted that their wives learn French, that they participate in the political actions, and I think that also changed something even when people went back to their homes. The proof: most of them found work afterwards. (Cissé and Quiminal 2000: 25)

It is not 'simply' the case that two struggles took place at the same time but that the friction between race and gender identities led to challenging (and continues to challenge) the French Republic and gender relations simultaneously, in fundamental ways that a Rancièrian perspective does not acknowledge.

Women in the movement challenged social as well as legal boundaries that ran along racial fault lines. Cissé documents in detail the types of coalition building that took place within the movement, particularly between women around a broader women's identity and community (Cissé 1999: 144–145). This included *sans papieres* from different countries – China, Turkey, Senegal, Mali – but also French women, many of whom were meeting 'foreigners' for the first time, a mutually enriching experience, with relationships that lasted beyond the mobilisation (Cissé 1999: 146). Christine Rasguissier describes the more recent *sans papieres* activism in similar terms:

> These women . . . are not (and do not think of themselves as) heroic activists. Most of them, in fact, happened upon collective action after having tried a variety of individual approaches to solving their situation. Most tried to work alone or with a private lawyer before reaching out to an NGO or a *sans papiers* collective. By becoming active in a social movement, the sans-papieres forge alliances with individuals and groups they might not have encountered outside of their social action. The unique analytical power, the potential coalitional work, and the impossible (unruly) politics that these alliances can generate are exciting. (Raissiguier 2010: 52–53)

The new relationships and coalitions that are formed simultaneously challenge gender relations, racial stereotypes and segregation and enable French women to become 'traitors' to the privileges of their citizenship status, and white French women to 'betray' their race privilege as well (Hill Collins 2000: 37). These are important forms of politics. And they do not spring up out of nowhere; they are the product of struggles at the intersections of race and gender that are sustained over time and are composed of less spectacular but no less important forms of action. These actions are deeply rooted in specific gender and racial hierarchies, and French and *sans papieres* women draw on these locations as a source of strength and motivation and as grounds for solidarity.

The dangers of experience

There are dangers in relying on experience, particularly ideas of personal suffering (Brown 1995). The idea of personal suffering and a sense of woundedness can bind groups and individuals to their own subjugation and risks not providing forward-looking alternatives. Instead, a politics of resentment and injury could be generated, which, in turn, can powerfully legitimise the state as protector (Brown 1995).

Detractors of the buzzword status of 'intersectionality' share some of these concerns and argue that this approach exacerbates the challenges of 'identity politics' – that is, fragmenting and destabilising political mobilisation – leading to further competition between sub-divided groups (Nash 2008); reifying and essentialising what are, in fact, fluid and multiple identities; and leading to a focus on how identities intersect in the individual, as opposed to the individual existing within and among overlapping identity claims and communities.[12]

Certainly there is a danger when 'politicised identity can see no future without the injury also constituting an aspect of that future' (Bhambra and Margree 2010: 65). Bhambra and Margree suggest instead not only that 'reformed' identity politics requires a desire for the future but also that 'that desire should actually be a desire for the dissolution (in the future) of the identity claim' (65). Rather than reifying identity politics around historical or contemporary suffering, a

> tomorrow [is needed] in which the social injustices of the present have been overcome. But identity politics also needs that tomorrow – today – in the sense that politicised identities need to inscribe that tomorrow into their self-definition in the present, in order to avoid consolidating activity around the maintenance of the identity rather than the overcoming of the conditions that generated it . . . That identity will no longer be required, is not a situation to be regretted, since it is rather the promise of success for any movement for justice. (Bhambra and Margree 2010: 65)

The relationship between identity, experience, knowledge and action is complex, and the transition from one to the other is not automatic.[13] For Hill Collins (2000: 114), 'identity is not the goal but rather the point of departure in the process of self-definition'. In the act of returning subjectivity to black women, humanity is recovered and disfiguring histories of oppression are cast off. This process is not exclusive to black women: by drawing from the specificity of black feminist epistemology, it is possible to generate knowledge about how others are affected by the same interlocking forces, through the 'ability to enrich our understanding of how subordinate groups create knowledge that fosters both their empowerment and social justice' (Hill Collins 2000: 269).

For the *sans papieres*, experience of race and gender oppression is the root of action, but its use as a source of knowledge is reflexive, constantly under review, and not the exclusive domain of any one group. And, drawing on Bhambra and Margree (2010: 64–65), it is embedded within politics today. 'Tomorrow' was already inscribed within this

---

[12] Thanks to Gurminder Bhambra for raising this point.

[13] See McNay's discussion of Jane Mansbridge's work (Mansbridge and Morris 2001) in McNay (2010: 520). Mansbridge argues that, at the outset, it is the most effective to engage individuals and groups through a direct appeal to their own experiences and narrower concerns of recognition and interest. This is an initial route into post-identity politics, providing marginal and oppressed groups with the opportunity to formulate politicised understandings of their identities, interests and needs. The challenge is to ensure that these enclaves do not become self-enclosed ends in themselves.

movement, as demonstrated by practices of engaging with others, learning and changing and participating in dialogues about what justice for all *sans papiers* should look like.

The coalition work of the *sans papieres* and French women involved in the movement is precisely this kind of work of inscribing 'tomorrow' in the heat of battle. Several French women's organisations were among the first to answer the call for solidarity (Cissé and Quiminal 2000). As Cissé describes this response,

they answered the call quickly, as they had also seen women on the TV with children. They came, they asked a lot of questions about women's situation, about their needs and the chain of solidarity worked quickly. As soon as they left they came back with duvets, milk etc. And it was there . . . that the contact was formed, and the relationships were very deep because we also had discussions between foreign and French women, that was important . . . complicity was easier between women. We understood each other quickly and today the result is a network for the legal independence/autonomy of foreign women. It was important because we were in the group but we had specific problems because we were women . . . I think our French friends learned a lot too. There were some who were spending time with African women for the first time. It was the first time they lived like that with us . . . we would go to their houses etc. For some it was a discovery and some even travelled to Africa. We have friends who went to Mali, and went to villages where there were *sans papiers* that we knew here. It was an enriching experience for everyone. Some took the children to play centres, some took the children to a Christmas tree . . . Some would take children to the hospital when they were sick . . . and organised day care. When we had tough actions/demonstrations, there were women who looked after the children while we occupied places or were evacuated by the CRS [police], it was a very interesting form of organisation. (Cissé and Quiminal 2000: 19)

This is not, therefore, an exclusive politics, nor is it a politics that focuses on one identity and experience of suffering as a political dead-end which, in turn, excludes the participation of others. Instead, different women drew on their respective resources to come together around objectives that evolved throughout mobilisation – for example, beginning with milk and duvets, shifting to childcare and hospital visits and culminating in a legal network for the rights of migrant women. While experience and embodied identity – as mothers, particularly – drew different women together, it was a resource rather than an obstacle and led to the practice of 'tomorrow' in the here and now of the movement.

Although, of course, power differences existed within the movement, Cissé suggests that no one group of women had a monopoly on action or speech. As Hill Collins argues,

each group speaks from its own standpoint and shares its own partial, situated knowledge. But because each group perceives its own truth as partial, its knowledge is unfinished. Each group becomes better able to consider other groups' standpoints without relinquishing the uniqueness of its own standpoint or suppressing others groups' partial perspectives... Partiality, and not universality, is the condition of being heard; individuals and groups forwarding knowledge claims without owning their position are deemed less credible than those who do. (Hill Collins 2000: 270)

Thus citizenship is expanded, but in new, unforeseen ways. By learning about the experiences of *sans papieres*, French women became sensitive to the ways in which systems that they had not realised were at work were oppressive to women outside the pale of citizenship. The knowledge that *sans papieres* women imparted in the struggle meant that they were in charge of their own thought and politics, but without excluding others (Hill Collins 2000: 18), and they certainly did not project separatist solutions to oppression because they were sensitive to how these same systems oppress others (Hill Collins 1986: S21). Women revitalised the movement and kept it together: 'a role of cement' (Cissé and Quiminal 2000). Cissé explains how women kept the group together, particularly when the government attempted to divide them, by offering to regularise the 'good files' of some families but not single men. *Sans papieres* very firmly opposed this proposal, arguing that, if single men were abandoned, they would never get their papers.

Through their sustained political action at the intersection of race and gender, which we see through Hill Collins's lens, the *sans papieres* used these identities as a political resource, simultaneously combatted multiple systems of domination and addressed the dangers of these identities becoming a political dead-end through dynamic coalition work with French women. Rather than exclusively focusing on a singular moment of rupture from racial hierarchies, their continuous struggles acting *as* undocumented, racialised migrant women situated within interlocking hierarchies formed the backbone of a movement that challenged multiple systems of domination.

Conclusion

Through a Rancièrian lens, we have seen an exciting vision of rupture from existing racial categories in which undocumented migrants act politically by demanding to be treated as equal speaking subjects in spaces and places where they were hitherto non-existent. Yet this is, in fact, a multidimensional form of politics in which undocumented migrant women contested their marginalised status both as racialised migrants and as women. They used race and gender identities as a political resource to carry out multiple struggles, both within and as part of the undocumented-migrant movement. The knowledge that came from the friction *between* identities at the intersections that Hill Collins draws into focus cannot be excluded because of its 'particular' roots in social identity and location: it was by acting *as* racialised migrant women that they were able to mobilise against different forms of domination. Reading the *sans papieres* through Hill Collins's lens tells us about the connections between knowledge, identity and action. This reading can generate knowledge about how others are affected by the same interlocking forces of race *and* gender, a vital prerequisite for understanding race and the politics of migration.

REFERENCES

Althusser, L. (1977). Ideology and ideological state apparatuses (notes towards an investigation). In L. Althusser, ed., *'Lenin and Philosophy' and Other Essays*. London: New Left Books, pp. 121–73.

Bassel, L. (2008). Citizenship as interpellation: refugee women and the state. *Government and Opposition*, 43(2), 293–314.

(2012). *Refugee Women: Beyond Gender versus Culture*. London: Routledge.

Bassel, L. and Lloyd, C. (2011). Rupture or reproduction? 'New' citizenship in France. *French Politics*, 9(1), 21–49.

Bhambra, G. K. and Margree, V. (2010). Identity politics and the need for a 'tomorrow'. *Economic and Political Weekly*, 45(15), 59–66.

Brown, W. (1995). *States of Injury: Power and Freedom in Late Modernity*. Princeton, NJ: Princeton University Press.

Chambers, S. (2010). Police and oligarchy. In J. P. Deranty, ed., *Jacques Rancière: Key Concepts*. Durham, NC: Acumen, pp. 57–68.

Cissé, M. (1997). *The Sans-Papiers: A Woman Draws the First Lessons*. London: Crossroads Books.

(1999). *Parole de Sans-Papiers*. Paris: La Dispute.

Cissé, M. and Quiminal, C. (2000). La lutte des 'sans-papières'. *Les Cahiers du CEDREF*, 8–9, 343–53. http://cedref.revues.org/220.

Cohen, D. (2004). Rancière sociologue, autrement. *Labyrinthe*, 17(1), 97–101. http://labyrinthe.revues.org.

Combahee River Collective. (1986). *The Combahee River Collective Statement: Black Feminist Organizing in the Seventies and Eighties*. New York: Kitchen Table/Women of Color Press.

Crenshaw, K. (1991). Mapping the margins: intersectionality, identity politics and violence against women of color. In M. Albertson Fineman, ed., *The Public Nature of Private Violence*. New York, Routledge, pp. 93–118.

Deranty, J. P. (2003). Jacques Rancière's contribution to the ethics of recognition. *Political Theory*, 31(1), 136–56.

Freedman, J. and Tarr, C. (2000). The sans-papiers: an interview with Madjiguène Cissé. In J. Freedman and C. Tarr, eds, *Women, Immigration and Identities in France*. Oxford: Berg, pp. 29–38.

Hancock, A. M. (2007). Intersectionality as a normative and empirical paradigm. *Politics and Gender*, 3(2), 248–54.

Hill Collins, P. (1986). Learning from the outsider within: the sociological significance of black feminist thought. *Social Problems*, 33(6), S14–S32.

(2000). *Black Feminist Thought: Knowledge, Consciousness and the Politics of Empowerment*. New York: Routledge.

Honig, B. (2001). *Democracy and the Foreigner*. Princeton, NJ: Princeton University Press.

hooks, B. (1981). *Ain't I a Woman? Black Women and Feminism*. Boston: South End Press.

(1984). *Feminist Theory: From Margin to Centre*. Boston: South End Press.

Jordan-Zachery, J. S. (2007). Am I a black woman or a woman who is black? A few thoughts on the meaning of intersectionality. *Politics and Gender*, 3(2), 254–63.

Lloyd, C. (1997). Struggling for rights: African women and the 'sanspapiers' movement in France. *Refuge*, 14(2), 31–34.

(2003). Anti-racism, racism and asylum-seekers in France. *Patterns of Prejudice*, 37(3), 323–40.

Mansbridge, J. and Morris, A. (2001). *Oppositional Consciousness: The Subjective Roots of Social Protest*. Chicago: Chicago University Press.

McNay, L. (2010). Feminism and post-identity politics: the problem of agency. *Constellations*, 17(4), 512–25.

McNevin, A. (2006). Political belonging in a neoliberal era: the struggle of the sans-papiers. *Citizenship Studies*, 10(2), 135–51.

Nash, J. (2008). Re-thinking intersectionality. *Feminist Review*, 89(1), 1–15.

Nordmann, C. (2006). *Bourdieu/Rancière. La Politique: Entre Sociologie et Philosophie*. Paris: Editions Amsterdam.

Raissiguier, C. (2010). *Reinventing the Republic: Gender, Migration, and Citizenship in France*. Stanford, CA: Stanford University Press.

Rancière, J. (1974). *La Leçon d'Althusser*. Paris: Gallimard.

(1998a). *Aux Bords du Politique*. Paris: Essais Folio/Gallimard.

(1998b). *Disagreement: Politics and Philosophy*. Minneapolis: University of Minnesota Press.

(2001). Ten theses on politics. *Theory and Event*, 5(3).

(2006). *The Politics of Aesthetics*. London: Continuum.

(2010). Racism: a passion from above. Paper given to the conference Les Roms, et Qui d'Autre? Montreuil, 11 September. http://blogs.mediapart.fr/edition/les-invites-de-mediapart/article/140910/racisme-une-passion-den-haut.

Stoler, A. L. (2011). Colonial aphasia: race and disabled histories in France. *Public Culture*, 23(1), 121–56.

Yuval-Davis, N. (2006a). Intersectionality and feminist politics. *European Journal of Women's Studies*, 13(3), 193–209.

(2006b). Belonging and the politics of belonging. *Patterns of Prejudice*, 40(3), 197–214.

7   Can race be eradicated? The post-racial problematic

Brett St Louis

> The idea [of race], although repeatedly killed, is nevertheless undying.
> – Jacques Barzun

After sponsoring death and despair over centuries and across continents, the scourge of race and racism was finally eradicated in the early twenty-first century. On a cold, late January day in 2009, the ceremony symbolising its end was conducted before a massed crowd of eager witnesses to history numbering almost 2 million, accompanied by a national and worldwide audience of many millions more. It was perhaps fitting that this rite took place in the United States, the nation where, arguably, race had been the most strongly entrenched and deterministic. And as the orator's words that day noted that America's 'patchwork heritage is a strength, not a weakness', not only was the enmity of race consigned to history but it was replaced with the audacious hope that 'as the world grows smaller, our common humanity shall reveal itself'.[1]

The 2008 general election success and inauguration of Barack Obama on 20 January 2009 as the 44th president of the United States signalled many things, often highly contestable. One of the most controversial aphorisms was and, indeed for some, remains a simple statement portrayed in the phantastical rendition that Obama's ascent confirmed the United States as a *post-racial* society. If, as the contention goes, an African American could be elected to the highest office in the land and become the 'leader of the free world', then race was no longer a barrier to progress and achievement in America. Moreover, if America was post-racial and had become truly meritocratic, then, by extension, it was also en route to becoming a post-racist society (Wise 2009).

But the suggestion of a post-racial shift has also been robustly contested. Obama is very much the exception that proves the long-standing

---

[1] Obama's inauguration speech, http://news.bbc.co.uk/1/hi/world/americas/obama_inauguration/7840646.stm.

rule of racial stratification and racism, evidenced by a series of socio-economic indicators, including African Americans' disproportionately high representation within the criminal justice and penal systems, higher rates of unemployment and lower average household incomes. Within this view, the post-racial society is not only a fiction but an extremely dangerous one that absolves profiteers of race and decrees they may keep their gains while threatening, once and for all, to end hopes of redistributive justice: the efficacy of post-racialism is thus questionable because

a moderate 'reformism' that bevels off the jagged edges of racial dictatorship but leaves the underlying social structure of racial exclusion and injustice largely untouched is in a poor position to claim that it has 'transcended' race. In many if not all respects it has reinforced the very system it claims to have surpassed. (Winant 2004: xix)

Despite its ubiquity, the term *post-racial* has been used in a rather super-ficial and impressionistic way within the news media, to the extent that Cornel West (2009: 240) argues that it is an 'empty media category' as well as 'an empty illusion'. Academic debates have tended to focus on this empty gesture toward an epochal shift and consider 'post-racial' as an illusory political artifice (Winant 2004). As a result, academic discussion of the post-racial has tended toward the cursory. This tendency is regrettable because, beneath the disingenuous realpolitik, vacuous utterance and straw man lie principles of great significance, with a profound practical resonance, that have a long and complex history. Toward this end, this chapter unpacks the term *post-racial* alongside the racial elimi-nativist ideal to develop a wider post-racial concept beyond the dishonest and vacuous utterance. Articulating the post-racial with racial elimina-tivism, I locate an uneven history of anti-race thinking across the human, social and life sciences that often attempts to reject racial categories and concepts.[2] I develop this post-racial framework to demonstrate the dif-ferent context-specific and objective-driven conditions of possibility for post-racial thinking. This reformulation – or rescuing – of the post-racial illustrates how sets of material interests and practices are tethered to assemblages of ideas and values to form practico-theoretical ensembles of post-racialism, of which there are distinct formations.

---

[2] In this chapter, I extend 'racial eliminativism' to refer to a critical practico-theoretical system oriented toward an eliminativist end that can also be characterised as post-racial. Post-racial and racial eliminativism are used interchangeably when the former is referred to as an idealisation and process with analytic value. This is also to distinguish post-racial eliminativism from reference to the post-racial as a gestural rhetorical stratagem synonymous with colour-blindness and/or an already existing state.

What is the post-racial?

ial is an extremely slippery term with various meanings within different contexts. As is the case with any *post*, *post-racial* can be read on a spectrum ranging from signalling a decisive break to being indicative of an unfinished and uneven process. In terms of the latter, the complexity of a putative post-racial process is compounded insofar as the diminution of race either *ought to be* demonstrable and/or *is* demonstrable; in other words, race is either disintegrating and/or ought to be actively dissembled. The dissimilarity between the post-racial as a break or as a process is crucial because it marks a key distinction between post-racial as an objective situation or an idealisation that is yet to be realised. For example, in post-racial terms, the Obama presidency might either signal the post-racial era as real, a decisive break with the racial past, or as an aspect of the destabilisation, but not eradication, of race.

The notion of the post-racial as a process is developed within philosophical debates on racial eliminativism. Paul Taylor (2004: 87) usefully defines a racial 'eliminativist' as 'a racial skeptic for whom race-talk is at best an egregious error, and at worst a pernicious lie... Adherents of this perspective usually insist that we strike – that is, eliminate – race from our ontological vocabularies.' So, the elimination of race here is not simply a process of atrophy, perhaps owing to its internal contradictions, but is instead an active process that is the result of purposive determinations. The contention that race *is* an erroneous and 'pernicious' category renders it indefensible, and that it therefore *ought to be* eradicated demonstrates racial eliminativ*ism* as praxis. Racial eliminativism, then, is a practicotheoretical ensemble that combines epistemological scrutiny, ethical critique and political prescription.

There is an important point of note here: some, indeed most, forms of racial scepticism are not eliminativist. Within the body of thought that David Theo Goldberg and Philomena Essed (2002) term 'race critical theory', the validity of 'race' as an empirical object as well as its divisive consequences are subject to strenuous critique. Race critical theory, then, can inform and provide a point of entry into a process-based post-racial perspective, as reflected in Taylor's observation of a productive synergy between racial scepticism and racial eliminativism. However, it must also be noted that some race critical theorists, while unconvinced of the efficacy of race and critical of its iniquitous applications, nevertheless retain the category and concept of race (sometimes in scare quotes) for various pragmatic purposes, including ontological, methodological and political. So, while some racial scepticism may result in a post-racial perspective, there is no logical correspondence between the two, and most race critical theory does not advocate racial eliminativism. The idea of post-racialism as an idealised process is a particularly strong and extreme form of race critical theory, critical to the point that it asserts that no concession can be made toward race and the only option is its elimination. Post-racialism, then, is most accurately applicable to the development of ideas and practices that might enable a process of racial elimination; it is an idealisation and an ambition.

The constitution of the post-racial is significantly impacted by an internal contradiction. As is the case with any *post-*, the relationship between the *post-* and its base word is extremely complex and often agonistic. If one thinks of post-feminism, post-colonialism and post-Marxism, for example, it is arguable whether the base word as the original formation is ever fully exceeded. The base word stands as the *post-*'s 'other' and therefore always remains, even if only in part, as a disruptive trace that always has to be accounted for and/or needs to be dismissed. So, even if the *post-* is meant to signify or aspire to a rupture, its other is always there − even the act of denial maintains its existence, however fragile. And in these terms, it is questionable whether the post-racial ideal can fully escape the spectre of race. The post-racial, like race, can also be characterised as comparative and relational; post-racial can in part be identified as non-race or anti-race. Obviously, post-racial is diametrically opposed to what is sometimes termed racial preservationism or conservationism − the notion that race ought to be retained, even if only for socially descriptive and analytical purposes. But race itself, albeit in the form of a profound dissatisfaction with it, is vital to formulating the post-racial as a process − the post-racial is conceptually dependent on race.

As an ambition, the post-racial is characterised and haunted by a constituent dilemma. On one hand, as is the current orthodoxy across the life, social and human sciences, race is not real − it does not exist as an empirical object in nature. This epistemological assertion is central to the eliminativist's rationale. But, on the other hand, race is a powerful normative idea that is believed to be real and acted upon as real and, as such, has practical effects and consequences. Therefore, to all intents and purposes, race *is* real. This situation raises the stakes for eliminativism to an acute pitch: How can the reality of race be denied and rejected when it can have grave, even fatal consequences? Does eliminativism not trivialise racially motivated homicide? Is such a stance not, at best, deeply insensitive toward and, at worst, a denial of suffering? Then again, are attempts at eliminating race not justified if the normalised idea of race helps to reproduce the governmentality and social conditions that have unjust and mortal consequences? Ultimately, as Colette Guillaumin (1995: 107) remarks, 'Race does not exist. But it does kill people.' This is a thorny problematic, for racial conservationists and eliminativists alike, that the post-racial ideal is unable to escape. Therefore, in addition to being an ambition, the post-racial is also a dilemma.

The actually existing post-racial society

Much current Anglo-American popular commentary suggests that the post-racial society is an emergent or actually existing form. Social indicators such as the increase of exogamous relationships and the expansion, normalisation and acceptance of mixed-race populations; the improvement of 'colour-blind' inter-racial contact as well as occupational and residential integration; and increased black and minority-ethnic social mobility and opportunity are cited as the empirical green shoots of racial transcendence and the colour-blind ideal (Mirza 2010; Payne 1998; Thernstrom and Thernstrom 1999). The election of Barack Obama is also held up as a bellwether and manipulated to represent the pinnacle of 'post-racial liberalism' (Wise 2010). In addition to the Anglo-American context, existent forms of post-racialism are also proclaimed in Brazil, South Africa and France as 'racial democracy', 'non-racialism' and 'racial differentialism', respectively (Winant 2001).

The already existing post-racial society is periodised as a relatively recent phenomenon. Barnor Hesse (2011) identifies the 'post-racial horizon' as a conceptual vista emerging in the mid 1990s with diverse individuals reconciling in an ecstasy of recognition, consumption and geniality as racism supposedly dissolves about them. Opting for a larger time frame, Tim Wise recognises post-racial liberalism as a decades-long project beginning with William Julius Wilson's (1978) provocation, *The Declining Significance of Race*. For Wise, Wilson's thesis that class had become an increasingly significant factor in determining black Americans' life chances and employment opportunities during the post–World War II industrial era because educational attainment and technical and professional skills were privileged within the economic sector has been central to the growth of post-racial liberalism. Indeed, Wise (2010: 16) argues that the liberal project to promote 'a de-emphasis of racial discrimination and race-based remedies for inequality, in favor of class-based or "universal" programs of uplift' is directly influenced by Wilson's work. Moreover, Munira Mirza's (2010: 31–32) statement in reference to Britain that 'race is no longer the significant disadvantage it is often portrayed to be' because, with regard to various indicators, such as 'educational attainment, career progression, rates of criminality, social mobility – class and socioeconomic background are more important', is also, in many ways, a restatement of Wilson's thesis.

For advocates of a more strident vision of the actually existing post-racial society, Wilson's intervention was wilfully circumscribed. Wilson's claim that the urban black lumpenproletariat was effectively an underclass deemed superfluous to an advanced capitalist economy purely because of its members' lack of education, training and skills ought not only to have noted the declining significance of race but also the diminution of racism. In his controversial work *The End of Racism*, Dinesh D'Souza (1995: 483) argued that Wilson's observation that cultural values emerge from and reflect social class position failed to call the so-called underclass to account for their moral and behavioural pathologies. Revisiting the 'culture of poverty' thesis previously advanced within the Moynihan Report, D'Souza accused Wilson of 'excusing' black pathologies as the product of poor life chances when instead they were the cause; Wilson and other apologists for black cultural pathology thus failed to account for the successes of black women and the black middle class as the sum of individual exceptions that disproved the disenfranchised underclass rule (D'Souza 1995: 519–20). In a supposedly ironic twist, the post-racist ideal portrayed here is undermined by the continued reification of race; although the putative underclass cannot claim to be victims of racism because their marginality results from their *cultural*, not their racial, pathology, the socially and occupationally mobile black middle class as the direct beneficiaries of affirmative action are castigated as having a deep material interest in maintaining racial categories and quotas. Thus blacks are both guilty of addiction to racial patronage as a secondary pathology and infantilised through the unjust charity of positive discrimination that assumes their inability to succeed.

These disingenuous claims to the actually existing post-racial and post-racist society are greatly exaggerated, and the oft-cited figure of Wilson is useful in determining why. The post-racial liberal consensus that Wise critiques is a Machiavellian use of a colour-blind ideal to deny the continued existence of racial discrimination and stratification that draws on Wilson's work without necessarily being endorsed by him. This is evident in Wilson's careful distinction between the declining significance of race in the economic sphere and its continued socio-political importance; for example, he recognised that the growing number of blacks in white-collar positions was not simply the result of progress and enlightened social attitudes but was assisted by 'the pressures of state affirmative action programs' (Wilson 1978: 151). Conversely, given that 'one of the legacies of the racial oppression in previous years is the continued disproportionate black representation in the underclass' (154), the black underclass is not simply a residual economic class but something akin to a racialised historical lumpenproletariat. Crucially, then, for Wilson, black workers and communities did not find themselves in a perilous position *because* they were black people, but nevertheless they inhabited their precarious social position *as* black people; the significance of race might be declining in the present, but its historical, cumulative effects are still being felt. If Wilson has any affinity with the post-racial, it is arguably in analytical terms; his intervention disputes the causal significance of race – where it is believed to exist, antagonistic race relations might be explained as a subjective manifestation of a material, class-based conflict. Nevertheless, while Wilson might be characterised as an eliminativist in economic terms, once faced with the post-racial dilemma, he accedes to the edifice of racial ideas that shape individual lives and the aggregated life chances of an underprivileged stratum that may be racially aggravated.

The critique of the 'actually existing post-racial society' and 'end of racism' theses as vacuous and spurious is compelling. Instead of the inexorable march of liberal democratic social perfectibility yielding the actually existing post-racial society, the persistence of racism testifies to the opposite, to the post-racial mirage. At best, reference to the existing post-racial represents a diversionary sophistry: for example, Obama's campaign team had counselled against the candidate giving a major speech on race, fearing that it might damage his 'post-racial brand' (Heilemann and Halperin 2010: 236), and, although this seems coldly instrumental, it is perhaps a response to the threat of a white backlash, as political pundits and commentators were prepared to view Obama as a post-racial figure of hope for as long as he avoided racial issues (Odell Korgen and Brunsma 2011). And, at worst, the 'actually existing post-racial society' and 'end of racism' are malignant tools that attempt to erase the reality of racial stratification, deny the effects of racist discrimination and, perhaps most importantly, seek to curtail the political and economic redistributive agenda that aims to ameliorate these ongoing injustices (Bonilla-Silva 2003; Winant 2001; Wise 2010). Ultimately, there is no material basis for the assertion that a post-racial era has been entered, given persistent and continuing racial inequalities, including within the criminal justice (Haney López 2010) and educational systems (Howard and Flennaugh 2011).

There is also another deep irony evident here. The declaration that race has been transcended and racism defeated is reinforced by the support garnered from the racialised commentariat: the post-racist/racial verbiage of D'Souza, Mirza and Tony Sewell, placed alongside 'black conservatives' such as Shelby Steele and the appropriation of Wilson as an advocate of post-racial liberalism, are presented as all the more compelling as spoken from mouths of colour. These commentators tend to utilise a liberal individualist framework that dismisses charges of racism as a form of victimology that conveniently blames 'white people' or 'society' instead of accepting individual and collective responsibility. However, the register of bitterness and loathing within this critique is particularly striking and difficult to explain: from D'Souza's caustic condemnation of black pathology to Tony Sewell's (2010) selection of black boys – for strategic extracurricular educational interventions – who were effectively 'shielded' from their peers and quarantined from their communities' 'negative values', the utter contempt and sheer disregard for fellow humans are palpable. But Steele's (1999: 5) almost poignant rendition of the 'greater exposure to contempt and shame' incurred by the black conservative both from 'their' racial group and within their mixed professional circle shows the price of admission into existent post-racial society. Ultimately, the very reliance on the racial tribunes to authenticate the colour-blind/post-racial declaration negates claims to the dawn of an actually existing post-racial society and only brings the post-racial mirage into sharp relief.

Proto post-racialism

If the actually existing post-racial society can be dismissed as a fiction – albeit a particularly dangerous one – it is necessary to look elsewhere to trace the genealogy of authentic post-racialism as an enduring dissention to normative racial ideas. As far back as the late eighteenth century, Herder (1968) disagreed with Kant's racial typology, asserting instead that races could not reliably be said to exist. And, in the following century, Darwin ([1879] 2004) stated that races could not exist as fixed, immutable types given the gradual and discontinuous evolutionary process. But, despite their scepticism toward racial taxonomy, neither Herder nor Darwin would move to reject the primordial basis and hereditary traits of race altogether – Herder (1997) still recognised the distinctive physical characteristics of 'ordinary Negroes', 'Kalmucks' and 'Mongols', amongst others, and Darwin ([1879] 2004: 195) concluded that there is 'no doubt that the various races, when carefully compared and measured, differ much from each other' in physical and physiological ways, amongst others. Nevertheless, taken together, their partial reappraisal of race contributed toward the development of race critical theories that would gather momentum and depth during the twentieth century as debates over the scientific validity of racial conceptualisation grew.

Stimulated in part by the rise of Nazism in Germany, the 1930s saw the publication of proto-racial eliminativist works in the human and social sciences; Julian Huxley and A. C. Haddon's *We Europeans: A Survey of 'Racial' Problems*, published initially in 1935, and Jacques Barzun's (1937) *Race: A Study in Modern Superstition* were followed by Ashley Montagu's ([1942] 1997) *Man's Most Dangerous Myth: The Fallacy of Race*. Each of these works stressed that the race concept was neither empirically secure nor methodologically reliable and that its continued usage was problematic. As a corrective, *We Europeans* and *Man's Most Dangerous Myth* both called for the discontinuation of racial terminology within scientific discourse and its replacement with ethnicity (Huxley and Haddon 1935: 107–8). Acutely aware of the durability of racial ideas and the immense difficulty of eradicating them altogether, Barzun stressed the need to purge all vestiges of race to the extent that he even recommended the reader to promptly forget his book once it had been read. Unlike Huxley, Haddon and Montagu, Barzun acknowledged the incipient dangers of nominating a substitute category such as ethnicity, which might be used to perform some of the same theoretical and political work of the race concept as well as leaving open the possibility of returning to a discussion of the relative merits of race vis-à-vis alternative concepts proposed, such as ethnicity and caste.[3]

It did not take long for the confirmation of Barzun's fears, his forewarning that 'one of the penalties of toying with the race-notion is that even a strong mind trying to repudiate it will find himself making assumptions and passing judgements on the basis of the theory he declaims' (Barzun 1937: 44), to prove apposite. After World War II and the realisation of the horrors of the Final Solution and the Holocaust, UNESCO convened a panel of experts to debate the race question. The panel, mainly composed of social scientists and with Montagu as rapporteur, met in Paris in 1949 and published their report, *Statement on Race*, the following year. *Statement on Race* reiterated much of the earlier proto-eliminativist works in asserting human common descent and genetic similarity, as well as rejecting the notion of any intrinsic inter-group intellectual and behavioural inequalities. However, by advocating the replacement of race with ethnicity '*within common usage*', the *Statement* left open the possibility that race might be maintained *outside* of common usage, a possibility which was swiftly exploited. The *Statement* also concluded that 'races' were effectively dynamic 'breeding groups' and that the associated scientific facts demonstrated that a clear distinction needed to be made between race as a 'biological fact', on one hand, and a 'myth', on the other (UNESCO 1975a).

---

[3] Extending this reservation, Michael Banton's chapter in this volume also addresses the efficacy of ethnicity within sociological analysis on the grounds that it is 'a spurious word, a failed concept that should be discarded'.

These qualifications and hesitancy in the 1950 *Statement* represented the fault line that Barzun feared, and once the breach had been opened, conservative life scientists dissatisfied with the 1950 *Statement*, which they considered to be liberal and ideologically driven, seized their moment and effectively lobbied UNESCO to convene a second panel (Graves 2001; Reardon 2005). The second UNESCO panel, comprising purely physical anthropologists and geneticists, met and published their report in 1951, with the revealing title *Statement on the Nature of Race and Race Differences*, dismissing the social scientists' views articulated within the 1950 *Statement* as unreliable and lacking the expertise of life scientists who were able to properly assess race as a biological entity unburdened by egalitarian dogma (Reardon 2005). The assertion that ethnicity should replace race was removed from the 1951 *Statement* and some stunning additions were made, including that race was a salient scientific *and* lay term:

The physical anthropologists and the man in the street both know that races exist: the former, from the scientifically recognisable and measurable congeries of traits which he uses in classifying the varieties of man; the latter from the immediate evidence of his senses when he sees an African, a European, an Asiatic and an American Indian together. (UNESCO 1975b: 349)

If the dependent clauses in the 1950 *Statement* were not enough of a compromise against a strong race critical – let alone eliminativist – declaration, the 1951 reactionary move away from the anti-racist tenor of the first *Statement* (Graves 2001) ensured that an important opportunity to seriously undermine race politically and scientifically in a significant historical moment was lost. This entire episode is instructive of a major problem facing racial eliminativism: the problem of properly moving beyond race. Hence, I refer to this period and these works – *We Europeans*, *Man's Most Dangerous Myth* and the UNESCO *Statements* – as 'proto' post-racialism. On one hand, to be continually brought back into the orbit of race within the social world for protean and pragmatic reasons, not least the misery and havoc wrought by racism, is understandable. But, on the other, the myopia and self-interest evident on both sides of the UNESCO strife – the proto-eliminativists' rejection of race but apparent inability to reconceptualise human phenotypical variation, and the racial conservationists' naked move to protect, amongst other things, their research careers, laboratories and grants – are all the more disappointing. Nonetheless, after the missteps of proto post-racialism, a major challenge for a racial eliminativist engagement with science, indeed the entire post-racial endeavour, is clear: to fully surpass race by dismantling it but not becoming fixated on its negation to the detriment of developing an affirmative humanistic project. Therefore, post-racial contributions to scientific debate are charged with escaping raciological norms and assumptions, while helping to fashion a new vocabulary and create the appropriate concepts for pursuing an accurate understanding of human biodiversity.

Post-racial biosciences

It would be wrong to overstate the academic inter-disciplinary warfare between life and social scientists that broke out in the corridors of UNESCO and the correspondence pages of *Man*. Biologists were not habitual racial conservationists, and all social scientists were not race sceptics. But for sceptics straddling the social and life sciences, the 'new synthesis' that emerged during the mid 1930s as a combination of Darwin's evolutionary theory and Mendel's thesis of the irregularity of genetic inheritance was particularly important to the development of the race critical theories that would underpin racial eliminativism. Under the new synthesis, the notion of blended inheritance central to classical racial explanation became untenable, and the existence of distinct racial types was declared forged instead of found (Livingstone 1962).

After the inter-war years and the new synthesis, the aftermath of World War II and beyond is the moment when some attempts to understand human biodiversity formally and consistently eschew the race concept. An element of the systematic study of human biodiversity generated in this moment is suggestive of an enterprise that I want to refer to as 'post-racial biosciences' – a methodological approach that matured beyond the hesitancy and contradictions of proto post-racialism to consistently deconstruct race. Numerous nominally post-racial scientists over an extended period declared the biological race concept redundant: influenced by Julian Huxley's (1938) concept of 'cline' as an expression of the frequency of genes within a given biological group across a gradient, the anthropologist Frank Livingstone (1962: 279) stated, 'There are no races, there are only clines'; the geneticist Richard Lewontin (1972) discovered that human biodiversity is greatest *within* so-called racial groups and that genetic similarity is evident *across* so-called 'races', 'the largest part by far of human variation being accounted for by the differences between individuals'; and J. Craig Venter, president and chief scientific officer of Celera Genomics, responded to the U.S. Food and Drug Administration approval of BiDil, a drug for heart disease developed specifically for African Americans, by saying, 'It is disturbing to see reputable scientists and physicians even categorizing things in terms of race . . . There is no basis in the genetic code for race' (cited in Brody and Hunt 2006: 557).

These indicative statements of falsification central within post-racial biosciences are not solely a critique of race but also constituted part of the affirmative basis for racial eliminativism: Livingstone (1962: 269) recognised that 'there are excellent arguments for abandoning the concept of race with reference to the living populations of *Homo sapiens*', while Lewontin issued his own firm rejection:

Human racial classification is of no social value and is positively destructive of social and human relations. Since such racial classification is now seen to be of virtually no genetic or taxonomic significance either, no justification can be offered for its continuance. (cited in Montagu 1997: 46)

This corrective is a robust rationale for a post-racial bioscience. For the racial sceptic, it is epistemologically and methodologically precise as well as ethically and politically compelling. And it is rigorous in neither resorting to offering the consolation of a replacement category nor vacillating in its recommendation.

Notably, the post-racial bioscientific intervention does not represent the death of race and the triumph of post-racialism. Lewontin's formulation, popularised as humans are 85 per cent similar and 15 per cent dissimilar regardless of 'race', has been critiqued as a 'fallacy' on the grounds that a population cannot be reasonably expected to be typified by genetic sameness because the frequency of particular genes is not measured at individual loci (Edwards 2003) – relatedly, it has been argued that even minute percentile genetic differences can be highly statistically significant (Sarich and Miele 2004) and that 'the greatest differentiation in the human population occurs between continentally separated groups' (Burchard et al. 2003: 1171). Race is also defended insofar as, methodologically speaking, assignment into genetic clusters consistent with racial groups on the basis of biological markers is probabilistic and need not be absolute. Consequently, race is also a meaningful category because it can be used to demonstrate a range of entrenched biological differences between populations – for example, 'there is overwhelming evidence that human populations exhibit probabilistic *differences* in specific genetic patterns associated with brain functions and sexual hormones' (Minkov 2011: 40). Leaving the validity and value of racial typification aside, variation within *Homo sapiens* is nonetheless discernible and constantly verified by studies noting the existence of population 'clusters' (Risch et al. 2002).

So, the broad set of critical and prescriptive insights gathered under the aegis of post-racial biosciences did not represent a consensus and therefore should not be overstated. But, even if Barzun's wish was not realised and race had not been 'killed', it was nevertheless seriously wounded. The contributions of post-racial bioscience normalised the demand that the continued use of race required thorough empirical justification and methodological defence and stimulated debate on its usefulness in pragmatic, strategic and social terms. Minkov (2011), for example, perhaps recognising that *overwhelming evidence* of a *probability* as opposed to proof of an absolute is not particularly compelling, concedes that population distributions may differ from racial distributions, thus invalidating race as a meaningful analytic concept. As a result, continued reference to race within health and biosciences by clinicians, epidemiologists and the like is often heavily qualified – amongst many things, race is, variously, 'a rough proxy' (Jones 2001), self-identified and thus contingent (Bonham et al. 2005), 'a product of an arranged marriage between the social and biologic worlds' (Cooper et al. 2003: 1169), 'generally highly statistically significant' (Nei and Roychoudhury 1982: 41) and a 'probabilistic marker' (see Kennedy 2001).

The routine attachment of such caveats to race can be regarded as demonstrating the significant post-racial bioscientific insights that genetic populations are changeable and subject to shifting migratory patterns which make them indefinable in *absolute* (read 'racial') terms. And the attempts to retain biological determinism, such as Minkov's argument that a discernible pattern might nevertheless be ethnic, thus justifying the analysis of biocultural correlations with an ethnic distribution that bisects racial lines, can be recognised as a desperate racial conservationism; changing the object from race to ethnicity, culture, population, target group and so on simply serves to maintain the possibility of somehow establishing a causal relationship or meaningful probabilistic correlation between genetic clusters and prevalent traits – race is known to be the answer, the 'correct' factors just need to be found. But, instead of accepting the burden of proof for the existence of the race concept it believes to be real, this naïve deductivism reveals its insecurity by trying to place a burden of disproof on racial eliminativism – in Popper's terms, then, race is no longer a scientific object; as it can be neither proven nor disproven, it is at best a cipher within health and the biosciences and at worst a paranormal entity that inspires faithful belief but can be neither empirically verified nor coherently known. As Michael Banton argues in this volume, there has been a long-standing false distinction between an inaccurate folk and a valid scientific concept of race. Banton shows that the conflation of outward appearance, phenotype and what it was taken to represent as a role sign – race – is not an indisputable scientific truth claim but is based on impressionistic speculation.

Cosmopolitan post-racialism

Methodological inconsistency and conceptual disorder aside, the critique of race initiated in the inter-war years demonstrated a strong political sense and ethical sensibility. The objection raised by Haddon and Huxley, by Barzun and by Montagu was not just that race was epistemologically problematic but that it furthermore gave rise to spurious racial 'sentiments' and was pressed into the service of pernicious political projects, including Atlantic slavery and Nazism. And, as the scientific community became increasingly diverse in gender and ethnic composition from the inter-war years onward, data were generated and arguments mobilised to refute judgments of reputed group 'inferiority' on egalitarian principles as well as metaphysical grounds (Barkan 1992). Therefore, as well as being epistemologically and methodologically problematic, race was also subject to social critique and deemed morally indefensible.

These incipient ontological and ethical concerns are taken up and developed within contemporary debates that illustrate the generalising principle at the centre of the race concept that refers to individuals only as the sum of a racial group. Kwame Anthony Appiah (1996) argues that normative racial typologies generate linked 'collective scripts' that determine the definitive mode of (racial) being. There is, then, an authentic racial personality and disposition that are maintained in part through the threat of being labelled as inauthentic – Richard T. Ford (2005) recognises this in the use of 'apple', 'banana' and 'oreo' as racial epithets for individuals who transgress against their given racial identity evident in their external appearance by being treacherously 'white on the inside'. Similarly, many mixed-race individuals have been miscategorised as black as a result of the one-drop rule of hypodescent (Zack 1993), and white people are automatically inducted at birth into the privileged club of whiteness (Ignatiev and Garvey 1996). As a result, these scripts constrain individuals and are limiting for personal development. Individuals feel pressurised to conform to normative racial behaviours for fear of ridicule and disapprobation should they resist (Hill 2000), and mixed-race people are 'trapped' in a past consumed with the dangers of miscegenation that does not allow them to create a future-oriented self (Zack 1993).

For many of these thinkers, the response to the tyranny of racial collective identities that 'go imperial' to the detriment of ontological complexity (Appiah 1996) is an eliminativist one: Zack (1993) argues for becoming 'raceless', whereby individuals are divested of race and invest in personal projects of becoming in relation to their own future desires; self-styled 'race traitors' and 'New Abolitionists' call for the abolition of whiteness by white peoples' disinvestment in white privilege under the slogan 'Treason to whiteness is loyalty to humanity' (Ignatiev and Garvey 1996); and Jason Hill (2000: 1) advocates the 'moral rejection of all forms of racial, ethnic, and national tribalism'. Instead, Hill calls for the development of a 'moral cosmopolitanism' centred around a radical ontological rebellion that abandons constraining collective racial identity in favour of cosmopolitan individuals' self-appointed status as 'eternal emigrants . . . who resent fixed standpoints, unreflective constitutive identities, and markers of completion as proof of a good life' (77). Therefore, stripped of the certainties of racial identity and its determining 'scripts', ready-made community and in-built solidarity, the cosmopolitan individual escapes the limitations of ascribed *being* and is able to enter a personal project of existential *becoming*. For Zack (1993: 164), such 'racelessness' as a disavowal of racial identity 'is more authentic than projections of the self onto "one hundred generations" that bear no relation to the self in the dimension to which one might turn for self-identification as a human being'.

For critics of racial eliminativism, the individual is figured rather differently. The everyday lived experience of racialised being means that race and racial identification are 'phenomenally real' and have an active embodied and affective dimension. Therefore, racial eliminativism might be regarded as unreflexive in trivialising and disregarding the intimate conditions of individual lives and its inability to account for the existential conditions within which 'race' becomes meaningful. Linda Martín Alcoff (2001: 271) argues for a phenomenology of racial embodiment based on a 'subjectivist contextualism' that recognises macro-level social relations that structure racialisation while also attentive to the micro-level interactions illustrating 'how race is constitutive of bodily experience, subjectivity, judgment, and epistemic relationships'. Alcoff acknowledges concerns that this approach might be seen as reifying racial experience as an epiphenomenon with self-evident meaning; however, she argues that the process of racialised perception is dynamic and has no intrinsic meaning. Therefore, instead of disregarding the existence of and reference to race as required by eliminativism, Alcoff (2001: 281) wants to 'make visible the practices of visibility' to understand the context that knowledge of ourselves and others emerges from in order to attempt 'to alter the associated meanings ascribed to visible difference'.

The strong constructivist critique central to racial eliminativism reverses this formulation – visible difference is constituted by the ascription of meaning instead of existing prior to that process. Therefore, the individualistic dimension of a cosmopolitan eliminativist formation is reinforced by a humanist ethics and related political concerns to critique and counter phenomenological justifications of race. The very notion of altering the 'associated meanings' of visible (racial) difference is strenuously contested by eliminativism. For Appiah (1990), the invention of race has propagated spurious racial differences that diminish or deny human commonalty, encourage the pathological suspicion of others and thus deny the 'moral unity of humanity'. Gilroy (2000) extensively argues that this promotion of racial exceptionalism is amplified by the phenomenological appeal to racial unanimity; the embodiment of racial subjectivity is suggestive of a collective identity, involuntary affinity and attendant solidarity that are found within an affective, subjective and experiential dimension and articulated through the grammar of visual imagery, as opposed to being forged through discussion and negotiation. One of Gilroy's key concerns is that this appeal to belonging found in the short-circuit signs of the body is not a democratic form of politics and thus creates a false solidarity based on racial authenticity that is redolent of authoritarian and fascistic motifs and can easily become absolutist. Consequently, race cannot escape its historical taint, it cannot be reconstituted or rehabilitated, and racial eliminativism is the only viable response: eradicating race is 'the only ethical response to the conspicuous wrongs that raciologies continue to solicit and sanction' (Gilroy 2000: 41).

Taken together, these ethical and political concerns form the basis of a dual justification for racial eliminativism: ethically, *racial eliminativism* is justified because 'race' creates harmful preferential distinctions between human beings; and politically, *racial eliminativism* is justified because 'race' encourages negative political projects not only in relation to subjugation but also ostensibly with regard to progressive politics – Gilroy (2000) suggests that even an anti-racist politics is a politics of negation, that is, *anti*-racism, and asks what sorts of projects a racial politics might *positively* seek. What progressive aims would it wish to *establish*? In this affirmative vein, Gilroy promotes 'strategic universalism' and 'planetary humanism', calling for a 'post-anthropological', common humanity that is predicated on an authentic fraternity and democratic ideal. This appeal to the 'cosmopolitan yet-to-come' as an ongoing process of negotiating a progressive political programme and its related social objectives is post-foundationalist and eviscerates appeals to particularised and insular phenomenology, be it the paradigmatic human, racial or masculine figures of Enlightenment rationality and imperial domination.

Whither post-racialism?

race should be irrelevant', writes Charles W. Mills, 'is certainly
tractive ideal, but when it has *not* been irrelevant, it is absurd to
:eed as if it had been' (Mills 1998: 41, original emphasis). This
rearticulation of the post-racial dilemma serves as a damning indictment
of racial eliminativism and the basis for manifold reservations about the
post-racial project, four of which I want to briefly outline. First, post-
racialism is considered utterly and irredeemably impractical. While it
may represent a well-intentioned and laudable ideal, it can never be
realised because race is so deeply socially embedded (Parker and Song
2001). Even when intended as a practical and theoretical project, the high
level of abstraction at which racial eliminativism is pitched questions its
material efficacy. Precisely how might race be eliminated? Is an edict to
be issued from on high? Or, alternately, does racial eliminativism allude
to the withering away of race – its declining significance? But, given the
organic, haphazard quality of withering away as a gradualist process,
it is not clear how this can be fostered. Withering away can be mapped
retrospectively but not directed. And, lastly, post-racial advocates develop
critiques of race but tend to offer little in the programmatic vein other
than the vague exhortation and pedagogical proclamations in the first
UNESCO *Statement* – even the thoroughgoing observations of Jacques
Barzun led him to unapologetically state that he had nothing to offer by
way of a post-racial strategy.

Second, it is not clear how, or whether, post-racialism would work
methodologically. The ascribed racial identities that racial eliminativists
wish to reject are not simply behavioural and existential 'scripts' but are
produced through and by deep social structures. Therefore, race is 'onto-
logically subjective but epistemologically objective', which is to say that,
although it has no natural existence, its use is socially produced and subject to societal conventions, making race a real object that is independent
of individual perception and not party to unilateral alteration or rejection
(Mills 1998; Taylor 2004). Micro methods of racial eliminativism such as
'ontological rebellion' (Hill 2000) and race traitors' rejection of the privileges of whiteness through mundane individual acts are insubstantial,
futile efforts in the face of enduring social structures.

Third, to all intents and purposes, post-racialism is apolitical – in the
sense of a radical, progressive politics. The lack of a prescriptive programme, as stated earlier, signals the largely theoretical orientation of
post-racialism that gestures toward but effectively disengages material
reality. The racial concepts rejected by post-racialism as a basis for invidious public policies such as racial profiling in policing are simultaneously

necessary for the longitudinal monitoring of discriminatory practices, such as profiling, to discern patterns and inform ameliorative strategies, so there may be a disconnect between post-racialism and anti-racism. Moreover, post-racialism's orientation toward the ideal-typical transcendent and autonomous individual liberated from racial communalism has significant consequences: the eliminativist appeal to individuated forms of labour – for example, intellectual and ethical – is divorced from the hard political work of movement building. Therefore, it is perhaps unsurprising that post-racialism could become a Trojan horse for an atomised colour-blindness that espouses individual free choice (Bonilla-Silva 2003) and reactionary laissez-faire liberalism.

Fourth, post-racialism is deracinating and inattentive toward what Alcoff (2001) conceptualises as the lived embodiment of racial identity as a subjectivist contextualism. Races are irreducible to biology and naturalistic understandings and can also be regarded as collective social identities forged through processes of racial formation; eliminating 'race' would attempt to erase significant histories of hard-fought political struggles. Post-racialism would also compromise the intra-racial moral obligation and solidarity forged through the racially stigmatised groups' historical travails that are also necessary for their ongoing struggles (Stubblefield 2005). And, at a more individual level, post-racialism can be unsympathetic toward the existential dimensions of racialised life. The dispassionate eliminativist objective to strip racialised individuals of a significant aspect of their sense of being, and the potential psychological dissonance that may result, seem somewhat incompatible with the ethics of care central to the humanist sensibility favoured by cosmopolitan formations of post-racialism.

These problems with the post-racial are only indicative and by no means exhaustive; as such they also highlight the gravity of the post-racial dilemma. Nevertheless, engaging the post-racial problematic – can race be eradicated? – is a fruitful exercise. The issue of the conceptual and practical status of race is seemingly intractable and confronting it elicits the customary rehearsals: race is real/unreal, an ideological construct, loose proxy and so on and so forth. But to think of racial eliminativism is a different project and invites alternative questions. Precisely what is to be eliminated? Why should race be eliminated? How can it be done? Even if these questions and related eliminativist queries are answered in a way unfavourable to the post-racial project, the common sense of race and its status as a dominant *episteme* is being disturbed. And similarly, for racial eliminativism to reckon with its constituent problems is to think through the coherence of the project and its conditions of possibility.

'It works in practice, but does it work in theory?'

Although its provenance is unclear, the question 'It works in practice, but does it work in theory?' is particularly appropriate to the post-racial problematic.[4] Racial eliminativism, on one hand, offers a developing critical theoretical framework that attempts to cogently link epistemological, ontological, methodological, ethical and political concerns, but its practicability is adjudged to be weak. Race, on the other hand, works well in practice, in the literal sense of functionality, but its theoretical coherence is admittedly poor. However, 'It works in practice, but does it work in theory?' can be considered more expansively: the question also suggests that we might not only require something to function but also *wish to understand how* it functions. And there is also the issue of whether the functioning object in question works in an *acceptable* way and the extent to which its functionality might be altered or improved by an enhanced theoretical understanding.

Applying 'It works in practice, but does it work in theory?' to the post-racial question is instructive. Race is undoubtedly practically effective. But the unacceptability of the invidious work it often performs might not be *despite* its inchoate theoretical premises but precisely *because* of them. The very spuriousness of the myths, legal doctrine, scientific claims, common sense and so on that have constituted the idea of race have facilitated its reproduction and transformation; the irrationality of race has enabled it to withstand the assault of reason. The theoretical weaknesses have enhanced its practical application and forestalled racial eliminativism by sponsoring the post-racial dilemma: Guillaumin's (1995: 107) 'Race does not exist. But it does kill people' is an effective summary. The practical and political stakes of this dilemma are severe. On one hand, the cessation of collecting statistical data on racial discrimination (such as that intended by Proposition 54 in California) would effectively eradicate race by leading to a 'no data, no problem' conclusion, whereas, on the other, the collection of such data is central to monitoring racial inequalities and informing the development of ameliorative strategies as a 'no data, no justice' formulation (Krieger 2010).

But to accede to the circularity of this racial reality is perhaps to submit also to the reproduction of its effects through being drawn into what Paul Gilroy (2000: 52) refers to as 'the pious ritual in which we always agree that "race" is invented but then are required to defer to its embeddedness in the world and to accept that the demand for justice requires

---

[4] The question is sometimes referred to as a joke or an apocryphal tale but, perhaps invoking the *philosophes*, often features a nonchalant Frenchman as the questioner in response to the observation of a new machine satisfactorily performing a mundane task.

us nevertheless innocently to enter the political arenas it helps to mark out'. Despite its practical shortcomings, then, an engagement with racial eliminativism might be worthwhile; to reflect on the post-racial instead of race poses an altogether different set of questions of race and racial eliminativism that step outside the circularity of racial realism. Do we *want* race? Why, and what do we want it for? And are we prepared to endure its effects in order to have it? Conversely, why might we want to eliminate race? And what transformations could be possible without race?

In a sense, racial eliminativism is a misnomer; essentially its pressing concern is not race but its effects, primarily racism – the data to which Nancy Krieger (2010) refer, for example, are not racial per se but the statistical capturing of racial inequality, discrimination, injustice; in short, racism, *not* race.

That the post-racial is deemed inimical to anti-racism is presented within Hesse's (2011) argument that, by constituting the actually existing post-racial society as performative, liberal and governmental in contradistinction to the (Eurocentric) formulation of racism as representational, anti-liberal and ideological, what he terms the 'post-racial horizon' is presented as a self-fulfilling prophecy – the emergent post-racial order heralds the defeat of racism. Therefore, for Hesse, the critique of the post-racial also requires the engagement of the problematic conceptualisation of racism, which invites a dramatic question – is there a formulation of the post-racial capable of assisting in the reconceptualisation of racism? Or, in other words, can there be an anti-racist post-racialism?

From a certain perspective, this is precisely the objective of racial eliminativism. The reification of race through complex networks, including administrative, legal, scientific, religious and cultural domains, has led to analyses implicating race within the causation of racism. Whether with regard to the race relations paradigm or theories of racial formation, the conceptual centrality of the race concept (even if qualified as 'social') continues to reify race 'because they seek to construct their analytical *concepts* to reproduce directly the commonsense ideologies of the every-day world' (Darder and Torres 2004: 41, original emphasis). Drawing attention to processes of racialisation or the governmental and performative aspects of racism is to move away from employing race as a determining empirical object in the production of racism, even if only as an incidental but necessary component. While this is not advocating an eliminativist approach to race, it tacitly admits its declining explanatory efficacy. 'The problems of coloured populations, of immigration and miscegenation, of anti-Semitism and national hatred', wrote Barzun (1965: 201), 'are not problems about a natural fact called race: they are problems of social life, of economic status, of educational policy, and political organization.' Therefore, racial eliminativism might be viewed as a means to accurately portray and understand human social existence. Eliminating the category and concept of race will not end racism but may enable a better understanding of the discriminatory practices performed in the name of the idea of race without the diversionary and obfuscating effects of epiphenomenal racial categories. And if this eliminativist theory works well, it might have a productive and useful impact on anti-racist practice.

So, the post-racial *is not* actually existing and yet it *is* many things: a process, an ambition, a dilemma, a mirage, an unfulfilled objective, a methodological scientific intervention, an ethical and political cosmopolitan calling and a utopian enterprise that invites an imaginative and affirmative meditation on the desired future society and alternative way of life. Whether post-racialism will ever be anything else, anything more 'substantial', is debatable. Howard Winant (2004: 165) argues that the world will 'probably' never 'get beyond' race, and he may be right. But there is also the question of whether scholars and researchers of 'race and ethnic relations' would ideally like to get beyond race and its effects.

REFERENCES

Alcoff, L. M. (2001). Toward a phenomenology of racial embodiment. In R. Bernasconi, ed., *Race*. Oxford: Blackwell, pp. 267–83.
Appiah, K. A. (1990). Racisms. In D. T. Goldberg, ed., *Anatomy of Racism*. Minneapolis: University of Minnesota Press, pp. 3–17.
   (1996). Race, culture, identity: misunderstood connections. In K. A. Appiah and A. Gutmann, eds, *Colour Conscious: The Political Morality of Race*. Princeton, NJ: Princeton University Press, pp. 30–105.
Barkan, E. (1992). *The Retreat of Scientific Racism: Changing Concepts of Race in Britain and the United States between the World Wars*. Cambridge: Cambridge University Press.
Barzun, J. (1937). *Race: A Study in Modern Superstition*. London: Methuen.
   (1965). *Race: A Study in Superstition*. New York: Harper and Row.
Bonham, V. L., Warshauer-Baker, E. and Collins, F. S. (2005). Race and ethnicity in the genome era: the complexity of the constructs. *American Psychologist*, 60(1), 9–15.
Bonilla-Silva, E. (2003). *Racism without Racists: Colour-Blind Racism and the Persistence of Racial Inequality in the United States*. Lanham, MD: Rowman and Littlefield.
Brody, H. and Hunt, L. M. (2006). BiDil: assessing a race-based pharmaceutical. *Annals of Family Medicine*, 4(6), 556–60.
Burchard, E. G., Ziv, E., Coyle, N., et al. (2003). The importance of race and ethnic background in biomedical research and clinical practice. *New England Journal of Medicine*, 348(12), 1170–75.

Cooper, R. S., Kaufman, J. S. and Ward, R. (2003). Race and genomics. *New England Journal of Medicine*, 348(12), 1166–70.

Darder, A. and R. D. Torres. (2004). *After Race: Racism after Multiculturalism*. New York: New York University Press.

Darwin, C. ([1879] 2004). *The Descent of Man, and Selection in Relation to Sex*. London: Penguin.

D'Souza, D. (1995). *The End of Racism: Principles for a Multiracial Society*. New York: Free Press.

Edwards, A. W. F. (2003). Human genetic diversity: Lewontin's fallacy. *Bio Essays*, 25(8), 798–801.

Ford, R. T. (2005). *Racial Culture: A Critique*. Princeton, NJ: Princeton University Press.

Gilroy, P. (2000). *Between Camps: Nations, Cultures and the Allure of Race*. London: Penguin/Allen Lane Press.

Goldberg, D. T. and Essed, P. (2002). Introduction: from racial demarcations to multiple identifications. In P. Essed and D. T. Goldberg, eds, *Race Critical Theories: Text and Context*. Oxford: Blackwell, pp. 1–14.

Graves, J. L. (2001). *The Emperor's New Clothes: Biological Theories of Race at the Millennium*. New Brunswick, NJ: Rutgers University Press.

Guillaumin, C. (1995). 'I know it's not nice, but . . . ': the changing face of race. In *Racism, Sexism, Power and Ideology*, London: Routledge, pp. 99–107.

Haney López, I. F. (2010). Post-racial racism: racial stratification and mass incarceration in the age of Obama. *California Law Review*, 98(3), 1023–73.

Heilemann, J. and Halperin, M. (2010). *Race of a Lifetime: How Obama Won the White House*. London: Viking.

Herder, J. G. (1968). *Reflections on the Philosophy of the History of Mankind*. Trans. T. O. Churchill. Chicago: University of Chicago Press.

(1997). *On World History: An Anthology*. London: M. E. Sharpe.

Hesse, B. (2011). Self-fulfilling prophecy: the postracial horizon. *South Atlantic Quarterly*, 110(1), 155–78.

Hill, J. (2000). *Becoming a Cosmopolitan: What It Means to Be a Human Being in the New Millennium*. Lanham, MD: Rowman and Littlefield.

Howard, T. C. and Flennaugh, T. (2011). Research concerns, cautions and considerations on Black males in a 'post-racial' society. *Race, Ethnicity and Education*, 14(1), 105–20.

Huxley, J. (1938). Clines: an auxiliary taxonomic principle. *Nature*, 142, 219–20.

Huxley, J. and Haddon, A. C. (1935). *We Europeans: A Survey of 'Racial' Problems*. London: Jonathan Cape.

Ignatiev, N. and Garvey, J., eds. (1996). *Race Traitor*. London: Routledge.

Jones, C. P. (2001). Race, racism and the practice of epidemiology. *American Journal of Epidemiology*, 154(4), 299–304.

Kennedy, R. (2001). Racial trends in the administration of criminal justice. In N. J. Smelser, W. J. Wilson, and F. Mitchell, eds, *America Becoming: Racial Trends and Their Consequences*, vol. II. Washington, DC: National Academy Press, pp. 1–20.

Krieger, N. (2010). The science and epidemiology of racism and health: racial/ethnic categories, biological expressions of racism, and the embodiment of inequality – an ecosocial perspective. In I. Whitmarsh and D. S. Jones, eds, *What's the Use of Race? Modern Governance and the Biology of Difference.* Cambridge, MA: MIT Press, pp. 225–55.

Lewontin, R. (1972). The apportionment of human diversity. *Evolutionary Biology*, 6, 396–97.

Livingstone, F. (1962). On the non-existence of races. *Current Anthropology*, 3(3), 279–81.

Mills, C. W. (1998). But what are you really? In *Blackness Visible: Essays on Philosophy and Race.* Ithaca, NY: Cornell University Press, pp. 41–66.

Minkov, M. (2011). *Cultural Differences in a Globalizing World.* Bingley: Emerald Group.

Mirza, M. (2010). Rethinking race. *Prospect*, 175, 31–32.

Montagu, A. ([1942]1997). *Man's Most Dangerous Myth: The Fallacy of Race*, 6th edn. Lanham, MD: Rowman and Littlefield.

Nei, M. and Roychoudhury, A. K. (1982). Genetic relationship and evolution of human races. *Evolutionary Biology*, 14, 1–59.

Odell Korgen, K. and Brunsma, D. L. (2011). Avoiding race or following the racial scripts? Obama and race in the recessionary period of the colourblind era. In A. J. Jolivette, ed., *Obama and the Biracial Factor: The Battle for a New American Majority.* Bristol, UK: Policy Press, pp. 191–204.

Parker, D. and Song, M. (2001). Introduction: rethinking 'mixed race'. In D. Parker and M. Song, eds, *Rethinking 'Mixed Race'.* London: Pluto, pp. 1–22.

Payne, R. J. (1998). *Getting beyond Race: The Changing American Culture.* Boulder, CO: Westview Press.

Reardon, J. (2005). *Race to the Finish: Identity and Governance in an Age of Genomics.* Princeton, NJ: Princeton University Press.

Risch, N., Burchard, E., Ziv, E. and Tang, H. (2002). Categorization of humans in biomedical research: genes, race and disease. *Genome Biology*, 3(7), 1–12.

Sarich, V. and Miele, F. (2004). *Race: The Reality of Human Differences.* Boulder, CO: Westview Press.

Sewell, T. (2010). Master class in victimhood. *Prospect*, 175, 33–34.

Steele, S. (1999). *A Dream Deferred: The Second Betrayal of Black Freedom in America.* New York: HarperPerennial.

Stubblefield, A. (2005). *Ethics along the Color Line.* Ithaca, NY: Cornell University Press.

Taylor, P. C. (2004). *Race: A Philosophical Introduction.* Cambridge: Polity Press.

Thernstrom, S. and Thernstrom, A. (1999). *America in Black and White: One Nation, Indivisible.* New York: Touchstone.

UNESCO. (1975a). Statement on race. 1950. In L. C. Dunn, N. P. Dubinin, C. Lévi-Strauss et al., *Race, Science and Society.* Paris: UNESCO/Allen and Unwin, pp. 343–47.

(1975b). Statement on the nature of race and race differences. 1951. In L. C. Dunn, N. P. Dubinin, C. Lévi-Strauss et al., *Race, Science and Society.* Paris: UNESCO/Allen and Unwin, pp. 348–54.

West, C. (2009). *Brother West: Living and Loving Out Loud – A Memoir.* New York: Smiley Books.

Wilson, W. J. (1978). *The Declining Significance of Race: Blacks and Changing American Institutions*. Chicago: University of Chicago Press.

Winant, H. (2001). *The World Is a Ghetto: Race and Democracy since World War II*. New York: Basic Books.

(2004). *The New Politics of Race: Globalism, Difference, Justice*. Minneapolis: University of Minnesota Press.

Wise, T. (2009). *Between Barack and a Hard Place: Racism and White Denial in the Age of Obama*. San Francisco: City Lights.

(2010). *Color-Blind: The Rise of Post-Racial Politics and the Retreat from Racial Equity*. San Francisco: City Lights.

Zack, N. (1993). *Race and Mixed-Race*. Philadelphia: Temple University Press.

Part II

Perspectives

Introduction to Part II

In the introduction to this volume, we set out the shift from classical sociological and anthropological theories and perspectives on race to the emergence of post-structralist theories concerned with language, identities, bodies, subjectivity and the politics of difference. The latter covers a wide range of approaches to race that challenge the kind of perspectives that featured in the 1986 Rex and Mason volume. In two particular ways, these approaches mark the shift from and challenge the picture set up in the 1980s. First, instead of grand structrual theories, they tend to be more like middle-range theories or perspectives. Second, they move beyond the boundaries of conventional social science disciplines such as sociology and signal the ways in which the field of race and ethnicity studies is now diversified in drawing on a range of traditions and themes. Consequently, in terms of their reach, some of these approaches map various kinds of intersectional theorising that link contemporary forms of race and racism with historical, cultural and literary analyses that are evident in a range of anti-foundational approaches in the social sciences and humanities. The perspectives that we have included in this section range from critical rationalism to critical race feminism, performativity, psychoanalysis/the psychosocial and critical whiteness studies. This section concludes with an analysis of what studying race in a trans-national or globalised environment should entail in terms of method and approach.

Chapter 8, by Michael Banton, is concerned with how the concepts of race and ethnicity have been understood in the social sciences and in everyday language. Banton's argument is that the concept of race is among those folk concepts – including racism, anti-Semitism, ethnicity, Islamophobia and multiculturalism – that are inadequate for sociological analysis because they are so marked by their political connotations and contexts. Drawing on social exchange and rational choice theories, Banton argues that the perspective of critical rationalism, rather than beginning with ideas and terms such as racism and ethnicity and using them as explanations, instead calls for a focus on developing and testing concepts that account for or explain observable variations in behaviours.

In Chapter 9, Adrien K. Wing highlights the contributions of critical race feminism (CRF). This is a development, and from the tradition, of critical race theory (CRT), which has been influential in the USA in particular. Originating in legal studies, CRT has been applied in fields such as education and sports in the United Kingdom. Drawing on CRT, Wing presents CRF as a multidisciplinary approach concerned with the legal status and rights of women of colour around the world, including where they are part of majority cultures. In keeping with the aims of activist scholarship, CRF, for Wing, is not solely a theoretical framework for scholarly analysis but also a means to address and improve the conditions for women of colour in various jurisdictions drawing on law but also going beyond that. This emphasis on political praxis puts CRF and the traditions on which it draws in stark contrast with Banton's approach.

This is followed by Chapter 10, by Shirley Anne Tate. This sets out the perspective of race performativity, drawing on the work of Judith Butler and Frantz Fanon. In its engagement with how mixed-race women, in particular, express and display raced identities, it shows how performativity both exposes and unsettles conventional racial binaries and hierarchies. Tate's approach to the ways in which mixed race is seen and how it is experienced and expressed shares some common ground with Miri Song's chapter in Part I of this book. Locating her view of performativity within a regime of normative whiteness, Tate argues that blackness provides a resource for anti-racist struggle and against post-race claims, even while the idea of authentic black identities is contested and renegotiated.

Tate's chapter, which touches on or engages with issues of identities, the psychic, whiteness and sexualities, connects to issues in each of the following three chapters. The emergence of psychoanalytic and psychosocial approaches to the study of racism is the focus of Chapter 11, by Simon Clarke. Drawing on Freud, Lacan and Klein, Clarke makes a number of suggestive links between sociological concerns and psychoanalytical ones. He develops a psychosocial approach which investigates and connects the structural and emotional dynamics between inner and outer worlds and between the individual and the social, without seeing these as binaries. In common with other approaches that stress embodiment, the psychosocial looks beyond and beneath the cultural theories drawing on language that were dominant through much of the past three decades.

An important and much contested aspect of research in the field of race and ethnicity studies in recent decades has been the question of whiteness and the ways in which it is or has been racialised and deracialised in various contexts. This issue is examined in Chapter 12, by Matthew W. Hughey, which is particularly concerned with the changing dynamics of white identity formation in the USA. While pointing to the hegemonic role of whiteness, he also draws attention to the ways in which it is homogenous and heterogeneous. His analysis draws both on ideologies of whiteness and on actual practice, and he uses this analysis to show how there is an idealised whiteness that demarcates those who are 'truly white'; this subtle analysis points to the complex dynamics of racial formations and racialisations.

In Chapter 13, Éric Fassin provides an insight into contemporary discussions about race and whiteness in France, a country where the issue of Muslim women wearing head scarves has starkly highlighted hostility to multiculturalism; this antipathy to religious symbols, and to Islam in particular, has been widespread in other European countries in the past decade. Although Fassin does not call his approach intersectional, he looks at the ways in which race, class and sexuality are linked in French political and public culture. In common with Hughey, Fassin shows how whiteness can be both visible and invisible and how a white victimology operates. French national identity, as Fassin shows, emerges through a complex interplay between class, race and sexuality, which plays out in public debates across a range of issues.

The final chapter in this part is by David Theo Goldberg; he draws our attention to the issue of how we study what we study in researching ethnicity, race and racism. In particular, he explores the limits of the comparative schema of analysing race and racism, which, he argues, has overstated the discreteness or uniqueness of national contexts. Instead of a comparative method, Goldberg argues for a relational framework that can grasp the complexities of race and the inter-connectivities of racial ideas and racisms across time and space.

8   Superseding *race* in sociology: the perspective of critical rationalism

Michael Banton

To qualify for the award of a PhD, a candidate has to demonstrate that he or she has made an original contribution to knowledge. This simple proposition encapsulates the most important characteristic of the philosophy which, after the work of Karl Popper, is known as critical rationalism. It focuses on the growth of knowledge. The candidate has to identify a segment of existing knowledge, examine its nature, present the results of new research and then show that he or she has, perhaps in small measure, expanded that knowledge.

This chapter reviews the origin of the academic study of racial and ethnic relations in Britain, noting how that study has broadened and how, within it, one line of inquiry has continued, acquiring new impulses. It contains an autobiographical component. Its ambition is to show that it is easier for a candidate to make a contribution to knowledge if he or she appreciates how previous contributions have come about, reflecting both the academic environment of the times and the imagination of individual researchers.

The chapter maintains that the study of racial and ethnic relations in British universities began in 1947 with the appointment, at the London School of Economics, of Dr Kenneth L. Little as assistant lecturer in anthropology, with special reference to race relations. As there was, in the British academic world of 1947, no agreement on what should be taught under this title, the appointment represented a major initiative on the part of Raymond Firth, the professor of social anthropology in the school.

The area of greatest disagreement concerned the explanatory value of the concept of *race*. Some of what passed as knowledge about race in 1947 has since been discredited. If *race* no longer has value for answering the sorts of questions of interest to sociologists, what can supersede it? The perspective of critical rationalism has a bearing on this problem too.

Race?

In the middle of the nineteenth century, some writers maintained that *Homo sapiens* was divided into five or more permanent racial types or species. This doctrine, which never gained acceptance from the leading scholars, appealed to some sections of the general public in Europe and North America (notably the whites, whom the typologists named 'Caucasians'). The scientific claims of racial typology were destroyed by Darwin's discovery of the theory of natural selection, but it took some 70 years for this to be properly appreciated. In the meantime, physical anthropologists continued to study comparative morphology, measuring variations in skull shape, eye colour, hair texture and other physical differences.

The Darwinian revolution in biology led to the discovery of the gene and then, in the 1930s, to the realisation that it was not the species but the gene that was the unit of natural selection. The new field of population genetics was being established. Most physical anthropologists nevertheless remained committed to the study of morphological variation, while social anthropologists spoke for alterative explanations of human diversity. So the Royal Anthropological Institute, with the support of the Institute of Sociology, established in 1934 a committee to report on the 'racial factor in cultural development'. As some would have predicted, it was impossible to reconcile explanations of diversity in terms of cultural difference with biological explanations, some of which classified the main human 'races' as separate species. Elazar Barkan (1992: 286–96) concluded that the publication of an unsatisfactory report was 'the only alternative to a declaration of failure, which was inadvisable since an agreement was needed for professional and political reasons'. Raymond Firth, a New Zealander, was a member of this committee, and the experience may have contributed to his initiative of 1947.

Beginnings

Kenneth Little graduated in anthropology at Cambridge in 1939 with an interest in comparative morphology. Having been found unfit for military service, he secured appointment as an assistant in the Duckworth Laboratory at Cambridge University. In the following year, he travelled to Cardiff to measure the physical characteristics of children at a school in the dockland neighbourhood who exemplified what he called the 'Anglo-Negroid cross'. Having found that children in the coloured category were somewhat taller and larger than the white children, he presented the results of this research in the *Eugenics Review* and in the *Journal of the Royal Anthropological Institute*.

In Cardiff, Little stumbled on a new and interesting research problem quite different from those featured in these two journals. It was the social exclusion of black and ethnic minority people in Britain. In 1948, his London PhD dissertation (which had been supervised by Firth) was published under the title *Negroes in Britain*. Following what was then regarded in his new department as the model structure for a dissertation in anthropology, the book was divided into a Part I on the current situation and a Part II on the history. Strikingly, the book contained only two footnote references to Little's initial studies in comparative morphology.

Little advanced an original theory about the cause of the social exclusion of black and ethnic minority people, arguing that it was a consequence of 'colour-class-consciousness'. 'Some English persons believe that they will jeopardize, if not lose, their social status in the eyes of their friends and acquaintances by association with a coloured person' (Little 1948: 232; 1972: 254). He described a widespread tendency to maintain social distance that was based on a scale of socioeconomic status in which a dark skin colour entailed a lower ranking. In addition to the two pages outlining this interpretation, the book contained an appendix summarising the results of an independent survey on the availability of accommodation for overseas students in London. Little discussed the reasons why the managers of guesthouses might be less willing than private landladies to offer accommodation to persons of another nationality or to 'coloured students', noting that there were considerations of a business nature as well as personal attitudes to be taken into account (Little [1948] 1972: 299–300).

This chapter traces my attempt to develop that theory, and the many mistakes I have made when trying to place it within a larger body of social and economic theory. For me as the author, it recounts a personal journey, yet, more than that, it is about a search for a particular kind of new knowledge that may well be continued by others in years to come.

The political environment

Although Little's book had made scant reference to race, and his theory was about differences in colour, he gave his lecture course at the LSE the title 'Racial Relations and Racial Problems'. From 1939 to 1945, the United Kingdom had been at war with a country which, under Nazi rule, had made a fateful use of pre-Darwinian theories of racial inequalities to send millions to gas chambers. This was not easily forgotten, and

Europeans were well aware of the conflicts associated with race in the USA. At the invitation of Charles S. Johnson, the sociologist who was president of Fisk University, Little had visited that university; he had learned about U.S. perspectives and had been particularly impressed by Oliver C. Cox's book *Caste, Class and Race*.

Initially, it had been believed that racial classification could be objective. Scientists might disagree about which was the best classification, but it had been assumed that the determination of a person's race was a task for an expert. This assumption was on the way out. In its place came the insistence that, in any event, the social relations between individuals could not be explained by concepts taken from theories about their biological makeup. A substantial body of informed opinion insisted that it was misleading to use race in a social context. An expert committee convened by UNESCO advised in 1950 that 'in popular parlance, it would be better when speaking of human races to drop the term "race" altogether and speak of ethnic groups'.

Educated opinion in Britain in the 1950s nevertheless favoured a shift in nomenclature such that, for example, references to 'the colour problem' were replaced by the expression 'racial problems'. In biology, race might be a failed concept, but others thought that, for non-biologists, the word had to be detoxified.

The case for better laws to protect Jews, as well as coloured people, from discrimination carried political weight. Opinion in Britain and other countries was moving toward the formulation whereby, in 1965, the International Convention on the Elimination of Racial Discrimination was to state that, for legal purposes, 'the term "racial discrimination"' covered any inequality of treatment 'based on race, colour, descent, or national or ethnic origin'. The adjectival form of the word *race* was used to designate a set with five members, while the noun designated the first of those five. Thus international law had endorsed a folk (rather than a scientific) concept of race and had used it both to designate a set with five members and to differentiate unequal treatment based on race from unequal treatment based on colour, descent, national origin or ethnic origin. The United Kingdom's law of 1965 repeated the international formula.

At this time, sociologists regarded this formulation as a legal nicety of only minor importance for their work. The focus of their research and teaching, in both Europe and North America, was on white discrimination against blacks. Looking back on their priorities after half a century, I regret that the sociologists in Britain (and their number could be counted on the fingers of two hands) did not more clearly distinguish their socioscientific objectives from their political objectives.

A critical rationalist perspective will hold that the social scientist should focus on the behaviour to be explained. Little had identified the social significance ascribed to differences of colour. These were visible and much simpler than the abstract and contested complexities of racial classification. When, much later, the law against discrimination in employment became effective, it was the perception of some people as 'black', and therefore of lesser entitlement, that was the instigator of cases before the tribunals, not their assignment to a race.

For the sociologist, *race* was an embarrassing word, yet it was a necessary word if the law against discrimination was to be of use. The critical rationalist solution is to distinguish the language of sociology from the ordinary language of everyday life, politics and measures of public policy like laws. The folk concepts of everyday life (sometimes called *emic* constructs) are flexible, with multiple and changing meanings. The inquirer can look up their definition in a dictionary. Scientific concepts (sometimes called *etic* constructs) have to be unambiguous and of stable meaning. Their definitions are decided by practice in research. The definition with *the* highest explanatory power is the one adopted. This is a retrospective view. For the moment, it is necessary to go back in time.

The academic impulse

The first defect of Little's 1948 formulation was that he did not explore the effects of the 'business' considerations. This was remedied by a later study, promoted by him after he had moved, in 1950, to the University of Edinburgh. This showed that coloured students, and particularly the darker-skinned ones, had either to pay more than white students to secure equal accommodation or to accept inferior facilities. The difference between the value of the accommodation in the white sector of the market, and what the coloured student had to pay, constituted a 'colour tax'. 'From the point of view of the landlady', it was said,

colour tax represents compensation for possible loss of social prestige; from that of an observer, it is an undesigned and unintended consequence of a social structure whose system of values includes the premise that association with coloureds is synonymous with 'low class' and generally disreputable behaviour. (Carey 1956: 68–71, 154–56)

From the point of view of the sociologist, the supposition that some kinds of identification could result in a loss of social status implied that the association imposed a cost. That cost could be offset by a corresponding benefit. Payment of a colour tax made possible a reciprocal relationship from which both the landlady and her lodger benefited. The landladies who wanted a higher rent to compensate for the loss of social prestige might not be aware that this was what they were doing. The theory advanced an explanation that did not depend upon the awareness of the parties involved.

This line of explanation was developed in a landmark essay by George Homans (1958) on 'social behaviour as exchange'. I referred to it in a draft paper about which, in early 1959, I sought the advice of a professor of moral philosophy who had displayed an interest in social anthropology. He singled out my sentence 'Any social action or series of actions can be treated as an economic transaction or series of transactions.' The professor put his thumb on this sentence, declared, 'This is *wrong*!' and refused to discuss the issue further. That was the university environment within which sociological explanation had to bid for attention.

The second defect of Little's formulation was that it neglected the possibility that someone might avoid associating with another person, not because of a concern about the judgments of the peer group but because of a suspicion that the other person would or could not observe the norms that would make the relationship beneficial to both parties. There would then be no reciprocity. As the risks of cost were too great, social contact was avoided.

In a follow-up study, I extended the theory to claim that avoidance could be motivated by a desire to avoid contact with anyone from whom reciprocity could not be expected. This was a characteristic of the stranger. I wrote that

strangers are not necessarily foreigners: the small child, the wealthy eccentric, the tramp, the village idiot, are all strangers to their society in that their behaviour cannot be predicted with any certainty, and the various informal pressures that usually produce conformity are not effective in their case ... In Britain the coloured man is not seen as a different sort of being but as the furthest removed of strangers. (Banton 1959: 73, 84)

This claim did not apply to relations governed by formal norms, like the relationship between an employer and an employee (Banton 1967: 332–33). The explanation of the social avoidance of inter-personal relations was analytically distinct from the explanation of the avoidance of social identification based upon distinctions of socioeconomic status.

Later I associated this embryonic theory with research into the expression of social distance. Social psychologists had differentiated between the expression of distance as a desire to avoid identification with another kind of person and the desire to avoid exposure to that person (Krech and Crutchfield 1948: 316). My differentiation was similar but added a hypothesis about when people might seek to avoid exposure to a socially strange person. The Bogardus measure of social distance was a scale of attitudes toward categories of persons; it did not explore the source of those attitudes (such as any scale of socioeconomic status). It raised questions about why some of the categories were ranked above others. Whereas sociologists inspired by the Marxist analysis of the structure of the labour market advanced explanations of why some categories were ranked low down, this was not a question pursued in the tradition deriving from Little's colour-class-consciousness hypothesis.

Little's explanation that 'some English persons' would avoid social identification with certain others because the costs might exceed the benefits connected it with a mode of explanation already established in the social sciences. Malinowski had highlighted the explanatory power of the concept of reciprocity, maintaining that 'give and take' pervaded the social life of the societies he had studied in the Pacific. Other anthropologists, including Edmund Leach, had followed. Fredrik Barth was soon to deepen the analysis of social relations as transactions. Later, in theorising about the generation of social forms, he was to stress 'the transactional nature of most inter-personal relations, in the reciprocity which we impose on ourselves and others' (Barth 1966: 3).

Further steps

My textbook *Race Relations* (Banton 1967) can be read as an elaboration of the intellectual tradition which Kenneth Little had initiated. Its title, though vulnerable to academic complaint, identified the thread of argument that ran through it, and it was immediately comprehensible to the book market. In the United Kingdom, a *Race Relations Act* had become law in 1965, and further acts with the same title were to follow.

Hoping to evade the uncertainty surrounding *race*, I stated that

an approach to race relations from the standpoint of social science requires that race be viewed not as a biological category but as a sign by which a social category is identified...When racial differences are used as a way of dividing up a population and different sets of rights and obligations (roles) are ascribed to the divisions, then these outward differences serve as signs telling others the sorts of privileges and facilities to which the person in question is conventionally entitled. (Banton 1967: 5, 57)

Race was a role sign. Later I acknowledged that, in this book, I had made two mistakes. The differences in appearance were differences, not of race, but of phenotype. No one can see another person's race. What people see is another's appearance, his or her phenotype. That is a first-order abstraction. *Race* is a second-order abstraction, an interpretation of what has been seen. My first mistake was to write of *race* when I should have written of *phenotype*. I used a folk concept of race instead of an analytical concept that grasped the nature of the outward difference. My second mistake was to present a classification of contact situations based on this first mistake (Banton 2005). Better use of *phenotype* in place of *race* would have been a step toward the supersession of the failed concept.

My next mistake, in the early 1970s, was to distinguish between the *'idea* of race' as expressing the folk concept and 'the *concept* of race' as summarising scientific knowledge about certain forms of human variation. This was wrong because, at no time, in either the nineteenth or the twentieth century, was there ever sufficient agreement among biologists about this kind of classification to justify the assumption that there was a scientific concept of race.

Social behaviour as exchange

A small revolution occurred in 1957 with the publication of Gary Becker's *The Economics of Discrimination*, a book primarily concerned with the employment market. Among the possible economic motivations for discrimination, he mentioned a desire to establish a monopoly or a monopsony but gave most attention to what he called a 'taste for discrimination' on the part of an employer. This was a personal sentiment with economic implications. Becker observed that, by declining to hire a certain category of worker (either because of his or her personal values or because of a fear that other workers might object), the employer was losing a possibly valuable opportunity. The employer paid a price for the exercise of this taste.

This was good economic logic, but, because employers might not actually enjoy discriminating, I contended that such behaviour was better represented as the exercise of a preference for association with co-ethnics. In Becker's examples, whites exercised such a preference, but in other circumstances, members of minorities would exercise their preferences, and sometimes people would prefer to avoid association with co-ethnics.

Becker (1957: 19–22) demonstrated that the nature of the relations between the discriminators and the discriminated could be more easily analysed if they were likened to the relations between two sets of people, each set being divided into capitalists and workers. This was to draw an analogy with international trade. So Becker pictured two 'societies', one he called W (to stand for whites) and the other N (to stand for negroes). W exported capital, while N exported labour. 'If members of W develop a desire to discriminate against labor and capital owned by N, they become willing to forfeit money income in order to avoid working with N.'

As a result, 'the return to W capital and N labor decreases, but the return to W labor and N capital actually increases.' Therefore discrimination *harms* W capitalists and benefits W workers. This was generalised in the proposition that 'trade between two societies is maximized when there is no discrimination, and it decreases with all increases in discrimination.'

At the Social Science Research Council's Research Unit in Ethnic Relations in Bristol, this model was used to guide research into housing inequalities. The structure of the British housing market was divided into four sub-markets: owner occupation; social (or 'council') housing, mostly provided by local authorities; unfurnished renting; and furnished renting. In the sector of owner occupation, one study concluded that real estate agents 'will be more likely to exclude coloureds from those areas in which they have a high stake' (Collard 1973: 288). Another found that 'Asian householders were paying more for their dwellings' and that this might be due to their investing less in the search for properties because they expected to encounter exclusionary practices (Fenton 1976). The attitude of those allocating social housing sometimes resulted in unequal treatment. Rent controls could be implemented more effectively in unfurnished than in furnished renting (Banton 1983: 346–60). Only by resort to economic reasoning could explanations for such differences be found.

This mode of explanation was in line with much that was written at the time in connection with the theory of social exchange elaborated by Peter M. Blau, Anthony Heath and others. It continues now in modified form under other names, such as the theory of social capital. Decisions in migrant-sending societies as to which family members should be financed to seek employment overseas, in which countries, which localities, which occupations and so on are explained as the outcomes of expected costs and benefits. Some more recent applications of this approach have been sampled in articles assembled by Boswell and Mueser (2008).

Groups and categories

Before going further, it is necessary to pause over the concept of *group*, because it is frequently misused. A social group is more than a social category. Moreover, the word *category* is used in more than one sense. If a research worker analysing demographic data chooses to abstract the figures on males aged 20–24, rather than on males aged 20–29, he or she creates a category appropriate to the purposes of the analysis. It is a *category* strictly speaking. There are also situations in which a research worker may study a set of persons customarily identified by a proper name, that is, a name that identifies this set of persons as distinct from all others. For example, in twentieth-century Bosnia, members of one population category were known as 'ethnic Muslims'. This is an example of a folk category, not a category *sensu stricto*, because some of those so designated did not consider themselves Muslims and, by reference to objective criteria, should not have been be so categorised. In the Bosnian case, it was outsiders who decided that some people were ethnic Muslims, and this designation was not, apparently, contested by those most concerned. In the first instance, a category has been constructed arbitrarily by an outsider. In the second instance, an outsider has taken over a category constructed by the local people.

The position in international law is now that, if individuals are to be categorised by race or ethnic origin, 'such identification shall, if no justification exists to the contrary, be based on self-identification by the individual concerned'. The person concerned can take over the role of the external adjudicator.

Unlike a category, a social group is constituted by its members; they recognise themselves as making up some sort of unit. Whereas categorical relations are unidimensional, social relations are multidimensional. Members of a group can interact with one another on the basis of different roles. There are always social exchanges within groups. For example, in any local community, there is usually some scale of socioeconomic status by which people are implicitly ranked. In such a scale, a low score on one social attribute can be traded off against a high score on another. This is a form of exchange and, if any group is to maintain a degree of closure vis-à-vis its social environment, such internal adjustments have to be made.

Because, within a group, social relations are multidimensional, each group is unique and any classification has to be arbitrary. In sociology and political science, group classifications are frequently based on folk categories. In Britain at the present time, it is conventional to refer to 'black and ethnic minority groups'. 'Black' is, strictly speaking, a colour category, but it is used as a folk category based on self-designation. Some sets of people, like Jews and Sikhs, identify themselves, and are identified, by both religion and descent or ethnic origin. This can be considered a form of 'intersectionality'.

A person has to be socialised within a family group to become properly human. While that person can later attain some of his or her ends by individual action, to attain other ends, he or she will have to cooperate with others. Outside the primary group, individuals can engage in exchange relations only if there are laws and institutions ('courts, codes, constables and central authority' – as Malinowski [1926] wrote). A reciprocal relationship is possible only if each party can be sure that the other will stand by a bargain. It may be a code rather than a law. Trust may grow gradually and may become a civic norm before it is given legal expression, so there are exceptions to Hobbes's assertion that 'There are no covenants without the sword.'

Because exchange is beneficial to both parties, it promotes economic growth, so the wider and greater the volume of trade, the more growth is possible. That is reciprocity in action. In the vocabulary of economics, the institutions that facilitate the growth of trade, such as the roads for the transport of goods by land, the lighthouses that protect transport by sea and the armies intended to ensure the defence of the realm, are public goods. They are goods because they provide benefits, and they are public because they are available to all. The benefits of trade underlie the increased importance of the state as an institutionalised body able to extend social and economic order and its ideological expression in the concept of the nation. The growth of state institutions exemplifies the principle of path dependence, in that new measures have, whenever possible, to be made compatible with the existing mode of organisation.

Competing perspectives

The year 1967 also saw the publication of *Race, Community and Conflict: A Study of Sparkbrook*, by John Rex and Robert Moore. It put forward a powerful argument that the social position of ethnic minorities in cities like Birmingham was, in significant measure, determined by their position in the housing market. It asked macro-sociological questions different from Little's focus on inter-personal relations, yet it saw nothing problematical in the use of the concept of *race*. This change, of course, later inspired an elaboration of the Marxist perspective.

At the end of the 1960s, a new generation within the ethnic majority population, together with the ethnic minority of Caribbean origin, was fascinated by news of the civil rights movement in the USA and the theses of those who spoke for black power. This movement utilised the concept of race in its strategy of polarising black and white. It claimed that the study of race relations should be superseded by the study of racism and thereby, unwillingly, gave new political support to a concept of which it was, very properly, decidedly suspicious.

In Britain, the conflict moved in the 1970s from the sociology classroom to the educational system. There, in the following decade, the campaign for an anti-racist approach to teaching was opposed by those who argued for multiculturalism and for the idiom of ethnicity in place of the idiom of race.

This move was strengthened in the 1970s and 1980s by the enthusiasm for a cultural studies perspective. The arguments that social behaviour could be explained as an exchange of benefits, that *race* served as a role sign and that people exercised preferences for association with co-ethnics identified causes of behaviour of which their parties might be unaware (just as Durkheim explained variations in suicide rates by underlying social causes in 1897). The cultural studies perspective, however, started from the conscious expression of attitudes influenced by racism and offered interpretations of their political significance. It was suspicious of explanations that relied on ideas of ethnicity.

Ethnicity?

One way in which the use of *race* in sociology might be superseded, and the 1950 UNESCO recommendation followed, was to separate cultural from physical differentiation and to identify an ethnic dimension to social relations. The essays collected in *Ethnicity: Theory and Experience*, edited by Glazer and Moynihan (1975), showed that much might be achieved by such a reorientation. In preparation for the conference that gave rise to the book, the editors inquired about 'situations in which ethnic groups distinguish themselves'. The chief thrust, however, appears to have been the editors' concern with the folk construct of 'ethnicity' as an *explanandum*. They wrote, 'We are suggesting that a new word reflects a new reality and a new usage reflects a change in that reality. The new word is "ethnicity"' (5). Many of the contributors provided analyses of particular situations that could be explicated by reference simply to ethnic groups and ethnic boundaries, and at least one concluded that the 'term "ethnicity" is clearly a confusing one' (156). Nevertheless, the editors postulated that 'ethnicity' was 'a new reality'. Their suggestion that the appearance on the political stage of 'ethnicity' was to be explained as the product of either primordialism or circumstantialism caught the attention of students of these matters and guided the course of much teaching and research for a quarter-century.

At the time, Glazer and Moynihan's argument appeared to be a significant and original contribution to sociological knowledge. In retrospect, it can be seen more clearly that Glazer and Moynihan's 'reality' was simply that some members of the public, particularly in the USA, were displaying a heightened appreciation of their ethnic origins and were using shared ethnic origin as a basis for mobilisation. European immigrants to the USA had initially associated with their co-nationals. Later, when they realised that they would not return to live in their countries of origin, and because of this, their co-nationals became their co-ethnics.

To write, as Glazer and Moynihan did, of 'ethnicity' was to represent ethnicity as a thing, to reify it. 'Ethnicity' is now freely used in popular speech, but from the standpoint of sociological knowledge, it is a spurious word, a failed concept that should be discarded. Its general acceptability has deceived some subsequent researchers who, as a result, have not defined their problems with sufficient precision.

In 1969, Barth had shifted the focus of investigation to the ethnic boundary that defines the group, instead of 'the cultural stuff that it encloses'. He inspired others to study the processes by which ethnic groups were created and maintained (even 'despite a flow of personnel' across their boundaries), and were sometimes dissolved (Barth 1969: 9, 15). His argument stimulated me to maintain that, instead of one ethnic boundary, there were two – an internal boundary for keeping members in and an external boundary for keeping others out. I suggested that folk beliefs about race were used in the maintenance of external boundaries. *Race* was a folk concept, not an analytical one. Beliefs about ethnic origin were used in the creation of internal boundaries. Yet I failed to consider whether *ethnicity* was a folk concept or an analytical one (Banton 1979: 130, 136).

By this time, I had started work on what I called a rational choice theory of racial and ethnic relations. In *Racial and Ethnic Competition*, I contended that 'When people compete as individuals this tends to dissolve the boundaries that define the groups, whereas when they compete as groups this reinforces those boundaries' (Banton 1983: 104). Trade across group boundaries occurs at prices influenced by the relative power of the groups, and a group that can present a united front can exercise more power than one that is divided; it can use its power to make it difficult for the other to mobilise its resources in collective action. If, in a situation like that of the U.S. Deep South in the 1930s, whites could control any breaking of ranks among their own number, tension between them and blacks would increase because trade was at prices very different from those that would prevail in a non-discriminatory market.

In that region at that time, the whites controlled state institutions and could set the prices at which blacks would be employed. There was, nevertheless, the possibility that, for example, a white farmer might calculate that it would be to his advantage to pay black workers at a higher rate to give them an incentive to work harder. Other whites would impose sanctions to prevent such a person breaking ranks. They could more easily prohibit equal-status relations between blacks and whites if they could call on an ideology that defined them as biologically different sorts of humanity.

It was relatively easy to regulate the relations between a white farmer and a black farm worker. Some other relationships were less simple. For example, a white man might operate a roadside filling station. When customers drove up, he would use the petrol pump to put fuel into the car. He would be serving his customer. What if the customer was a black motorist? This potential difficulty was dealt with by exempting this relationship at the pump from the norm of white superiority and by defining it as one of 'business'. The transaction was then regulated by the definition of the situation as one that did not call into question the premise of social inequality.

In a two-category situation, the parties are involved in a bargaining relationship. In the Deep South, this had some of the features of a zero-sum game. One party could make a gain only if there was an equivalent loss to the other party. Rioting, or disorder, could, in the short term, make it resemble a negative-sum game, in which both parties lost. In the longer term, changes might follow, especially if relations were altered by intervention from outside. In some circumstances, bargaining can stimulate both parties to greater output, and the outcome then resembles a positive-sum game in which exchanges have benefited both parties.

The interest of the members of a category as a whole is unlikely to coincide with the interests of individual members. Successful mobilisation depends upon leaders so committed to their cause that they are willing to take personal risks. Some of those who might join them will be tempted to take a 'free ride', benefiting from the investments of others. Therefore a mobilisation movement is more likely to succeed when the would-be free riders can be forced to join, becoming captive travellers (Banton 1985: 19–21). In developing this argument, I held that positive-sum relations between ethnic categories constitute a public good. The practice of racial discrimination, by contrast, could be accounted a public bad.

A social boundary, whether based on ideas of race or on some other social attribute, constitutes an obstacle to trade. That obstacle can be overcome by a special exemption or by trading at a price outside the usual range. This line of reasoning about reciprocity, transaction or exchange led in turn to two alternative theories. One was the rational actor (or rational agent) theory, which treated the human person as a rational agent with intelligible goals, choosing between them as potential courses of action. The other was the theory of rational choice; this made no assumption about the actor's state of mind but evaluated his or her choices against the criterion of rationality, that is, whether it maximised his or her net advantages. The rational actor theory assumed that the actor was making decisions on the basis of positive preferences, the nature of which could, in principle, be verified by research. The rational choice theory relied on the view that the actor's behaviour revealed his or her preferences and did not seek independent verification of them.

Therefore it was not affected by the evidence from psychological research about the unconscious sources of errors in reasoning or by the results of research into motivation. A psychologist who was awarded a Nobel Prize in Economics has reported that 'for the billionaire looking for the extra billion, and indeed for the participant in an experimental economics project looking for the extra dollar, money is a proxy for points on a scale of self-regard and achievement' (Kahneman 2011: 342). Those points could be more important than the extra dollar. Though propositions based on a concept of revealed preference may be tautological, they can still be instructive.

Multidimensionality

The belief that racial classification could be objective had brought with it the assumption that humans belonged in racial categories for all purposes. If two people were of different race, then any relationship into which they might enter would be affected. Experience suggested otherwise. If, in some relationships, racial assignment could be irrelevant, then this called into question the concept of 'race relations'. Attempting to clarify what had been called the 'race relations problematic', I therefore sought to answer the question 'When is a relation *racial*?' I took a lead from legal proceedings in which the tribunal has to decide whether someone had acted on racial grounds.

It would have been better had I started from the multidimensionality of relations within social groups that has been noted earlier. Each relationship in which someone is involved is based on a norm. There are civic norms stating expectations that individuals will conform to the customs of the community and the laws of the state. There are norms relating to particular social categories, stating expectations of how an individual shall behave in relations with persons of the same or different race, colour, descent, national origin, ethnic origin, gender, religion and so on. The observance of norms is rewarded, and their neglect is punished, but the benefits flowing from conformity and the costs on account of deviance impact individuals differently.

Faced with alternatives, one individual may prefer a civic option and the approval of other members. Another person may choose to seek his or her personal advantage. A third person may choose an ethnic option, bringing the approval of persons who share that ethnic origin.

Research in Malaysia has shown how it is possible, in surveys interviewing a sample of members of the general public, to study the preference for association with co-ethnics set against alternatives of personal gain and personal obligation. Persons were asked to predict how they thought others would decide in certain situations. In one situation, they were told that Husin Ali, a representative Malay-Malaysian, bought his groceries from Ah Kow's grocery shop, noted for its cheapness and being close to his house. He had been told that someone called Ahmad was about to open a second grocery in the neighbourhood. Respondents were asked whether they thought that Husin Ali would transfer his custom to the new shop. Nothing in the interview said that Husin Ali was of Malay origin, or Ah Kow of Chinese origin. Those interviewed will have made this inference. In research elsewhere, the names, or photographs, of representative persons can be varied to discover more about the processes of social cognition.

There was a common belief that Chinese-origin shopkeepers sold groceries more cheaply. Would Husin Ali shop with his co-ethnic (Ahmad), or would he buy where prices were lower (Ah Kow)? Were he to patronise Ahmad instead, this would be taken as an expression of social alignment based upon a preference for association with a co-ethnic. The strength of such a preference could be measured, for example, by finding whether Husin Ali was predicted to continue shopping with Ahmad if, other things being equal, his prices were 2, 4, 6 or 8 per cent higher. In a shopping situation, some individuals will have a preference for association with a co-ethnic of zero; others may have a higher preference, depending perhaps upon their personalities, their financial circumstances or the social pressures they experience.

A prediction that Husin Ali would prefer to shop with his co-ethnic could be seen as an estimation of his individual likes and dislikes or as reflecting his solidarity with the co-ethnics who have made him the person he is. This latter aspect was measured in the research by asking respondents how they thought Husin Ali's mother would wish him to act in the situations studied. The questions were varied to measure the preference for association with a co-ethnic by comparison with an expected financial gain, a gain in social status and the sense of obligation to a fellow employee. They were repeated in a study of the predicted ethnic preferences of a Chinese-Malaysian (Banton 2000).

Just as many individuals will have a preference, in given situations, for association with a co-ethnic, so they may have preferences for association with someone of the same national origin, the same religion or the same gender or social class, or with a speaker of the same language. These preferences will not necessarily be of positive value. In some circumstances, people wish to avoid co-ethnics, co-nationals, co-religionists and so on. Their preferences will then be a negative value. This perspective shows that the forms of behaviour that some have considered 'racial' can be explained without use of that failed concept.

If a research worker asks questions about an interviewee's experiences of relations with blacks, or whites, or Indians or Muslims, he or she frames the question in a way that evokes a particular kind of answer. There is no check on whether the subject has categorised the other person in any of these ways. In a heterogeneous neighbourhood, a shop assistant at the till collecting payments for purchases may pay little attention to the social attributes of customers passing rapidly through. Variations in social categorisation have rarely, as yet, been studied systematically.

To question subjects in a way that makes it possible to compare the strengths of their various preferences is to make an elementary use of experimental method. It opens the possibility of uncovering causes of behaviour of which the parties are not conscious, as Durkheim (1897) did in his famous study of the causes of suicide.

Conclusion

The history of the growth of knowledge in this branch of sociology, as in any other academic field, is a history of the problems identified and the explanations that have won acceptance. To some biologists, *race* once seemed to have explanatory potential, but they were found to be wrong. The concepts of eugenics and of comparative morphology also once seemed to offer something of value for the study of racial and ethnic relations. They have been superseded.

Kenneth Little, in 1948, sought to explain why 'some English persons' avoided 'association with a coloured person'. This chapter has traced a 60-year line of research into the problem which Little identified. It concludes that this line can fruitfully be extended by study of the preferences expressed by members of both ethnic majorities and minorities for association with co-ethnics in different circumstances. If that research makes use of experimental methods, it should be possible to discover causes of behaviour underlying the level of consciousness.

Such research does not need to employ any concept of *race*. Nor does much of the current research into macro-sociological questions. Indeed, its use may be a source of confusion. Why, then, does it persist – as in the title of this volume? In the academic journals, there are still many publications about 'theorising race' and suchlike. Its persistence is surely due to the importance of ideas of race in the perception of matters thought to be politically important.

International and national laws against discrimination are designed to protect all persons from unfavourable treatment 'on racial grounds'. For certain purposes, these laws, and other instruments of public policy, rely on the assumption that persons can be classified by 'race, colour, descent, or national or ethnic origin'. In this sphere, as in the discussion of social policy, the idiom of race will continue to be used.

Race is a member of a class of folk concepts, freighted with multiple meanings, that are vital to the discussion of political issues but lack the precision needed for sociological explanation. This class of concepts includes racism, anti-Semitism, ethnicity, Islamophobia and multiculturalism. The continued use of, and meanings given to, these words depend upon political leaders, journalists and public figures of many kinds, not upon the qualifications which sociologists might like to introduce.

If the distinction between the two kinds of vocabulary is observed, it should be possible to distinguish the study of sociology from that of social policy and to supersede the use of *race* within sociology. Many teachers of sociology would disagree. They prefer to start from ideas, like those of 'racism' and 'ethnicity', and to use them to interpret everyday experience. From a critical rationalist standpoint, this is back to front. The sociologist should start from the *explananda* and use whichever concepts best account for them. The central *explanandum* for racial and ethnic studies is that of the differential behaviour associated with physical and cultural differences. Accounting for that behaviour is a challenging task because there is so much variation in individual behaviour.

Anyone studying everyday experience encounters a sampling problem. How can the research deal with the great variations in individual sentiment and behaviour? The research in Malaysia points to a solution. By asking for predictions about the preferences for association with co-ethnics that others will display in imagined situations, and permuting a variety of possible variables, it should be possible to find which concepts display the greatest explanatory power. In this way, the research problem can be transformed and a new conceptual framework established.

As Durkheim (1897: 310) acknowledged, people are reluctant to accept new concepts; new knowledge may offend common sense. He went on, 'If there is such a science as sociology, it can only be the study of a world hitherto unknown.' Without going as far as that, I conclude that, in this particular field at least, there is a world as yet unknown and that, if sociologists utilise experimental methods, they will be able to step into it.

REFERENCES

Banton, M. (1959). *White and Coloured: The Behaviour of British People towards Coloured Immigrants*. London: Jonathan Cape.
(1967). *Race Relations*. London: Tavistock.
(1979). Analytical and folk concepts of race and ethnicity. *Ethnic and Racial Studies*, 2(2), 127–38.

(1983). *Racial and Ethnic Competition*. Cambridge: Cambridge University Press.

(1985). *Promoting Racial Harmony*. Cambridge: Cambridge University Press.

(2000). Ethnic conflict. *Sociology*, 34(3), 481–98.

(2005). Finding, and correcting, my mistakes. *Sociology*, 39(3), 463–79.

Barkan, E. (1992). *The Retreat of Scientific Racism: Changing Concepts of Race in Britain and the United States between the World Wars*. Cambridge: Cambridge University Press.

Barth, F. (1966). *Models of Social Organization*, Occasional Paper 23. London: Royal Anthropological Association.

ed. (1969). *Ethnic Groups and Boundaries: The Social Organization of Culture Differences*. Bergen-Oslo: Universitets Forlaget.

Becker, G. S. (1957). *The Economics of Discrimination*. Chicago: University of Chicago Press.

Boswell, C. and Mueser, P. R. (2008). Introduction: economics and interdisciplinary approaches to migration research. *Journal of Ethnic and Migration Studies*, 34(4), 519–29.

Carey, A. T. (1956). *Colonial Students*. London: Secker and Warburg.

Collard, D. (1973). Exclusion by estate agents – an analysis. *Applied Economics*, 5(4), 281–88.

Durkheim, E. (1897). *Suicide: A Study in Sociology*. Engl. transl., London: Routledge and Kegan Paul, 1962.

Fenton, M. (1976). Price discrimination under non-monopolistic conditions. *Applied Economics*, 8(2), 135–44.

Glazer, N. and Moynihan, D. P., eds. (1975). *Ethnicity: Theory and Experience*. Cambridge, MA: Harvard University Press.

Homans, G. (1958). Social behavior as exchange. *American Journal of Sociology*, 63(6), 597–606.

Kahneman, D. (2011). *Thinking, Fast and Slow*. London: Allen Lane.

Krech, D. and Crutchfield, R. S. (1948). *Theory and Problems of Social Psychology*. New York: McGraw-Hill.

Little, K. L. ([1948] 1972). *Negroes in Britain: A Study of Racial Relations in English Society*. London: Routledge.

Malinowski, B. (1926). *Crime and Custom in Savage Society*. London: Routledge/Kegan Paul.

Adrien K. Wing

This chapter introduces critical race feminism (CRF) as an analytical tool to assess the legal plight of women in various jurisdictions. Developed primarily by U.S. legal authors, CRF draws from several other jurisprudential trends. After a general discussion of the various interwoven themes, the chapter applies a CRF analysis to the recent situation confronting Arab and/or Muslim women during the age of the continued War on Terror as well as the post–Arab Spring – what I have termed the 'Arab season'. These women have been stigmatized and have faced substantial discrimination both in Western countries, where they are a minority, and in their countries of origin. The chapter concludes that a nuanced CRF approach reveals both the positive and the negative realities of Muslim/Arab women's lives, and there is room for optimism as well as pessimism for the future.

CRF is a term originally coined by Professor Richard Delgado (1995a), then of the University of Colorado Law School, in the first edition of his anthology *Critical Race Theory: The Cutting Edge*. CRF describes an emphasis on the legal status and rights of women of color around the world. I produced two editions of an anthology using this term – *Critical Race Feminism: A Reader* (Wing 1997, 2003). CRF poses two fundamental questions. First, what is the de jure and de facto legal status of women of color, whether they be minorities within the United States or Europe or part of majority cultures in the developing world? Second, what can a focused theoretical framework do to beneficially affect their condition? These queries are posed about this group because women of color are disproportionately stalled at the bottom of every society – economically, socially and politically – no matter what country they call their own. CRF seeks to identify and theorize about these issues and formulate relevant solutions as well. Furthermore, CRF may use a multidisciplinary approach that considers the law to be a necessary, but not sufficient, basis to formulate solutions to social justice dilemmas. Fields including history, sociology, psychology, criminology and education may be particularly relevant, and scholars in these disciplines are using CRF approaches (Pratt-Clarke 2010).

Critical race feminism defined

CRF derives from a broad set of jurisprudential movements – most notably critical legal studies (CLS), critical race theory (CRT) and feminist jurisprudence. The first of these movements, CLS, developed in the late 1970s by politically progressive white male academics who were a 'collection of neo-Marxist intellectuals, former New Left activists, ex-counterculturalists, and other varieties of oppositionists' (Crenshaw 1996: xvii). Some of them became professors in elite law schools. This group of scholars founded CLS, endorsing a progressive class analysis on the role of law – critiquing both conservative orthodoxies and legal liberalism ideals. The CLS movement used a deconstruction methodology to challenge the conception that law is neutral, objective or determinate. CLS was very much influenced by European post-modernists like Jacques Derrida and Michel Foucault (Boyle 1992; Fitzpatrick and Hunt 1987; Hutchinson 1989; Kelman 1990). CRF agrees with these tenets of CLS and uses this framework to expose how the law has served as a tool in perpetuating not only unjust class hierarchies, which was a CLS concern, but also race and gender hierarchies. Most significantly, CRF draws from CLS the challenging of ideals of law as inviolable and objective – laws that have, in practice, oppressed women and people of color for centuries. CRF scholars, however, find that CLS fails in adequately representing the identities of women and people of color. CRF focuses on moving beyond the marginalization of these communities, expanding past the worldview of these progressive white male elites.

The second movement from which CRF derives is CRT, which emerged within the legal academy as a self-conscious entity in the late 1980s. Its intellectual foundations can be found in the works of then Harvard University law professor Derrick Bell and in those of other scholars from the mid 1970s and onward. CRT challenges narrow approaches to providing social and economic justice and addresses relevant and contentious sociolegal racial issues, including affirmative action in education and employment, hate speech, racial profiling and immigration law (Crenshaw 1996; Delgado and Stefancic 1999, 2012). The CRT movement developed a growing set of affiliated networks, including LAT-CRIT, which emphasizes Latinos and Latinas (Delgado and Stefancic 1998a). AsianCrit focuses on Asians and the discrimination facing them (Chang 1993). QueerRaceCrit focuses on gays and lesbians of color (Arriola 1994; Valdes 1995). Critical white studies focuses on the

way whiteness functions as a social organizing principle (Delgado and Stefancic 1998b).

CRT has several basic tenets which are part of its approach and which are shared by CRF. The first is that racism is a normal and ordinary part of our society rather than an aberration. A second tenet is that the subordination existing within the white-over-color hierarchy is a critical aspect of how our society develops both psychologically and materially. Third, race is a social construct and is not a fixed or biological reality. Fourth is that race is constructed and reconstructed to meet the needs and demands of the dominant society. Fifth is that identity is unique to the individual and should be considered holistically. A sixth tenet is that there is a 'unique voice of color' among groups who have faced oppression (Delgado and Stefancic 2001). A seventh tenet is that law may be a necessary but not always a sufficient approach to resolving racial hierarchies. Other disciplines may have much to contribute, especially from fields like sociology, political science, history, economics and other liberal arts fields. Interestingly, the legally situated CRT theorists prefer to cite those within the legal academy and may be less likely to embrace multidisciplinarity than those in the social sciences. Another tenet is that CRT endorses the CLS notion that legal rights are indeterminate, but it vehemently disagrees that rights are therefore not important (Williams 1987). In fact, CRT and CRF consider the struggle to attain human rights as a critical step for people of color such as American minorities.

Additionally, both CRT and CRF endorse critical race *praxis*, the combination of theory and practice (Wing 1990: 91). This perspective acknowledges that progressive scholars of color cannot afford to adopt the classic detached ivory-tower model of scholarship, when so many from their respective communities are suffering, sometimes in their own extended families. This praxis may take many forms – such as working with various public interest and non-governmental organizations, engaging in law reform both domestically and internationally, coalition building, political activism, board memberships, speeches and even writing op-eds and blogs. These efforts enrich scholarship and teaching, have practical significance and expand opportunities for understanding and growth.

While drawing greatly from it, CRF scholars have critiqued CRT approaches that essentialize the treatment of people of color. CRF constitutes a gender intervention within CRT by noting that men of color may face different kinds of discrimination to their female peers. Issues that require separate analysis may include, among others, female health, sexuality, pregnancy, motherhood and domestic violence.

The final major movement from which CRF draws is the modern-day feminist jurisprudence developed as a response to the gender oppression faced by middle-class and affluent white women (Kramer 1995; Olsen 1995; Weisberg 1993). Feminism addresses gender oppression within a system of patriarchy. Mainstream feminism, however, has been found by many to essentialize all women, often at the price of silencing the unique or varied experiences of women of color (Harris 1990). For this reason, while CRF has adopted much of the theory and focus of feminist jurisprudence, some critical race feminist scholars may have refused to associate themselves with the mainstream feminist movement. As a result, CRF is a race intervention with respect to feminism and uses its perspectives to expose the unique and varied experiences of women of color as distinct from white women or men of color.

Additionally, CRF has drawn from the energy and ideas of black and 'womanist' feminism of those outside the legal academy to address the concerns for equality and treatment of women of color. Among the important non-legal figures in this area are the late Audre Lorde (1995), Patricia Hill Collins (2008), Toni Morrison (2004) and Alice Walker (1982).

CRF has also introduced its own distinct analytical contributions within these jurisprudential movements. Most notable is the concept of anti-essentialism. CRF contradicts the traditional feminist ideology of the 'essential female or minority voice' and instead relies on the theory of intersectionality, popularized by UCLA/Columbia law professor Kimberle Crenshaw. CRF considers the anti-essentialist perspectives of women of color by analyzing the intersection of their race and gender identities. Demarginalizing women of color has led to the development of CRF perspectives on various issues, including criminal justice, constitutional law, employment discrimination, torts, domestic violence, sexual harassment, reproductive rights, family law, the Internet and even tax law. Scholars who have written in the American legal context have shown particular reverence for CRF foremothers like Crenshaw, Mari Matsuda, Angela Harris and Patricia Williams, who laid out fundamental principles.

Related to intersectionality is the term *multiple consciousness*, coined by University of Hawaii law professor Mari Matsuda, which is used to describe the intersectional identities of women of color (Matsuda 1989). These women view the world simultaneously from both a gendered and a racialized perspective, and many may also have a class perspective disproportionally based on lower-income or working-class status. In earlier scholarship, I have chosen to use the word *multiplicative* to configure identity. In this sense, some CRF scholars understand identities of individuals to include their race, gender and other identifying characteristics such as class, age, color, disability, marital status, religion or nationality. The multiplicative equation also acknowledges that individuals must be taken as the whole of their identity. For example, an African American woman may not be considered a white woman color or a black man gender. Every day, she is a holistic black woman (Wing 1990: 91).

CRF also brings to the analytical table the importance of public international and comparative law, international business transactions and human rights. My anthology entitled *Global Critical Race Feminism: An International Reader* (Wing 2000) gathered together materials in these fields. GCRF has contributed to the development of international law, global feminism and post-colonial theory by moving women of color away from the margins and putting them in the centre, in both a theoretical and a practical sense. Global CRF authors – ranging from Professor Penelope Andrews, who has written about South African and Australian women confronting domestic violence, to Professors Isabelle Gunning and Leslye Obiora, who have deconstructed issues relating to female genital surgeries – have explored a wide array of topics. Berta Hernandez has critiqued *marianismo*, the cult of the Virgin Mary in Latin America, whereas Leti Volpp has explored the global workplace (Wing 2000).

Critical theory generally, including CRF, has often been considered by many as too soft or not 'legal enough' to fully incorporate into legal discourse. When attempting to define CRF, it is not unusual to be met with an unwelcoming or condescendingly polite response – as the conversation quickly returns to 'real law'. This uncomfortable exchange, however, is important in that it communicates the implicit skepticism toward CRF. The reasoning that prompts this response is often sparked by questions such as, Are the concerns of this sub-category of people not covered adequately by 'real law' or, rather, race- and gender-neutral law? Or, does the race movement not adequately protect women of color? Does the post–World War II international legal regime that has developed principally since the First World decolonization of most of the Third World not encompass the legal problems of Third World women? The answer to these questions, when using a critical race feminist perspective, is a resounding *no*. The existing legal frameworks under U.S., foreign and international law have allowed women of color to fall between the cracks – to become both literally and figuratively voiceless and invisible. CRF uses a conscious, anti-essentialist inter-disciplinary approach to provide women of color a voice and place in legal and social discourse (Wing 2000).

Another critique of critical theory, including CRF, comes from one of the methodologies used – the narrative or storytelling technique. Authors ranging from Derrick Bell and Richard Delgado to Patricia Williams have used fictional and non-fictional stories to tell important truths affecting the lives of people of color (Bell 1987; Delgado 1995b). Opponents have challenged the validity of this approach, claiming it lacks intellectual rigor and is overly emotional and too subjective to rely on (Farber and Sherry 1997). CRF, however, finds this approach necessary and significant – as many of us prize our heritages in which oral tradition has had historical significance and where vital notions of justice and the law are communicated, generation to generation, through the telling of stories. Perhaps even more significantly, this narrative approach enables us to connect with those who do not understand the hypertechnical legal language but may nonetheless seek understanding of our distinct voices (Delgado 1990; Matsuda 1989). CRF acknowledges and attempts to break down the privileged wall created by academics and scholars, which shuts out those who are less educated or outside the designated field.

Now that this chapter has provided an overview of CRF, it will use CRF analysis to discuss the status of Arab and/or Muslim women. In the context of the War on Terror, it discusses the negative stigmatization of these women who have been essentialized in the West as voiceless, faceless, exploited people whose customs and religion cast them in an inferior status. Arab male patriarchy is seen as ensuring that the women stay subordinated. On a more positive side, the chapter then discusses the more upbeat portrayals of some women during the early phase of the Arab Spring events. As the Arab Spring turned into the Arab autumn and now the Arab season, women have been portrayed as sunken back into the essentialized victim role.

War on Terror

Western law enforcement has been racially profiling anyone who looks like an Arab/Muslim in the age of the War on Terror. The pan-ethnicity term *Arab* and the religious signifier *Muslim* have been socially constructed as synonymous with *race*. Although there are more than 1 billion Muslims worldwide, only 15 per cent are Arab. There may be 3 million Arabs in the USA, originating from 22 countries, and the majority may be Christian (PBS, n.d.). In the important case *St. Francis College v. Al-Khazrahi*, 481 U.S. 604 (1987), the U.S. Supreme Court acknowledged that Arabs can be discriminated against on account of their race.

In the West, this Arab/Muslim group has been socially constructed not only as a race but as a disfavored race, that is, 'black'. It does not matter what the skin colors of the various individuals are or the actual differences in cultures and religions. The Arab/Muslim category as a whole gets lumped together and stigmatized. Equally, it does not matter to the West that, in the Arab world or among Muslims globally, there may be a totally different conception of race or an outlook that race is irrelevant. Western, or certainly U.S., policy may be based in large part on trying to make things fit within a black–white binary. Who are the whites? Who are the blacks? For Americans, this approach can also manifest as, Who are the cowboys and who are the Indians? In the Middle East region, Israelis will be seen as the socially constructed whites against the dark Arab hordes. Among Arabs, Christians may be seen as white versus Muslim. Among Muslims, Sunnis may be seen as white compared to Shias.

Whereas blacks have been stereotyped as criminals in the U.S. context, the Arab/Muslim group has been even further essentialized as criminals writ large – global terrorists. They are 'forever disloyal and imminently threatening', whether they are citizens or not (Saito 2001: 12). Of course, the law enforcement essentialization of this group has proved ineffective in the War on Terror, because Muslims can look like or be anyone. Richard Reid, the mixed-race British shoe bomber, did not look like a Muslim, and neither did the young white man from Marin County, California, John Walker Lindh, who was caught on the battlefield with the Taliban.

It should also be noted that Islamophobia and the demonization of Arabs/Muslims predates 11 September 2001. They have been physically attacked, blacklisted in academia, restricted from political participation and so on. Modern movies have used terms that would never be tolerated today if applied to blacks or Jews. Jack Shaheen found the following characterizations: 'assholes', 'bastards', 'camel-dicks', 'pigs', 'devil-worshippers', 'jackals', 'rats', 'rag-heads', 'towel-heads', 'scumbuckets', 'sons of dogs', 'buzzards of the jungle', 'sons of whores', 'sons of unnamed goats' and 'sons of she-camels' (Shaheen 2001: 11).

While many male Arabs or Muslims may be able to 'pass' as many other ethnicities, depending on their individual skin color, clothing and so on, those Muslim women who chose to wear Islamic dress of some kind are immediately identifiable as Muslim. For them, there will be no 'passing' as something else. In countries like France, girls have not been able to wear the head scarf (*hijab*) in state school since a 2004 law was passed (Wing and Smith 2006). A 2011 law has banned the wearing of the *niqab* in public altogether, even though fewer than two thousand women may have been wearing such attire. The fines are small for women but quite draconian for men who make a woman wear a *niqab* – 30,000 euros. Other European states have passed or are considering such laws.

The chapter will now demarginalize Arab/Muslim women and look specifically at how the ongoing War on Terror affects many of them.

These women and those who look like them (i.e., many Indians, Latinas, African Americans) may be socially constructed as black by the West in various ways in this age of endless war against terror. The chapter de-essentializes the women and considers four roles: woman as terrorist, woman as terrorist sympathizer, woman as family member of terrorists and all other women. The categories are not linear but can intersect. Thus a woman could be regarded as a terrorist, a terrorist sympathizer and a family member of terrorists as well.

The American media has not reported any incidents of Arab/Muslim women being directly regarded as terrorists themselves in the USA. Abroad, there have been reports of Palestinian, Jordanian and Iraqi women who have engaged in or attempted suicide bombings. Because arrests under the USA Patriot Act and other security legislation are very hush-hush, it could be that women are being arrested and held in incommunicado detention. Men were definitely held for undetermined periods of time in a legal limbo after 11 September.

Historically speaking, there have not been many women regarded as 'terrorists'. I remember the case of Joanne Chesimard, also known as Assata Shakur, a member of the Black Panthers and later the Black Liberation Army back in the 1970s. She was convicted of killing a police officer in 1973. Some of her colleagues 'liberated' her from a New Jersey prison, and she went into exile in Cuba, where she remains today (Shakur 1987).

In the case of women who are actually accused of being terrorists themselves, they have to deal with all the problems that any criminal defendant does, plus the consequences of the intersection of their identities, especially the perception of their political opinions as a socially constructed terrorist. If a woman is actually apolitical, she is unlikely to be believed in such a highly charged era. If the woman is a Muslim, the prison may not be equipped to be sensitive to her religious and dietary restrictions. If she wears a head scarf, would she be permitted to wear it in prison? If she is more modest than the average woman, can any of her sensitivities be respected in prison? If she is a wife and mother, her family will be bereft of her efforts in these areas. Are the authorities likely to treat her more harshly than other prisoners because of the intersectionality? A street criminal would get better treatment than a terrorist. If she is a non-citizen, she has even less protection than citizens or permanent residents. She may be deported before or after serving her sentence.

Rather than being actual terrorists, it is more likely that many Arab/Muslim women are regarded as terrorist sympathizers. The authorities may regard them as tacit backers of terrorism – even though the women may be citizens. They may be subject to unknown government surveillance and private-sector discrimination.

One of the most famous cases of a terrorist sympathizer outside of a Muslim context was that of UCLA black philosophy professor Angela Y. Davis, who was put on trial for providing weapons for convicted Black Panthers Jonathan Jackson and others. A judge ended up being murdered, and Jackson was killed fleeing the Marin County, California, courthouse. Professor Davis was acquitted and is an emerita professor at the University of California, Santa Cruz campus (Davis 1989).

Arab/Muslim women who fit into this category of terrorist sympathizer may be wives, girlfriends, mothers, siblings or other relatives of terrorists. They may be under scrutiny because it is perceived that they will have knowledge relating to the terrorist or terrorist activities. When Osama bin Laden was killed, 3 of his wives and 12 of his children were taken into custody, and the wives were questioned extensively about his activities. After many months, Khairiah Sabar, Siham Sabar and eight of the children were eventually repatriated to Saudi Arabia. His fifth wife, Yemeni Amal Ahmed al-Sadah, was sent to Qatar (Burke 2011).

Conversely, it may be assumed that such women are passive, silent and voiceless – and likely to know little. When I co-authored an article on the 2004 French law that banned the wearing of ostentatious religious garb (mainly head scarves), I was astonished by how little the French public and media engaged in actually asking for the opinions of Muslim women (Wing and Smith 2006). A debate about Muslim female behavior occurred without any public participation by them in the political sphere.

Women in this category may be left bereft if a male family member is taken into custody. This man is likely to have been the main breadwinner, upon whom some women relied. If a woman does not know the language of the country she is in, or does not have as high a level of education as the man taken away, she has less ability, if any, to recoup the lost income. She may have been a spouse who did not have equal knowledge of the family finances. She may not even be a citizen with a work permit. She may also have children to now support who are acting out emotionally in school – owing to the loss of their father. Perhaps other children have been calling them 'terrorists' or other derogatory terms for a long time.

Most women are not terrorists, terrorist sympathizers or family members of terrorists. Yet this simple fact is probably lost as they are socially constructed into one or more of the preceding categories. Those committed to praxis in wanting to improve the treatment of these women must realize the intersecting complexity of their issues that arise from their multiple perceived identities. Legal and social services must be made available to assist them. Such programs should ideally be designed by women from the communities involved – that is, from the bottom up – rather than totally designed by well-intentioned outsiders who lack understanding.

Additionally, legal and service providers must understand not only the various roles that women may simultaneously inhabit but that the Arab/Muslim category cannot be essentialized. Services will have to be culturally relevant and specific to the various religious and ethnic communities involved.

Each religious community will face unique issues within each religion. Lebanese, Syrian or Coptic Christian Egyptians will each have distinct issues among Christians, for example. Shiites from Hezbollah will be different from Shiites from Iran, not to mention any of the differences with the various Sunni nationalities/ethnicities. Class issues are relevant as well. Secular upper-class, second-generation women in France, such as Rachida Dati, the former minister of justice, would be in a very different position from an Algerian refugee woman who is an undeclared second wife in Marseille, with her husband detained indefinitely on no charges.

Now that the chapter has used a CRF analysis to deconstruct aspects of the treatment of Arab/Muslim women in the War on Terror, it will discuss some positive as well as negative aspects concerning these women arising from the Arab season events.

Arab season

The events of what has become known as the Arab Spring 2011 took the world by surprise. The quick downfalls of the Tunisian ruler Zine ben Ali and the 30-year reign by Egyptian president Hosni Mubarak were energizing to the rest of the region. The subsequent NATO-assisted toppling of Libyan four-decade-long ruler Colonel Muammar Gadhafi and the routing of Yemenite leader Ali Abdullah Salah gave hope to those in Syria and other countries where the leaders brutally hang on to power.

The Arab Spring helped the West to stop essentializing Arab women as silent, oppressed victims in some cases. Instead of being socially constructed blacks in the Western sense, some women were able to counter those stereotypes and take on unprecedented public roles. The international community acknowledged this fact when Yemeni Tawakkul Karman was one of three activist women who won the 2011 Nobel Prize for Peace. U.S. secretary of state Hillary Rodham Clinton praised the awardees: 'The unflinching courage, strength and leadership of these women to build peace, advance reconciliation and defend the rights of fellow citizens in their own countries provide inspiration for women's rights and human progress everywhere' (Cowell et al. 2011). Ms Karman, who is a mother of three, led a human rights advocacy group called

Women Journalists without Chains. Arrested by the regime, some have called her the 'Mother of Revolution' (Cowell et al. 2011).

Other women were also on the front lines of their revolutions, breaking norms and fighting for the freedom of their fellow citizens. For example, the Tunisian blogger Lina Ben Mhenni chronicled the revolution in her country via social media. Israa Abdel Fattah of Egypt, a founder of the April 6th Youth Movement, was a key player in the Egyptian uprising (ALBAWABA 2011). An Egyptian female journalist, Bothaina Kamel, ran for president (Davies 2011).

In Libya, women have been mentioned in various roles. There were women like Aisha Gdour, a school psychologist, who smuggled bullets in her brown leather handbag. Fatima Bredan, a hairdresser, tended wounded rebels. Hweida Shibadi, a family lawyer, helped NATO to find airstrike targets. Amal Bashir, an art teacher, used a secret code to collect orders for munitions: small-caliber rounds were called 'pins', larger rounds were 'nails' and a 'bottle of milk' meant a Kalashnikov (Barnard 2011).

Women have faced severe backlashes when they have asserted their rights. Human Rights Watch obtained statements from women who described how they were detained at an Egyptian military base and the personnel there subjected them to virginity tests. An official confirmed that the military had performed the tests, which constitute unlawful assault under both Egyptian and international law. They charged the women with prostitution, but one woman is suing – strongly defying cultural norms (Coleman 2011).

Whether suing or protesting, these activities counter pre-existing stereotypes of Arab/Muslim women as meek, passive, subordinated people. Whether they were young or old, hair exposed or in head scarves, lawyers, mothers, wives or workers, the incredible courage displayed illustrates that essentializing such women is a massive disservice to their individuality and their strength.

During the Arab Spring, there were other attacks on women. On International Women's Day 2011, a month after the fall of Mubarak, a march for women's rights filled Tahrir Square. The marchers were met by crowds of men shouting abuse and sexually harassing them. At one stage, they held up a woman in full *niqab* face veil and chanted, 'This is a real Egyptian woman' (*Think Africa Press* 2011).

As the spring rolled into the autumn and winter, women experienced victories and defeats. Women made up half of the candidates for the Tunisian elections and then earned 24 per cent of the Constituent Assembly seats. Conversely, an important section of the draft constitution referred to women as 'complementary' to men rather than equal

(Wing 2012). In December 2011, Egyptian military police attacked a woman in full Islamic dress, stamped on her and left her exposed on the street with her blue bra showing. Women responded by doing a giant demonstration to protest against this violence (Coleman 2011). The Egyptian constitutional draft of autumn 2012 is worse on women's issues than its 1971 predecessor, and women make up only 2 per cent of the parliament, far fewer than during the Mubarak years, when legislative quotas ensured greater female representation.

Assisting women during the Arab season will be enhanced if policy makers and non-governmental organizations (NGOs) used CRF praxis. For example, crafting relevant programs will require not lumping women in with men in certain contexts. It will mandate getting an assessment of female needs directly from women themselves or their NGOs and not letting men talk for them. For example, some may want politicization training to be able to actively participate in the political process. Many will want to understand the constitution making options as each nation engages in that process for the first time in many years. Holding an evening session during dinner time that is open to both genders may result in a dearth of women. Why? Women still predominantly do the cooking and child care around the world and will be too busy in that time slot. It is unlikely that a significant number of their husbands will relieve them of these responsibilities to enable the women to attend meetings. Alternatively, holding a small local session in the community while the older children are in school or providing day care for small children may enable more women to attend. Holding sessions in female safe spaces such as private homes or embroidery or women's centers may work in some cases. For those with Internet capabilities, being able to do distance learning via Skype or another similar carrier may be viable. For women who work outside the home, it could be that a lunch-break session would be best. For some women, mosques or churches may be acceptable places to have sessions.

Regardless of the political changes under way in their respective countries, an anti-essentialist approach of consulting women directly may reveal that they would prioritize efforts focusing on the improvement of their economic situation rather than their political knowledge. The global economic crisis affects employment in certain groups in many of the Arab/Muslim countries to a larger degree than in many Western nations. Micro-finance may continue to have more salience than constitutional models. Some may prefer general educational assistance or health information. They may prioritize the avoidance of forced or child marriages. They may want to not become the victim of an honor killing or suffer domestic abuse. Conversely, such concerns may seem irrelevant to their particular lives. Outsiders cannot presume that such women are ignorant and must be given political information whether they want it or not. Outsiders cannot decide that whether or not a woman is wearing Islamic dress is a priority just because such an issue has received major attention in the West.

The delicate issue of psychological or emotional aid is often neglected but hard to provide when culturally competent care is unavailable or stigmatized. With respect to a country like Syria, facing severe destabilization, foreign efforts may be geared to assisting refugees who make it out to nations like Turkey, Lebanon or Jordan, which provide basic food, shelter and security needs. Women may be disproportionally among the refugee population without resources, without male relatives at all or with males who have lost their breadwinner status.

Conclusions

This chapter has provided an overview of CRF, a jurisprudential theme that focuses primarily on the legal status of women of color, whether the women are based within Western nations or elsewhere in the world. CRF has been greatly influenced by progressive trends in CLS, CRT and feminism theory. After presenting an overview of CRF, the chapter used a CRF analysis to explore the condition of Arab/Muslim women with respect to two areas – the War on Terror and the Arab season. CRF praxis is necessary to de-essentialize and de-marginalize women who are in need of a wide variety of assistance based upon their intersectional and multiplicative identities. While law is one aspect of their needs, more urgent help may be required in areas of security, health, education and employment. Often left out of the laundry lists of needs may be psychological and emotional aid in societies where such help is unavailable and/or stigmatized.

CRF is still in its infancy as a means of analyzing the legal status of women of color. As more young scholars join the academy, it is hoped that some of them will be attracted to improve upon the embryonic efforts of those critical race feminist foremothers who wrote some of the seminal pieces more than 20 years ago. CRT held a 20th anniversary conference at the University of Iowa College of Law, and there were a number of junior professors interested in CRF perspectives. They faced the usual challenges of getting tenure and balancing their personal lives with their professional ones. Many remain the only or one of the few faculty of color, much less women of color, at their respective institutions. They are advised, as we were, to stick to traditional doctrinal subjects and to stay away from controversial or even irrelevant things like CRT or CRF.

After all, we have two black lawyers in the White House as president and first lady and a black female billionaire, Oprah Winfrey, who is one of the most influential and popular Americans. In what would surely be a shock to him if he were alive, Malcolm X is even featured on a U.S. postage stamp.

It could be that CRT and CRF may be going or have gone the way of CLS – ideas that had their heyday in a certain historical moment within a small subset of progressive scholars but never caught on in the mainstream academy, much less the bar and bench. It may be that invoking CRT or CRF is like invoking the Black Panthers or the black power movement – interesting historical oddities where relatively few see the relevance to twenty-first-century post-racial society.

Whether or not the names 'critical race theory' or 'critical race feminism' continue to be used at all in the future, the principles that they helped to crystallize remain valid. Ideally, those scholars and activists committed to global social justice will not marginalize or essentialize the concerns of women of color. Among the many needs, I will only mention a few. There is a need for people of every background to enhance their understanding of the situation of such women, without stereotyping them. In particular, because men and patriarchy will continue to dominate most societies for the foreseeable future, it is important that our sons as well as our daughters, husbands as well as wives, learn of the issues and needs. For people living in the West with resources, it is important to visit other societies in a serious way – not just hit the famous tourist spots for a few days. Scholars and activists in the West and in the societies targeted can help to create informational materials, especially in this technologically savvy age, which can educate people of all ages, from primary school pupils to senior citizens, on the status of women of color. Scholarships and travel grants can assist those interested of all backgrounds. NGOs can enhance their targeted fund-raising. The image of the Pakistani teenager Malala Yousafzai, who was attacked for daring to want an education, may inspire even young children to want to contribute to the cause of female education.

Because the needs are so vast, it is important that major resource allocation be implemented. These resources, of whatever level, should be placed in part in the hands of women themselves. If women can handle hundreds or thousands of dollars responsibly in micro-finance, what might they do with billions of dollars? Surely they will not be any more incompetent or corrupt than many of the men who have had sole access to spending societal resources?

Meanwhile, although billions are useful, the very micro-giving that comes from one's own pocket can be priceless. I visited a Tunisian family a number of times and saw how difficult it was to wash the family of eight's clothes in an ancient tub. The machine I bought for a few hundred dollars locally saved countless hours of the family time. Small donations over a long period enabled the family to renovate the entire main-floor living space – a permanent improvement for them and for their social status in their family and the community. A 100 euro wedding gift gave a young couple one of their largest contributions to start their new life. Although I cannot talk directly to the family matriarch in her language, her French-speaking children make sure I get my point across.

While targeting women of color in our efforts, it is equally important not to neglect the needs of men and male children. Many well-intentioned projects have failed when the men in control forbade their women from participating or when the men sabotaged the project. It is essential that traditionally respected men buy into the program. Village leaders demanding that their daughters get an education has defanged the Taliban, for example, in a way that would not be the case if the only ones calling for education were well-meaning Westerners like *Three Cups of Tea* author Greg Mortenson (Mortenson and Relin 2006) or the U.S. State Department.

Another major priority for those interested in CRF praxis is the improvement of language capabilities on both sides. Girls and women in poor societies need more access to global language-learning facilities. Likewise, more Westerners need to decide from a younger age to undertake language study in Arabic, Farsi or Chinese, for example. There have been many occasions in my life when I wanted to talk to the spouses of my male lawyer colleagues but I did not speak their local language, and they did not speak mine. Assessing their needs through male filters is often impossible and counterproductive. A favorite activity of mine has been going shopping or learning local cooking from women, even though our language capabilities may be weak. I have learned much in these safe female spaces.

Another CRF-inspired need is humility. Those of us in the West who have the luxury of professional careers or lives in the academy need to be sure that we are operating from a position of humility when we are eager to assist. Our lives can be taken from us by death, disease, natural disasters or the global economic meltdown. Some of us face racism and sexism or other -isms as well. Nevertheless, we may still be in a vastly more secure economic position that many of the women we wish to help. Arrogance is counterproductive and may be very ingrained in even the most humble of us. We may presume that, because some of us come from communities of color and have higher levels of education than most people in the world, we are qualified to dictate to others what is best for them. I have found that, if I deal with people as if they were my own family and respect them for their insights, whether they have a PhD or no degree at all, everyone benefits more.

In conclusion, CRF can provide a theoretical framework that is helpful in improving the lives of women of color. All those concerned with social justice should also engage in CRF praxis with our sisters and our brothers, rallying together for a brighter future, whether we are in Tahrir Square, Trafalgar Square or Times Square.

REFERENCES

ALBAWABA. (2011). Arab Spring poet and blogger tipped for Nobel Prize nominations. 2 October. www.albawaba.com/editorchoice/arab-spring-poet-and-blogger-tipped-nobel-prize-nominations-394710.

Arriola, E. (1994). Gendered inequality: lesbians, gays, and feminist legal theory. *Berkeley Women's Law Journal*, 9(1), 103–43.

Barnard, A. (2011). Libya's war-tested women hope to keep new power. *New York Times*, 13 September. www.nytimes.com/2011/09/13/world/africa/13women.html?_r=1&ref=africa.

Bell, D. (1987). *And We Are Not Saved: The Elusive Quest for Racial Justice*. New York: Basic Books.

Boyle, J., ed. (1992). *Critical Legal Studies*. New York: New York University Press.

Burke, J. (2011). Osama bin Laden's wives told they are free to leave Pakistan. *The Guardian*, 8 December. www.guardian.co.uk/world/2011/dec/08/osama-bin-laden-wives-free.

Chang, R. (1993). Toward an Asian American legal scholarship: critical race theory, post-structuralism, and narrative space. *California Law Review*, 81(5), 1241–323.

Coleman, I. (2011). 'Blue bra girl' rallies Egypt's women vs oppression. 22 December. http://edition.cnn.com/2011/12/22/opinion/coleman-women-egypt-protest/index.html.

Cowell, A., Kasinof, L. and Nossiter, A. (2011). Nobel Peace Prize awarded to three activist women. *New York Times*, 7 October. www.nytimes.com/2011/10/08/world/nobel-peace-prize-johnson-sirleaf-gbowee-karman.html?pagewanted=all.

Crenshaw, K. (1996). Introduction. In K. Crenshaw, N. Gotanda, G. Peller, and K. Thomas, eds, *Critical Race Theory: The Key Writings That Formed the Movement*. New York: New Press, pp. xiii–xxxii.

Davies, C. (2011). The woman who wants to be Egypt's first female president. *CNN*, 16 September. www.cnn.com/2011/09/13/world/meast/egypt-bothaina-kamel/index.html.

Davis, A. (1989). *An Autobiography*. New York: International.

Delgado, R. (1990). When a story is just a story: does voice really matter? *Virginia Law Review*, 76(1), 95–111.

ed. (1995a). *Critical Race Theory: The Cutting Edge*. Philadelphia: Temple University Press.

(1995b). *Rodrigo Chronicles*. New York: New York University Press.

Delgado, R. and Stefancic, J., eds. (1998a). *The Latino/a Condition: A Critical Reader*. New York: New York University Press.

eds. (1998b). *Critical White Studies: Looking behind the Mirror*. Philadelphia: Temple University Press.

eds. (1999). *Critical Race Theory: The Cutting Edge*, 2nd edn. Philadelphia: Temple University Press.

(2001). *Critical Race Theory: An Introduction*. New York: New York University Press.

(2012). *Critical Race Theory: An Introduction*, 2nd edn. New York: New York University Press.

Farber, D. and Sherry, S. (1997). *Beyond All Reason: The Radical Assault of Truth in American Law*. New York: Oxford University Press.

Fitzpatrick, P. and Hunt, A., eds. (1987). *Critical Legal Studies*. Oxford: Basil Blackwell.

Harris, A. (1990). Race and essentialism in feminist legal theory. *Stanford Law Review*, 42(3), 581–615.

Hill Collins, P. (2008). *Black Feminist Thought: Knowledge, Consciousness, and the Politics of Empowerment*. New York: Routledge Classics.

Hutchinson, A., ed. (1989). *Critical Legal Studies*. New York: Rowman and Littlefield.

Kelman, M. (1990). *A Guide to Critical Legal Studies*. Cambridge, MA: Harvard University Press.

Kramer, M. (1995). *Critical Legal Theory and the Challenge of Feminism: A Philosophical Reconception*. New York: Rowman and Littlefield.

Lorde, A. (1995). *Sister Outsider*. New York: Crossing Press.

Matsuda, M. (1989). When the first quail calls: multiple consciousness as jurisprudential method. *Women's Rights Law Reporter*, 11, 297–99.

Morrison, T. (2004). *Beloved*. New York: Vintage.

Mortenson, G. and Relin, D. (2006). *Three Cups of Tea*. New York: Penguin.

Olsen, F., ed. (1995). *Feminist Legal Theory*. New York: New York University Press.

PBS. (n.d.). Caught in the crossfire: Arab Americans. www.pbs.org/itvs/caughtinthecrossfire/arab_americans.html.

Pratt-Clarke, M. (2010). *Critical Race, Feminism, and Education: A Social Justice Model*. New York: Palgrave Macmillan.

Saito, N. (2001). Symbolism under siege: Japanese American redress and the 'racing' of Arab Americans as 'terrorists'. *Asian Law Journal*, 8(1), 1–29.

Shaheen, J. (2001). *Reel Bad Arabs: How Hollywood Vilifies a People*. New York: Olive Branch Press.

Shakur, A. (1987). *An Autobiography*. London: Zed.

Think Africa Press. (2011). Egypt's quiet gender revolution. 24 August. http://thinkafricapress.com/egypt/egypt-quiet-gender-revolution.

Valdes, F. (1995). Queers, sissies, dykes, and tomboys: deconstructing the conflation of 'sex', 'gender', and 'sexual orientation' in Euro-American law and society. *California Law Review*, 83(1), 1–377.

Walker, A. (1982). *The Colour Purple*. New York: Harcourt Brace.

Weisberg, D. (1993). *Feminist Legal Theory: Foundations*. Philadelphia: Temple University Press.

Williams, P. (1987). Alchemical notes: reconstructing ideals from deconstructed rights. *Harvard Civil Rights – Civil Liberties Law Review*, 22(2), 401–33.

Wing, A. (1990–91). Brief reflections toward a multiplicative theory and praxis of being. *Berkeley Women's Law Journal*, 6(1), 181–202.

   ed. (1997). *Critical Race Feminism: A Reader*. New York: New York University Press.

   ed. (2000). *Global Critical Race Feminism: An International Reader*. New York: New York University Press.

   ed. (2003). *Critical Race Feminism: A Reader*, 2nd edn. New York: New York University Press.

   (2012). The 'Arab fall': the future of women's rights. *University of California at Davis Journal of International Law and Policy*, 18(2), 445–68.

Wing, A. and Smith, M. (2006). Critical race feminism lifting the veil? Muslim women, France and the headscarf ban. *University of California at Davis Law Review*, 39(3), 743–86.

10   Performativity and 'raced' bodies

Shirley Anne Tate

Judith Butler's (1990, 1993) groundbreaking work has led to the permeation of performativity into other theorisations of difference. This chapter engages with the (im)possibilities of the black body's 'race' performativity as it comes up against the 'race empire'. It does this by focusing on the question of whether 'mixed-race' naming as black, as well as performances of blackness, can unsettle 'the certainties of race'. Using data on identification and beauty drawn from British black 'mixed-race' women, the chapter shows that they performatively construct identities as black by drawing on hypodescent – the one-drop rule. It also shows that, as discursively constructed categories, the black–white binary is made mobile through everyday acts of resistance such as naming oneself as black and practices on/of the body – such as fake tanning – which question identity positionings in those racialised hierarchies in which the visual is central to recognition. The fact that black–white remains the binary that keeps the black social skin in place points to the continuation of a 'race empire' that draws its certainties from both master signifiers – blackness and whiteness. This 'race empire' has instituted an informal and extra-legal anti-miscegenation regime (Thompson 2009) based on hypodescent – from at least the time of slavery and colonialism – that continues in twenty-first-century Britain. The chapter concludes with a discussion of how Frantz Fanon's (1967) racial epidermal schema and its racialising technology of dissection (Haritaworn 2009) continue to operate at the levels of the psyche, the social and the nation as 'race' haunts performativity's (im)possibilities. Let us now consider what constitutes 'race' performativity before looking at the 'race empire' and how 'race' performativity can help us to theorise 'race' in the twenty-first century.

Race performativity

'"Race" is a social construct' is somewhat of a twentieth-century mantra. However, we know that it continues to very powerfully weave its discontents, desires and exclusions into people's lives. Lola, who, at the time of her interview,[1] was a 38-year-old social worker, deals with the commonplace assumption that 'mixed-race' people are confused about their identities in the following extract. She also shows that, for a black 'mixed-race' girl child, racialised criteria of beauty can be very effective in shaping a wish to be white. This is especially so for her as someone who grew up in 1970s Britain, when there were no black beauty role models:

I'm not confused you know. I have never had a problem with my identity. I have always known I was black. But it didn't stop me wishing I was white when I was younger because I saw no positive black role models. I never saw beauty in blackness, do you know what I mean? But that doesn't mean to say I was never confused. I was. I wondered if I was white. Or what I was. I always knew I was black but it didn't stop me wishing I was other than that when I was younger.

She never had a problem with her identity because she 'always knew [she] was black'. How could she be so certain of her blackness when the norm for her, at the time she was growing up, was a whiteness that produced a regime of truth which permeated the psyche, politics and practices on/of the self as it did in colonial times (Clarke, this volume; De Vere Brody 1998; Fanon 1967)? This norm precluded both the possibility of black beauty and of being the *white* child of a *black* father. Precluding whiteness underlies the dominant black–white binary which explained 'race', so that, even if mixedness was a source of confusion as a child, blackness was always a certainty because of the fact of her father's 'race'. To wonder if you were white or what you were points to the impact of the skin – its materiality, social construction and meanings – on the psyche.

The skin ego (Anzieu 1990; Prosser 1998) needs 'race' certainty to function in a once-and-for-all way to establish identity. Lola highlights the pervasiveness of hypodescent – the one-drop rule – that locates her as black because of her father's 'blood', halts the movement of her body toward whiteness and nullifies any identity claim to whiteness itself. Whiteness was a haunting question on/of belonging as the only possible naming for her was black. If we think about the question on/of belonging, as an integral part of the dominant 'race' regime of hypodescent, then, drawing on Foucault, as does Butler (2005: 22), we can see that there is

always a relation to this regime [of hypodescent], a mode of self-crafting that takes place in the context of the norms and, specifically, negotiates an answer to the question of who the 'I' will be in relation to these norms... This does not mean that a given regime of truth sets an invariable framework for recognition;

---

[1] The data drawn on here are from research on black identity and black beauty conducted in the late 1990s and early 2000s in the United Kingdom.

it means only that it is in relation to this framework that recognition takes place or the norms that govern recognition are challenged and transformed. (emphasis added)

The dominant 'race' regime of hypodescent is productive of bodies, subjectivities, psyches and politics. It has been a long time in the making, as shown by Jennifer De Vere Brody's (1998) account of the use of the bodies of black 'mixed-race' women in the making of English subjectivity as white, male and pure in Victorian times. The Victorian era's iconic trans-racial couple were the black woman and the white man, whose offspring – the 'mulatto', 'quadroon' or 'octoroon' – were marked by the inherited impurity of 'black blood' (De Vere Brody 1998). Mixing was seen to produce degeneration and illegitimacy, to support the illusion of white purity and legitimacy. However, mixing and its mark on the body also 'comments on the "illegitimate" sources of English wealth and the unseemly origins of English imperial power' (De Vere Brody 1998: 18). As such, then, mixing must be continually disavowed, erased to keep the black–white binary firm. This points to the normative function of hypodescent and its colonial corporeal classification systems – contained in names such as 'mulatto', 'quadroon' and 'octoroon' – in maintaining the purity of the white citizen body. However, hypodescent's framework for recognition can be challenged and transformed, even though it is, at the same time, crucial for racialised recognition. Lola's words reveal not only the place of the racial epidermal schema in the making of identities within the dominant 'race' regime of hypodescent but also the possibility for a movement otherwise – that is, a movement away from 'identity confusion' and toward the 'race' certainty of blackness through projective identification (see Clarke, this volume).

What Lola talks about in the preceding extract is how, as a black girl, she was fixed bodily and biologically (Clarke, this volume) as ugly, which then led to her desire for whiteness as a child. As a child, she engaged in the process of constructing Fanon's (1967) white mask in which 'black is white is black' (Clarke, this volume). However, as an adult, she challenges the racial epidermal schema by constructing a position of 'black is black is black', as she produces black skin, black mask (Tate 2005), because she always knew she was black and never had a problem with her identity. Her movement toward 'race' certainty also involves projective identification, in which she rids herself of 'unpalatable parts of the self' (Clarke, this volume) into the child who wished to be white. This shedding of that which is abject, the desire to be other than oneself, enables new namings to emerge. That is black but/and 'mixed race'. Such naming produces whiteness as other, erects a boundary between the sameness of black community and the otherness of whiteness. This naming refuses the border identification of a mixed category (Song, this volume) while, at the same time, highlighting the social constructedness of blackness as it troubles its boundaries and fixed binary relationship to whiteness.

Lola's movement toward blackness as 'race' certainty points to the possibility of an understanding of performativity as *both* 'the act by which a subject brings into being what she/he names [and] that reiterative power of discourse to produce the phenomena that it regulates and constrains' (Butler 1993: 2). Blackness is such a 'race' discourse which, whether from within black Atlantic diaspora anti-racist politics or whiteness, facilitates certain black identifications and disavows others. We can see this facilitation in Lola's certainty of blackness, even though she wished to be other than black when she was young, because of the workings of whiteness as the ideal. Lola also makes us recall that identifications – or what she names herself – are regulated practices that are given meaning by individual acts of recognition and the translation of identity discourses. Subjects engage in the translation of identity discourses in the process of identification/dis-identification with blackness/whiteness to

fashion, stylize, produce and 'perform' these [identity] positions, [but] they never do so completely, for once and all time, and some never do, or are in a constant agonistic process of struggling with, resisting, negotiating and accommodating the normative rules with which they confront and regulate themselves. (Hall 1996a: 14)

If we look at Lola's extract again, we see that the power of discourse to regulate and constrain resides in the claim to blackness itself, which shows that she is both discursively located and bodily embedded in a 'race' regime which precedes her and in which she is always already known as black because of hypodescent. The example speaks to us very powerfully about the significance of recognition, projection and naming. To say 'I am black' is, at one and the same time, to locate oneself politically, socially, intellectually, philosophically, culturally, 'racially', psychically and affectively, no matter how contested 'black' is itself (Hall 1996b). Naming is identity constituting; as it 'orders and institutes a variety of free-floating signifiers into an "identity", the name effectively sutures the object' (Butler 1993: 208). 'I am black' sutures Lola to specific diaspora histories, genealogies, bodies and affective economies through which racialised recognition is set in train. Thus, irrespective of the translations of identity discourses in which we engage, recognition as black is significant for identification because

recognition is not conferred on a subject, but forms that subject. Further, the impossibility of a full recognition, that is, of ever fully inhabiting the name by which one's social identity is inaugurated and mobilized, implies the instability and incompleteness of subject-formation. (Butler 1993: 226)

Recognition forms the subject as black, but incompleteness and instability point us toward anti-essentialism and the possibility for the emergence of new identifications. However, when Lola says she is black, she anchors herself within a 'race' essentialism 'without which [she] cannot speak' (Butler 1993: 226). This is so because even her 'mixed-race' body and the multiracial/cultural conviviality within which she lives cannot contest this essentialism because of hypodescent. Indeed, for Song (in this volume), evidence suggests that black 'mixed-race' people are consistently assigned as monoracial, as black. Furthermore, the necessity of black politics for strategic essentialism has the unintended consequences of keeping hypodescent in play and refusing the possibility of the free flow of hybrid identities. However, if the naming of oneself as black amounts to the very constitution of blackness, then its 'descriptive features will be fundamentally unstable and open to all kinds of... rearticulations' (Butler 1993: 210). Thus, 'black' would be capable of extension to take rearticulations of mixedness and hypodescent into account in a manner in which a whiteness which seeks to remain 'pure' is not (Zack 1993). Black, then, would not seek to deny mixing but rather to see itself as an inclusive identification within a society which is decidedly not post-race. Here black rearticulations would enter into the dynamic process of deconstructing blackness and reconstructing its relationalities and affective attachments.

Within black rearticulations, to identify as black implies an agency '[which] would then be the double movement of being constituted in and by a signifier, where "to be constituted" means "to be compelled to cite or repeat or mime" the signifier [black] itself' (Butler 1993: 220). To say 'I am black' does this work of constitution. However, within this miming of the signifier, it always fails 'to produce the unity it appears to name... [which is] the result of that term's incapacity to include the social relations that it provisionally stabilizes through a set of contingent exclusions' (Butler 1993: 220–21). One such contingent exclusion is that of whiteness, as Lola shows, because of the black–white binary as a point of certainty. One way in which this certainty is maintained is through the constant dialogue between the white-originated discourse on hypodescent and impurity and the black nationalist discourse of 'purity' as a sign of cultural and political authenticity. This continues to be the case even though, as we have seen in the discussion thus far, such purity is a collective fiction within the 'race empire'.

The race empire

Paul Gilroy (2004: 32) notes that 'while the political order of "race" endures, the character of racial and ethnic groups is seen to be at stake in attempts to overthrow it'. This political order, which I would like to call here the 'race empire', produces a structure of feeling that proceeds as a regime of truth on 'race' as authentic culture, body, consciousness and politics and establishes the boundaries of the black community's psychic and social skin in the black Atlantic diaspora (Banks 2000; Candelario 2007; Pinho 2010; Tate 2005). As a deterritorialising system of rule, 'empire', for Michael Hardt and Antonio Negri (2001), has no territorial power centre or fixed boundaries. The 'race' empire flows within the black Atlantic diaspora through its connective circuitry (Gilroy 1993) and reproduces recognisable black bodies, psyches, identities and politics through the connectedness of hypodescent to 'race' politics. The 'race' empire incorporates the global as it manages hybrid identities, hierarchies and exchanges through its discourses on 'race' which continually circulate. For example, through this circulation, the threat to both 'pure' whiteness and blackness posed by mixedness is dealt with through the discourse of hypodescent. This operates at the levels of the psyche, the social, the national and the global, so that embodiments have an incommensurable blackness–whiteness as the binary which aids in their racialised recognition.

Such incommensurability produced by, for example, black nationalism, Rastafarianism, negritude, Latin American Afro-descent politics, black power and white supremacy dictates the boundaries of the black social skin. In states which aim to be tolerant, multicultural, racial democracies or, indeed, post-'race', quotidian boundary maintenance is achieved through what Fanon (1967) terms 'dissection' – that is, 'a racialising technology which entitles some to gaze at and define others according to colonial archives of knowledge' (Haritaworn 2009: 123). I want to extend dissection further to include those regimes of truth on 'race' that came out of black diasporic experience, intellectual endeavour, philosophies and political activism. This is important because the question 'What are you?' so often asked of black 'mixed-race' women can be even more excluding if uttered by one with whom a connection is felt because of what is perceived as a shared black social skin.

Although an essential aspect of anti-racist aesthetics, nation building and decolonisation within black politics in the twentieth century, we must critique the political and intellectual legacy of black nationalism, negritude and black power for their avoidance of the gender question.

With regard to W. E. B. DuBois, Aime Césaire, Leopold Senghor and Frantz Fanon, Michelle Wright (2004) shows that feminist and queer rereadings of the black Atlantic diaspora are necessary to counter the heteropatriarchal discourse of nationalism, where black women do not exist and, indeed, where they can only be heterosexual. Wright (2004: 11) argues that 'the counterdiscourses of Du Bois, Césaire, Fanon and Senghor speak of the Black subject as "he" and allocates to that subject full agency, leaving little room for (and even less discussion of) the Black female subject'. For Michelle Stephens (2005), early-twentieth-century pan-Africanist Caribbean intellectuals and activists based in the USA (C. L. R. James, Marcus Garvey and Claude McKay) developed a masculinist diasporic global imaginary in which the battle was between African diasporic and 'Western' masculinities and in which black women were represented as 'the race's' passive nurturers. Furthermore, black politics also set in train black Atlantic body ideologies, such as those of Garveyism, Rastafarianism and Brazilian Afro-aesthetics, which valorised more-'African' beauty at the expense of other black beauties (Tate 2009). Nothwithstanding this critique, Fanon's (1967) racial epidermal schema and its attendant racialising dissection are still active in the twenty-first century, and the problem of the colour line continues unabated (Gilroy 2004). We should also extend usual understandings of 'the colour line' to incorporate what Marcus Garvey (2004: 143) called an 'aristocracy based upon caste of colour and not achievement in race', which tries 'to get away from pride of race into the atmosphere of colour worship'. That is, the colour line seeks to maintain chromatism in the twenty-first century as part of its racialised embodied orders.

Within these racialised embodied orders, the history of the objectified black body is linked to the history of normative whiteness, for instance, as fear, desire, terror and phantasy (De Vere Brody 1998; Yancy 2008). Blackness calls forth whiteness, and vice versa. However, blackness also calls forth blackness in the recognition of authenticity or exclusion from the black social skin. Indeed, black-Atlantic diaspora politics have shown the possibility for newness to emerge from the 'race' performativity of, for example, Rastafarianism's valorisation of darker skin and natural hair, black power's 'Black is beautiful' and the emergence of Afro-aesthetics in Brazil in the 1970s. This illustrates that the 'black body is a historical project and as such is capable of taking up new historical meanings through struggle and affirmation' (Yancy 2008: xxii). The black 'mixed-race' female body's struggle for affirmation cannot remake the 'race' empire, but we should perhaps look for the small ruptures that signal meaning change in racialised hierarchies. This leads us to question whether black 'mixed-race' naming can unsettle 'race' certainties through 'denaturalising biologistic notions of the "mixed race" body' (Haritaworn 2009: 123), so firmly a part of the 'race' empire's reification of hypodescent.

Can black 'mixed-race' naming and performativity unsettle 'race' certainties?

We have seen that Lola places her 'mixed-race' body as black but that this has been a process of struggle. The struggle for naming is also contained in Mark Christian's (2008) account of the Fletcher Report (1930), which placed Britain as a modern racialised state much before Hazel Carby's (2007) Second World War timeline. This report was researched and written by Muriel Fletcher between 1928 and 1930, supported by the Association for the Welfare of Half-Caste Children and the University of Liverpool. It cemented the derogatory term *half-caste* into the social perception of Liverpool, which, by the end of World War I, had a well-established black community which was viewed as a social problem. It also supported previously held negative stereotypes of black families through a supposedly 'objective' sociological analysis. Christian blames anti-black 'race' riots in June 1919 in Liverpool on class, poverty, racism and the white population's anxiety about sexual relations between black men and white women. The problem of 'half-caste' children in Liverpool took on greater significance after these riots and meant that the 'mixed-race' population was problematised. The report focused on 'mixed-race' children as 'genetically abnormal', repeated eugenicist ideas and established the black man's family as poverty-ridden and immoral, with dysfunctional children because of 'the fusion of different outlooks and cultures' (Christian 2008: 230). Fletcher created a moral panic about trans-racial sexual intimacy in the media of the day and left a lasting legacy in terms of stereotypes of Liverpool's black 'mixed-race' population.

The war prompted racialised responses by the British government to the presence of black civilian and military personnel, because of the interaction of mobilised white British women and mobilised men from the colonies and the problem of 'half-caste children' (Carby 2007).[2] As early as 1942, the British Colonial Office worried about what the future population of Britain would look like in the face of the sexual invasion of black soldiers (Carby 2007). By 1947, 'mixed-race' orphans became 'the

[2] In the first wave, 125,000 volunteers, mostly Jamaican, joined the RAF or worked in munitions factories and in forestry in Scotland. By 1942, there were 3 million American troops, 130,000 of whom were African American. The British government responded with measures to curb the flow of non-white soldiers. From these policies we can see the emergence of Britain as a modern racialised state (Carby 2007).

lonely picaninny' and, as a British subject was constructed in opposition to this abject other (Carby 2007), a clear warning was given on the dangers of trans-racial heterosexual intimacy.

By World War II, the perils of 'mixed race' were removed from the colonies into the bosom of the very nation from which it was to be, and continues today to be, set apart. This setting apart operated through the informal and extra-legal anti-miscegenation regime (Thompson 2009) and continued in the mid-twentieth-century colour bar in public spaces. The colour bar sought to segregate white and black populations and thus minimise the possibility of trans-racial sexual intimacy,[3] primarily between black men and white women. The informal and extra-legal anti-miscegenation regime from the 1930s operated on the basis of a principle of 'biracialization [that] dictates that separate inferior Black and superior White social and symbolic designations determine subjectivities and define specific and exclusive group memberships. Moreover, these interdependent cohorts co-exist in symbolic opposition' (Ifekwunigwe 1999: 13). Therefore, in everyday understandings, 'mixed-race' individuals are often tolerated and/or pitied, as they are seen as marginal because of their blackness or because they are in between racially defined groups (Stoler 1995). In both Carby's and Christian's accounts and the colour bar, we have echoes of Phillips in the twenty-first-century. In 2006, Phillips, the then chair of the Commission for Racial Equality, laid out what was necessary for a Britain of the future: more racial equality, less racial discrimination and the real integration of all Britain's diverse people.[4] He also constructed 'mixed-race' Britons as a problem, because of 'more-than-average' 'mixed-race' family and individual pathology and dysfunction in terms of lone parenthood, family breakdown, drug treatment and

---

[3] The first full-length television documentary programme (on the BBC) to examine the problems faced by black immigrants in Britain was *Special Enquiry: Has Britain a Colour Bar?* (31 January 1955). The programme implied that the primary reason for discrimination and a colour bar was 'cultural' difference rather than racism. Nevertheless, it provoked emotive responses from many white viewers, who felt that it was a defence of black people in its acknowledgement that racial discrimination existed in Britain.

[4] For the first time, more than half of all ethnic-minority Britons are British-born; however, of even greater significance is the astonishing rise in the number of mixed-race Britons – 674,000 in 2001. New projections based on the census suggest that this number will grow to 1.24 million by 2020. By the end of that decade, they are almost certain to overtake those of Indian origin to become the single largest minority group in the country. I welcome this, but, as with all the changes we face, it is not an uncomplicated prospect. The mixed-race Britons are young, and they show the highest employment rate of any minority group. But they also exhibit the highest rates of lone parenthood and family breakdown – in some cases three times the average. They suffer the highest rates of drug treatment. We do not yet know why this should be so, though many people talk now of identity stripping – children who grow up marooned between communities.

'identity-stripping', because they are 'marooned between communities'. Furthermore, Phillips collapsed 'mixed-race' multiplicity into a single minority group based on the shared 'racial' difference of being 'not quite white'.

His words alert us to the (im)possibilities of 'the right to be different' and 'the duty to integrate' which underpin 'racial' tolerance in the United Kingdom and which stick to black 'mixed-race' bodies always already designated as a problem for state governance because of individual pathology and family dysfunction. The state rhetoric of tolerance of 'the right to be different' which underlay New Labour's (1997–2010) approach to managing internal racial colonies is still actively generating a racial nomos into the twenty-first century, in which tolerance silences the operation of racism. This frees 'race', as 'bad black blood', to continue to be constructed as 'breeding' dysfunction, pathology and difference. Such a racial nomos creates affective economies which both govern black 'mixed-race' people and show the limits of a politics of tolerance which continues to use disgust and contempt to shore up the citizenship boundaries of a 'post-multiculturalist' British state. The emergence of the identity category 'black mixed race' asserts 'the right to difference' as a decolonial antidote to the continuing state governance strategy of contemptuous tolerance. Black 'mixed-race' identifications act against informal and extra-legal anti-miscegenation regimes that speak, as in colonial times, of the need for 'proper', 'respectable', white sexuality and family life as a requirement of citizenship.

Black 'mixed-race' identifications continue to be constituted in essentialised ways based on enduring ideas about the immutability of 'race'. Indeed, even when ambiguous, the body must be interpellated through recognisable 'racial' categories so that we can become known. Rhona shows in what follows how the complexities of shade can cause unease for racial dissection if the body refuses to be fixed as either–or but instead occupies the space of both–and:

Growing up in a predominantly white neighbourhood, because I am slightly darker than what everyone assumes to be the average 'mixed-race' person, I was automatically assumed to be black without any white parentage at all. I still am, even in predominantly black neighbourhoods. I still am. There tends to be massive ignorance when it comes to skin shade and ethnicity. Also because of my skin shade and maybe features as well, I am not sure, a lot of Asian people take me to be Asian and begin speaking to me in Hindi or maybe Punjabi. I can't understand so I have to say 'Sorry I am not Asian. I am 'mixed race', I am black'. I think, with 'mixed-race' people, if you are a dark 'mixed-race' person then black people can be ignorant in regard to shade and ethnicity and when you are kind of a brown- or red-skinned person or really light-skinned black 'mixed-race' person, white people can be extremely ignorant in regards to ethnicity.

Rhona shows that it is not just the white gaze that dissects her black 'mixed-race' body in its constant search for origin in 'race' scopophilia. Knowledge of one's origins, one's 'race' and ethnicity, is a feature of a twenty-first-century racial nomos (Gilroy 2004) in which we cannot defy categorisation because the always already known of blackness–whiteness is an essential aspect of our stock of 'racial' knowledge. Rhona's body resists easy categorisation and causes unease to the black social skin, so she is always incited to name herself. Our felt sense of the body's surface, its skin, also has to be read as black 'mixed race' for us to have a contiguous connection between ourselves and the physical body as it is perceived from the outside. Skin is, therefore, a key interface between the self and the other, between the psychic, biological, political and social body and its others (Prosser 1998).

As Rhona illustrates, black 'mixed race' is an identification that must be continually performed bodily, culturally, inter-personally and communally, to come into being. The performativity of black 'mixed race' (Tate 2005) challenges 'race' immutability at the same time as it reifies 'race'. However, the very appellation 'black mixed race' performs 'disalienation' (Césaire 2000; Fanon 1967). That is, it unmakes racialised bodies and remakes them, restoring them to human modes of being in the world through the very juxtaposition of black with 'mixed race', which refuses the primacy of whiteness as an identification category. Black 'mixed race' as identity, thus, undoes compulsory raciality and raciology (Gilroy 2004) by putting 'race' and how it is read on the body itself into question. It undoes the colonial power reinscribed in the British context which puts each racial/ethnic type in its place and questions a racialisation in which black and white must be binaries (Gilroy 2004), without privileging any aspect. Black 'mixed race' as an identification shows us that we need to theorise beyond 'race', even whilst we keep in view the significance of naming and a reading of skin as a necessary, though ambiguous, marker of 'race'. If skin's materiality continues to be significant in racialised identification, recognition and dissection, how can performativity help to theorise 'race' in the twenty-first century?

How can performativity help to theorise 'race' in the twenty-first century?

If we go back to Rhona's extract, we can see that her everyday struggle is to be seen as black 'mixed race' because her 'darker-than-expected' skin shade belies her heritage and creates an-other identity location. Discourses of shade speak of her as black or Asian, and she has to name herself as black 'mixed race' to assert her chosen identity positioning. The dialogism contained in body ambiguity, the differences of identification's address, can lead to mobility within the category 'black'. This would make us question anew the certainties of twenty-first-century blackness and see it as necessitating that performativity come into being. Such ambiguity unsettles the always already known of blackness as fixed, immutable, whilst also reiterating 'race-empire' ideologies in the claim to blackness itself.

For other black 'mixed-race' women, like Shaza, who are light skinned, the process of naming oneself involves bringing blackness to life on the surface of the skin through beauty practices:

SHA: The reason I wear fake tan in summer is because I am very pale...
SH: Mhm...
SHA: ... and I'd like a glow to my skin and unfortunately this British weather...
R: Yeah.
SHA: ... isn't very good and it isn't very hot.
R: Believe.
SHA: So therefore I have to go out and buy fake tan. Now it's better than using a sun-bed which I used to do because, you know, skin cancer...
R: Oh!
SHA: ... and I have a mole on my back; I don't want it to get cancerous. I know quite a few people that are mixed race that wear fake tan. I don't wear it so much on my face because I don't want to get a streaky complexion but I do put it all over my body and if I did have enough money I would go for the spray tan.
R: Would you spray it? Dread you're not romping.
SHA: I'd go for a spray tan. A lot of white girls wear it because they like to be brown and 'mixed-race' people wear it because they like to be just a bit darker. I use J—'s Holiday Skin which is quite expensive. It's almost £10 a bottle, £8 something and I also use N—é, which is a facial and body moisturiser as well as fake tan. However, J—'s does leave quite a funny smell!
SHA: Look how dark my feet are.
R: Yeah I know.
SH: Is that from your fake tan then?
SHA: Yeah.
R: Yeah, look at her face.
SH: Very ni– I know, but Shaza just looks natural I mean...
R: Look at her face.
SHA: It's fake tan.

In the extract, Shaza talks about bringing blackness into view as giving a 'glow to the skin' through fake tan or sun-beds. This 'glow to the skin' is about being darker, erasing light skin and making herself recognisably black through bodywork on the surface of the skin. She claims that other 'mixed-race' people whom she knows also use fake tan. So this making of blackness through bodywork is not the practice of just one woman. Furthermore, she would have a spray tan if she had the money. She contextualises her use of fake tan in the practices of others – white women use it because they want to be brown, and 'mixed-race' women use it because they want to be a bit darker. Notice here she does not equate black 'mixed-race' women's practices with white women's because the desire for 'skin' is different. The skin desire is to be undeniably black. Irrespective of the prohibitive cost of the brands she uses, she would not be without her fake tan. The black beauty model she is aiming for here is 'browning' beauty (Tate 2009). Browning is a black beauty category that emerged in 1980s Jamaica, most possibly through dancehall lyrics (Mohammed 2000). From its modern, black, urban Jamaican heritage, it has spread to the Jamaican diaspora in the black Atlantic (Tate 2009). As a breakaway from the brown phenotype of colonialism and early independence in Jamaica, browning asserts the process of beautification and stylisation as technologies for becoming acceptably black as a possibility for all black women (Tate 2009). Thus, for Shaza, the black beauty category 'browning' can come from a bottle when it is carefully applied. As Shaza shows, approaching skin as a light-skinned black 'mixed-race' woman who wants to be in the browning category means that one also has to fake it but look natural at the same time. Fake tan is used by her to provide a veneer of browning, to erase the traces of her light skin so that she can mimic the browning successfully and become undeniably black in this process.

For Homi Bhabha (1994: 86), mimicry within the colonial context is about a 'desire for a reformed, recognizable Other, *as a subject of a difference that is almost the same, but not quite*'. However, mimicry in the twenty-first-century post-colonial United Kingdom also speaks to other desires, such as the disruption of the cultural, racial and historical sameness of post-colonial discourses which valorise white beauty and indeed recognise it as the iconic ideal. The other disruption, of course, is to a black anti-racist aesthetics, born from black nationalism that sees only dark-skinned, more 'afro-haired', more-'African-featured' natural beauty as black (Tate 2009). The gaze of the browning returns to displace the 'raced' boundary making of these discourses through its dissection of both black and white skin ideals. The mimicry of twenty-first-century browning produces 'race' scopohilia with a difference, as

the representation of identity and meaning is rearticulated along the axis of metonymy. As Lacan reminds us, mimicry is like camouflage, not a harmonization of repression of difference, but a form of resemblance, that differs from or defends presence by displaying it in part, metonymically . . . Under cover of camouflage, mimicry . . . is a part-object that radically revalues the normative knowledges of the priority of race. (Bhabha 1994: 91–92)

In black 'mixed-race' scopophilia, 'race' continues to be reproduced, but with a difference, because it is the black subject who is the object of the gaze. As well as this, black 'mixed-race' scopophilia works here to radically revalue blackness itself.

Based on its black working-class Jamaican heritage, browning is a resemblance that challenges normative whiteness and opens up a becoming-space of blackness. As such, browning's mimicry rearticulates the presence of 'race' in terms of whiteness as its disavowed other, even while it seeks the camouflage of the black same as a becoming-space of black identification. Browning does not harmonise with the background of whiteness; rather, it comes into being as the translations of the black beauty category are made manifest through the bodily practices of 'brownings', like using fake tan to become the right shade of black. The skin desire is to be darker than one is, to wear a beauty camouflage to become a browning, to become black. Fake tanning is another aspect of the mimetic labour of browning in which one is taken into 'the magical power of the signifier [browning] to act as if it were indeed the real, to live in a different way with the understanding that artifice is natural' (Taussig 1993: 255). In this way, mimetic labour imparts the black beauty capital of browning onto the bodies of the young women who use fake tan to reproduce the browning shades of blackness. The colonial priority of 'race', in which white was right, and the only beauty was white – as for Lola as a girl – has now been overturned. However, 'race' performativity does not have the possibility of endless citation because of the (im)possibilities of recognition, racialised skin, psyche and politics that bring it up against the 'race' empire.

Conclusion: the (im)possibilties of 'race' performativity

As Gilroy (2004: 137) says, 'to have mixed is to have been party to a great civilizational betrayal. Any unsettling traces of the resulting hybridity must be excised from the tidy, bleached-out zones of impossibly pure culture.' Furthermore, rather than being post-'race', we are still in the grip of a 'racial nomos – a legal, governmental, and spatial order' (Gilroy 2004: 42) – in which 'mixed race' is still reified as embodiment and genetic inheritance as well as a determinant of one's current life chances and future prospects. The racial nomos denies the connection of identities to history and agency (Brah and Phoenix 2004; Gilroy 2004; Hall 1996a; Tate 2005; Tizard and Phoenix 1993) and erases centuries of conviviality and 'trans-racial' intimacies. Within the United Kingdom's racial epidermal schema, 'black' is infinitely extendable, whereas 'white' stubbornly maintains its boundaries against that which appears to be mixed with that designated black (Zack 1993).

What is significant is the continuation of the 'racial' category 'black' as a prefix to 'mixed race' at the level of identification and politics (Ali 2003; Tate 2005, 2009). In terms of Caribbean-heritage people, this interpellates a skin colour, African/African Caribbean/Indian Caribbean, diasporic connection and anti-racist politics in the forging of an identity that refuses whiteness and essentialist blackness to come into being. However, subjects still continue to reach for the black social skin and its concomitant essentialisms as the basis of their recognition as 'racialising' and 'raced' subjects (Tate 2005). Indeed, to become 'raced', they also have to subject themselves to the anatomical, psychic and affective economies of 'the black community' that judges the (im)possibilities of their admittance through its recognition regimes. For Rey Chow (1999: 35), admittance operates in several senses as

the person who is or is not *admitted bears on him or her the marks of a group in articulation* . . . Admittance . . . is a permission to enter in the abstract, through the act that we call validation. To be permitted to enter is then *to be recognized as having a similar kind of value* as that which is possessed by the admitting community. Third, there is admittance in the sense of a confession . . . Insofar as confession is an act of repentance, *a surrender of oneself in reconciliation with the rules of society*, it is also related to community.

As a performative discourse, 'the black community' and indeed 'the black Atlantic diaspora', which is marked with reference to its otherness from whiteness, does construct 'racial' and cultural difference through marking the inner and the outer in terms of admittance. This performativity still functions even when the collective identity 'black' is contested, and has to be constantly negotiated, and the very notion of 'the black community'/black Atlantic diasporic connectedness is itself questioned. Indeed, within 'the black community', the inner and the outer are marked – as we have seen in the preceding extracts – through recognised embodiment, through one's very skin. It is through recognition within the racial epidermal schema that it is possible to be hailed into position as authentically black. However, black 'mixed race', simultaneously to being hailed, also refuses authenticity, which becomes, instead, a

critical search for a third space that is complicitous neither with the deracinating imperatives of Westernization nor with theories of a static, natural, and single-minded autochthony . . . [It] is an invention with enough room for multiple rootedness . . . There need be no theoretical or epistemological opposition between authenticity and historical contingency, between authenticity and hybridity, between authenticity and invention. (Radhakrishnan 2003: 316)

It is our skin's recognition, and recognition's projection of a connection–disconnection to the social skin of blackness–whiteness and our psyches, that refuses the endless citation of performativity. This refusal is the case even within 'third-space' thinking, as subjection to blackness–whiteness is demanded for our very recognition as 'raced' subjects. Such subjection returns us to the culturally instituted 'race' melancholia (Butler 1997) of the racial nomos, with its racial epidermal schema and regime of hypodescent. In such culturally instituted 'race' melancholia, both *becoming* black and *being* black are framed by hegemonic blackness and whiteness that are still focused on 'blood', 'culture', 'consciousness' and 'purity'. We become black within an anatomical economy based on 'race', and this demands dis-identification to become a subject, if you place yourself in the position of black 'mixed race'. As we dis-identify, we assimilate the loss of the possibility of authentic blackness. This frees us from a melancholia in which the [im]possibility of blackness is a 'nagging return of the thing lost [blackness] into psychic life' (Khanna 2003: 16). Dis-identification with the (im)possibility of 'authentic blackness' means that, rather than profound ambivalence being generated around blackness, it becomes a site of social skin, a home. Such dis-identification enables the dismantling of the 'race empire's' binary of racial authenticity/inauthentic invention and takes us back to Radhakrishnan's (2003) multiple rootedness.

Notwithstanding its contested nature, blackness continues to be a vital aspect of the continuation of anti-racist politics and the psychic, social, intellectual and political connectedness gleaned from a shared structure of feeling in the black Atlantic diaspora. The continuing dynamic construction of a black commonality at once shows the workings of 'race' performativity as it also highlights its limits. The limits are shown as 'race' itself continues to question the possibility of performativity. This is the case because, in the same instance that we call ourselves into being, we are also powerfully hailed into position, interpellated as black through skin, 'consciousness', 'blood', politics and racialised histories.

REFERENCES

Ali, S. (2003). *Mixed-Race, Post-Race: Gender, New Ethnicities and Cultural Practices*. Oxford: Berg.
Anzieu, D. (1990). *A Skin for Thought: Interviews with Gilbert Tarrab on Psychology and Psychoanalysis*. London: Karnac Books.
Banks, I. (2000). *Hair Matters: Beauty, Power and Black Women's Consciousness*. New York: New York University Press.
Bhabha, H. (1994). Of mimicry and man: the ambivalence of colonial discourse. In H. Bhabha, ed., *The Location of Culture*. London: Routledge, pp. 85–92.
Brah, A. and Phoenix, A. (2004). Ain't I a woman? Revisiting intersectionality. *Journal of International Women's Studies*, 5(3), 75–86.

Butler, J. (1990). *Gender Trouble: Feminism and the Subversion of Identity.* London: Routledge.

(1993). *Bodies That Matter: On the Discursive Limits of Sex.* London: Routledge.

(1997). *The Psychic Life of Power: Theories in Subjection.* Stanford, CA: Stanford University Press.

(2005). *Giving an Account of Oneself.* New York: Fordham University Press.

Candelario, G. (2007). *Black behind the Ears: Dominican Racial Identity from Museums to Beauty Shops.* Durham, NC: Duke University Press.

Carby, H. (2007). Postcolonial translations. *Ethnic and Racial Studies*, 30(2), 213–34.

Césaire, A. (2000). *Discourse on Colonialism.* Trans. J. Pinkham. New York: Monthly Review Press.

Chow, R. (1999). The politics of admittance: female sexual agency, miscegenation and the formation of community in Frantz Fanon. In A. Alessandrini, ed., *Frantz Fanon: Critical Perspectives.* London: Routledge, pp. 34–56.

Christian, M. (2008). The Fletcher Report 1930: a historical case study of contested black mixed heritage Britishness. *Journal of Historical Sociology*, 21(2/3), 213–41.

De Vere Brody, J. (1998). *Impossible Purities: Blackness, Femininity and Victorian Culture.* Durham, NC: Duke University Press.

Fanon, F. (1967). *Black Skin, White Masks.* London: Pluto Press.

Garvey, M. (2004). *Selected Writings and Speeches of Marcus Garvey.* New York: Dover.

Gilroy, P. (1993). *The Black Atlantic: Modernity and Double Consciousness.* London: Verso.

(2004). *After Empire: Melancholia or Convivial Culture?* London: Routledge.

Hall, S. (1996a). Introduction: who needs identity? In S. Hall and P. duGay, eds, *Questions of Cultural Identity.* London: Sage, pp. 1–18.

(1996b). What is this 'black' in black popular culture? In D. Morley and K. Chen, eds, *Stuart Hall: Critical Dialogues in Cultural Studies.* London: Routledge, pp. 468–76.

Hardt, M. and Negri, A. (2001). *Empire.* Cambridge, MA: Harvard University Press.

Haritaworn, J. (2009). Hybrid border-crossers? Towards a radical socialisation of 'mixed race'. *Journal of Ethnic and Migration Studies*, 35(1), 115–32.

Ifekwunigwe, J. (1999). *Scattered Belongings: Cultural Paradoxes of 'Race', Nation and Gender.* London: Routledge.

Khanna, R. (2003). *Dark Continents: Psychoanalysis and Colonialism.* London: Duke University Press.

Mohammed, P. (2000). 'But most of all mi love me browning': the emergence in eighteenth and nineteenth century Jamaica of the mulatto woman as desired. *Feminist Review*, 65(1), 22–48.

Pinho, P. (2010). *Mama Africa: Reinventing Blackness in Bahia.* Durham, NC: Duke University Press.

Prosser, J. (1998). *Second Skins: The Body Narratives of Transsexuality.* New York: Columbia University Press.

Radhakrishnan, R. (2003). Postcoloniality and the borders of identity. In L. Martín Alcoff and E. Mendieta, eds, *Identities: Race, Class, Gender and Nationality*. Oxford: Blackwell, pp. 312–29.

Stephens, M. A. (2005). *Black Empire: The Masculine Global Imaginary of Caribbean Intellectuals in the United States, 1914–1962*. Durham, NC: Duke University Press.

Stoler, A. L. (1995). *Race and the Education of Desire: Foucault's History of Sexuality and the Colonial Order of Things*. London: Duke University Press.

Tate, S. (2005). *Black Skins, Black Masks: Hybridity, Dialogism, Performativity*. Aldershot, UK: Ashgate.

(2009). *Black Beauty: Aesthetics, Stylization, Politics*. Aldershot, UK: Ashgate.

Taussig, M. (1993). *Mimesis and Alterity: A Particular History of the Senses*. London: Routledge.

Thompson, D. (2009). Racial ideas and gendered intimacies: the regulation of interracial relationships in North America. *Social and Legal Studies*, 18(3), 353–71.

Tizard, B. and Phoenix, A. (1993). *Black, White or Mixed Race? Race and Racism in the Lives of Young People of Mixed Parentage*. London: Routledge.

Wright, M. (2004). *Becoming Black: Creating Identity in the African Diaspora*. Durham, NC: Duke University Press.

Yancy, G. (2008). *Black Bodies, White Gazes: The Continuing Significance of Race*. Plymouth, UK: Rowman and Littlefield.

Zack, N. (1993). *Race and Mixed Race*. Philadelphia: Temple University Press.

11 Racism: psychoanalytic and psychosocial approaches

Simon Clarke

In this chapter, I want to explore the relationship between the inner world of the psyche, the construction of ethnicity and cultural identity and the way this relationship plays out in racist attitudes and beliefs. In particular, I want to highlight how psychoanalysis adds to our understanding of racism beyond that of traditional sociological explanations giving a different (not better) understanding of the psychosocial dynamics of ethnic hatred. I do this by charting some of the history of psychoanalytic theories of racism before offering some contemporary ideas.

I feel that it is difficult to separate the complex amalgam of dynamics involved in racisms, ideas of Othering, fear and loathing of others, identity construction in relation to who we are not and the often exclusionary practices of community building, all interacting to form emotive and irrational ideas about others. The highly charged emotional dynamics, affective reasoning and bouts of seemingly irrational hatred all work together to fuel some of the virulent racisms, but, conversely, we have racisms that act in subtle and stealthy ways, often gnawing at individuals and groups – for example, institutional racisms. Psychoanalysis as a discipline deals directly with the emotional affective forces, using conceptual tools such as projection and projective identification to identify emotional and largely unconscious communications, and, as such, is well placed to build on, and add to, our understanding of racism. We all know that there is a social construction of our realities as much as we know that we are emotional people who construct our 'selves' in imagination and affect. Neither sociology nor psychoanalysis, nor psychology for that matter, provides a better explanation of the world than the other, but together they provide a deeper *understanding* of the social world.

I have previously argued (Clarke 2003) that, if we are to understand racism, then a perspective approach is wanting in explanation. Sociological explanations of racism concentrate on the structures of modern life that facilitate discriminatory practices and hierarchies of inequality and have been very good at pointing to and identifying them (see Back 1996; Back and Solomos 2000; Banton 1997; Gilroy 1997; Mirza 1992).

The problem remains, though, that sociology fails to address some of the central issues surrounding racism: first, the ubiquity of forms of discrimination and the emotional component of hatred; second, the sheer rapidity, the explosive, almost eruptive quality of ethnic hatred and the way in which communities which used to coexist together, as in the former Yugoslavia, Rwanda and Sierra Leone, come to hate and destroy each other; third, sociology fails to address the visceral and embodied nature of racism and the content of discrimination; and finally, the psychological structuring of discrimination is ignored in this emphasis on social structure, therefore we are unable to look at the psychological mechanisms that provide the impetus for people to hate each other. In other words, sociologists are very good at explaining *how* discrimination arises but not *why* affect – emotion – is left in the sociological cupboard. I believe that there is a complex inter-relationship between sociostructural and psychological factors. Both need to be addressed in parallel if we are to *understand* the ubiquity and visceral elements of racism.

It is to this end that I have developed a psychosocial approach in my work (Clarke 2003, 2006; Clarke and Hoggett 2009; Clarke and Garner 2010). To put it quite simply, a psychosocial approach looks at both the structural and the emotional dynamics of social life and the mediation between our inner and outer lives, and this affects both society and the individual. I have argued (Clarke et al. 2008) that there is something quite distinct about a psychosocial approach toward social research – it is more an attitude, or a position toward the subject(s) of study, than just another methodology. Since the 1990s, partly because of the impact of feminism, the social sciences have been changing. Traditional models of human rationality which opposed reason to passion are being challenged. The preoccupation with language and cognition has started to give way to an equal interest in emotion and affect. The familiar split between 'individual' and 'society', psychology and sociology, is now recognised as unhelpful to the study of both. And as ways have been sought to overcome such splits, psychoanalysis has increasingly appeared in the breach. Drawing also on some aspects of discourse psychology, continental philosophy and anthropological and neuroscientific understandings of the emotions, 'psychosocial studies' has emerged as an embryonic new paradigm in the human sciences in the United Kingdom.

Psychosocial research can be seen as a cluster of methodologies which point toward a distinct position, that of researching beneath the surface and beyond the purely discursive – in other words, to consider the unconscious communications, dynamics and defences which exist in the research environment. This may entail the analysis of group dynamics, observation and the co-construction of the research environment by researcher and researched – we are all participants in the process. From this we derive the idea of the reflexive researcher, where we are engaged in sustained self-reflection on our methods and practice, on our emotional involvement in the research and on the affective relationship between ourselves and the researched (for a full history of this emergent paradigm, see Clarke and Hoggett 2009).

Thus I start this chapter by examining the Freudian theory of the Frankfurt School, and the way in which it is used to analyse anti-Semitic behaviours, before going on to look at the seminal work of Frantz Fanon (1967) and his Freudo-Lacanian analysis of the colonial condition and black identity construction. I conclude by offering a contemporary Kleinian reading of these works and introduce the idea of projective identification as a powerful conceptual tool for the understanding of the psychodynamics of racism. I also proffer the idea that the much talked about concept of community cohesion is often a catalyst, in an emotional sense, for exclusionary practices in relation to identity construction.

Freudian theory: projection and ethnic hatred

Horkheimer and Adorno's (1994) *Dialectic of Enlightenment* is the first useful text in the examination of racism and Othering that uses a psychoanalytic schema – in particular, the chapter titled 'Elements of Anti-Semitism'. Horkheimer and Adorno inter-weave Freudian drive theory with Marxism and the Weberian notion of rationalisation to explain the pathological nature of anti-Semitism. After Freud (1969), Horkheimer and Adorno argue that civilisation – the modern world – has slowly and methodically prohibited instinctual behaviour. Horkheimer and Adorno concentrate on the instinctual mechanism of mimesis, the way in which we mimic nature to survive – for example, freezing when we sense danger. This, they argue, has become perverted in modern times. In the modern world, mimesis has been consigned to oblivion. For Horkheimer and Adorno, those blinded by civilisation experience their own repressed and tabooed mimetic characteristics in others. Gestures, nuances, touching and feeling are experienced as embarrassing remnants from our prehistory that have survived in the rationalised environment of the modern world. Horkheimer and Adorno draw our attention to Freud's ([1919] 1961) paper 'The Uncanny' ('Das Unheimlich') – 'What seems repellently alien is in fact all too familiar.' We start to see what Horkheimer and Adorno (1994) suggest when they talk about mimesis and false projection, as Freud argues that the uncanny fulfils the condition of 'touching' the residues of our animistic mental activity and bringing them to expression. The notion of the 'uncanny' is a useful metaphor which

I have myself used to explore the colonial condition, in particular the relationship between white settlers and indigenous peoples (see Clarke and Moran 2003).

Anti-Semitism is based on what Horkheimer and Adorno (1994) describe as false projection, which is related to a repressed form of mimesis. In mimesis proper, we see an imitation of the natural environment – a mechanism of defence which enables camouflage and protection; we make ourselves like nature that we may become one with nature. False projection, conversely, tries to make the environment like us – we try to control and rationalise nature, projecting our own experiences and categories onto natural things and making that which is not natural natural, through a reification of scientific categories and constructions. Inner and outer worlds are confused and perceived as hostile. Central to this argument is projection. The product of false projection is the stereotype, the transference of socially unpalatable thoughts from subject to object. Projection is a pivotal idea in psychosocial research, where we can determine that one person disowns his or her own emotion or feeling – of disgust or hatred – and perceives it as belonging to some other: 'It's not me, it's him!'

Moving on to an account of colonial othering, in *Black Skin, White Masks*, Fanon (1967) argues that the black person is both objectified and denigrated at a bodily level and psychologically blinded or alienated from his or her black consciousness and cultural identity by the effects of colonialisation and racist culture. In *Social Theory, Psychoanalysis and Racism* (Clarke 2003), I have argued that this is the premise of much of Fanon's writing and argumentation. The black person becomes a phobogenic object – in other words, a stimulus that causes anxiety. In a psychoanalytic interpretation of phobias, Fanon notes that there is a secret attraction to the object that arouses dread in the individual. Fanon argues that it matters little whether this image of the black man is real; the point is that it is cognate. In the same way that the Jew was perceived as a danger through the projection of a stereotype, the black person has suffered the same form of projection with an emphasis placed on sexual phenomena. To understand racism from a psychoanalytic perspective, argues Fanon, we have to concentrate on sexual phenomena. As Bulhan (1985) notes, there are strong reminders of Freud's (1969) *Civilization and Its Discontents* throughout *Black Skin, White Masks* and, more generally, Freud's notion of 'sublimated instinctual energies that must find socially acceptable means of expression' (Bulhan 1985: 70). Thus, revered for his or her sexual powers and potency in popular mythology, the black person becomes a phallus symbol: 'When a white man hates black men, is he not yielding to a feeling of Impotence or of sexual inferiority? Since his ideal is an infinite virility, is there not a phenomenon of diminution in relation to the Negro, who is viewed as a penis symbol?' (Fanon 1967: 159).

Fanon argues that the white person has a secret desire to return to an era of 'unrestricted sexual licence' and 'orgiastic' scenes of rape and unrepressed incest: everything he sees, creates and projects in the image of the black person. This is reminiscent of Max Horkheimer and Theodor Adorno's (1994) thesis in *Dialectic of Enlightenment*. The fascist longs to return to a presocial state of nature, seeing in the Jew what he really *feels* in his 'self'. For Fanon, the white person projects desire on the black person, the white person behaves as if the black person were the owner of these desires: 'What appears repellently alien, is in fact, all too familiar' (Horkheimer and Adorno 1994: 182). The Jew is associated with wealth and power; the black person has been fixated at a bodily, biological, genital plane.

The main reference to psychoanalysis in Fanon's work appears in an extended footnote, where he discusses the work of Jacques Lacan (1977a, 1977b). Fanon suggests that it would be interesting to investigate how the image of the white person develops with the appearance of the 'negro', with reference to Lacan's idea(l) of the mirror stage. Lacan (1977a, 1977b) argues that the infant, at between 6 and 18 months, becomes aware of its own body as a totality, by seeing in the mirror its own image. Thus, for Lacan, 'we only have to understand the mirror stage *as an identification,* in the full sense that analysis gives to the term: namely the transformation that takes place in the subject when he assumes an image' (Lacan 1977b: 2). The child sees its own image in a mirror; at first, it will try to grasp this image as if it were real. There is then some recognition of similarity in this image, proceeded by a realisation that the image is indeed the child's own. The child at this age is unable to fully coordinate its movements and has to be held in front of the mirror by some 'other'. The child is able to look in the mirror and say, 'That is me,' whilst turning to the parent and perceiving a sense of separation, a sense of identity. This process, Lacan argues, is a drama. The individual moves from a state of insufficiency to one of anticipation – that is, anticipation of the individual's image as an adult. It is a metamorphosis from a fragmented body image to a totality that Lacan describes as orthopaedic – orthopaedic in the sense that the mirror stage adds a 'prop' that enables the child to metaphorically stand up straight in the identity of a subject. This, however, for Lacan, is 'the armour of alienating identity, which will mark with its rigid structure the subject's entire mental apparatus' (Lacan 1977b: 4). The subject is therefore alienated by the rigid structure of the mirror. image, imprisoned by its own identity. There is no doubt that the image we see in a mirror is never real – it is always the reversal of a projected image of the self. Bowie (1991: 26), after Lacan, describes the mirror image as a *mirage of* 'I':

The child, itself so recently born, gives birth to a monster: a statue, an automaton, a fabricated thing . . . From spare parts, an armoured mechanical creature is being produced within the human subject, and developing unwholesome habits and destructive appetites of its own.

Lacan is suggesting that what the child creates is an *identification* rather than an *identity*, a fiction, an imaginary projection, the *ideal-I*. As Sarup (1992) indicates, this gestalt is more stable than the child, giving an illusion of control. Crucially, self-identification represents a permanent tendency in the individual to seek and foster this 'imaginary wholeness of an ideal ego' (Sarup 1992: 65). In other words, the ego has only an illusion (or delusion) of strength, which has to be constantly reinforced throughout life. It could be suggested that, if this sense of self can only be validated in the realm of reality by the presence of some 'other', in the first instance, then this must continue throughout the subject's existence, as the ego is constantly reinforced. Can this be what Fanon meant when he makes reference to the formation of the image in the mirror stage? Can it be that the 'other' for the racist will always be the black person, as Fanon intimates? If we return to Lacan's theory, the 'other' warrants the existence of the child, marking a separation and difference in which subjectivity is based. In other words, the self is defined in relation to some other, and other is not what 'I' am. The 'other' is idealised in the mirror on the level of a body image. The image of the black person, as we have seen, is threatening, based in myths of sexual prowess and potency. Aggression is directed at the 'other' in two forms: first, aggression which separates and defines who 'I' am, or perhaps more importantly, who 'I' am not; second, who 'I' would like to be: powerful, sexual, potent. Desire, for Lacan, is always desire for the 'other'. Instinctually, 'I' desire what the 'other' is, but 'I' cannot have it, so 'I' will destroy it. The mirror stage, for Fanon, has a double edge. The black person, he argues, perceives in terms of 'whiteness'. The 'I' is constructed with reference to 'white', and 'black' is both 'other' and 'I'. In this sense, the black person is doubly disadvantaged. He or she is both persecuted as 'other' and, in the same instance, oppressed by making his or her 'I' a white mask – black is white is black.

In the next section of this chapter, I want to suggest how we may start thinking about Fanon's work psychoanalytically from a Kleinian perspective. This is because I feel that, despite the insights that a Lacanian perspective can and does give to Fanon's writings, there are some basic theoretical and epistemological problems which need to be highlighted.

Fanon's treatment of Lacan is interesting, but it is still subject to some of the huge theoretical and conceptual problems present in Lacan's ideas.

First, Anthony Elliott (1994) draws our attention to Lacan's failure to specify the processes which enable the individual to misrecognise his or her self in the mirror stage. Surely the individual must have some sense of self and some capacity for emotional response to be able to respond in this way to the mirror? Similarly, Ferrell (1996) concludes that the mind must be active in its interpretations of the mirror image. Again, there must therefore already be some sense of self. Second, as Bowie (1991) has noted, Lacan's use of language and frequent puns leaves the reader in a state where much has to be speculated about, or inferred, as the language becomes more impenetrable. Third, as Francois Roustang (1990) has noted, Lacan is prone to splitting and setting up irreconcilable dichotomies.

The final, and perhaps most troubling, aspect of Lacan's work is articulated by Elliott (1994), who focuses on an epistemological dilemma with specific implications for freedom and anti-racism. If the self is illusory, a trick, something imaginary and alienating, then any political project aimed at emancipation and freedom would be caught in the same illusory trap.

This Lacanian perspective is taken up in the work of Slavoj Žižek's (1993) analysis of the collapse of the former Yugoslavia and the way in which ethnic identities are very much tied in with difference and projections of phantasy. Žižek introduces us to the idea of the *theft of enjoyment*. Žižek argues that the bond which holds a given community together is a shared relationship to a Thing – 'to our enjoyment incarnate'. The relationship we have to our Thing is structured by phantasy and is what people talk of when they refer to a threat to 'our' way of life. This nation's Thing is not a clear set of values from which we can refer but a set of contradictory properties that appears as 'our' Thing. This Thing is only accessible to us but is tirelessly sought after by the other. Žižek argues that others cannot grasp it, but it is constantly menaced by 'them'. So, this Thing is present, or is in some way to do with what we refer to as our 'way of life', the way in which we organise our rituals, ceremonies, feasts – 'in short, all the details by which is made visible the unique way a community *organises its enjoyment*' (201). Žižek cautions, however, that this Thing is more than simply a set of features which compose a way of life; there is something present in them, people *believe* in them or, more importantly, 'I believe that other members of the community believe in this Thing.' The Thing exists because people believe in it; it is an effect of belief itself:

We always impute to the 'other' an excessive enjoyment: he wants to steal our enjoyment (by ruining our way of life) and/or he has access to some secret, perverse enjoyment. In short, what really bothers us about the 'other' is the peculiar way he organises his enjoyment, precisely the surplus, the 'excess' that pertains to this way: the smell of 'their' food, 'their' noisy songs and dances, 'their' strange manners, 'their' attitude to work. (Žižek 1993: 203)

Thus, Žižek notes the paradoxical nature of this Thing; on one hand, the other is a workaholic who steals our jobs and labour; on the other, he or she is an idler, a lazy person relying on the state for benefits. Our Thing is therefore something that cannot be accessed by the other but is constantly threatened by 'otherness'. What Žižek's work highlights is the role of myth and phantasy in the construction of cultural and national identity and, more importantly, the way in which this identity is imagined rather than grounded in some reality. As Žižek notes, what we cover up by accusing the other of the theft of our enjoyment is the 'traumatic fact' that we never possessed what we perceive has been stolen in the first place. It is a fear of the theft of enjoyment, a fear of the theft of imagination, of phantasy, of myth.

What I think we can take from the work of both Fanon and Žižek is that identities are both socially and psychosocially constructed. They are filled with passion and emotion and are multiple. As we construct the identity of others, others construct our identity. Imagination and passion are integral parts of our perception of self and others but can also be destructive and alienating (see Lane 1998 for an extended discussion of Lacanian perspectives on racism).

Kleinian theory: splitting and projective identification

Kleinian psychoanalytic theory provides a powerful basis for our understanding of the ubiquitous and visceral elements of racism and discrimination. Concepts such as splitting, phantasy and projective identification help us to understand the unconscious dynamics at work in the construction of black and ethnic identity and the psychodynamics of racism. Projective identification is, for Klein (1997a), a crucial mechanism of defence. Whereas projection per se is a relatively straightforward process in which we attribute feelings and parts of the self to some other, projective identification involves a deep split, a ridding of unpalatable parts of the self *into* rather than *onto* some other. Klein (1997a: 8) explains:

Split off parts of the ego are also projected on to the mother or, as I would rather call it, *into* the mother . . . Much of the hatred against parts of the self is now directed towards the mother. This leads to a particular form of identification which establishes the prototype of an aggressive object-relation. I suggest for these processes the term projective identification.

It is important to note that the concept of projective identification becomes more complex as it is unravelled and sits in relation to the paranoid-schizoid and depressive positions. Put simply, in the paranoid-schizoid position, we tend to split the world into dichotomies, good and bad, and project the bad out into others. In the depressive position, splitting lessens, and we tend to see both good and bad in others. The depressive position is as good as it gets, but in times of high anxiety, we may return to paranoid-schizoid functioning. It is not just bad parts of the self which are split off and projected into others but also loving parts of the self. The point, for Klein, is that a balance can be struck between the expulsion of good and of bad, which is essential for the development of 'healthy' object relations. It is when this balance becomes one-sided that things start to go wrong. The introjection and reintrojection of the bad object is at the very heart, for Klein, of paranoia. Forcibly entering an object in phantasy stimulates anxieties which threaten the subject; the fear of being controlled and persecuted inside it leads to the fear of being imprisoned in another body (or culture), or the fear of the object (or another culture) forcing its way inside the self. The implication of this is that, by using projective identification to expel our 'bad bits' into others, we live in fear of being consumed *by* others, thus perpetuating the cycle of persecution.

Robert Young (1994) has suggested that projective identification is the most fruitful psychoanalytic concept since the discovery of the unconscious. I have argued that projective identification involves the forcing of a feeling or emotion into some other. Bott-Spillius (1988) takes a wide approach, arguing that projective identification is used and directed at both internal and external objects. Hanna Segal (1964: 14) defines projective identification in terms of projection into an external object: 'Parts of the self and internal objects are split off and projected into the external object.' Julia Segal (1992) uses the term to describe a mechanism which is designed to evoke a response in others. Bion (1962) develops Klein's ideas, introducing the concept of 'container' and 'contained'. Indeed, for Bion, projective identification is crucial and central in the thinking process. Ogden (1986) argues for a communicative account of projective identification which is designed to elicit a response, either consciously or unconsciously, from the recipient, a manipulative form of the mechanism in which unwanted feelings are dumped on others by inducing the experience in some other. Robert Hinshelwood (1989, 1994) positions all these interpretations on a continuum from a violent prototype of the aggressive relationship to empathy:

> If projective identification varies from expulsion to communication, then at the very furthest point on the benign end of the scale is a form of projective identification underlying empathy, or 'putting oneself in another's shoes' . . . In this case the violence of the primitive forms has been so attenuated that it has been brought under the control of the impulses of love and concern. (Hinshelwood 1994: 133)

Hinshelwood quite rightly highlights the parallel between this continuum and the movement between paranoid-schizoid and depressive positions. A number of forms of projective identification can be used or employed which are closely related to the notions of positions and phantasy. Phantasy is deeply unconscious at one level but is also an integral part of perception. Projective identification is the vehicle or tool which enables phantasy to become reality by projecting our perception and emotion into others. Klein, herself, uses the term *projective identification* in several ways as her work evolves, but in 'Some Theoretical Conclusions Regarding the Emotional Life of the Infant' (Klein 1997b), she is clear that projective identification plays a vital role in the interaction between internal and external worlds.

I have differentiated between projection and projective identification and discussed several forms of this mechanism. These interpretations range from the prototype of a violent aggressive relationship to empathy. I have argued that the most important aspect of projective identification is the nature of the projection, in that it involves putting *into* rather than *onto* the recipient. The implication of this is clear: the projection has some affect on the object. It would be unwise to view projective identification as any less than a combination of the ideas that I have discussed. Different forms of projective identification are used in differing psychological situations, and this is relational to the paranoid-schizoid and depressive positions implicit in Klein's work. The concept of projective identification is crucial in a psychoanalytic understanding of racism and ethnic relations. It shows us how feelings and ideas are forced into others to make them feel inferior, different and excluded. If we return to the work of Fanon, we can see these processes at work.

A major feature of Fanon's understanding of the psychology of oppression is that inferiority is the outcome of a double process, both socio-historic and psychological: 'If there is an inferiority complex, it is the outcome of a double process: primarily economic; subsequently, the internalisation, or better, the epidermalization of this inferiority' (Fanon 1967: 13). There is a link between the sociogenesis and psychogenesis of racism, and these processes are violent and exclusionary. Fanon illustrates this internalisation of projection: 'My body was given back to me sprawled out, distorted, recoloured, clad in mourning in that white winterday. The negro is an animal, the negro is bad, the negro is ugly' (113). If we understand the reference to the breaking up of bodies, to being sprawled out and distorted, in terms of more than mere metaphor but as felt feeling, then, from a Kleinian perspective, these processes – which have consequences on the sociogenic level – are the outcome of processes of projective identification. The white person makes the black person in the image of the white person's projections, literally forcing identity into another, as Fanon notes: 'The white man has woven me out of a thousand details . . . I was battered down with tom-toms, cannibalism, intellectual deficiency, fetishism, racial defects, slave ships' (112).

The black person lives these projections, trapped in an imaginary that white people have constructed – trapped both by economic processes and by powerful projective mechanisms which both create and control the other. This highlights the paradoxical nature of projective identification. White people's phantasies about black sexuality, about bodies and biology, are fears that centre on otherness – otherness that they themselves have created and brought into being. This is what Fanon means when he says that he was 'battered down', 'woven out of a thousand details': identity is a stereotype of the black person constructed in the mind of the white person and then forced back into the black person as the black historical subject – a false consciousness (see Dalal 2002; Macey 2000).

This kind of analysis focuses on the virulent and violent, perhaps more aptly called 'visible', face of racism, but projective identification is useful in the analysis of more subtle, but no less dangerous, forms of racism. This is typically the case with, for example, institutional racism, where projective identification is often subtle, a gentle nudge – almost covert – but, nevertheless, the recipient is made to feel uncomfortable, anxious and different. These forms of projective identification induce in the recipient a feeling of not belonging to an institution and ultimately a sense of exclusion. In a study of the experience of black and Asian students in higher education (see Clarke 2000), I argued that there is evidence of subtle forms of projective identification in which ethnic-minority students are made to feel, by their white peers, that they do not belong in the institution. There is a complex interaction between the projection of individual anxiety at one level and the macro-social environment of the institution as a promoter of projective identification at another. This is reinforced by stereotypical constructions of 'black' and 'difference' which induce in the student a feeling of not belonging. If we are to address institutional racism, then we need to understand the subtle processes and emotional mechanisms which underpin this form of social exclusion.

More recently, Clarke and Garner (2010), in a major research project that investigated the construction of 'white' identities and ethnicity in relation to home and community, found that a person's perception of his or her own 'self' and the selves of others was based largely in phantasy. This was particularly the case for other groups who people knew very little about, and these groups were often the object of projections that emanated from fear and anxiety about access to housing, welfare and community or ideas (ideals?) about community. There has, of course, been a major change in perception about immigrants. Those who come to this country and 'steal' our jobs, our houses and our benefits no longer fit the traditional stereotype – rather, they are largely white, and of course, the focus has changed to that of asylum and asylum seeking. Legitimate forms of cross-European economic migration are seen as an illegitimate threat. There is now a new politics of fear.

The sociopolitics of fear has added a new psychodynamic dimension to asylum. The asylum seeker represents not only our own fears of chaos and displacement but also the possibility of being destroyed from within by both our own phantasies of terror and the terrorist in our midst. The terrorist in our midst is now a concrete reality, and it is even more important that ideas of asylum and anti-immigration not be conflated and confused with terrorism. The asylum seeker represents all our own fears of displacement, of potential chaos and of living with ambiguity in the modern world. The asylum seeker is the contemporary version of this. The Jew, the gypsy, the migrant and so on can also serve this purpose, but the actual contemporary of it focuses on specific circumstances such as the decline of the welfare state, 'mass migration on the march' and increased awareness of these things as global phenomena. The press and politicians tap into our inner world of anxiety and imagination, placing a stress on difference which is irreconcilable and incompatible with 'our' ways of life, which threaten our ethnicity, our whiteness. In some sense, it is a more sophisticated version of Barker's (1981) *New Racism* thesis, in which ideas about cultural difference, identity and attachments to 'our way of life' come to the fore. We start to see yet another spiral of racism, ethnocentrism and Islamophobia, but this is not coming from right-wing individuals but from the centre, as anti-immigration policy becomes mainstreamed. Projective identifications and phantasy abound.

The nature of belonging, identity, community and ethnicity is a complex amalgam of socioeconomic factors and deeply psychological, often unconscious, ideas about the other. When asked how people feel they create and maintain their identities and how this relates to community, many of the ideas were based in what we might call 'tradition' and an emotional attachment to certain ways of life, whether real or imagined, to intimate relations rather than instrumental ones. In our research, we found that there was very little talk of what we might term fluid post-modern consuming selves, narratives in which the individual is sovereign and the community is of little importance. Rather, there is an empha-sis on the family, class and geographical locations which were, in turn, linked to ideas about outsiders and defining your 'self' by who you are not. Interestingly there was a strong emphasis on the notion of a shared identity that linked in with the notion of community. There is also a deeply psychosocial element where people often create their perceptions of others in their own imagination, which helps them to create who *they* are. This was exemplified in the emotional dynamics involved in notions of contempt, acceptance and tribalism between geographical areas and groups of people. Identity or identities in contemporary Britain are cer-tainly complex and often contradictory. Community is often expressed as a feeling or as something concrete like a building. When you look at the notion of identity and community together, then there is a very strong sense of boundary, both physically and psychologically (Clarke and Garner 2010). We have ideas of belonging and not belonging, a sense of who we are in relation to others, of in-groups and out-groups and of shared values and ideas. Finally, there is also the notion of familiarity and a certain yearning to return to more traditional forms of community, albeit forms of community that are often imaginary and unreal. This raises questions about the notion of community cohesion (Department for Communities and Local Government 2007; Joseph Rowntree Foun-dation 2008), as I believe one of the paradoxes of community is that at the very heart of the concept is a circle of exclusion and inclusivity that enables one ethnicity to define itself at the expense of others.

Some thoughts and conclusions

In this chapter, I have tried to show how both psychoanalytic and psy-chosocial ideas are different to traditional explanations but add to our understanding of racism and othering. At the very heart of psychoanal-ysis is the notion of the unconscious. This is a key area in which this tradition differs, for example, from sociology. This is a hugely contested notion and is predicated on the belief that there is an unconscious mind. The theory I have presented started with basic Freudian models and then moved to a more complex Kleinian approach, in which we have seen how key conceptual tools, such as projective identification, can help us to understand the psychodynamics of racism, colonialisation and othering – in other words, how people are made to feel the way they do, whether through a process of psychological or of economic oppression. I feel that both go hand in hand, which is why sociology is so important in psychoanalytic analysis.

I firmly believe that, if we are to continue to address questions of racism, discrimination and hatred of the other, then we need to look at the huge emotional dynamics that are at work in society. Racism is often driven by the most irrational, emotive experiences of people, often simply in their imagination; a psychosocial approach is the only discipline that looks at both in tandem. In my more recent work (Clarke et al. 2007; Clarke and Hoggett 2009; Clarke and Garner 2010), I have tried to acknowledge some of the problematics with psychoanalytic thought and to address them. For example, the language and theory of psychoanalysis are hugely complex and confusing. Another paradox, in some sense, is that we are all used to talking about our, or other people's, egos, and there is, of course, the classic phrase 'Don't project your inadequacies on me.' I now tend to use phrases such as 'imagination' rather than 'phantasy', or at least I try to make readers aware of the link. I am starting to develop the idea of what I term an 'emotional community', something that binds together the bricks and mortar of the group, something that operates at both unconscious and conscious levels and is responsible for solidarity and hostility, cohesion and disintegration. Finally, I would like to stress, perhaps after Fanon, that there is both a sociostructural and a psychological dynamic within race and ethnic relations; both need to be addressed together if we are to understand more about this issue in the coming years.

REFERENCES

Back, L. (1996). *New Ethnicities and Urban Culture: Racisms and Multiculturism among Young Lives*. London: UCL Press.

Back, L. and Solomos, J. (2000). *Theories of Race and Racism*. London: Routledge.

Banton, M. (1997). *Ethnic and Racial Consciousness*, 2nd ed. London: Longman.

Barker, M. (1981). *New Racism: Conservatives and the Ideology of the Tribe*. Toronto: Junction Books.

Bion, W. R. (1962). *Learning from Experience*. London: Karnac Books.

Bott-Spillius, E. (1988). *Melanie Klein Today: Developments in Theory and Practice: Vol. 1. Mainly Theory*. London: Routledge.

Bowie, M. (1991). *Lacan*. London: Fontana.

Bulhan, H. (1985). *Frantz Fanon and the Psychology of Oppression*. London: Plenum Press.

Clarke, S. (2000). Experiencing racism in higher education. *Journal of Socio-Analysis*, 2(1), 47–63.

(2003). *Social Theory, Psychoanalysis and Racism*. London: Palgrave.

(2006). Theory and practice: psychoanalytic sociology as psycho-social studies. *Sociology*, 40(6), 1153–69.

Clarke, S. and Garner, S. (2010). *White Identities: A Critical Sociological Approach*. London: Pluto.

Clarke, S. and Hoggett, P. (2009). *Researching beneath the Surface*. London: Karnac Books.

Clarke, S. and Moran, A. (2003). The uncanny stranger: haunting the Australian settler imagination. *Free Associations*, 10(1), 165–89.

Clarke, S., Garner, S. and Gilmour, R. (2007). Home, identity and community cohesion. In M. Wetherell, M. Lafleche, and R. Berkeley, eds, *Identity, Ethnic Diversity and Community Cohesion*. London: Runnymede Trust/Sage, pp. 87–101.

Clarke, S., Hahn, H. and Hoggett, P. (2008). *Object Relations and Social Relations: The Implications of the Relational Turn in Psychoanalysis*. London: Karnac Books.

Dalal, F. (2002). *Race, Colour and the Process of Racialization: New Perspectives from Group Analysis, Psychoanalysis and Sociology*. London: Brunner Routledge.

Department for Communities and Local Government. (2007). What works in community cohesion? www.communities.gov.uk/documents/communities/pdf/whatworks.pdf.

Elliott, A. (1994). *Psychoanalytic Theory: An Introduction*. Oxford: Blackwell.

Fanon, F. (1967). *Black Skin, White Masks*. London: Pluto Press.

Ferrell, R. (1996). *Passion in Theory: Conceptions of Freud and Lacan*. London: Routledge.

Freud, S. ([1919] 1961). The uncanny. *Standard Edition*, 17, 219–52.

(1969). *Civilization and Its Discontents*. London: Hogarth Press.

Gilroy, P. (1997). *There Ain't No Black in the Union Jack*. London: Routledge.

Hinshelwood, R. D. (1989). *A Dictionary of Kleinean Thought*. London: Free Association Books.

(1994). *Clinical Klein*. London: Free Association Books.

Horkheimer, M. and Adorno, T. (1994). *Dialectic of Enlightenment*. London: Continuum.

Joseph Rowntree Foundation. (2008). Community engagement and community cohesion. www.jrf.org.uk/sites/files/jrf/2227-governance-community-engagement.pdf.

Klein, M. (1997a). Notes on some schizoid mechanisms. In *Envy and Gratitude and Other Works 1946–1963*. London: Vintage, pp. 1–24.

(1997b). Some theoretical conclusions regarding the emotional life of the infant. In *Envy and Gratitude and Other Works 1946–1963*. London: Vintage, pp. 61–93.

Lacan, J. (1977a). *The Four Fundamental Concepts of Psychoanalysis*. London: Tavistock.

(1977b). *Ecrits: A Selection*. London: Tavistock.

Lane, C., ed. (1998). *The Psychoanalysis of Race*. New York: Columbia University Press.

Macey, D. (2000). *Frantz Fanon: A Life*. London: Granta Books.

Mirza, H. S. (1992). *Young, Female and Black*. London: Routledge.

Ogden, T. H. (1986). *The Matrix of the Mind: Object Relations and the Psychoanalytic Dialogue*. London: Karnac Books.

Roustang, F. (1990). *The Lacanian Delusion*. Oxford: Oxford University Press.

Sarup, M. (1992). *Jacques Lacan*. London: Harvester-Wheatsheaf.

Segal, H. (1964). *Introduction to the Work of Melanie Klein*. London: Heinemann.

Segal, J. (1992). *Melanie Klein*. London: Sage.

Young, R. M. (1994). *Mental Space*. London: Process Press.

Žižek, S. (1993). *Tarrying with the Negative*. Durham, NC: Duke University Press.

12 The sociology of whiteness: beyond good and evil white people

Matthew W. Hughey

> It might even be possible that what constitutes the value of those good and respected things, consists precisely in their being insidiously related, knotted, and crocheted to these evil and apparently opposed things – perhaps even in being essentially identical with them.
>
> – Friedrich W. Nietzsche

Recent discourse on white racial identity centers on the contemporary 'crisis' of whiteness – the progressive movements and their corresponding neoconservative backlashes. Taken at face value, whites are splintering into antagonistic groups, possessive of differing worldviews, resources and ideological stances. This perspective assumes a social continuum polarized by 'racists' and 'anti-racists'. Additionally, our dominant narratives frame whiteness as a uniform racial category replete with social privilege and material power. This arrangement poses a puzzle: How do we conceptualize an understanding of white identity that accounts for the long-term staying power of white privilege alongside the heterogeneity and fracturing of whiteness? Animated by this background, this chapter presents a new theory of white racial-identity formation.

In what follows, I first present an abbreviated overview of the extant debates in contemporary sociological theory concerning white racial identity. Next, I advance my theory of 'hegemonic whiteness': how an ideal type of whiteness is actually shared between and across white racial actors in divergent social worlds. And third, I demonstrate how members of two white organizations commonly thought to be opposed and entirely different – a white nationalist group and a white anti-racist group – attempt to embody a shared ideal of white identity formation. They pursue that ideal through an ongoing process of inter- and intra-racial boundary construction. Members of both groups (1) use racist and reactionary narratives to make inter-racial boundaries ('whites' from 'non-whites') and (2) mark certain whites' inability to adhere to dominant white expectations to make intra-racial boundaries ('hegemonic' or 'ideal' whites from 'lesser' whites').

Lawrence and Patrick: case studies on the Janus face of whiteness

A committed white nationalist, a 55-year-old man that I call Lawrence,[1] leans toward me. Focusing his gaze on a nearby bookshelf, he points at a copy of Herrnstein and Murray's (1994) *The Bell Curve* – a controversial text that discusses intelligence, racial identity and socioeconomic success. Lawrence says, as he fixes his eyes on me:

The only thing we are trying to say is that there are both social and biological causes to blacks, and Latinos, low levels of wealth, success, intelligence for that matter. Whites, on average, are just more moral, together, socially. There are genetic differences and non-whites, their cultures are impoverished, dysfunctional if you will. Whites are more organized and intelligent. It's foolish to work for, or even desire, some kind of racial equality. That's not racist. That's just reality.

Walking down a city street with a 28-year-old white man whom I call Patrick, a member of a white anti-racist organization, we see an inter-racial couple holding hands. After we pass them by, Patrick turns to look at them. 'See, that's great. Not everyone is a racist, not everyone is closed-minded.' Patrick beams. We resume walking as he continued to speak:

I mean, it's real tough, though. There are just some inherent differences between us. We've been conditioned that way. I tried dating a few black women, but they really didn't get me. Don't want to say they were 'ghetto' but... I don't know if it's biological or cultural or social or whatever, but it's real. I mean, they've measured IQ differences between the races... Whites just seem to have their things together and it's easier to handle or navigate groups of white people. You want to be with someone that can carry on an intelligent conversation with you, you know? There's just something special about white people.

The two preceding examples pose an interesting dilemma. On one hand, one expects such words from Lawrence, a lawyer by trade and an active member of National Equality for All (NEA), a nationwide *white nationalist* organization that advocates the legal separation of races from one another. On the other hand, how do we make sense of a young writer named Patrick, an active member of a nationwide *white anti-racist* organization called Whites for Racial Justice (WRJ)? Is Patrick an aberration within his organization and anti-racist worldview? Do we dismiss his words either as a momentary gaffe or as an unintentional display of ignorance? Should we not expect the discourse of these two white actors to be more different than similar?

---

[1] All names of persons, places and organizations are pseudonyms employed to protect the confidentiality of the research participants.

Such data are confounding because they do not comport with our predefined narrative about whites and racism. Although there is debate over who the 'racists' and the 'anti-racists' are, there is little debate over the fact that they exist as two stable, divergent and opposing sides. Alastair Bonnett (2000: 10) wrote that the story of racism and anti-racism 'is staged with melodrama, the characters presented as heroes and villains: pure anti-racists versus pure racists, good against evil'. So, also, did Jack Niemonen (2007: 166–67) remark that we often 'paint a picture of social reality in which battle lines are drawn, the enemy identified, and the victims sympathetically portrayed . . . [distinguishing] between "good" whites and "bad" whites'. And after the 2008 election of Barack Obama, racial dualism proved prevalent among many, as they celebrated a white anti-racist triumph over racism in the political mainstream. Journalist Tim Wise (2009: 84) penned, 'While it may be tempting . . . to seek to create a dichotomy whereby the "bad whites" are the ones who voted against the black guy, while the "good whites" are the ones who voted for him, such a dualism is more than a little simplistic.'

In our contemporary moment, categorizing people as fundamentally belonging to one side of a specific polarity is a meaningful enterprise. Binaries are a cornerstone of our social structures and a road map for our navigation of everyday life. However, descriptions of reality are quite arbitrary and depend on the strategies we use to classify social life by temporal, spatial and contextual variation. Categories do not merely sort our experiences but instead help to infuse everyday life with specific meanings. So how do we make meaning of Lawrence's and Philip's striking similarities?

A brief primer on white racial identity

In recent years, an overwhelming litany of scholarship concerned with white racial identity, especially in a U.S. context, has burgeoned. A large part of the early scholarship on whiteness explored the notion that whites generally have a lower degree of self-awareness about race and whiteness than do non-whites (Delgado and Stefancic 1997; Frankenburg 1993; McIntosh 1988). As Richard Dyer (1988: 44) wrote in an early and key essay on white racial identity, 'white power secures its dominance by seeming not to be anything in particular.' After approximately two decades of research, arguments about whiteness as a formation of invisible privileges and norms remain well rehearsed. However, with the declining size of white demographics in the USA, coupled with increasing birthrates and the immigration of non-whites into North America (Vickerman 2007), not to mention the increased prominence of non-whites in various public spheres, whiteness renders itself more visible and less of a synonym for invisible normality (Hughey 2012). Indeed, the current study of whiteness is moving away from its initial coupling with 'privilege and power' (Andersen 2003).

For example, Charles Gallagher (1995) found that whites display high levels of racial awareness either when they are the racial minority or if they perceive their resources to be threatened by another racial group. Indeed, challenges to the racial status quo can activate defensive and reactionary white racial awareness like that of the Ku Klux Klan or White Citizens' Councils (Daniels 1997; Dobratz and Shanks-Meile 1997; Ezekiel 1996, 2002). So, too, can changes to established racial hierarchies both raise and marshal white racial consciousness in ways that seek to bring about racial equality and increased opportunities for people of color (Bonnett 2000; George 2004). Hence, the dominant trend in contemporary research on white racial identity now centers on the relationships between white racial (un)consciousness, the diversity and intersectionality of whites across various social axes and whites' relationship to inequality and racism (McDermott and Samson 2005: 249).

Whether in historical context (Allen 1994; Brodkin 1998; Jacobson 1998), various environmental situations (Hartigan 1997), differing socioeconomic circumstances (Buck 2001; Hartigan 1999) or varied sexual orientations (Berube 2001), it is now agreed that whiteness is a constantly morphing identity refracted by context (Duster 2001; Twine and Gallagher 2008). The recent work of Howard Winant is emblematic of this approach. Winant (2004: 5–11), in his essay 'Behind Blue Eyes', argues that whiteness is best understood as a series of 'white racial projects' that resemble a bifurcated political spectrum. Winant distils white identity into five categories 'along a political spectrum, according to explicit criteria drawn from the meaning each project attaches to "whiteness" . . . far right, new right, neoconservative, neoliberal, and new abolitionist'.

While this paradigm remains an efficacious approach to the study of various white racial identities, the dominant meanings attached to whiteness – and race *writ large* – are not always reducible to political ideology or local context but are semi-autonomous schemas shared across formal social locations (Hughey 2012). Moreover, such reductionism may threaten the conceptualization of whiteness as a 'group' (Lewis 2004) or how differing processes of white identity formation across varying contexts are intimately connected with, and coalesced through, a reliance on similar repertoires, scripts and material practices of domination (Doane 1997). Failure to synthesize how seemingly disparate and opposed white identity formations are constituted by, and help to reinforce, strategies of social control and ascendancy may unnecessarily rob the study of white identity of critical, conceptual and explanatory purchase. Providing an answer for the 'changing sameness' (Gilroy 1993) of whiteness is a question of paramount import today (McDermott and Samson 2005: 256). Rather than focusing on political *ideology* or individual *attitudes* on race, much can be gained from shifting attention toward the shared meanings that white people hold about their own white racial *identity*.

National Equality for All and Whites for Racial Justice: an ethnographic comparison of white racial identity

I survey the details of the methodology and data employed in this study in other venues (cf. Hughey 2010, 2011, 2012) and cover the challenges of employing a cultural sociological standpoint (cf. Hughey 2009). It should suffice to say that, for little over one year (May 2006 to June 2007), I spent at least one day a week with either or both members of the white nationalist organization NEA and the white anti-racist organization WRJ.[2]

Though there were many similarities between these two groups, the differences should be obvious. NEA members identified themselves with pride and exuberance as 'white' and explicitly advocated racial segregation. They argued that predisposed genetic and cultural differences between racial groups are catalysts for racial antagonism. In their view, white people should separate from non-whites so as to preserve their moral, intellectual and cultural 'superiority'. NEA represents a larger neoconservative backlash (inclusive of neo-Nazis, militia movements, variants of the Christian Identity Church and more 'refined' groups like the National Association for the Advancement of White People) against the victories of the U.S. civil rights movement. They hold in common a reaction to whites' perceived decline in demographics, political control and cultural influence in the USA (Daniels 1997; Ezekiel 1996, 2002).

Conversely, WRJ members come together to fight the aforementioned views of race and whiteness. Together they promote activities for whites to try to curtail or eliminate racism: from the active disruption of white

---

[2] I triangulated the data (Downward and Mearman 2007; Golafshani 2003; Olson 2004) via
- ethnographic fieldwork (I attended their meetings, 58 meetings in total; $n = 31$ with NEA, $n = 27$ with WRJ)
- semistructured in-depth interviews with members ($n = 41$)
- content analysis inclusive of newsletter issues ($n = 7$), flyers ($n = 22$) and any textual information such as e-mails and office memos ($n = 467$)

nationalist events to mainstream activities such as counseling and education. Today's white anti-racist movement is one of various goals and organizations: from groups like the Alliance of White Anti-Racists Everywhere (AWARE) and Caucasians United for Reparations and Emancipation (CURE) to the White Anti-Racist Community Action Network and Skin Heads against Racial Prejudice (SHARP). These groups promote the view that whites receive undeserved and unasked-for privileges and powers at the expense of people of color and thus work to confront, eradicate and/or ameliorate racism and racial inequality (Bonnett 2000).

Dominant forms of white racial identity: 'hegemonic whiteness'

Members of both groups hold eerily similar understandings of an ideal, or 'hegemonic',[3] form of white racial identity thought to be idyllic, proper and desirable. As Amanda Lewis (2004: 624) wrote,

whiteness works in distinct ways for and is embodied quite differently by homeless white men, golf-club-membership-owning executives, suburban soccer moms, urban hillbillies, antiracist skinheads, and/or union-card-carrying factory workers . . . In any particular historical moment, however, certain forms of whiteness become dominant.

While the meanings of an idealized and dominant white racial identity are reformed in localized interactions, it is clear that local settings do not exist in isolated vacuums. Rather, the processes by which actors come to interpret white racial identity are guided by larger sets of shared expectations and authoritative meanings. As Schwalbe et al. (2000: 442) wrote, 'the power to hold others accountable in one setting depends upon relationships, that is, a larger *net of accountability* with actors outside the setting.' In this sense, adherence to racialized expectations of what it means to be 'white' is not entirely reducible to local context. Although a range of *whitenesses* exists, white actors across formally different political groups hold similar notions of an ideal and hegemonic whiteness.

---

[3] I specifically employ the term *hegemonic* – via Antonio Gramsci – to emphasize that dominant cultural scripts neither turn actors into identical robots nor remove the possibility for variation in meaning making. Rather, throughout this research, when members of WRJ and NEA spoke to me about white racial identity, they often said things akin to 'Matthew, of course that's so, isn't it?' Those 'of course' statements are indicative of hegemony. That is, members were the least aware that they were consenting to a particular cultural view of the world, and when schemas and scripts become accepted as little more than 'common sense', they become hegemonic.

And this shared understanding constitutes a 'net' – simultaneously constraining and guiding the ongoing formation of one's white racial identity throughout everyday social interactions.

From this perspective, the hegemonic form of whiteness is neither essential nor innate but appears 'natural' and 'common-sensed'. All racialized individuals are compelled to adhere to culturally valorized mythologies taught in social interaction and which, over time, are accepted as a priori reality (Hughey 2010, 2011). For example, throughout an average young white male's formative years, he is encouraged to adopt a special vision of white manhood as strong, autonomous, rational, neutral, objective and meritocratic – characteristics that commonly (yet never exclusively) characterize a dominant, idealized or hegemonic form of masculinity and whiteness (Connell 1987; Lewis 2004; Hughey 2010). And it is from these shared schemas, internalized as the natural and existential background of who one is – *and should be* – that a host of actions are simultaneously enabled and constrained.

Hegemonic whiteness: inter- and intra-racial differences

By building upon the concept of 'hegemonic whiteness' (Hughey 2010; Lewis 2004), I argue that meaningful racial identity for whites is produced vis-à-vis the reproduction of, and appeal to, racist, essentialist and reactionary *inter-* and *intra-*racial distinctions:

- *inter-racial difference and superiority*: positioning whites as essentially different and superior from those marked as non-white
- *intra-racial distinction and marginalization*: marginalizing practices of being white that fail to exemplify dominant white racial ideals and expectations

Within the context and setting of both NEA and WRJ, hegemonic ideals about white racial identity are collectively shared by members and function as seemingly neutral yardsticks against which discourse and action are measured. In what follows, I detail various dimensions of the hegemonic form of white racial identity.

Inter-racial difference and superiority

> There are no white people, only people who think they are white.
>
> – J. Baldwin

The first mechanism for the pursuit of an ideal form of white identity remains tethered to the construction of a 'normal' form of whiteness in relation to 'dysfunctional' non-whites. Members of NEA and WRJ who adhere closely with the ideal forms of white racial identity are those who accept such a framing and reproduce it in their everyday speech and action. Specifically, I cover here three shared configurations thought to embody the ideal form of white racial identity: victimology, pathology and white debt/color capital.

White victimology

I find that both NEA and WRJ construct and perform their racial selves as victimized and culturally stigmatized. Members of NEA understand themselves to be under the yoke of a culture that is increasingly 'politically correct' and 'anti-white'. As Daniel (registered nurse, 32 years old, 4 years in NEA) said in an interview,

> this politically correct nation has become so hostile toward any expression of white pride or even any subtle attempts at whites claiming their rights that it is a distinctly racist society toward whites. While there is surely prejudice toward all people, that is nothing new, that's what happens when races mix: there's trouble. But now, things have changed so that it's just not accepted for whites to stick up for themselves . . . *It's like we are the new black people of a couple hundred years ago.* Except that now blacks and Mexicans are the ones that get to say whatever they want. (emphasis added)

Although one should remember that both groups have vastly different political agendas and worldviews of their place as white men, of equal import is the illumination of how different political orientations failed to negate similar racial meaning-making processes. In an interview with WRJ member Duncan (corporate salesperson, 30 years old, 2.5 years in WRJ), he expresses a view analogous to NEA's worldview:

> Being in [WRJ] is a commitment that I love. I get a lot out of it, but you know . . . at the same time it gets old real quick. Whenever I bring up how I feel [about racial issues] it seems that I'm attacked. I mean [long sigh] it just doesn't just seem that way, *I am attacked* [said with emphasis]. Being white with these beliefs puts me on center stage, right in the line of fire. People of color think I'm crazy and wonder what my ulterior motives are and other white people, well they think I'm crazy too and that I'm a communist or something or other [long pause]. It's like being white with these beliefs, like I said, makes you a target *just like black people* [my emphasis].

Duncan's supposition that white identity is a 'target just like black people' is parallel to NEA's ideas that whites are 'the new black people'.

As evidenced, the understanding of white identity as victimized by a racial double-standard justifies the actions of people of color while simultaneously demonizing whites. This worldview is a powerful tool in the maintenance of white self-marginalization. It is especially prevalent because of racist beliefs that people of color are exploiting the 'social system' en masse, thereby unfairly displacing whites.

Black and brown pathology

The evocation of a powerful anti-black rhetoric of 'pathological behavior' reigns as a powerful tool for whites to 'talk nasty about blacks without sounding "racist"' (Bonilla-Silva 2002: 41). Members of both NEA and WRJ commonly use such a discourse of black pathologies to relationally construct a sense of the white self. The subtle difference between the two groups is that members of NEA advance an understanding of people of color (especially blacks and Latinos) as biologically – thus essentially – inferior. Conversely, members of WRJ promote a worldview in which non-whites are culturally inferior. One member of NEA whom I call Joey (salesperson, 36 years old, 3 years in NEA) stated,

Like on education, look at what happened in California after we got rid of affirmative action. Standards rose, quality of education went up. When you put different races together, conflicts rise, standards fall. That's the way it is. Now we have to suffer through this mess even though we all know the truth. It hurts whites the most. We are the ones that pay for it.

Although members of WRJ reject the aforementioned argument whole-sale, they still express similar understandings that black and brown populations drive standards down. In an interview, WRJ member Michael (banker, 36 years old, 4.5 years in WRJ) mentioned how anxious he was that his child's school was becoming 'less white', which, in turn, would bring an array of 'dysfunctional behavior' to the school. Andre (graduate student, 24 years old, 1 year in WRJ) also spoke of his experiences in graduate school: 'I believe in diversity, but I'm tired of having to pick up the slack for the black students in all my group work. I mean, it's not their fault, I know they are oppressed by racism and that their behaviour is all a product of it, but I suffer too.'

Comments of this ilk were not uncommon. There was an overarching belief in the cultural inferiority of blacks that was effectively and unfairly burdening whites through decreased standards – from education to job performance to morality. Such belief in the *naturally* low standards of black and brown populations is laced with racist ideologies that only work to reassert the *normality* of whiteness. As a NEA member whom I call Chris (business manager, 44 years old, 4 years in NEA) stated to me in an interview,

It's simply not fair. What do you want me to say? The reality of it is: black people steal, cheat, lie . . . they have corrupt values . . . they are killing each other . . . their culture is dysfunctional and damn near demonic . . . Why won't anyone in the mainstream say it [said rhetorically]? Because it's not P.C. [politically correct] and then that person, if they're white, would be burned at the stake . . . Being white means dealing with this time after time.

In similar fashion, a WRJ member, Philip (grocery store owner, 53 years old, 5 years in WRJ), stated,

Racism is a fundamentally corrupt and wasteful action . . . For example let's take slavery. It's important to examine the methods that were used to enslave Africans and bring them here. Look at what was done to the family structure, destroying homes, taking their religion, corrupting their values, the violence in black urban areas. Now fast-forward to today, look at the problems with being black, the crime rates, lack of education, et cetera. These things are engrained in black culture now, and it's important for me to stand up and fix these things . . . being a white antiracist means I'm under assault for wanting to fix that. That's what I mean by duty. Black people are in a screwed up predicament; they've been crippled because of racism.

Pathology discourses are widespread among whites (Bonilla-Silva 2003: 40–41). In a world dominated by white supremacist discourse that has become 'natural' and 'common-sensed', varied beliefs in the cultural or biological inferiority of non-whites work as powerful catalysts in the meaning making of white racial identities.

White debt and color capital: perceptions of empty whiteness

Across both contexts of NEA and WRJ, whiteness is understood as 'normal', 'dull', 'boring' or 'inauthentic'. As a remedy to these feelings, members often use social relationships with people of color and/or claim ownership or knowledge of objects and traditions symbolically coded as non-white. Though members of both groups hold various negative views of non-whites, they also possess many critiques of whiteness that fit within the scope of stereotypical racial distinctions: whites are overly logical and intellectual and lack in physical prowess, emotional passion and sexual potency, and are – as one WRJ member constantly stated – 'stale'.

I label this meaning-making process with the terms 'white debt' and 'color capital' because NEA and WRJ members work to fill in their perceived white debt by converting relationships with people and objects symbolically coded non-white into a kind of credentialing capital. The possession of color capital temporarily allows the white actor to re-create the meaning of whiteness as legitimate and valorized. As NEA member Will (real estate agent, 37 years old, 6 years in NEA) said,

I often try to hang out at a bar around the corner from my house. . . It generally has a lot of race mixing in it, . . . now you know I don't agree with that or think that's the best for anyone, but it gives me an advantage. [*Author:* 'How so?'] Because I have lots of black friends, I learn a lot about things I wouldn't otherwise know about, . . . in the end it shakes up what people think of white nationalists as 'bigots' and whatnot. I know all the latest [black] music, sayings, and what their community is thinking about. I'm far from a dull white guy . . . and I can use that information if anyone wants to equate white nationalism with racism. Ha, it's like a get out of jail free card [laughing].

A WRJ member named Samuel (music store employee, 26 years old, 2 years in WRJ) stated,

I came to this organization because, I mean, I don't know if you feel this way, but I often wanted to be less white, like it's empty or has a hole in it or something. . . I mean, being in WRJ brings me in contact with lots of history about African Americans, music, styles, . . . I learned about Cesar Chavez in our ed [educational] session a few weeks ago. And now I get to use that information, it's a part of me, I feel more 'real' somehow, . . . I know it sounds crazy [laughing], . . . no one can say I'm racist or boring.

For members of both organizations, whiteness was sometimes configured as a lack of positive authenticity. Sean (gardener, 62 years old, 6 years in WRJ) stated,

It is difficult being in WRJ. Our decision has stigmatized us to a certain extent. Just because we are all white and that other whites are not flocking here means we are somehow different. It's an intense feeling of realness. To many of us, being white is a part of the problem . . . Becoming less white is losing something, but also about gaining something real. [*Author:* 'How do you become "less white"? What does that actually look like?'] Well, there is something more real, I think because of oppression and racism . . . that has made people of colour more human. So, if I had to spell it out, being less white is being more like them.

Sean's comment established a connection between the social-constructivist nature of whiteness and the authenticity of 'others'. WRJ's construction of whiteness was nearly identical among NEA members. As one NEA member, Harry (lawyer, 39 years old, 6 years in NEA), told me,

Because of many whites' approaches to white civility, they have made it dull, sold out its character, made it plain. In many ways that style transferred to blacks hundred of years ago, . . . they stole many white styles and passed it off as 'African'. Now we're in a situation that needs to reclaim our passion. Look at jazz, I love Miles Davis . . . so what if he's black? I'm filling in what was taken from me. The creativity of jazz is because of white people thousands of years ago. Now we are at a point where white nationalism has to be more open to the authenticity of others.

As Harry makes clear, the authenticity (that was once white but since has been lost or stolen) is now manifested in the color capital of black cultures that are usable by whites.

On a certain level, such inter-racial connectivity and tolerance appear like a step toward racial inclusivity and even unity. Yet, Bryson (1996: 895) wrote, 'Cultural tolerance should not be conceptualized as an indiscriminate tendency to be non-exclusive, but as a reordering of group boundaries.' Instead of laboring to transform social arrangements, both groups co-opt 'otherness' to remedy 'white debt'.

Intra-racial distinction and marginalization

> The ideal white man was one who knew how to use his head, who knew how to manage and control things and get things done. Those whites who were not in a position to perform these functions nevertheless aspired to them.
> (Cleaver 1989: 80)

While the aforementioned findings demonstrated one side of the proverbial Janus face of 'hegemonic whiteness' (positioning whites as essentially different and superior to non-whites), there is a second side. The meanings of white racial identity are not based simply on distinctions between white and non-white but also on different types of whiteness. For example, in her study of white women, Ruth Frankenberg (1993: 198) found that her subjects thought there were two types of white: 'those who are truly or only white, and those who are white but also something more or is it something less?' Such intra-racial boundary work between those thought to be 'truly white' and those thought to be 'more or less white' works to maintain the ideal form of whiteness by marginalizing the latter and framing the former as a superior form of white racial identity. Within NEA and WRJ, I find that members distinguish between forms of whiteness not so much in terms of color, bodily feature or even political views but in terms of everyday-life shared expectations. In particular, I outline three shared alignments of ideals thought fundamental to the performance of a 'proper' white identity – affectation, consciousness and simplicity.

Affective whiteness

Sociologists have long suggested that the appropriate sort of emotional display greatly assists in distinguishing between groups and helping to solidify collective identity (Bourdieu [1979] 1984; Hochschild 1983).

Within both NEA and WRJ, I found that certain emotional displays were expected with patterned frequency. Specifically, the ideal of white emotional expression in WRJ was that of a regular display of sadness in regard to the pain of racism, whereas NEA members were expected to exhibit anger over a perceived anti-white bias. Those members who did not exhibit these dominant emotional performances were not seen as simply abnormal; rather, their racial identity was understood as inferior and deficient.

For example, after one particularly charged WRJ meeting at which one member – Malcolm (consultant/counselor, 44 years old, 5 years in WRJ) – admitted that living an anti-racist life was incredibly difficult, another WRJ member, Cassandra (marketing agent, 31 years old, 3 years in WRJ), spoke with me about the meeting:

I guess I just don't see what the big deal is, I mean, not that I want to be insensitive, but what does he [Malcolm] expect? Yes, it's hard sometimes, but I just don't see what good the crying is for all the time. I get that it's a positive release, but what does it *actually do* [said with emphasis]?

Overhearing Cassandra's comment, Patrick (writer, 28 years old, 2 years in WRJ) immediately stepped toward us and said in a harsh tone,

You just don't get it, do you? Racism hurts. It hurts. It just hurts. Get it? And it's not easy to talk about in that way. Anyone can step back and analyze it scientifically [turning to look directly at me as he spoke], but understanding how it affects you . . . better yet, how it forms you, or misshapes you that is, is hard to do. Until you try to see it that way, I'm not sure you'll get it . . . Until then, you have no idea what your whiteness is and what it does to you. [Malcolm] does [know what whiteness 'is'].

The dominant ideal that adequate emotions of sadness and hurt should be overtly expressed was used as a marker for the idealized form of 'affective whiteness'. If a member did not express such emotion (or at least agree with the ideal), then he or she was understood (paraphrasing Cassandra) as having little to no idea what his or her whiteness 'is'.

Among NEA members, the dominant ideal of affective whiteness both constrained and enabled members' social construction of white identity. At NEA meetings, there were frequent emotional displays of anger encapsulated within, and aroused by, the understanding of 'reverse racism' against whites. In this sense, those who failed to regularly express 'righteous anger' were often devalued. That is, the expression of anger framed the *racialized value* of members. Indeed, as I entered into the second half of the 14-month-long ethnography with the white nationalist organization NEA, my perceived lack of anger and consciousness that I was a 'victim of reverse racism' led several members to confront me: 'I'm not even sure you're really white. If you were, you would have to get angry sooner or later.' Conversely, in WRJ, I relayed a sad story of an early childhood experience in which I became cognizant of racial inequality. Upon the completion of my story, one WRJ member took me aside and, wrapping his arm around me in a supportive manner, stated, 'I think you're starting to understand whiteness.'

Conscious whiteness

Another shared cultural ideal was that of 'conscious whiteness', or those whites able to see through the 'propaganda' of society to adopt, willingly and without coercion, the NEA or WRJ worldview. In this ideal, the principles of individualism, equality, freedom, rationality and objectivity were the most prized. In relation to the two groups, whites who either were brought by friends or joined the organization more recently than others were often viewed as susceptible to 'mainstream' thought. My field notes are full of observations I made regarding 'gossip and backbiting' about such members – as their ability to make decisions and their commitment to the 'movement' were in doubt. For example, one afternoon in the headquarters of NEA, a senior member I call Derek (marketing agent, 34 years old, 6 years in NEA) and a younger member – Charles (graduate student, 25 years old, 3 years in NEA) – were discussing an upcoming event for which press packets had to be designed. Such a job was viewed as vital to the growth and continued existence of NEA. In discussing who could be assigned to oversee the work, the following exchange took place:

CHARLES: [Robert] is nice, he'll get it done quick, at least I think so.
DEREK: Well, I would say that we hand it over to, uhhh, [Paul] but he, ummm, you know . . . he's not the strongest at wading through all the, uhhh, information out there. [Laughing] I wonder if he knows who he is. He just seems confused sometimes . . . like you know, autopilot.
AUTHOR: What do you mean by 'autopilot'?
DEREK: I mean he buys into the mainstream view of race too much. He has no idea what it means to be white in this day and age. That brother is lost, lost right now, anyway. It depends, I think he can make it, but he's got a long way to go.
CHARLES: OK, well, I'll be in early tomorrow. I'll see what else he can do.
DEREK: Yeah [muttering under his breath, but just loud enough to hear], he can make the coffee.

By framing Paul (police officer, 49 years old, 5 years in NEA) as too easily swayed, his racial consciousness was called into question and his low status in the organization was made explicit. Although there were whites in both NEA and WRJ who were marginalized and subordinated owing to their lack of ability to act out various aspects of the idealized (hegemonic) forms of whiteness, they still tried to accomplish the hegemonic white ideal. That is, rather than rebelling against these hegemonic ideals, members accept them via their consent and continual attempts toward status ascendancy.

Simplistic whiteness

The third pattern by which both groups create intra-racial distinctions is observable through their valorization of simplicity. Specifically, the ideal white member understands both race and race relations as simple, material observations, to be clouded neither by overly theoretical paradigms nor by lengthy explanations. In one of my first WRJ meetings, Michael explicitly told me,

We don't engage in theory here. Our basic approach is that racism is an irrational behaviour that causes negative feelings and interferes with cooperation between the races. Instead of working through these feelings, we tend to bottle them up, which exacerbates the situation. We work to get through this, it's simple. No grand designs of society or sociology or whatever. It's simple and effective . . . No overblown abstract theorizing.

In a manner akin to WRJ, Derek, of NEA, stated,

People call it 'racial realism'. It's simple. Blacks are more likely to steal, more likely to commit violent crimes; whites have higher IQs. It's not rocket science. People try to explain these realities away with statistics that adjust and skew the numbers, at least that's what many of your colleagues do in the universities. Then they apply all kinds of ridiculous theory to it. Take Stokely Carmichael, the thug, you know he invented 'structural racism' in order to shift the blame for black violence and no education to whites?

Explanations for racial inequality which included sociological theories grounded in empirical evidence were often coded as clouding the real issues that – for both groups – were little more than simple observations that required no particular education or insight. Those whites who availed themselves of more complex explanations were not understood as simply engaging in abstract reasoning or relying on erroneous assumptions. Rather, their white racial identity was interpreted as deficient. Because the ideal form of white racial identity was coupled with understandings of the world as plain, matter-of-fact and clearly observable, discussions of social complexity were perceived as windows into the soul of a lacking whiteness. Those white members who made simplistic and reductionist accounts of race relations – whether white supremacist or white anti-racist in orientation – often sat atop the social hierarchy in their organization and were viewed as good and proper white people.

Conclusion

This study's implications suggest that white anxiety over changing race relations and expectations is widespread and resonates strongly in diverse, even supposedly antithetical, locations. It cannot be distilled into static political formations that are distinct and separable. It shares a common allegiance to dominant racial (and often racist) ideologies and expectations that transcend differing belief systems.

I advance an understanding of the processes of white identity formation that is sensitized to both white homogeneity and heterogeneity. By conceptualizing whiteness as a configuration of ideological meanings and actual practices, white racial cohesion and difference are seen as a two-pronged process: through positioning those marked as 'white' as essentially different and superior from those marked as 'non-white', and through marginalizing practices of 'being white' which fail to exemplify dominant ideals.

This study of NEA and WRJ members' words and performances is not definitive. Yet, the task of such an ethnographic study does not pause with the recovery of basic situational knowledge but seeks to aggregate the situational knowledge to reveal important mechanisms of social process – here related to the meaning-making process of white racial identity. Each of these actors' statements and actions bears the imprint of racialized expectations. Hence, while such folkways are contextually specific, they also transcend contexts to cohesively bound white racial identity via the pursuit of the ideal or hegemonic form.

With these findings in mind, they gesture toward several implications and future directions for research. First, more empirical, firsthand study is required to validate the reach of hegemonic whiteness in cross-national settings. Second, more work must be done to tease out the junction of hegemonic whiteness, class, gender, sexuality and age. That is, do such intersections with the ideals of whiteness temper or add to the robustness of the hegemonic whiteness model? Third, the practice of hegemonic whiteness is not static or ahistorical but, rather, operates within the regime of 'color-blindness' and 'post-racialism' which is becoming a defining hallmark not only of the USA but also of the global village. Examining the processes by which hegemonic whiteness is mutually constitutive of this dominant logic (via education, religion, the media, the military etc.) is certainly germane for those concerned with its ability to obfuscate the material realities of racial inequality.

REFERENCES

Allen, T. W. (1994). *The Invention of the White Race: Racial Oppression and Social Control*, vol. 1. New York: Verso.

Andersen, M. (2003). Whitewashing race: a critical perspective on whiteness. In E. Bonilla-Silva and A. W. Doane, eds, *White Out: The Continuing Significance of Racism*. New York: Routledge, pp. 21–34.

Berube, A. (2001). How gay stays white and what kind of white it stays. In B. B. Rasmussen, I. J. Nexica, E. Klinenberg, and M. Wray, eds, *The Making and Unmaking of Whiteness*. Durham, NC: Duke University Press, pp. 234–65.

Bonilla-Silva, E. (2002). The linguistics of colour blind racism: how to talk nasty about blacks without sounding 'racist'. *Critical Sociology*, 28(1–2), 41–64.

(2003). *Racism without Racists: Colour-Blind Racism and the Persistence of Racial Inequality in the United States*. New York: Rowman and Littlefield.

Bonnett, A. (2000). *Anti-Racism*. New York: Routledge.

Bourdieu, P. ([1979] 1984). *Distinction: A Social Critique of Taste*. London: Routledge and Kegan Paul.

Brodkin, K. (1998). *How Jews Became White Folks and What That Says about Race in America*. New Brunswick, NJ: Rutgers University Press.

Bryson, B. (1996). 'Anything but heavy metal': symbolic exclusion and musical dislikes. *American Sociological Review*, 61(5), 884–99.

Buck, P. D. (2001). *Worked to the Bone: Race, Class, Power, and Privilege in Kentucky*. New York: Monthly Review.

Cleaver, E. (1989). *Soul on Ice*. New York: Dell.

Connell, R. E. (1987). *Gender and Power*. Sydney: Allen and Unwin.

Daniels, J. (1997). *White Lies: Race, Class, Gender and Sexuality in White Supremacist Discourse*. New York: Routledge.

Delgado, R. and Stefancic, J. (1997). *Critical White Studies: Looking behind the Mirror*. Philadelphia: Temple University Press.

Doane, A. W. (1997). Dominant group ethnic identity in the United States: the role of 'hidden' ethnicity in intergroup relations. *Sociological Quarterly*, 38(3), 375–97.

Dobratz, B. A. and Shanks-Meile, S. L. (1997). *White Power, White Pride! The White Separatist Movement in the United States*. New York: Twayne.

Downward, P. and Mearman, A. (2007). Retroduction as mixed-methods triangulation in economic research: reorienting economics into social science. *Cambridge Journal of Economics*, 31(1), 77–99.

Duster, T. (2001). The 'morphing' properties of whiteness. In E. B. Rasmussen, E. Klinenberg, I. J. Nexica, and M. Wray, eds, *The Making and Unmaking of Whiteness*. Durham, NC: Duke University Press, pp. 113–33.

Dyer, R. (1988). White. *Screen*, 29(4), 44–65.

Ezekiel, R. S. (1996). *The Racist Mind: Portraits of American Neo-Nazis and Klansmen*. Harmondsworth, UK: Penguin.

(2002). An ethnographer looks at neo-Nazi and Klan groups: the racist mind revisited. *American Behavioral Scientist*, 46(1), 51–71.

Frankenberg, R. (1993). *The Social Construction of Whiteness*. London: Routledge.

Gallagher, C. A. (1995). White reconstruction in the university. *Socialist Review*, 24(1–2), 165–87.

George, M. P. (2004). Race traitors: exploring the motivation and action of white antiracists. PhD thesis, University of New Mexico, Albuquerque.

Gilroy, P. (1993). *The Black Atlantic: Modernity and Double Consciousness*. Cambridge, MA: Harvard University Press.

Golafshani, N. (2003). Understanding reliability and validity in qualitative research. *The Qualitative Report*, 8(4), 597–607.

Hartigan, J., Jr. (1997). Locating white Detroit. In R. Frankenberg, ed., *Displacing Whiteness: Essays in Social and Cultural Criticism*. Durham, NC: Duke University Press, pp. 180–213.

(1999). *Racial Situations: Class Predicaments of Whiteness in Detroit*. Princeton, NJ: Princeton University Press.

Herrnstein, R. J. and Murray, C. (1994). *The Bell Curve: Intelligence and Class Structure in American Life*. New York: The Free Press.

Hochschild, A. R. (1983). *The Managed Heart: The Commercialization of Human Feeling*. Berkeley: University of California Press.

Hughey, M. W. (2009). The Janus face of whiteness: toward a cultural sociology of white nationalism and white antiracism. *Sociology Compass*, 3(6), 920–36.

(2010). Navigating the (dis)similarities of white racial identities: the conceptual framework of 'hegemonic whiteness'. *Ethnic and Racial Studies*, 33(8), 1289–309.

(2011). Backstage discourse and the reproduction of white masculinities. *The Sociological Quarterly*, 52(1), 132–53.

(2012). *White Bound: Nationalists, Antiracists and the Shared Meanings of Race*. Stanford, CA: Stanford University Press.

Jacobson, M. F. (1998). *Whiteness of a Different Colour: European Immigrants and the Alchemy of Race*. Cambridge, MA: Harvard University Press.

Lewis, A. (2004). What group? Studying whites and whiteness in the era of colourblindness. *Sociological Theory*, 22(4), 623–46.

McDermott, M. and Samson, F. L. (2005). White racial and ethnic identity in the United States. *Annual Review of Sociology*, 31, 245–61.

McIntosh, P. (1988). *White Privilege and Male Privilege: A Personal Account of Coming to See Correspondences through Work in Women's Studies*. Working Paper 189. Wellesley, MA: Wellesley College Center for Research on Women.

Niemonen, J. J. (2007). Antiracist education in theory and practice: a critical assessment. *The American Sociologist*, 38(2), 159–77.

Olson, W. K. (2004). Triangulation in social research: qualitative and quantitative methods can really be mixed. In M. Holborn, ed., *Developments in Sociology: An Annual Review*. Ormskirk: Causeway Press, pp. 103–21.

Schwalbe, M., Godwin, S., Holden, D., Schrock, D., Thompson, S. and Wolkomir, M. (2000). Generic processes in the reproduction of inequality: an interactionist analysis. *Social Forces*, 79(2), 419–52.

Twine, F. W. and Gallagher, C. (2008). The future of whiteness: a map of the 'third wave'. *Ethnic and Racial Studies*, 31(1), 4–24.

Vickerman, M. (2007). Recent immigration and race: continuity and change. *The Du Bois Review*, 4(1), 141–66.

Winant, H. (2004). Behind blue eyes: whiteness and contemporary US racial politics. In M. Fine, L. Weis, L. P. Pruitt, and A. Burns, eds, *Off White: Readings on Power, Privilege, and Resistance*. New York: Routledge, pp. 3–16.

Wise, T. (2009). *Between Barack and a Hard Place: Racism and White Denial in the Age of Obama*. San Francisco, CA: City Lights Books.

13 (Sexual) whiteness and national identity: race, class and sexuality in colour-blind France

Éric Fassin

In 2009, Manuel Valls, then a rising star on the right wing of the French Socialist party who was to become, in 2012, an omnipresent minister of the interior after François Hollande's election as president of the republic, raised some eyebrows when the television channel Direct 8 released, on 8 June, footage of a racial comment he had made. While touring downtown Évry, a city outside Paris associated in the national imaginary with social and racial tensions, the young mayor sarcastically complained to one of his aides about a flea market run by black immigrants: 'Such a pretty picture of this town!' He went on to call for action: 'Do put in a few Whites' – or, as he put it in French, for emphasis (with virtuoso linguistic variations), 'quelques Blancs, quelques Whites, quelques Blancos'.

When asked about these words, characterised by TV journalist Valérie Trierweiler (soon to rise to first lady) as 'definitely not politically correct', Valls did not back down: 'We must bring in social diversity', that is, make room in the inner city for the middle class, 'whether of immigrant origin or not'. However, this last comment, though couched in a colour-blind rhetoric that today reconciles in French public discourse Republican universalism and Marxist class, was undermined by the next sentence, which only confirmed the racial dimension of his argument: 'We need a mix. What has killed part of the Republic is clearly the ghettoisation, the reality of spatial, social, ethnic segregation. A true apartheid has developed that self-righteous people occasionally see blow up in their faces, as was the case in 2005 during the riots in the suburbs.' Valls concluded, 'Everyone thinks this way, so we have to say it clearly. While we kept denying problems, we left this issue to others – in particular extremists – thus fueling political despair.'

Indeed, 2005 can be considered a turning point in the racialisation of France (Fassin and Fassin 2006). Not that race did not exist before, obviously – and recent studies, in English even before French (Chapman and Frader 2004; Peabody and Stovall 2003), have emphasised the historical importance not only of racism (Noiriel 2007) but also of race itself as a defining category, whether in the colonies (Dubois 2004; Saada 2007)

233

or in metropolitan France (Ndiaye 2007). However, in the aftermath of World War II, following Claude Lévi-Strauss's (1952) *Race and History*, it became an illegitimate category in French intellectual life. It even became 'un-French', as it was associated with (so-called) Anglo-Saxon culture. Thus, as historian and anthropologist Ann L. Stoler has made clear in her work, though race has always already been pivotal in imperial France, its enunciation became and still remains problematic: hence her concept of 'colonial aphasia', to be distinguished from 'amnesia' (Stoler 2011). This erasure of race even applies to Foucault's work on biopolitics – as if sex relegated race to the margins of the French philosopher's work (Stoler 1995).

The novelty today is not race itself, then, but the fact that, starting in 2005, racial categories could be invoked explicitly once again, and (not surprisingly) in reference to the past. In January of that year, a new radical movement, Les Indigènes de la République, published a manifesto speaking in the name of racialised, underprivileged *banlieues* to reclaim and reverse the colonial stigma of the 'native'. A few months later, the urban riots coincided with the creation, on 26 November, of a black movement in France, the Conseil représentatif des associations noires (CRAN): it gave a name to a colour that had, until then, remained largely unspoken in political terms (Fassin 2008). But race is not solely about 'others': in fact, although in France, this new awareness still tends to focus on non-whites (in particular blacks and Arabs, though the latter seem more reluctant than the former to identify in such racial terms), it is worth bearing in mind, as Valls makes explicit, that the racialisation of France in public discourse simultaneously contributes to the emergence of a new category: whites.

Whiteness, visible and invisible

It is important to bear this in mind if one is to understand the passions revealed, or rather unleashed, by French discussions of race. Think, for example, of the controversy surrounding 'racial statistics' – and even their name, as they are sometimes called 'ethnic' or 'ethno-racial' or even (euphemistically) 'statistics of diversity' (Fassin 2010a). Not only is race absent from the French census, along with religion, which makes it impossible to evaluate the number of blacks and Arabs, or Jews and Muslims (not to mention whites or Christians); in addition, these categories cannot be used explicitly in research conducted by state institutions. The Constitutional Council forcefully reiterated this legal obligation at the end of 2007, thus constraining INSEE (in charge of statistics) and

INED (specialised in demography) to abandon two questions concerning skin colour and religion in a major joint survey about immigration and discrimination.

Anti-racist organisations played a crucial role in the polemic – interestingly, on both sides. While the CRAN[1] cleverly used the presidential campaign in spring 2007 to advocate racial statistics to combat discrimination, its older rival, SOS Racisme, successfully mobilised in the autumn, after Nicolas Sarkozy's election confirmed his anti-immigrant stance – from their point of view, the racist instrumentalisation of race categories only confirmed that they are inherently suspect. The struggle between the two organisations reveals different histories: while SOS Racisme was created in 1984 in reaction to the rise of the openly racist National Front, the CRAN arose in the 2005 context of a new awareness of structural racism. The former focuses on explicit racist ideologies, the latter on racial discrimination – whether intentional or not.

While SOS Racisme insists that we are all the same, regardless of colour or religion, the CRAN insists that the experience of everyday racism contributes to the differential racialisation of subjects – some of whom can be called blacks, not on account of their origin or skin colour, but insofar as they are treated as such. Race is here defined not in biological terms (by genes), nor even in ethnic terms (by culture); it is the experience of discrimination that contributes to the subjectivation of racialised subjects. This helps us to understand the virulent opposition to racial statistics in French society – especially (though not surprisingly) among intellectuals (including social scientists) whose dominant professional ideology is universalism. From their perspective, the problem is probably not so much that such statistics would name blacks or Arabs (although of course the difficult question of the definition of such categories was raised): those are precisely the people who are used to being called (those) names and, conversely, they are accustomed to naming themselves thus.

During the debate on racial statistics, the idea of filling out a state questionnaire with racial categories often evoked, especially among white intellectuals who are confronted with the globalisation of race as well as academia, the unpleasant discovery of immigration forms in the United States – not the boxes 'African-American' or 'Latino' though, but rather 'Caucasian', that many ridiculed and refused to check. Interestingly, French anthropologists of sub-Saharan Africa and the French Caribbean – that is, of societies in which race is most explicit – were among the most virulent in their rejection of the introduction of racial categories in Continental France (as their actual existence in French

[1] http://www.le-cran.fr/.

New Caledonia was hardly ever acknowledged). Thus, they rejected any suggestion that the racialised world they studied in the French or former colonies had anything to do with France itself: they refused the repatriation of whiteness. Post-colonial could only mean *after* colonisation, as if the colonial logics of race only belonged to the past and not the present: hence also their rejection of the post-colonial Indigènes de la République that immediately reached considerable media visibility – and still does through its attacks on 'whiteness'. The movement's spokeswoman is being sued for a pun she made on television in 2007, making up the term *souchiens*, supposed to characterise the French stock, *Français de souche*, while also evoking *sous-chiens*, or 'sub-dogs'.

The question of racial visibility (and invisibility) became apparent, though unspoken, with the importation, in the late 1990s, of the Canadian term *minorités visibles*. The metaphor of visibility, while it has met with mixed reactions, especially on the part of those it is meant to name, proves enlightening through its very paradoxes. First, what defines (so-called) visible minorities is not simply their physical appearance; it is also their social disappearance, that is, their invisibility – how they are made invisible, and how they struggle to become visible. One could interpret the rising public existence of Islamic veils, which purportedly hide the women wearing them, as 'ostensible signs' (according to the 2004 law which bans it from public schools) which make those socially invisible women politically visible, both individually and collectively. Think also of the academic and political debates concerning the meaning of the urban riots of 2005: were they political, proto-political, apolitical or even anti-political? One could argue that the fires which devastated the projects also illuminated them: they staged them for the media and thus gave visibility to the 'invisible man', namely, the growing presence of blacks in France revealed to some, even among social scientists, through such threatening images (Fassin 2011a).

But visible minorities also suggest the existence of an invisible majority. One can argue that, in France, the problem which (still) dares not speak its name is whiteness – not blackness or any other colour. Racial privilege is not only founded on unequal access to resources of all kinds, whether material or symbolic, nor exclusively on the exemption from stigmatisation and segregation that relies on structural domination. The ultimate privilege of whiteness is blindness to one's privilege. One need not think about oneself as 'white'. Indeed, one has no colour. One is simply a human being. Of course, this is not specific to race: contrary to women, men have no gender; they, too, are just human beings. And the same would apply to all distinctions between majority and minorities, sexual or otherwise.

The paradox is that such arguments have gained currency in English, rather than French, whereas they apply to the situation in France so much better than in English-speaking countries – especially as far as race is concerned. While there are now (as we have seen) occasional references to 'whites' (though seldom in a critical vein), 'whiteness' itself is hardly ever named in French; actually, the word itself is only beginning to be used: *négritude* is as common and old as *blanchité* is rare and new. But one could argue that, while 'colour-blindness' clearly remains the dominant rhetoric in French society, there is no equivalent 'gender-blindness': on the contrary, sexual difference is often opposed to the supposedly American concept of gender, and in reaction against the lack of differentiation allegedly promoted by feminism. The real 'invisible men' in France may be neither 'visible minorities' nor men in general, but *white* men.

Anti-white racism?

Whites may not exist in France, but apparently 'anti-white racism' does. On 16 March 2005, the newspaper of record, *Le Monde,* published an article ominously titled 'The Ghost of Anti-"White" Violence'. The scare quotes were soon to be forgotten, as the incident (young, white, middle-class demonstrators attacked by working-class blacks and Arabs, in part for racial reasons, according to the article) was picked up over a week later by a group of intellectuals and public figures who joined a zionist group to launch a manifesto 'against anti-white lynching' (in French, *ratonnade,* a term associated with anti-Arab attacks since the Algerian war of liberation from France in the 1950s). They worried that whites were attacked simply 'because they are French' – thus conflating, or purporting to reflect the conflation between, nationality and race, Frenchness and whiteness. The phrase 'anti-white racism', which had, until then, been identified with the extreme right, was thus appropriated by public figures who were not – whether they were supposed to be on the left (like historian Jacques Julliard and Doctors without Borders founder Bernard Kouchner) or not (like philosopher Alain Finkielkraut and political scientist Pierre-André Taguieff).

This elevation of 'anti-white racism' to mainstream political discourse only confirmed the growing influence of extreme-right politics in French public discourse (just as in much of Europe, of course). A September 2012 polemic only confirms this evolution: while competing to become leader of the right-wing party UMP, Jean-François Copé published a book advocating 'an unrepentant right' (*une droite décomplexée*) – a phrase associated with former president Nicolas Sarkozy. One anecdote captured his political strategy as it ignited controversy: a woman who complained to her neighbours about a theft perpetrated by their teenage son against her own only received insults in return. 'She now feels like a foreigner in her neighbourhood of many years. An "anti-white racism" has developed in our cities, in the projects, as certain individuals – some of whom are French – despise French people whom they label "Gauls" under the pretext that they do not share the same religion, skin colour or origins.'

The polemic that ensued centred on the main opposition party's shift toward the extreme right. However, the concept of racism was effectively reversed and displaced. Even on the left, those who denounced this new step in the direction of the National Front seldom mentioned the obvious fact that whites are not the main target of discrimination in French society, nor that those who are attacked because they 'do not share the same religion, skin colour or origins' are usually Muslims, blacks, Arabs and Roma. In addition, the new terms of discussion overlooked the major role that political parties have played in legitimating xenophobia and racism, especially under the presidency of Sarkozy: the creation of a Ministry of Immigration and National Identity in 2007 was to occupy centre stage during most of his term, as he and his government kept the focus on 'unwelcome migrants' (*immigration subie*) and various 'others'.

More insidiously, the response of anti-racist associations to the political staging of 'anti-white racism' tended to be framed in universalist terms: while siding with the venerable, Dreyfus Affaire–era Ligue des droits de l'homme in refusing to use the term, SOS Racisme made a generous declaration that 'racism knows no border, no nationality, no skin colour'. On the occasion of what may be the first trial for anti-white racism, which was to open a month after the Copé controversy, Alain Jakubowicz, the president of Ligue internationale contre le racisme et l'antisémitisme (LICRA), was to use exactly the same phrase ('racism knows no borders') – with an equivalent list: 'national, religious, or ethnic'. Even the Mouvement contre le racisme et pour l'amitié entre les peuples (MRAP), departing from its emphasis on Islamophobia, joined the lawsuit to confirm its new strategy: anti-racism should combat 'all forms of racism' – including against whites. The new political rhetoric had then succeeded in erasing the structural dissymmetry of racial domination, thus eviscerating the concept of 'racism'.

The emergence of 'anti-white racism' in political discourse serves to demonstrate several points. First, race is not just about 'others'; it has to do with the norm, thus affecting whites at the same time as non-whites – those who embody the norm just as much as those whom it marginalises. Second, race is not just an empirical fact; it is inseparably a representation. This is why it is not only a social reality but also, at the same time, a political issue. Politics and policies do not just reflect a pre-existing given; they construct race and thus bring it to existence. This is why race has little or even nothing to do with biology and everything to do with society. Third, French exceptionalism notwithstanding, France is no exception: the colour-blind rhetoric is not in any way incompatible with the actual racialisation of society and politics. This discourse should be understood as part of the nationalisation of racial rhetoric. Indeed, this requires taking the politics of national identity to understand both blindness to race and actual racialisation in the French context.

How the French became white

Whiteness is 'good to think', especially in the French context, not only as a way of shedding light onto the blind spot of colour-conscious race studies but also to resist any naturalisation of racial categories. The Irish provide a classic example in whiteness studies. Noel Ignatiev analysed *How the Irish Became White* (Ignatiev 1995) – that is, how these immigrants reinvented themselves in the context of nineteenth-century America through the confrontation with racial hierarchy: far from siding with abolitionist movements, they embraced racism. In other words, they gained acceptance as whites at the expense of blacks. One reason for this book's impact is that it helped by questioning the obvious, thus revealing how race remains imbued with biological assumptions: Are not the Irish *really* white? The fact is that, even before race as we know it, the British colonial situation defined the Irish as 'savages', so much so that they were to serve as a prototype for thought about 'native Americans' or blacks (Schaub 2008). Conversely, our perception today of the Irish as manifestly white owes something to the transformation of Ireland itself – from a land of emigration to a country of immigration. The new whiteness of the Irish, who thus join the evolution of much of the European Union, is defined in contrast to migrants categorised as 'non-whites' (Garner 2007).

The case of France is certainly different. The French were probably never categorised as non-white, and they only had to identify as whites in the colonial context – in Continental France, their whiteness had little relevance in their self-definition. This is precisely what is changing today: race is coming home. With his colleague Michel Pialoux, sociologist Stéphane Beaud has been studying the French working class for more than two decades – that is, after the reference to the 'working class' all but disappeared from political discourse, in the wake of the collapse of communism and following the decline of trade unions (Beaud and Pialoux 1999). Workers who had, until then, been defined primarily in terms of class, even at a time of massive Maghrebian immigration, were now deprived of this traditional identity. The discourse of the extreme-right National Front, whose rise coincided with the decline of the Communist Party, has ever since offered an alternative identification which is inseparably national and racial. The French working class is becoming white, one could argue – not in the Irish sense, because its whiteness had never been questioned, but rather because class is no longer available as a primary identification.

While resisting the facile denunciation of working-class racism, Beaud and Pialoux have tried to make sense of this racialisation (though they might not use the term) in sociological terms (Beaud and Pialoux 2006: 89):

The group of 'white' workers also includes those who come from older waves of immigration (whether Italian, Spanish, or Portuguese) which have been redefined as 'European' once their cycle of integration came to an end. This redefinition has been favored by the contrast with the difficult professional integration of youths of more recent migrations, especially from the Maghreb.

In France, any reference to race is exposed to the suspicion of racism: the quotation marks around the word 'white' indicate caution. This leaves open the question of whether this emic category might also be an etic one – used sociologically as well as socially. The two sociologists reverberate their main informant's 'metaphors': 'There is this old working-class population, they are "French", they are "white white"; they are driven by demons: in order to make it, they are ready to trample others – that's all a little scary' (89).

However, Beaud and Pialoux go further: not only does this contribute to the racialisation of those 'non-Europeans' who are targeted, and who thus identify as 'non-whites'; 'in return, working-class racism plays a major role in making those who express it identify as white, French workers – racial identification compensating through its symbolic dividends the strong devaluation of working-class identity' (89). This is especially true of the recent generations – some of 'the children "of French stock" are all the more prone to thinking of themselves as "white" for having experienced situations in which they lost face as they were dominated by these other youths – "Arabs" and/or "Blacks", who now comprise locally a majority of the young working class' (Beaud and Pialoux 2006: 89). What is particularly clear here is that, once again, 'white' and 'non-white' are inseparable; whiteness is both a consequence and a condition of racialisation.

This analysis can be read as a response to what is often presented, especially in the United States, as a French predicament: according to this narrative, traditional France, described as ethnically homogeneous, cannot cope with the new multicultural world – hence a 'crisis of identity'. In fact, racialisation works the other way around: the crisis of identity (to be understood in terms of class rather than of culture) opens the way for racialisation (both the imposition of race on others and self-identification in racial terms), which redesigns France simultaneously as a multiracial society and as a white nation. Of course, this does not imply that race replaces class: on the contrary, race is about class – in this instance, about working-class identity. The rising significance of race is not to be understood as the declining significance of class. What is at stake is not simply race and class as empirical realities but also, once again inseparably, as representations.

Remarkably, these French sociologists unwittingly replicate arguments earlier developed in the United States, as if this social and political logic superseded that of national cultures. The 'symbolic dividends' of racial identification echo the 'wages of whiteness' that David Roediger ([1991] 2007) borrowed for the title of his book from this sentence by W. E. B. Du Bois: white workers' low wages were 'compensated in part by a . . . public and psychological wage' (12). Roediger thus revised traditional Marxist approaches, arguing that 'the most pressing task for historians of race and class is not to draw precise lines separating race and class but to draw lines connecting race and class'. The similarity in argument (and vocabulary) results from parallel histories: while the American social historian acknowledged in his afterword how much his book was written 'in reaction to the appalling extent to which white male workers voted for Reaganism in the 1980s' (188), Beaud and Pialoux attempt to make sense of the racist temptation among working-class whites that was and still is at the centre of the new right-wing populisms in France: so-called Reagan Democrats thus anticipated what some might label 'Le Pen Communists'.

However, some of the response to this work reveals its potential political ambiguities. Roediger makes it clear that, while his argument is 'anti-whiteness', it should not be construed as 'anti-whites'. On the contrary, it calls us 'to consider not only how racial identity leads some whites to deal out misery to others but also how it leads them to accept misery for themselves'. Hence the historian's acknowledgement that the tone of his book might be 'bleak', 'despairing', even 'tragic' (Roediger [1991] 2007: xv–xvi). In the French context, Beaud and Pialoux's analysis should be read as a defensive reaction against accusations of racism levelled by self-righteous, privileged anti-racists against the white working class. However, populists who go beyond the sociological explanation to politically justify working-class racism and xenophobia have also appropriated this defence.

In France today, some appropriate the work of Beaud and Pialoux's students, whether it be the sociology of rural working-class youths or that of lower-middle-class or middle-lower-class suburbans (Cartier et al. 2008; Renahy 2005), to make a plea for 'autochthony' (by contrast to those whom the Dutch call 'allochthonous') – left-wing populism (Guilluy 2010) sometimes converges with its right-wing counterpart to support the 'cultural identity' of 'poor whites' against 'visible minorities'. Once more, the risk derives from the dissociation of the social and the political. Considering the former as 'infrastructure' and the latter as 'superstructure' makes it possible to legitimate political xenophobia as a mere response to white, working-class 'cultural insecurity', instead of acknowledging how social identities are inextricably political; actually, 'top-down xenophobia' contributes to the production of racialised identities – and thus of working-class racism (*Cette France-là* 2012).

From French whiteness to white Frenchness

Whiteness makes sense in French society – as it should in studies of France – just as much as, if not more than, it does in English-speaking countries where this field of research first developed, as it is even more invisible because of the illegitimacy of race talk. As a consequence, France is not to be considered in the usual terms of national exceptionalism. However, the question of the nation certainly does not become irrelevant: it is to be understood not in a culturalist perspective but in the context of the politics of national identity. As whiteness becomes visible in France, it grows possible to think about white Frenchness, that is, the colour of the nation. After all, it is significant that 'Gaul' and 'French' have become synonymous with 'white' (all usually with scare quotes when in writing): it is not only a code word for race; it also says something about the racialisation of the nation.

An obvious example is that of football, which is – more than most sports – a site of national communion while simultaneously riven (and driven) by race. It has already been carefully examined from the perspective of race, class and national identity, confronting the 'changing face' of multiracial teams in multiracial nations with the near-absence of black spectators in English stadia: 'There is a tension between, on the one hand, the way football provides a means to define Englishness within a pageant of white nationalism; while on the other hand, the involvement of a minority of black England fans points to the possibility of decoupling Englishness from a seemingly compulsory whiteness' (Back et al. 2001: 254). These ambiguities, including the phantasy of transcending race thanks to nation (and the disillusionment that can follow), have a lot to do with the British context: 'The World Cup showed that a "protean sense of black Englishness" is emergent alongside the disavowal of that identity' (Back et al. 2001: 254, 275). But they are certainly not specific to Britain: in France, the post-colonial present of race and nation is as much steeped in a colonial history as was manifested in 1998, when (so-called) *black, blanc, beur* (black, white, French-born North African) France won the World Cup in a brief moment of national euphoria and (post-)racial reconciliation (Dubois 2010).

In that perspective, the French fiasco of 2010 is at least as telling as the 1998 triumph. What was at stake during the World Cup in South Africa was not simply the humiliating defeat but also the national embarrassment caused by the attitude of the players displayed on the international stage. Not only did they play poorly on the field; in addition, they behaved miserably off the field, or so everyone, from politicians to journalists, seemed to think, including some of the victorious players of the past. In a gesture of solidarity toward one of the players excluded for (allegedly) insulting the coach, his teammates decided to go on strike – in such a context, a most unusual labour practice that discredited the whole team, while the 'leaders' of the rebellion became the focus of public animosity. Stéphane Beaud wrote a book trying to make sense of this major scandal, in which players were publicly labelled 'scum' and considered un-French, as if they were 'traitors to the nation' (Beaud 2011). Did not these 'immature' teammates resemble the new 'dangerous classes', those young men of colour, and/or of foreign origin (for the most part), from the projects, who had rioted in 2005?

The scapegoating did not start then – and even less in 2010. Although 1998 may have briefly suspended the sarcastic attacks levelled by Jean-Marie Le Pen against a team of 'recent French stock', controversies soon resumed. In 2001, a symbolic game between France and Algeria was disrupted after tens of thousands of spectators hissed the French national anthem – reconciliation had failed. This incident reverberated through the presidential campaign of 2002, in which the National Front candidate reached the second round of the election at the expense of the outgoing prime minister, Socialist Lionel Jospin. The incident was not isolated, and this was generally interpreted as a sign of the failure to integrate 'second-generation immigrants' (a frequent oxymoron in French that reveals much about the racialisation of immigration). A 2003 law against social unrest initiated by future president Nicolas Sarkozy then criminalised offenses against national symbols such as the anthem or the flag.

The national anxieties do not only bear on spectators. Players are also the targets of attacks on account of their colour – not only by some racist fans but also by public figures, and not just on the extreme right. During the 2005 riots, philosopher Alain Finkielkraut speculated in the Israeli press about the evolution of French society, drawing a parallel with the national team which, he explained, far from being '*black, blanc, beur,*' had now become 'black, black, black' – thus turning it, or so he claimed, into an object of ridicule throughout the world. Even on the left, a prominent (though controversial) socialist figure from Montpellier in the south of the country, Georges Frêche, bitterly complained in 2006, 'In this national team, there are nine blacks out of eleven players. If there are so many, it is because whites suck. I am ashamed for this country.'

This declaration helps us to realize that, for these men, the problem is not just 'visible minorities'; at the same time, or even prior to this, it is about the 'invisible majority' – the fears about ridicule and shame reveal a great deal about national whiteness. The scandal hurt French pride – that is, the pride to be French, a 'symbolic wound' that Beaud considers even deeper among working-class Frenchmen whose symbolic gratifications are scarce. Such an argument about national identity parallels others heard about manhood (another essential dimension of football) or whiteness, of course. Should one not speak, then, of the wages of Frenchness? Hence a defence of football itself – in all its social dimensions, including coaches and managers (and not just players and spectators) – among those (including sociologists) for whom the joys of this sport compensate for the dividends, symbolic and otherwise, that are denied to the working class by society.

This became apparent in a later scandal that also concerns football, race and national identity. After the fiasco in South Africa, a new, widely respected coach was appointed: Laurent Blanc, a former player of the 1998 team whose surname was unfortunately to acquire symbolic resonance. In 2011, the publication of the transcript of a secretly recorded meeting of 8 November 2010, attended by all the national heads of the profession, revealed that they openly talked about race; worse, they did so in professional terms. The figures thus exposed, including the coach, denied that the discussion had anything to do with race: it was, they argued, about players with dual citizenship. Blanc and others resented the fact that players who had been trained and supported in France could eventually play for another national team – in particular (as was clear in the 2010 World Cup) for Algeria. This worry is paradoxical: the situation only concerns players who are not selected for the French national team. It probably reflects anxieties outside the world of football: only a few weeks earlier, the radical wing of the conservative party UMP, in the wake of the 'debate' on national identity launched by President

Sarkozy's minister of immigration, called for the disappearance of dual citizenship.

But dual citizenship is not just about nationals and foreigners; beyond this denotation, the connotation is race. This was made clear in the conversation held during this same meeting. As the national coach pointed out, 'all the Blacks, with the exception of Caribbean French, are of African origin. So, they can all go to an African team.' Laurent Blanc later went on, while denying that the quotas he envisaged would 'eliminate foreigners' (i.e., French players with dual citizenship), by positing that such quotas would help to diversify the players' morphologies. He complained that there was now only one 'prototype' (he also said 'stereotype') of player – 'tall, sturdy, powerful. And today, who's tall, sturdy and powerful? Blacks.' 'Small, white builds' were needed: 'The game is about intelligence, hence, other kinds of players – it's all connected!'

These explicit statements did not meet with universal disapproval in France – far from it. Many criticised the critics, deploring that such accusations of racism only served to discredit anti-racism, as a man like the national coach had nothing to do with the likes of the minister of immigration and national identity, who had just been exposed for making a racist joke. Historian Gérard Noiriel and sociologist Stéphane Beaud thus jointly wrote an opinion piece in the left-of-centre daily *Libération* (6 May 2011 – my critical response was published on 9 May): they argued that the concern about dual citizenship was justified (what if Zidane had played for Algeria instead of France?) and even that, in football circles, 'Blacks' was really 'less a racial than a social category' meaning 'working class'. This defence was ultimately grounded in the idea that 'football is probably today the one social practice that best contributes to mixing youths of working class background, regardless of their origins': therefore, they opposed the actual 'immersion of football in the working class' to the 'elite institutions' of 'critical intellectuals'.

These social scientists (both mentioned earlier for their important scholarly contributions to our understanding of racist mechanisms) certainly did not intend to condone racist political discourse associated with President Sarkozy's government. However, on this occasion, their effort was meant to resist the introduction of race as a critical tool, thus blinding them to Blanc's politics and policies of whiteness – as if football were simply about the working class, and as if race ultimately boiled down to class. Conversely, reintroducing the national dimension of whiteness in the analysis developed here is not a way to evacuate class. On the contrary – it is a starting point for a redefinition that does not narrow 'class' to 'working class': whiteness is about the class structure of the nation.

Sexual whiteness

Finally, one more term now needs to be introduced in the discussion of race, class and national identity: sex – in its double meaning of gender and sexuality. Let us go back to the 2010 French debacle in the World Cup. The media reported on tensions within the team, in particular between two players, one presented as a bully (Franck Ribéry), the other as his victim (Yoann Gourcuff), as if this were a school yard fight between the bad student and the good one. Whereas the former was often presented as one of the leaders of the strike, the latter was generally exempted from such suspicion. The two men do stand in sharp contrast: Ribéry comes from the working class, Gourcuff from the middle class – his conformity to good football manners reflecting the fact that he is the son of a well-known coach. The latter is a shy presence, always on his best behaviour, whereas the former, well known for his loudness, is regularly accused of misbehaving.

Of course, one might say that both are white, but it all depends on the definition of whiteness. Going beyond mere skin colour – as the classic example of the Irish taught us – makes it possible to understand that Gourcuff embodies a kind of whiteness that certainly does not define Ribéry. For one thing, Ribéry converted to Islam in 2006, thus crossing a clearly racialised line in today's French society – the three children he had from a woman of Algerian parents have Muslim names. It is also worth noting not only the large, visible scar on his face but also his deliberate choice not to have it removed surgically. By contrast, Gourcuff is considered very handsome, if not pretty. Beyond that, discussions about both men's sexual lives have played an important role. A sexual scandal erupted concerning the former a few months before the World Cup: Ribéry was sued for having sex (as a birthday present) with an underage Algerian escort who went on to have a career in sexy lingerie. Gourcuff is said to be the opposite: he is not one to brag about sexual adventures. Rumour has it that he is single.

Actually, several commentators (including his father) insisted that the harsh treatment he received on the national team was about 'more than football': this young man was perceived as 'different'. How different? After gay magazine *Têtu* elected him in 2009 'hunk of the month', rumours about his sexual orientation developed. He denied being gay, while adding, 'Even if I were, I don't see where the problem would be.' The question may not be homosexuality, after all, but rather homophobia – as another commentator explicitly invoked, 'which is rich, considering that the guy is not even gay. It's bad enough when you are, but if you aren't, it's even more incomprehensible.' To make this comprehensible, though, one could argue that, in the homosocial world of football, manliness in its most macho version is crucial for the affirmation of compulsory heterosexuality.

One question remains: How does homosexuality, or rather homophobia, relate to race, or class, not to mention national identity? Indeed, homophobia, like racism, is heard all the time in football games – with a difference: whereas race is likely to be visible, homosexuality may not be, hence the permanence of the gay closet in the locker room. A club president, Louis Nicollin, from the city of Montpellier (a man close to the socialist powerhouse Georges Frêche, mentioned earlier), regularly makes the news for his racist, sexist and, in this case, homophobic comments. However, this is generally considered, not without amusement, as idiosyncratic. Conversely, when a tiny amateur Muslim club from the projects (Bebel Créteil) declined in 2009, less than a year before the World Cup, to play against an openly homosexual team (Paris Foot Gay), the scandal was considerable: this kind of homophobia was supposed to have a very serious meaning, reflecting a deep cultural problem.

The explanation is that homophobia has been racialised in the years since 2000. For example, two books came out in 2009 focusing on homophobia in the suburbs (*banlieues*). This is not a specifically French issue: throughout Europe, and beyond, one witnesses the rise of what has been called (in the wake of 11 September 2001) 'homonationalism' (Puar 2007). In broader terms, the opposition between 'us' and 'them' plays out in what we might call the *sexual* clash of civilisations (Fassin 2010b) – which is, in fact, about both (homo-)sexuality and gender (and, in particular, women). Hence the broader category of 'sexual nationalisms', particularly relevant in Europe; old nationalisms relied on models of virility, in contrast to women, gays and Jews, and the new nationalisms claim to make room for gender equality and sexual freedom (Fassin 2011b).

This started in the Netherlands, with the Islamophobic populism of Pim Fortuyn, an openly gay leader – but it reverberated elsewhere, including in France. National Front leader Marine Le Pen famously proclaimed in 2010 that 'in some neighbourhoods, it is hard to be a woman, gay, Jewish or even French or white' (in his attack on 'anti-white racism', UMP leader Copé was to abridge this remarkable list in 2012 – 'there are neighbourhoods where it is hard to be a woman, or to be white'). 'We' consider 'them' homophobic; in return, 'they' see 'us' as homosexuals. In the same way, 'they' appear to 'us' as sexist; conversely, 'we' look effeminate to 'them'. This is how it becomes plausible, if not necessarily true, that a man like Ribéry might reject the alleged homosexuality of another, like Gourcuff, thus proclaiming, as a sign of class identity, his homophobia – and confirming to many what his conversion to Islam had already indicated: Ribéry's renunciation of whiteness just as he validates that of Gourcuff.

One advantage of adding sex, after national identity, to the equation of race and class is that it helps us to think differently about whiteness. Once again, race is both a reality and its representation. Instead of apprehending it exclusively as the last resource of the working class, we can simultaneously approach this cultural identity as a political project that permeates society as a whole. This is why it has to do with the nation. But, once again, this in no way rehearses old, culturalist versions of French exceptionalism. On the contrary, it is clear that the politics of sexual whiteness are not specific to France. The rhetoric of national identity plays in parallel, today, throughout Europe, and paradoxically, that which seems to define each nation the most intimately turns out to be the European common denominator – in contrast to racialised others. The only true specificity of the French situation may still be not colour-blindness itself but the shared representation of France as 'colour-blind' – that is, a denial of race which contributes to the efficiency of whiteness as a category of power.

It becomes clear, then, that national identity is not to be understood merely in terms of class identification; it is also an operation of power that plays in class relations – in terms both of inclusion and exclusion. Here the reference is no longer so much Roediger but rather Ann L. Stoler, already mentioned earlier (Stoler 2010). Carnal knowledge talks about the power, not the wages, of whiteness. Colonial history thus teaches us that race traces social boundaries in the sexual intimacy of subjects – just as sex draws lines between racialised groups. Whiteness is not just that; it is always, in fact, *proper* whiteness. This is why class cannot be reduced to working class, and also why race cannot be reduced to class. Racial politics implies the sexual policing of racial boundaries.

REFERENCES

Back, L., Crabbe, T. and Solomos, J. (2001). *The Changing Face of Football: Racism, Identity, and Multiculture in the English Game*. Oxford: Berg.
Beaud, S., with Guimard, P. (2011). *Traîtres à la Nation? Un Autre Regard sur la Grève des Bleus en Afrique du Sud*. Paris: La Découverte.
Beaud, S. and Pialoux, M. (1999). *Retour sur la Condition Ouvrière. Enquête aux Usines Peugeot de Sochaux-Montbéliard*. Paris: Fayard.

(2006). Racisme ouvrier ou mépris de classe? Retour sur une enquête de terrain. In D. Fassin and É. Fassin, eds, *De la Question Sociale à la Question Raciale?*, pp. 72–90.

Cartier, M., Coutant, I., Masclet, O. and Siblot, Y. (2008). *La France des Petits-Moyens. Enquête sur la Banlieue Pavillonnaire.* Paris: La Découverte.

Cette France-là, ed. (2012). *Xénophobie d'en Haut. Le Choix d'une Droite Éhontée.* Paris: La Découverte.

Chapman, H. and Frader, L., eds. (2004). *Race in France: Interdisciplinary Perspectives on the Politics of Difference.* New York: Berghahn.

Dubois, L. (2004). *A Colony of Citizens: Revolution and Slave Emancipation in the French Caribbean, 1787–1804.* Chapel Hill: University of North Carolina Press.

(2010). *Soccer Empire: The World Cup and the Future of France.* Los Angeles: University of California Press.

Fassin, É. (2008). Actualité de la 'question noire'. In A. Boubeker and A. Hajjat, eds, *Histoire Politique des Immigrations (Post)Coloniales. France, 1920–2008.* Paris: Amsterdam, pp. 275–88.

(2010a). Statistiques raciales ou racistes? Histoire et actualité d'une controverse française. In D. Fassin, ed., *Les Nouvelles Frontières de la Société Française.* Paris: La Découverte, pp. 427–51.

(2010b). National identities and transnational intimacies: sexual democracy and the politics of immigration in Europe. *Public Culture*, 22(3), 507–29.

(2011a). 'Immigration et délinquance': la construction d'un problème entre politique, journalisme et sociologie. *Cités*, 46(2), 67–83.

(2011b). From criticism to critique. *History of the Present*, 1(2), 265–74.

Fassin D. and Fassin, É., eds. (2006). *De la Question Sociale à la Question Raciale? Représenter la Société Française.* Paris: La Découverte.

Garner, S. (2007). *Whiteness: An Introduction.* London: Routledge.

Guilluy, C. (2010). *Fractures Françaises.* Paris: François Bourin.

Ignatiev, N. (1995). *How the Irish Became White.* New York: Routledge.

Lévi-Strauss, C. (1952). *Race and History.* Paris: UNESCO.

Ndiaye, P. (2007). *La Condition Noire. Essai sur une Minorité.* Paris: Calmann-Lévy.

Noiriel, G. (2007). *Immigration, Antisémitisme et Racisme en France (XIXe–XXe Siècle). Discours Publics, Humiliations Privées.* Paris: Fayard.

Peabody, S. and Stovall, T., eds. (2003). *The Colour of Liberty: Histories of France.* Durham, NC: Duke University Press.

Puar, J. K. (2007). *Terrorist Assemblages: Homonationalism in Queer Times.* Durham, NC: Duke University Press.

Renahy, N. (2005). *Les Gars du Coin. Enquête sur une Jeunesse Rurale.* Paris: La Découverte.

Roediger, D. R. ([1991] 2007). *The Wages of Whiteness: Race and the Making of the American Working Class.* New York: Verso.

Saada, E. (2007). *Les Enfants de la Colonie. Les Métis de l'Empire Français entre Sujétion et Citoyenneté.* Paris: La Découverte.

Schaub, J. F. (2008). *Oroonoko, Prince et Esclave. Roman Colonial de l'Incertitude.* Paris: Seuil.

Stoler, A. L. (1995). *Race and the Education of Desire: Foucault's History of Sexuality and the Colonial Order of Things*. Durham, NC: Duke University Press.
    (2010). *Carnal Knowledge and Imperial Power: Race and the Intimate in Colonial Rule*. Berkeley: University of California Press.
    (2011). Colonial aphasia: race and disabled histories of France. *Public Culture*, 23(1), 121–56.

14   Racial comparisons, relational racisms: some thoughts on method

David Theo Goldberg

The prevailing academic paradigm in analyzing race and racism, ethnic and racial relations, has been comparative. Analysts contrast and compare different societies, historically or contemporarily, to reveal similarities and differences regarding popular ethnoracial expression as well as state formulations, structures and responses. In this chapter, I suggest that this dominant paradigm overlooks a more compelling mode of critical analysis regarding race and racism, namely, the influencing and reinforcing *relations* between different national expressions of racial and ethnic commitment. Noting the relative methodological strengths of comparativism and relationalities, I map out what a relational critical countermethod looks like, arguing that it incorporates comparative considerations, where they arise, within its scope.

Much of the work on race and racism has been indexed to local national contexts. This mode of analysis has ranged across historical, sociological, political, legal, cultural and, indeed, critical contributions. It marks a great deal of what goes under the designation of critical race studies. Racial conception and racist social arrangements, at least on first blush, seem indelibly tied to specific national sociopolitical, economic, legal and cultural conditions. Racial arrangements and their implications are overwhelmingly considered a response to and a product of local arrangements, relations of power and historical legacies. They seem to acquire meaning and take on significance only as a function of the specific contexts contained and constrained by the fabric of life, meaning making and administrative arrangements indexed to a specific society, a state configuration, at a given place and time. In this, racial studies, in the broad, follow the dominant strand of ethnic studies quite faithfully.

Here whiteness studies is a contemporary case in point (Twine and Gallagher 2008): think of its emergence over the past 20 years in the USA, Britain, Canada, Australia, South Africa and, more recently, various European countries. How the Irish, Jews, Italians, East Europeans, working class or, for that matter, Indians ('Hindu'), Syrians, Lebanese

251

or Indonesians (the latter in the Netherlands) became white has been narrowly tailored to the relevant legal and political histories in this place or that. Perhaps understandably so, as the histories differ from one site to the next, the status and privilege associated with 'being white' ascribed, 'earned' or denied very much a matter of where and how. But whiteness studies simply represents what has long been at play in thinking about racial matters more generally.

It follows from this that, where studies seek a larger frame of reference for thinking about race and racism – both, note, in their singularity – they have resorted to a methodology of comparativism. They seek to compare the histories of, for the most part, discretely conceived state experiences. And the comparisons have tended to draw together almost exclusively those states considered to exhibit the most extreme and extremely different modes of state racism.

These dominant examples of compared racisms are taken either to indicate that their differences are not as extreme as first thought or to reveal that, at least tentatively, there are a limited number of different models for state-based racisms. So the USA and South Africa have been repeatedly placed besides each other to reveal their similarities – Jack Cell (1982) on histories of segregation, Massey and Denton (1998) on American apartheid and so on. Or Brazil and the USA have been juxtaposed to reveal both their relatively significant distinctions and their overlaps – from Pierre van den Berghe (1967) to Carl Degler (1971) and, more recently, Anthony Marx (1998). Today, many are turning to apartheid South Africa as the appropriately revealing comparison point for the structures of oppression imposed by Israel on Palestinians (Carter 2006; Davis 2004; Glaser 2003).

There is no doubt that these studies have been useful, revealing similarities and differences, bringing to notice the ways in which racial governmentalities from one state to another converge and diverge, how racial consciousness can take hold, the work it does, the power it expresses, the shaping of national consciousness which it effects and so on. The specificity of the local, then, has been important, even crucially so, in the development of critical studies of race and racism. And local conditions, given the structures of political, economic, social, cultural and legal life, in the main have been configured throughout modernity at the state or even at the more local level.

Such a comparativist frame, resting as it does on a presumptive model of geographic discreteness, on incontrovertible and reductive cultural, sociopolitical and legal uniqueness, however, is deeply connected to the structuring assumptions of post-war area studies (Spivak 2003: 2–3). It may hide as much as it reveals. Accounts restricted to these frames of

relative localism actually seem to miss a crucial dimension for compre-
hending racial significance and racist conditioning in all their complexity.

Theoretically driven critical work on race and racism can be traced
genealogically to those such as W. E. B. Du Bois, Ruth Benedict, Oliver
Cromwell Cox, Frantz Fanon, Albert Memmi, Jean-Paul Sartre, Hannah
Arendt, Edward Saïd and Stuart Hall. Together, and among others,
they have forged a different analytic to the comparativist one. I will call
this counterdisposition *relational* and interactive rather than discretely
comparativist. Crucial to note is that the work of each of these analysts
grew out of linking racial conception and racist expression constitutively
to the colonial condition.

It is not that racism is reducible only to some narrow connection to
colonial subjection and repression, ordering and governmentality. But
colonial outlooks, interests, dispositions and arrangements set the tone
and terms, its frameworks for conceiving and thinking about, the horizons of possibility for engaging and distancing, exploiting and governing,
admitting and administering those conceived as racially distinct and different – and, relatedly, for elevating and privileging those deemed racially
to belong to the dominant.

Racial conception and racist practice are *relational*. They are to be fully
comprehended, then, only once the constitutively relational aspects are
not just integrated into but centered in the account. The conceptions and
comprehensions, as well as the institutional arrangements and exclusionary expressions, are no doubt deeply local in the exact meanings and
resonances they exhibit, as well as the effects and implications to which
they, in the end, give rise. But these local resonances, nevertheless, are
almost always tied to extra- and trans-territorial conceptions and expressions, those that revolve in wider circles of meaning and practice.

Local expression may both be prompted by and may prompt interactive expressions elsewhere. They come and go with travelers, commerce, governing ideas, mail and media (newspapers, books, comics,
magazines, journals, sermons, lectures, radio and television programming etc.). Terms circulate, practices are shaped and fail, only to be
taken up and refined in environments that prove to be more conducive
to their articulation. Ideas and practices from one place interact with
conditions and expressions tried and tested elsewhere.

A comparativist analytic might enable one to indicate how ideas and
practices in one place – a nation-state – have taken on a meaning, a
nuance, a 'color' or an impact different to expression elsewhere. But it
fails to account for the interactive relation between repressive racial ideas
and exclusionary or humiliating racist practices across place and time,
unbounded by the presumptive divides of state boundaries. Indeed, a

comparativist account pays attention to the relational only as an observed outcome of the compared states, failing for the most part to consider the constitutive condition of the relational components for their very possibility, historically and manifestly. Race and racisms are also, and at least as importantly, as globally circulating, interacting, relational conditions as they are locally indexed, resonant, impacting.

Frank Dikötter has gestured at something like a relational account, at least at first blush. He dismisses standard accounts of racism as trading on understanding it 'as a uniform phenomenon, as if there were only one form universal in its origins, causes, meanings and effects'. In contrast, he insists, racisms are not 'fixed or static entities' but 'interactive', taking 'appropriation, differential usage and re-signification as key to understanding the rapid spread of racist worldviews in parts of the world outside Europe' (Dikötter 2008: 1482).

Dikötter at least points in the right direction. But, upon starting out well, he all too quickly seems to choose the cul-de-sac turn in the road. His account bogs down in an argument for recognizing the unique national traditions of racist articulation in areas of the world outside Europe – such as Japan, China and parts of West Africa. Far from enabling a robust relational account, Dikötter's is an 'interactionism' among already constituted discrete national configurations, suggesting perversely exactly the sort of universalism of racisms he claims to reject. 'People across all continents', he concludes, 'express profound interest in the outward appearance of people and are likely to divide people along some sort of racial classification, "white" and "black" being poles now adopted almost everywhere.' Indeed, he even gives title to this: 'The *racialization of the globe*', from 'Latin America to East Asia' (Dikötter 2008: 1494, emphasis added).

In contrast, the relational account I am suggesting takes leave from this universalizing of racial naturalization bound to finding color prejudice recurrent from Latin America to East Asia. Racial relationality turns, by contrast, on two *interactive* claims. Dikötter loosely recognizes the first, only to pull back from its development and ignore its implications.

In the first instance, racial ideas, meanings and exclusionary and repressive practices in one place are influenced, shaped by and fuel those elsewhere. Racial ideas and arrangements circulate, cross borders, shore up existing or prompt new ones as they move between established political institutions. Ideas and practices emanating from elsewhere are made local; local practices that appear homegrown more often than not have a genealogy at least in part not simply limited to the local. The local may provide a particular timbre and color to the ideas' reference or application, their sound and style. It gives *voice* to racial expression and racist arrangement in specific ways. But while the accent may be unique, as, too, the semantic content and even the syntax, their influences and implications most often are not.

Who counts as 'black' and who 'white' differs from one place to another, as do specific meanings attached to the designations and their placements. Nonetheless, in the main, their relational conditions – to each other as concepts, to the pragmatics of those concepts wherever in use – strongly suggest that, once so designated and determined, conditions of privilege and disprivilege, power and vulnerability, will pertain.

Second, racist arrangements anywhere – in any place – depend, to a smaller or larger degree, on racist practice almost everywhere else. In the absence of racist institutionalization virtually everywhere else, local racist expression, if not disposition, would certainly be less resonant and impactful, if it did not (quite) cease in significance altogether. The support which racial thinking and racism 'here' get from 'there', both as a symbolic matter and materially, sustains and extends the impacts. This, in short, might better be characterized as the *globalization of the racial* rather than the racialization of the globe.

The globalization of the racial is predicated on the understanding that racial thinking and its resonances circulated by boat in the European voyages of discovery and was imported into the impact zones of colonization and imperial expansion. Racial ordering, racist institutional arrangement and racial control were key instruments of colonial governmentality and control. Made local to apply to lived conditions of the everyday, the colonies became, in turn, sites of state experimentation, as Bernard Cohn (1996) argued, laboratories for metropolitan class rule, the maintenance of order and rehearsals in the intimacies and morals of class life (Stoler 2002, 2006). Reimported as the baggage of colonial administrators and the 'return' of the imperial repressed of colonial charge, strands of racial governmentality seeped into and ordered the imaginations of metropolitan burghers too. The racial out there came, by extension and connection, default and design, to shape home rule, if with local specificity. Cohn insisted that 'the metropole and colony have to be seen in a unitary field of analysis' (Cohn 1996: 4). I am urging, by extension, that this unitary field of analysis be deeply, if differentially, heterogeneously, relational.

A relational account accordingly reveals something not otherwise comprehensible. It signals how state formations or histories, logics of oppression and exploitation, are linked, whether causally or symbolically, ideationally or semantically. A comparativist account undertakes to reveal through analogy; a relational account reveals through indicating how effects are brought about as a result of historical political or

economic, legal or cultural, links, the one acting upon another. A comparativist account may choose to contrast racially conceived or ordered relations of production in one place and another. A relational analysis will stress the (re-)production of relational ties and their mutually effecting and reinforcing impacts. A comparativist account contrasts and compares. A relational account connects.

For example, an account in which contemporary Israel is compared with apartheid South Africa aims to tell us something about the Israeli treatment of Palestinians analogous to the white treatment of blacks in apartheid South Africa. And the comparison then serves to sustain the implication that the same sort of response to apartheid South Africa – economic sanctions and cultural boycotts, for instance – may properly be in order in the case of Israel. The account makes a point through likenesses and implications from those analogical connections.

But the account can obscure as much as it reveals, seeking to establish likenesses by ignoring distinctions. So, although the Palestinian territories seem like Bantustans or Homelands, there are also ways in which they are not quite like them. The territories no longer provide labor to Israel in the way Homelands did to white South Africa and were set up always intending to do so. Apartheid was about formalized *segregation*; contemporary Israel seems wedded to a policy of more or less absolutized *separation*, economically and socially, to invoke a distinction John Hope Franklin made useful when talking about his experiences growing up in the American South.

To press the point, making the occupied territories like Bantustans ignores the distinctions between the West Bank and Gaza. The former remains akin to a colony, settlers and all; Gaza is more like a highly policed, very oppressive concentration or prison camp. Gazans are concentrated into a persistently locked enclosure with little access to the basic resources of life, comparable in some basic ways to that to which so many European Jews were subjected, awkward as some might find that connection (Agamben 2002; Goldberg 2009).

Israel's unqualified supporters – the strident critics of Israel's critics – find it easier to respond to comparativist than to relational accounts. To object to a comparativist account requires simply pointing out disanalogies, for example, that Palestinian Israelis have many of the rights which Jewish Israelis have (of course, they do not have equal rights, a point often side-stepped in the name of security); they vote for Knesset representation; they can own property, etc. Often, the response takes on the indignation of the 'How dare you compare?': Israel couldn't possibly be like apartheid South Africa, let alone Nazi Germany, as Israeli existence has been threatened as South Africa's never was; Jews were subject to the exterminating angel of Nazi final solution – another point of contextual comparison – while Israel is simply defending itself from the exterminating angel (once again)!

Evidence of this preference for the counter-comparativist resides in the fact that such supporters of Israel will attempt to reduce relational critics to comparativist accounts. Some relationalists will cite instances of Israel's own military officers urging that the control of Palestinian refugee camps such as Jenin tactically should follow or learn from the Nazi vice-grip of the Warsaw ghetto. Others have long pointed out apartheid South Africa's support for Israel, militarily and economically, in reciprocating Israel's willingness to consort with the apartheid state and in criticism of the ANC's long-standing support for the Palestinian cause. Relationists, here, are especially concerned to reveal how new formations look to older modes of repression for resources of control and domination, relating new circumstances to the experiences of the tried and tested elsewhere, no matter the 'pedigree'. Their pro-Israel critics will react with horror, chiding them for comparing victims (Israelis, Jews) to villainous exterminators and arch-racists.

For relational accounts, accordingly, specificity is important, the micro-details of the considerations related revealing of the conditions needing to be accounted for, to be explained. For comparativist accounts, the broad stroke is more likely to be revealing. If the latter works through drawing on impressions, the former reveals by showing how movement in one place ripples through impacts in another, and how structures at one time are taken up and put to work in another elsewhere.

Here it is not just that Gaza is *like* (or, depending on one's point of view, unlike) the Warsaw ghetto, a comparison point. Rather, that Israeli military officers are on record for explicitly invoking the Warsaw ghetto as a model for thinking about how to regulate the Palestinian refugee camps suggests that the Warsaw ghetto provides a model. It is an experiment the process of which can and has been taken up by later repressive regimes to suppress an ethnoracially identified population considered dangerous and expendable. Just as early-twentieth-century British and German concentration camps in Africa – the British camp imprisoning Boer enemies during the Anglo-Boer War, for instance, or the Germans rounding up Herero in German South West Africa, first to exploit their labor and then to exterminate them – became models for the Nazis almost half a century later (cf. Gilroy 2000).

Comparativist methodological dispositions are unlikely to reveal this sort of connection, its efficacy and productivity, in helping to produce the technologies of repression and control. Or, if they did, it would only be indirectly, as an inductive inference after the fact, at best, not a

constitutive connection. That could only be composed and comprehended relationally.

Comparisons, as I say, are generated outward from within the parameters – the bounded reference points – of states. Within these parameters,
comparisons, of course, may be especially revealing. To take a different reference point, comparisons can indicate that the average wealth of
blacks, say, is significantly less than that of whites in a given society or
social domain, that blacks are unemployed traditionally at twice the rate
and are charged more for insurance, automobile purchases, mortgages
and so on. But all this tells us, as such, is the *fact* of inequality. To determine whether there is discrimination at work, patterns would have to be
established, a connection to interests or intentions, dispositions or repro-
ductions, of treating the racially differentiated differently. In short, the
move from comparison to a conclusion regarding racial discrimination
or racisms requires the establishment of certain sorts of relation.

To go back to drawing a link between Auschwitz's Musselmanner and
Gaza's Muslims, then, this reveals two further considerations. First, I
concede that comparisons of this kind can be powerful rhetorically and
morally. It is hard to remain unmoved by the degradation experienced
in the Nazi death camps. Those unmoved are probably in some sort of
deep denial. An analogical comparison of a set of experiences at another
time and place shown to be like the one at hand in relevant respects is
likely to effect at least a critical response, to move to action of some kind
those who feel the analogical force. It is revealing, perhaps, that, for a
related reason, if pulling in the opposite direction, the analogy may be
resisted. There can be no analogy here because the Nazi death camps
were unique, the Holocaust exceptional. But the larger point, one lost in
the resistance to the analogy, as the Israeli military officers demonstrate,
is that comparisons like this can also be taken up for their more nefarious
lessons in 'effective' repressive state apparatuses.

Second, there can be a thin line sometimes between comparison and
relation, bridged perhaps by some other form of argumentation or insight.
That the ghetto of Gaza today may be (somewhat? sufficiently?) like
the one in Warsaw in the late 1930s and early 1940s might be turned
into something more causally connected via, say, a group psychoanalytic
account that attempts to explain the former as a consequence of lingering
psychic trauma fixating on a fantasized sense of ongoing victimization. I
am less concerned here with the propriety or content of this argument
than with its form, the ways in which analogicality can be taken up as a
mode of causality, comparativism in the service of relationality.

That comparativism can service the relational rather than the reverse
reveals that relational accounts, even in their specificity, offer a wider,

more telling purview. The relational undercuts the reach of the comparative, outstripping it. It subsumes comparison in a way in which the reverse cannot. Comparison can reveal an initial insight probably hidden from view but for the comparison. But it takes the relational to make evident the deeper connection constitutively unavailable to comparison.

The relational outstrips the comparative disposition precisely because it puts the elements in question into play, causally and productively, in relation to each other. The comparative holds the elements apart, insisting upon, because assuming, their discreteness. In this, the relation of the comparative disposition to the relational is reminiscent of the differing elements to which Descartes famously drew attention in his *Discourse on Method*. The first stage of philosophico-scientific method, Descartes insisted, was to decompose the constituent components of the object under analysis, breaking the object down into its most basic discrete elements to comprehend them in their simplest, barest formation (Descartes 1637). In this, comparison consists of one-to-one (to one, reiterative) assessments of relevant conditions or social arrangements characteristic of each site. Relationality, by methodological contrast, involves mapping conditions in their interactivity, drawing out their transforming impacts. Relationality, in short, offers a cartography of reiterative impacts, of their transformations and redirections.

The supposed discreteness of the compared elements, as I have hinted, is nevertheless a product of the artifice of national (or local) boundaries. It is curious how the national continues to figure the analytic imaginary, to structure its possibilities, to limit its analytic capacity and force. The national or state frame privileges comparison over the relational, perhaps because the comparativist frame analytically preserves by presupposing established boundaries, the sociostructural givens, in turn helping to fix them in place. Likewise, comparativism and the positivity of reductively empirical accounts of racial phenomena turn out to be mutually reinforcing, the boundary conditions of one mapping onto those of the other.

In service to the relational, then, the comparative is accordingly put to productive purpose, its insights extended, its inherent, because presumptive and narrowing, limits prized open. The comparative operates, at (its) best, at the level of first-order insight, uncovering what calls for extended exploration and ultimately what requires explanation. On its own, the comparative stops short, at the border – of the nation-state, perhaps of discipline and disciplinarity itself.

What, then, of the connection of the racial to the colonial raised in passing at the outset? As a point of comparison, the contrast of, say, contemporary racism in the USA, South Africa, Latin America, Europe or, yes, also Israel-Palestine, with colonial modalities of racial governance and control, can tell us something about how things looked then and how they operate now. This can be revealing as much about the differences as about the similarities. What a relational account adds, however, is not just the historical legacy. It enables one to see how the colonial shaped the contemporary, planted racism's roots in place, designed its social conditions and cemented its structural arrangements. It reveals how what, today, social agents might take as given, as supposedly natural conditions of the social, were socially composed by the relatively powerful over the backs of the relatively powerless, how far from natural they became naturalized, cemented and retained in place by a mix of design, default, ongoing social labor, habitus and carelessness – by the (re-)production of relationalities. The traces of those formations run very deeply, both directly and by extension.

This is not to say that contemporary racisms are colonial; it is to point, by contrast, to the constitutive connection of the contemporary to the colonial, even as racism's immediate prompts and expressions may have morphed over time. Given these contemporary contrasts, nevertheless, the horizons of possibility were set in place a good while ago, the modes of racial governance and the orders of racist exclusion, humiliation and death deeply rooted in the sorts of disposition, social and personal, to which coloniality gave rise.

Today this may tell us only half the story, the half captured by the clichéd phrase 'We are here because you were there.' The 'here' now, especially across urban localities almost everywhere – not least in the global north – is composed in part by the presence of the 'there' in it, whether 'you were there' or not. The often denied or resisted hetero-geneities making up the urban embody the connectivities to elsewheres and other times, the local also constituted anew by the distant in place and time. 'Home' is reinvented in the complex and morphing relations between the familiar and the strange, the local and the distant, the here and the there (Simone 2008).

So comparativism alone can tell us little about contemporary racial Europeanization, little, for instance, about what has brought about the indignities which Europe's contemporary peoples of color – those peoples once thought to have no history – continue to suffer (through). Why are Europe's peoples of color so readily reduced in imagination, if not by explicit reference (though that, too), to 'non-Europeans?' Why do Europe's supposedly 'non-Europeans' continue to be so readily discriminated against in the employment and housing markets, and why are they so relatively absent from its institutions of higher learning – as students, faculty and staff? Perhaps the quickest and most direct way to make such connections is to point out that a people thought historically to have no history come to have thrust upon them, relationally, a history only racial fabrication can shape.

The challenge, then, is to trace the intercoursing connectivities of the ethnoracial (Goldberg 1993) across their geographies and temporalities. It is to comprehend their complexities, the possibilities and challenges, the convivialities but also the dangers and violence that heterogeneous socialities conjure and condition. And it is to sense the prompts and implications, fabrics and effects, fragilities and ambiguities that the transnational networks' ethnoracialities have long conceived and created.

I do not mean by all of this, either, to romanticize relationality, to cloak its constitutively deep historicity in an inevitable teleology of presumptive sameness. The substantive knowledge which I am suggesting relationality, as a method, is concerned to produce will not be the same across different points or streams of connection, between different histories or their space-time *loci*. That the abstract methodological form of relationality – its logic – may be common across cases (that is what method amounts to) does not entail that this is an instance of what Paul Gilroy (1997), in a different theoretical context, has called the 'changing same'. From the fact that the form of knowledge formation is common, it does not follow that the substantive knowledge thus produced must be so too. Knowledge, all knowledge, is a product of form and content, as Kant made so clear.

Comparison without relationality, then, inevitably falls short, hypostatizes, sets the analytic horizons close to the vest. A comparativity open to relational extension, in effect, is a different mode of comparativity. Relationality reveals, pulls productively together, connects prompting and causal conditions across otherwise seemingly discrete instances, offers an explanatory account where otherwise there is likely none. Race critical theory thus calls for a more complexly nuanced relationality as its method. The challenge is to place the method in play, in a methodological and theoretical practice at once self-conscious and systematic.

REFERENCES

Agamben, G. (2002). *Remnants of Auschwitz: The Witness and the Archive*. Cambridge, MA: Zone Books/MIT Press.

Carter, J. (2006). *Palestine, Peace Not Apartheid*. New York: Simon and Schuster.

Cell, J. (1982). *The Highest Stage of White Supremacy: The Origins of Segregation in South Africa and the American South*. Cambridge: Cambridge University Press.

Cohn, B. (1996). *Colonialism and Its Forms of Knowledge: The British in India*. Princeton, NJ: Princeton University Press.

Davis, U. (2004). *Apartheid Israel: Possibilities for the Struggle Within*. London: Zed Books.

Degler, C. (1971). *Neither Black nor White: Slavery and Race Relations in the United States and Brazil*. New York: Prentice Hall.

Descartes, R. (1637). *The Discourse on Method*. http://records.viu.ca/~johnstoi/descartes/descartes1.htm.

Dikötter, F. (2008). The racialization of the globe: an interactive interpretation. *Ethnic and Racial Studies*, 31(8), 1478–96.

Gilroy, P. (1997). Diaspora and the detours of identity. In K. Woodward, ed., *Identity and Difference*. London: Sage, pp. 299–346.

(2000). *Against Race: Imagining Political Culture beyond the Colour Line*. Cambridge, MA: The Belknap Press.

Glaser, D. (2003). Zionism and apartheid: a moral comparison. *Ethnic and Racial Studies*, 26(3), 403–21.

Goldberg, D. T. (1993). *Racist Culture: Philosophy and the Politics of Meaning*. Oxford: Basil Blackwell.

(2009). *The Threat of Race: Reflections on Racial Neoliberalism*. Oxford: Wiley-Blackwell.

Marx, A. (1998). *Making Race and Nation: A Comparison of the United States, South Africa and Brazil*. Cambridge: Cambridge University Press.

Massey, D. and Denton, N. (1998). *American Apartheid: Segregation and the Making of the Underclass*. Cambridge, MA: Harvard University Press.

Simone, A. (2008). Emergency democracy and the 'governing composite'. *Social Text*, 26(2), 13–33.

Spivak, G. C. (2003). *Death of a Discipline*. New York: Columbia University Press.

Stoler, A. (2002). *Carnal Knowledge and Imperial Power: Race and the Intimate in Colonial Rule*. Berkeley: University of California Press.

(2006). *Haunted by Empire: Geographies of Empire in North American History*. Durham, NC: Duke University Press.

Twine, F. W. and Gallagher, C. A., eds. (2008). Special issue on whiteness and white identities. *Ethnic and Racial Studies*, 31(1).

Van Den Berghe, P. (1967). *Race and Racism: A Comparative Perspective*. New York: John Wiley.

15   Conclusion: back to the future

Karim Murji and John Solomos

This book opens with a discussion of race and racism in a new genomic era and concludes with a debate about method in the study of ethnicity and race. In between these two poles, the chapters in this volume have examined ethnicity, race, post-race and racism across a range of national contexts, chiefly the USA but also France and the United Kingdom. The coverage in this volume – such as mixed-race identities, critical race feminism and intersectionality, sexualities, psychoanalytical and performativity perspectives, critical rationalism and critical whiteness studies – offers an insight into the extent and variety of lively debates and investigations in contemporary race theorising and research. This summary reflects the organisation of this book around a range of contemporary debates and perspectives. Although no book can provide a comprehensive global outlook on the wide and expanding scope of debates and perspectives in which ethnicity, race and racism are key issues, the array of views in this book is intended to highlight a number of key questions in their study. Collectively, the chapters underscore one of these: the extent to which there is recurring and continuing debate about what race is and whether it can, or should, be transcended. This is a theme reflected across both parts of this book. Looked at as a whole, the chapters specify the multiple, sequential and contradictory processes at play in contemporary social science approaches to race.

A brief run-through of one key issue illustrates the complex and contradictory elements that permeate current race debates. At one level, there are critiques of the reification and essentialisation of race; this is most commonly attributed to biology but also occurs in social science analyses. However, the social constructionist alternative to essentialism is challenged on the grounds that it ignores the need for measures to advance political and social justice, which, it is argued, requires race categories (Krieger 2010). While social scientists are critical of folk and science versions of race, they are themselves accused of holding on to race in quasi-essentialist ways (Daynes and Lee 2008). At the same time, arguments drawing on 'machinic' (Saldanha 2006), phenomenological

(Monahan 2011) and sociohistoric and biological perspectives (Halady 2011) assert the reality of race in different ways. The authors in this volume cover the use of performative approaches (Tate) as well as the expanding field of mixed-race studies (Song) and genomics (Lee), and debates following critical race theory (Wing) and critical whiteness studies (Hughey, Fassin) explore the fluidity and stretch of racial ideas and formations, while others criticise the overreach of the race concept in research (Banton). Critiques of post-race arguments (Bonilla-Silva and Ray, Gallagher, St Louis; see also Meer and Nayak 2013) criticise colour-blind perspectives that fail to grasp the extent and depth of racism, which some post-race views overlook or are intended to erase.

From race relations to racialisation

Rather than reviewing this book's contents chronologically, given the range of perspectives and arguments that it covers, this concluding chapter takes up the question of race again. To set this in context, we return to a book that appeared nearly 30 years ago (Rex and Mason 1986), as we discussed in the introduction. Some of the continuities, but also the contrast between that book and this one, will be evident to anyone who just glances at their respective contents pages. The reason for referring back to Rex and Mason now is that, in the period in which their volume appeared, it was common to refer to a field called 'the sociology of race relations'. In the 1980s and before, race relations was a term that appeared in everyday language, in Britain at least. It was the term used in two landmark pieces of anti-discrimination legislation passed in the 1960s and 1970s and their updating in 2000 as the *Race Relations Amendment Act*. Yet race relations now rarely appears as an idea or a phrase with which to capture and explain 'relations between races' or as an expression employed in policy and legislation, in the social sciences or in the humanities. In U.K. legislation, at least, this may be due to the thinking that informed the 2010 *Equality Act*, which brought together the various strands of anti-discrimination legislation – race, gender, disability, age and so on – into a common framework, and the intersectional approaches to inequalities which informed it. In the European Union (EU), the *Racial Equality Directive* of 2000 was also informed by an intersectional approach and a concern with 'mainstreaming' equality and anti-racism and, latterly, human rights (Bell 2008).

Perhaps, more than that, race relations sounds anachronistic and has been replaced by more familiar terms such as multiculturalism (or inter-culturalism; see Meer and Modood 2012) in U.K. or EU policy in the past decade, and in debates about integration and community cohesion. Other terms and words – *incorporation, assimilation, citizenship* and *belonging* (Faist 2009; Kyriakides 2008), as well as *superdiversity* (Vertovec 2007) – float about in the same cloud, making the boundaries of what is and what is not race-specific challenging. Despite some changes in language, some of these words and the policies associated with them have connotations that look rather like race-relations policy in the 1970s and 1980s which made 'minority' communities into social problems and placed the emphasis on them to integrate into the 'majority', 'indigenous' or 'national' culture (Rattansi 2011). At the same time, continuing arguments for and about addressing inequalities and their economic, social and cultural underpinnings, encompassing but also going beyond traditional social class–based arguments, as well as developments in intersectional theorising, further call into question the extent to which race serves as a marker of identities and exclusions; significantly, much of this predates current 'post-race' debates.

With regard to scholarly debates, one of the main drivers in the academic field was the shift that informed the critique of race relations. Robert Miles was a significant figure in this, and his main approach is summed up in his book *Racism after 'Race' Relations* (Miles 1993), which also bookended the key arguments he made in the 1980s. Miles developed an important political economy of race in the United Kingdom in reaction to the sociology of race relations as derived from the USA and as it developed in the United Kingdom through the analyses of John Rex and Michael Banton. Rex's (1970) Weberian approach led him to make an argument for 'race-relations situations' occurring in conditions of structural conflict and discrimination. Banton (1967) offered a historical and comparative framework of race relations. These approaches have been widely debated and criticised, not least by Miles (1993) (for a defence of his view, see Rex and Mason 1986; for an acknowledgement of the critique, see Banton 1991; for continuing criticisms of the race-relations paradigm and the view that it obscures racial inequalities, see Steinberg 2007).

A key part of Miles's approach was the argument that the term *race* in *race relations* could not serve as an analytical category; indeed, it actually obscures the important task of analysing racism. Race, he argued, is fundamentally ideological; it is not founded on or based in science. It is the process of racialisation through which ideas about race are made. Miles's influential proposition was that the reason *why* some differences are coded as race lies in social structures and relations of domination and subordination. Race is a historically and politically contingent construction that has changing meanings over time:

The visibility of somatic characteristics is not inherent in the characteristics themselves, but arises from a process of signification by which meaning is attributed to
certain of them. In other words, visibility is socially constructed in a wider set of
structural constraints, within a set of relations of domination. (Miles 1993: 87)

For Miles, considerations of racial difference are linked to the distinction
between the outer, observable differences between people – or phenotype – and the underlying genetic inheritance, or genotype. The idea of
race does correspond in some way to phenotypical differences among
human populations, though the relationship between them is open to
variation and not clear-cut. There may be any number of phenotypical differences between groups – for example, hair colour, facial features,
body size. Because these are not necessarily coded as 'racial' differences, it
is clear that phenotypical differences are not inevitably equated with race.
They are, as Jenkins summarises, 'different orders of things . . . phenotype
is the material product of the interaction of genetic endowment (genotype) and environment, "race" is a cultural fiction' (Jenkins 1997: 78).
In other words, race differences are not located in nature, and race is
not the same as observable visible differences between peoples, because
there are any number of clear differences; only some are seen to count
as race. In recognising the critique of race relations, Banton (1991: 117)
made the point in this way: 'People do not perceive racial differences.
They perceive phenotypical differences of colour, hair form, underlying bone structures and so on. Phenotypical differences are a first order
abstraction, race is a second order abstraction.'

Beyond the prominent black–white dichotomy framing race, particular
and diverse groups have come to be named as 'racial' in various national
and regional contents, such as China (Dikötter 1992), Latin America
(Hanchard 1999; Wade 1997) and Eastern Europe (Boatca 2007; Turda
2007) as well as socialist/communist nations (Law 2012). Indeed, Bourdieu and Wacquant's (1999) excoriating view of the dominant and dis-
maying effect of the U.S. sociology of race relations in framing race in
the social sciences along black and white lines is based on what they
saw as the lack of recognition in the U.S. academy of such diversity in
racial formations and schemas (though, for various critical responses to
Bourdieu and Wacquant, see subsequent issues of *Theory, Culture and
Society*). Indeed, Miles's critique of race relations was also that it treated
the black–white dichotomy as defining the subject of race, and it did not
recognise the ways in which Jews, Irish and Poles, among others, had
been racialised in Europe (Kay and Miles 1992; Miles and Brown 2003).

Miles's perspective combined Marxist political economy with social
constructionism in ways that have not always sat comfortably together

(Virdee 2010). The constructionist element led him to argue that race should always be written as 'race' to signal its problematic status. For some years, and to this day to an extent, this became something of an orthodoxy in academic writing. It is reflected in the titles of books such as *'Race' in Britain Today* (Skellington 1996), *'Race', Ethnicity and Difference* (Ratcliffe 2004) and *Researching 'Race' and Ethnicity* (Gunaratnam 2003), among many other publications. Whether referring to race in this way is still needed is a matter that seems to be more of an issue in Britain than in North America or mainland Europe. The exact purpose of the quotation marks around race is still sometimes debated, particularly in teaching. The case for the use of the scare marks around race in those books is usually based on Miles's proposition that it places 'under erasure' (though that is not a term that Miles uses) any biological basis for race. Thus, 'race', so used, in the social sciences signifies a term that has been tainted by its roots in biology and disavowed and discredited in the twentieth century. The critique of racial constructs, particularly in biology, is a key object of these arguments, which maintain that race is not real but invented by science and reproduced through processes of racialisation.

Scientific method – particularly the observation and classification of regularities – is, indeed, itself fundamental to the schemas and hierarchies of racial typologies. As a means for ordering human populations, racial knowledge acquires its apparent authority from science; indeed, there is an intimate inter-relationship between them, as Goldberg maintains: 'Race has been a basic categorical object, in some cases a founding focus of scientific analysis' (Goldberg 1997: 28). However, neither Goldberg nor Glasgow (2009), in a more recent argument for freeing race of any biological associations, speak of race in quotation marks, even though the latter comments that 'when I first mention to civilian friends and students that many academics think race is nothing but an apparition, one common reaction is incredulity' (4); he adds that this 'departure from conventional wisdom . . . might make academics appear to be unglued from the real world'. Yet, developments in science, especially the Human Genome Project and genomics, as well as the question of the relationship between nature and society, and human and non-human worlds (Latour 1993), have altered – at the very least – or, perhaps, transformed the landscape and the context in which these issues are considered.

Race, biology and social constructionism

Investigations under the banner of science have produced a multitude of racial classifications, ranging from 3 to 10 to 30 categories in which human beings are sub-divided according to definable physical characteristics (Blackburn 2000; Stepan 1982). Though the content of racial schemas has varied, the modes of classification have been more consistent, as Whitmarsh and Jones (2010) point out. The variability of the classes demarcated, and of the phenotypical characteristics used to denote race, signals its basis in historical and social processes rather than unvarying rules of biology (Omi and Winant 1994). However, though the variability and inconsistency of these schemes can be regarded as self-evidently undermining the idea of race, the ability of racial classification 'to integrate divergent, sometimes contradictory contents . . . has been foundational to its extensive scientific and medical use' (Whitmarsh and Jones 2010: 4). Or, to approach this another way, the relationship between what is regarded as fixed (in nature) and what is regarded as variable (in the social) is itself paradoxical, as Wade (2002: 14) indicates:

> Racial ideas do make reference to human biology, nature and phenotype but those ideas do not always straightforwardly invoke fixity or permanence. This means that what may appear to be a discourse of fixity may actually allow a measure of malleability and change, but it also means that a discourse of malleability can acquire meanings of permanence.

Wade (2002, 2010) is among those race scholars who take seriously Latour's (1993) important and influential critique – arguably insufficiently acknowledged within race and ethnicity studies – of the way in which modernity and the social sciences drew sharp distinction between 'nature' and 'society' or culture. Despite this, the natural and cultural realms have always interlocked and shaped one another in ways which involve, as Wade says, the naturalisation of culture and the culturalisation of nature. In regard to race, it indicates that 'the whole apparatus of race (racial categorizations, racial concepts, racisms) has always been as much about culture as it has about nature, that race has always been about shifting between these two domains' (Wade 2010: 45; see also Monahan 2011: Chapter 3). Influential as the analysis of and for the 'new racism' was (Barker 1981), it is commonly read as suggesting that the use of culture-difference arguments was a new – rather than a revived – component of racism.

In the last decades of the twentieth century, differences in sporting ability and achievements in intelligence tests became two of the most prominent interfaces where academic and popular conceptions of race differences were raised and contested. In that period, there was, on one hand, the well-known and controversial view around *The Bell Curve*, in which Herrnstein and Murray (1994) argued that disparities in intelligence scores between blacks and whites were due to a combination of environment and genetics. On the other hand, in relation to different sporting abilities or, rather, the superior achievements of some black athletes, Entine (2000) dismissed as 'political correctness' any denial of what he takes to be self-evident: that black people are better equipped, physiologically and genetically, to excel at sport. Whatever the changes in representations of race in media and cultural sectors, these formulations seemed to return race to a base level rooted in physiology and genetics.

However, in the period since the last decade of the twentieth century, health, law and genealogy – through the use of specific drugs for particular populations, the forensic uses of DNA and its role in genealogy tracing – have come to the fore in ways which combine and cut across divisions of commerce and governance (Whitmarsh and Jones 2010). Commerce around race-specific items has advanced beyond the cultural consumption of designer goods that cultural studies scholars identified (Gilroy 2000) and on to 'designer' drugs. The best-known of these is still BiDil (Kahn 2013), a combination of two existing medicines for treating heart failure which has received support, following a clinical trial, from a range of black groups in the USA. It became the first medical product to be approved in the USA specifically for a particular racial or ethnic group, African Americans. Despite criticisms, the trade in race-specific products moves on – from particular vitamins to jogging shoes and more common uses in popular genealogy and ancestry. All of these signal a part of the ways in which 'the relevance of race as a social, legal and medical category has been reinvigorated by science, especially genetics' (Whitmarsh and Jones 2010: 2). Less than a decade after Craig Venter, one of the key mappers of the Human Genome Project, announced, in 2000, that 'what we've shown is that the concept of race has no scientific basis . . . racial research has remerged and proliferated to occupy scientific concerns to an extent unseen since early twentieth-century eugenics' (cited in Bliss 2012: 2).

Social scientists have analysed and criticised these developments as a 'molecular reinscription' (Ossorio and Duster 2005) of race, as 're-biologisation' (Kahn 2013), as race science (Whitmarsh and Jones 2010) or as a further stage in scientific racism (Carter 2007). The extent to which race science is marked by greater continuity with or change from the past is open to debate, as these sources indicate. There is, though, some agreement that the forms of race science in a genomic age mark a new and significant frontier in racial formations (Lee, this volume). Despite claims that they can be understood and explained within the templates of social science critiques of racial science, we suggest that debates about the 'reality' of race occur in a different space from the blood-and-bones discourses established in the nineteenth century and continued, in some form, in twentieth-century arguments around differential sports and educational attainment, to a sub-molecular level that introduces new elements and complexities. While the ways in which scientists understand and justify their work do not have to be taken at face value, research on their practices does bring out a picture that takes us well beyond claims about scientific racism as a means of understanding the values and assumptions of scientists themselves. In passing, it is worthy of note that, while the discussion focuses on science, disciplines other than the sciences, such as philosophy, have also played a significant role in constructing race (Bhatt 2010; Goldberg 1993) in ways which, like science, have seemingly clarified while simultaneously mystifying the meanings of race and informed racist ideologies.

The research on the practices and attitudes of scientists that we referred to earlier come up with quite distinct views of what race science means and entails in the early twenty-first century. On one hand, Bliss's (2012) work presents a view of scientists staking a claim for focusing on race through social justice arguments. While it would be naïve to accept this as merely good – even some racial scientists of the past claimed to be working in the public interest to improve the general status of populations – they do mark a departure from the stark exclusionary logic of eugenics and scientific racism (Barkan 1992) and the claim of fixed characteristics and innate hierarchies propounded in various racial typologies. However, those who see more continuity with the past have to take into account that the modalities of the production of racial difference have altered and now use equality arguments drawn from claims for inclusion rather than exclusion (Bliss 2012; Epstein 2007). Hence, Bliss (2012: 15) argues,

It is time to rethink the character, aims, and implications of scientific knowledge. Formerly, scientists used biological inquiry into race to naturalize social difference in essential biological difference . . . Biology was used to obscure social explanations for race. By contrast, contemporary inquiry into race begins with the concept of social disparities and hierarchies and explores biological differences in order to correct those disparities. Instead of arguing that racial difference is impervious to social reform, scientists are expanding the definition of biology to include social actors, using their position to draw attention to inequalities; and applying scientific tools to create social change.

Catherine Bliss argues that seeing racial science as racist and as a form of biological essentialism is to miss the nuances of contemporary genomic research. She uses the term *anti-racist racialism* to refer to an 'idea that there is no rank to races but that there are nevertheless discrete populations worth studying' (Bliss 2012: 15). Instead of the post-race retreat from race – criticised by several contributors to this volume – she suggests that an anti-racist post-racialism, underlined by genomics, may become the framework for addressing racial disparities.

In contrast, Outram and Ellison (2010) provide a different view of scientific practice. They argue that scientists selectively engage with arguments about the use of racialised categories. Unlike Bliss's interviews with scientists, their perspective is based on a systematic citation-based literature search. They identified 335 papers which discussed the question of and issues about the use of racialised categories in biomedical research. Given the foundation of some of these categories in scientific racism and various racial typologies from the eighteenth century, it would be reasonable, as they state, to assume that 'geneticists and biomedical researchers would be only too pleased to abandon racialized categories' (Outram and Ellison 2010: 110). Asking why that is not the case and whether the use of everyday racial categories in research is a source of concern leading to the reproduction of conventional ideas about race is their starting point. Their thematic analysis found five main arguments against using racialised categories at all: that there is genetic variation within all racialised groups; that only a small amount of variation bunches within racialised groups; that there are no pure populations; that variations in phenotype do not necessarily mean underlying genotypic variations; and that the use of the terms and categories tends to reify and essentialise them. As for the use of racialised categories in biomedical research, their review confirms a lack of agreement about the definition of any of the categories. It also highlights concerns about the ways in which the use of racial categories may erroneously infer genetic causality and lead to inappropriate and stigmatising services to particular groups.

Scientists – despite their awareness of the extensive criticisms of the use of racialised categories – are, Outram and Ellison (2010) suggest, involved in a process of 'selective engagement' which enables them to square the circle of recognising the criticisms made while also maintaining the value of using the categories. This selective engagement includes the use of a wide range of racialised categories which remain largely unclear and unspecified, making them 'unexamined, common sense entities, sustained without critical examination by their frequent appearance in the genetic and biomedical literature' (Outram and Ellison 2010: 111). Furthermore, they argue that scientists' lack of attention to the conceptual basis for using racialised categories produces a self-perpetuating and self-referential framework in which the use of those categories makes it difficult to interpret disparities in health, for example, as anything other than genetically based. Consequently, the preoccupation with genetic causes narrows down the diagnostic and treatment options for racialised groups. Despite this critique, instead of an either–or approach which treats racialised categories as sociopolitical or biogenetic constructs, Outram and Ellison (2010) argue for a biosocial or bi-cultural approach that crosses over the natural and social sciences and the scientific and sociopolitical arenas (see also Malik 2008). From this perspective, they argue, racialised categories may be important for understanding and addressing the causes and consequences of disparities and injustices within racialised formations.

There are a number of parallels to this 'pragmatic' approach to race and racialised categories, arising from the unexpected and unpredictable consequences of arguments for and against using race classifications for policy purposes, social and biomedical research and equality claims (Epstein 2007; Krieger 2010). Goldberg (1997), for instance, argued that, for all the racialised power-knowledge behind their construction and application in the U.S. Census, the use of such categories remained a significant basis for the measurement of racial inequalities and any assessment of their change. Krieger (2010) criticised Proposition 54 in the state of California – an attempt to remove the use of racialised categories altogether – on the basis that it was motivated by a 'no data no problem' outlook in which not taking account of race would make racial disparities disappear from view, at least officially. Glasgow (2009) calls arguments to stop counting by race a form of 'political eliminativism', which he mentions alongside 'public eliminativism' and 'global racial eliminativism'. The contention that race could or should be made to disappear by not using the word or the idea comes in both radical and conservative guises; a common thread between them is that 'race talk' is both misleading and damaging for people so racialised, because the appeal to racism breeds a victim culture (D'Souza 1995) or narrows identity politics into singular and exclusive forms (Gilroy 2000). As the chapters in this volume by Bonilla-Silva and Ray and by Gallagher maintain (see also St Louis, this volume), a colour-blind or race-neutral view that informs post-race arguments shares some of this outlook. For others, the language of race is so corrupted by its antecedents and its folk uses that social scientists should adopt a different vocabulary to avoid the problem of contamination and misunderstanding (see Banton, this volume; Glasgow 2009).

Racial reality/unreality

The biosocial or biocultural approach that Outram and Ellison (2010) advocate calls for a changed understanding of the relationship between the natural and the social sciences. Its implications for race theorising go well beyond the social-constructionist critique of race as a term and a category to be placed under erasure. Beyond the either–or genetic or

sociopolitical models and explanations of, for instance, health disparities, the emerging field of epigenetics – itself as development beyond
genomics – provides a view that straddles both 'nature' and 'culture'.

While the genome is inherited and does not change, except for mutations, the epigenome is the result of the genome interacting with the
environment, thus showing how the social environment can become
embodied as a biological and developmental pattern trans-generationally
(Kuzawa and Sweet 2009). Taking the case of black–white disparities
in cardiovascular disease, the authors assess the link between that and
the greater incidence of premature and low-birth-weight births among
African American mothers. They suggest that the impact of this has consequences for developmental pathways which continue into adulthood
and across generations. While some culturalist approaches may attribute
it to maternal behaviour patterns, they argue that the main predictors of
low birth weights are factors such as racism, discrimination and stress,
which are structural issues beyond individual control; this, therefore, calls
for social and economic changes.

On one level, these developments and debates across the natural and
social sciences call for a more detailed understanding of the relationship
between 'natural' and 'social' realities. Social scientists arguing that race
is not real because it is not founded in biology clearly cede too much
ground to natural science as a basis for determining what *is* real. Social
science understandings of biology can veer between blank dismissal and
naïve acceptance. In the former case, social science perspectives in relation to the natural sciences can look like a kind of 'turf war in which social
scientists claim to have superior racial optics and measures' (Bliss 2012:
204). In a similar vein, Monahan (2011) regards such social science takes
on biology as relying on positivist and essentialist views of science. Social
science arguments for avoiding any reference to or suggestion of biology
in race maintain that to do so smacks of essentialism, a view which takes
limited or no account of the essentialisms in and across social science
perspectives of race (see also Sayer 1997). As Brett St Louis signals in his
chapter in this book, social scientists seem as unwilling as anyone to give
up on race, whether for progressive or for other reasons. Indeed, Daynes
and Lee (2008) go as far as to attribute this 'desire for race' to a psychic
fixation (for a different approach to the psychosocial, see Clarke, this
volume), where, for all their critiques of essentialism, social scientists of
all theoretical hues are unable to abandon race. In any case, as we have
seen, the grounds of biology are changing in ways that cross over into
sociopolitical fields (and perhaps they always have; Wade 2002), while
providing resources for an array of commercial and forensic applications
that outstrip the resources of the social sciences. As the controversies

about science, genomic and biomedical research and their uses in health, law and genealogy indicate, the issue of the 'reality' of race is not a matter that looks likely to be settled soon

It is, perhaps, arguable that it is the 'real' rather than race that should be placed in quotation marks as the key problematic term in relation to the wide and numerous debates about the ontology of race. Argument for 'race' in quotation marks can include the claim that the word needs to be demarcated so that other people know that 'we' are not treating race as real; this implies a 'they' who still believe the commonsense view that it must be biologically based. Imputing positions to an undifferentiated 'other' is an oddly orientalising move from socially progressive social scientists. A corresponding view that failing to put race in quotation marks means that it must be being treated as real fails to address what kind of social reality it may have, as well as implying that race could only be 'real' if it had some basis in nature.

Glasgow (2009) partially clarifies the discussion of natural and social realities through his distinction between realism and anti-realism. While he personally takes the anti-realist view, following Appiah (1996) and Zack (2002) (but see Monahan 2011 for a critique), for now the issue is the distinction he draws between two forms of realism – biological realism and constructivism. The latter broadly refers to a view that something like race may be real because of its social construction through the 'sociohistorical relations that have been produced by widespread, significant and long-standing race based practices' (Glasgow 2009: 114), rather than having any biological foundation. As Glasgow indicates, this is a view that has a wide purchase, particularly in the USA, among scholars such as Outlaw (1996) and Mitchell (2012). However, drawing on Du Bois's view that race involves both a 'badge of colour' and a set of sociohistorical relations, Glasgow argues that, because constructivists usually tie racial identifiers and race-making processes to physical differences, they continue to refer to race as a visible physical feature. While his own anti-realist perspective can accept that there are real social kinds, Glasgow maintains that race is not one of those things because, while race is not biologically real, constructivist arguments are unable to show that they can advance a notion of race that has no referent linked to biology (Glasgow 2009; for a critique, see Halady 2011).

As previously indicated, the concept of racialisation, particularly the process of signification in relations of domination, was for Miles (1993) a way of understanding the processes through which race making and identification occurred. His own work on the 1905 *Aliens Act* and the response to Jews fleeing the pogroms in Eastern Europe (Miles and Brown 2003) and the European voluntary workers scheme following the

Second World War (Kay and Miles 1992) were intended to show how Jewish and white communities were racialised selectively, in ways which drew on and combined elements of biological and cultural separateness. Like his view on 'race', Miles's (1993) approach to racialisation has been influential and widely used. But whether it achieved the intended break with race is questionable; analyses drawing on racialisation are not always clear on whether or in what ways race, in the more specific sense which Miles intended, is being invoked in discourse or, to put it the other way, what makes something 'racial' (see Murji and Solomos 2005). In a recent interview, Miles himself has reflected on these issues in these terms: 'The concept of racialization presumes that there is a product of the process of racialization. I resist talking about the concept of "race" . . . and I try consistently to talk about the ideas of "race."' Miles's distinction between a concept and an idea enables him to accept that 'there is an idea of "race" that is a historical reality'; the concept of racialisation seeks to 'explain the origin, development and use of that idea' (in Ashe and McGeever 2011: 2018).

Miles's stress on processes of race making is important (see also Omi and Winant 1994) and broadly equivalent to Blum's (2002) argument that talking in terms of racialised groups, rather than of race, is preferable because the former designates a social kind without inherent characteristics, unlike the link to biology that race contains. Speaking in terms of racialised groups is preferable to suggesting that there are races. However, it does not quite address the difficulty to which Outram and Ellison (2010) pointed, namely, that racialised categories and terms are used selectively; in practice this means that the processes of race making are overlooked or not referenced. Consequently, analyses and explanations produced in biomedicine tend to speak in terms of race-based explanations of, for example, variations in health and illness, which reaffirms a biologically real basis for race as an explanatory category that fails to address Banton's (1991) long-standing plea for a clear distinction between an *explanandum* and *explanans*.

In calling Blum's (2002) argument 'substitutionism', Glasgow (2009) instead proposes what he calls 'reconstructionism'. This entails a conception that race (or, rather, race*, he suggests) can be used as long as it is free from any biological association. As Mitchell (2012) suggests, race with an asterisk (race*) is presumably unlikely to be adopted widely in everyday use. Although Mitchell does not say so, in this sense, race in quotation marks ('race') has been more widely adopted in Britain – though much less in the USA – among scholarly communities and, to a lesser extent, in some policy fields. However, demarcating race in this way takes us back full circle to the issue of the boundaries and cross-over between biological and social realities and the natural and social sciences. In any case, Mitchell argues for a view that retains the links between race and elements of genealogy and 'bloodlines'. These, like other ancestral linkages, would fail Glasgow's (2009) test because of their biological roots. Despite the link to bloodlines and biology, Mitchell's main argument seeks to steer a course between the options of treating race as either real or unreal. Rather, drawing on psychoanalytical theories, he argues that race is both phantasy and reality (cf. Clarke, this volume; Daynes and Lee 2008), rather than natural or cultural. Race, he argues, is a medium we see *through*, rather than *with*. It is 'an intervening substance . . . something we see through . . . a repertoire of cognitive and conceptual filters through which forms of human otherness are mediated' (Mitchell 2012: xii).

In various guises, others take a stronger stance against racial eliminativism in asserting the reality of race as distinct from racialised ideas and discourse. Halady (2011), for instance, seeks to make a case for the reality of race which combines biological and social construction. A different approach, in which race is a real kind, comes from a Deleuzian-derived attempt to 'reontologise' race. In contesting the predominant discursive and cultural approaches to race in the social sciences, Saldanha (2006) makes the case for an embodied materiality of race based on the 'viscosity of bodies'. Other approaches which draw on a materiality perspective do not necessarily insist on the reality of race, though they do share Saldanha's view that materiality provides a means beyond treating nature–culture as a duality and that this duality is an alternative to social constructionism (Papadopoulos and Sharma 2008; Sharma 2012).

Conclusion

Although developments in social theory, biomedicine and genomics and commerce and governance have profoundly altered the landscape in which we consider the issues of ethnicity and race, some of the questions they raise are perennial ones in the field. Chief among these are the problems of what race is biologically or socially, its real or other status, and the frameworks within which race in contemporary societies can be analysed and explained. Hence, in this concluding chapter, we have returned to some quite-well-established themes in the field of race and ethnic studies, particularly the question of what is meant by race and how we should discuss it. We have updated the discussion through the lens of science, biology and genomics and pointed out that the social-constructionist tradition – which, in various guises, has been influential and dominant for several decades – has been challenged from numerous directions in the past decade. These include the rapid developments in genomics and epigenetics, psychosocial and biocultural approaches and materiality which criticise the sharp division or dualisms between nature and culture, on which some social science perspectives on race have relied for some time. Some share the view that the reality or unreality of race is another unhelpful duality. Alongside the growth of ontological debates about race in recent decades, these views all underscore the extent to which race theorising is a lively and diverse field, with parallel and overlapping debates across and beyond the social sciences. It makes it challenging to integrate all these approaches within any single discipline and raises the question of the extent to which the field of race and ethnic studies can encompass all that goes under the banner of race research. In our view, the state of the field at present is that it combines elements of disciplinary perspectives, alongside a measure of inter- and trans-disciplinarity. The latter is more evident in areas such as diaspora and migration studies, which are concerned with the mobility of populations, though, even then, there are sometimes quite narrow approaches.

While acknowledging the vibrancy of these developments and debates, in closing this volume, we make this final point. Although the ontological arguments are important, as is the relationship between natural and social scientific views on race (and their interconnections), a clearly distinct and significant body of work takes as its focus not what race is per se but, rather, what race *does* and what is done in the name of race. These perspectives point us, at one level, to debates and approaches with feminist and intersectional politics about racial identities, subjectification and the reproduction of racialised formations and inequalities – with which several chapters in this volume engage. These work alongside important arguments about the ways in which race is summoned and mobilised in racist imaginaries that position racialised groups as inferior, other or different – evident in a range of sociological, historical, post-colonial and decolonial scholarship attuned to particular ways in which race is made to matter, sometimes intersectionally. Both historical and contemporary scholarship point to the ways in which race and racism are articulated in specific and wider contexts – for instance, the war on terror and global racisms, debates around slavery and reparations, unequal development and exploitation and the policy and politics of anti-discrimination measures such as affirmative action in the USA or the mainstreaming of race equality and fundamental rights in the EU. At the same time, the focus of these approaches on effects rather than definitions is also reflected in new battleground issues such as the approach of European states to the wearing of head scarves, international migration and the politics of welfare and the ways in which these things have been wrapped in anti-multiculturalist 'xenologies' (Bhatt 2012), all of which highlight the dynamism of racism and social inequalities founded on ethnicity and race. We can also point to Islamophobia, anti-Semitism and whiteness as areas that stress the mobilisation and operation of racial and racist imaginaries. For all the appeal to post-race arguments, these trends and perspectives indicate that ethnicity and race remain fertile issues of scholarship; in turn, such work can only be significant if it draws and speaks to the wider public and political contexts in which race and racism remain live issues and concerns.

REFERENCES

Appiah, K. A. (1996). *Colour Conscious: The Political Morality of Race*. Princeton, NJ: Princeton University Press.

Ashe, S. D. and McGeever, B. F. (2011). Marxism, racism and the construction of 'race' as a social and political relation: an interview with Professor Robert Miles. *Ethnic and Racial Studies*, 34(12), 2009–26.

Banton, M. (1967). *Race Relations*. New York: Basic Books.
  (1991). The race relations problematic. *British Journal of Sociology*, 42(1), 115–30.

Barkan, E. (1992). *The Retreat of Scientific Racism: Changing Concepts of Race in Britain and the United States between the World Wars*. Cambridge: Cambridge University Press.

Barker, M. (1981). *The New Racism*. London: Junction Books.

Bell, M. (2008). *Racism and Equality in the European Union*. Oxford: Oxford University Press.

Bhatt, C. (2010). The spirit lives on: races and disciplines. In P. H. Collins and J. Solomos, eds, *The Sage Handbook of Race and Ethnic Studies*. London: Sage, pp. 90–128.
  (2012). The new xenologies of Europe: civil tensions and mythic pasts. *Journal of Civil Society*, 8(3), 307–26.

Blackburn, D. (2000). Why race is not a biological concept. In B. Lang, ed., *Race and Racism in Theory and Practice*. Lanham, MD: Rowman and Littlefield, pp. 3–26.

Bliss, C. (2012). *Race Decoded: The Genomic Fight for Social Justice*. Stanford, CA: Stanford University Press.

Blum, L. (2002). *'I'm Not a Racist, but . . .': The Moral Quandary of Race*. Ithaca, NY: Cornell University Press.

Boatca, M. (2007). No race to the swift. negotiating racial identity in past and present Eastern Europe. *Human Architecture: Journal of the Sociology of Self-Knowledge*, 5(1), 91–104.

Bourdieu, P. and Wacquant, L. J. D. (1999). On the cunning of imperialist reason. *Theory, Culture and Society*, 16(1), 41–58.

Carter, B. (2007). Genes, genomes and genealogies: the return of scientific racism? *Ethnic and Racial Studies*, 30(4), 546–56.

D'Souza, D. (1995). *The End of Racism*. New York: Free Press.

Daynes, S. and Lee, O. (2008). *Desire for Race*. Cambridge: Cambridge University Press.

Dikötter, F. (1992). *The Discourse of Race in Modern China*. London: Hurst.

Entine, J. (2000). *Taboo: Why Black Athletes Dominate Sport and Why We Are Frightened to Talk about It*. Boston: Public Affairs.

Epstein, S. (2007). *Inclusion: The Politics of Difference in Medical Research*. Chicago: University of Chicago Press.

Faist, T. (2009). Diversity: a new mode of incorporation? *Ethnic and Racial Studies*, 32(1), 171–90.

Gilroy, P. (2000). *Between Camps: Race, Identity and Nationalism at the End of the Colour Line*. London: Allen Lane.

Glasgow, J. (2009). *A Theory of Race*. New York: Routledge.

Goldberg, D. T. (1993). *Racist Culture: Philosophy and the Politics of Meaning*. Oxford: Blackwell.

(1997). *Racial Subjects: Writing on Race in America*. New York: Routledge.

Gunaratnam, Y. (2003). *Researching 'Race' and Ethnicity*. London: Sage.

Halady, S. (2011). *The Reality of Race: Against Racial Eliminativism*. Ann Arbor, MI: Proquest.

Hanchard, M., ed. (1999). *Racial Politics in Contemporary Brazil*. Durham, NC: Duke University Press.

Herrnstein, R. J. and Murray, C. (1994). *The Bell Curve: Intelligence and Class Structure in American Life*. New York: Free Press.

Jenkins, R. (1997). *Rethinking Ethnicity: Arguments and Explorations*. London: Sage.

Kahn, J. (2013). *Race in a Bottle: The Story of BiDil and Racialized Medicine in a Post-Genomic Age*. New York: Columbia University Press.

Kay, D. and Miles, R. (1992). *Refugees or Migrant Workers? European Volunteer Workers in Britain, 1946–1951*. London: Routledge.

Krieger, N. (2010). The science and epidemiology of racism and health: racial/ethnic categories, biological expressions of racism, and the embodiment of inequality – an ecosocial perspective. In I. Whitmarsh and D. S. Jones, eds, *What's the Use of Race?*, pp. 225–58.

Kuzawa, C. and Sweet, E. (2009). Epigenetics and the embodiment of race: developmental origins of US racial disparities in cardiovascular health. *American Journal of Human Biology*, 21(1), 2–15.

Kyriakides, C. (2008). Third way anti-racism: a contextual constructionist approach. *Ethnic and Racial Studies*, 31(3), 592–610.

Latour, B. (1993). *We Have Never Been Modern*. Trans. from the French by Catherine Porter. London: Harvester Wheatsheaf.

Law, I. (2012). *Red Racisms: Racism in Communist and Post-Communist Contexts*. Basingstoke, UK: Palgrave.

Malik, K. (2008). *Strange Fruit: Why Both Sides Are Wrong in the Race Debate*. London: Oneworld.

Meer, N. and Modood, T. (2012). How does interculturalism contrast with multiculturalism? *Journal of Intercultural Studies*, 33(2), 175–96.

Meer, N. and Nayak, A. (2013). Race ends where? Race, racism and contemporary sociology [online]. *Sociology*, no. 2. doi:10.1177/0038038513501943.

Miles, R. (1993). *Racism after 'Race' Relations*. London: Routledge.

Miles, R. and Brown, M. (2003). *Racism*, 2nd edn. London: Routledge.

Mitchell, W. J. T. (2012). *Seeing through Race*. Cambridge, MA: Harvard University Press.

Monahan, M. J. (2011). *The Creolizing Subject: Race, Reason, and the Politics of Purity*. New York: Fordham University Press.

Murji, K. and Solomos, J., eds. (2005). *Racialization: Studies in Theory and Practice*. Oxford: Oxford University Press.

Omi, M. and Winant, H. (1994). *Racial Formation in the United States*, 2nd edn. London: Routledge.

Ossorio, P. and Duster, T. (2005). Race and genetics: controversies in biomedical, behavioral, and forensic sciences. *American Psychologist*, 60(1), 115–28.

Outlaw, L. J. (1996). *On Race and Philosophy*. New York: Routledge.

Outram, S. and Ellison, G. (2010). Arguments against the use of racialized categories as genetic variables in biomedical research: what are they, and why are they being ignored? In I. Whitmarsh and D. S. Jones, eds, *What's the Use of Race?*, pp. 91–124.

Papadopoulos, D. and Sharma, S. (2008). Editorial: race/matter – materialism and the politics of racialization. *darkmatter* 2. www.darkmatter101.org/site/2008/02/23/racematter-materialism-and-the-politics-of-racialization/.

Ratcliffe, P. (2004). *'Race', Ethnicity, and Difference: Imagining the Inclusive Society*. Maidenhead, UK: Open University Press.

Rattansi, A. (2011). *Multiculturalism: A Very Short Introduction*. Oxford: Oxford University Press.

Rex, J. (1970). *Race Relations in Sociological Theory*. London: Weidenfeld and Nicolson.

Rex, J. and Mason, D., eds. (1986). *Theories of Race and Ethnic Relations*. Cambridge: Cambridge University Press.

Saldanha, A. (2006). Reontologising race: the machinic geography of phenotype. *Environment and Planning D: Society and Space*, 24(1), 9–24.

Sayer, A. (1997). Essentialism, social constructionism, and beyond. *The Sociological Review*, 45(3), 453–87.

Sharma, S. (2012). Black twitter? Racial hashtags, networks and contagion. *New Formations*, 78, 46–64.

Skellington, R. (1996). *'Race' in Britain Today*, 2nd edn. London: Sage.

Steinberg, S. (2007). *Race Relations: A Critique*. Stanford, CA: Stanford University Press.

Stepan, N. (1982). *The Idea of Race in Science: Great Britain 1800–1960*. Basingstoke, UK: Macmillan.

Turda, M. (2007). The nation as object: race, blood, and biopolitics in interwar Romania. *Slavic Review*, 66(3), 413–41.

Vertovec, S. (2007). Super-diversity and its implications. *Ethnic and Racial Studies*, 30(6), 1024–54.

Virdee, S. (2010). Racism, class and the dialectics of social transformation. In P. H. Collins and J. Solomos, eds, *The Sage Handbook of Race and Ethnic Studies*. London: Sage, pp. 135–66.

Wade, P. (1997). *Race and Ethnicity in Latin America*. London: Pluto Press.

(2002). *Race, Nature and Culture: An Anthropological Perspective*. London: Pluto Press.

(2010). The presence and absence of race. *Patterns of Prejudice*, 44(1), 43–60.

Whitmarsh, I. and Jones, D. S., eds. (2010). *What's the Use of Race? Modern Governance and the Biology of Difference*. Cambridge, MA: MIT Press.

Zack, N. (2002). *Philosophy of Science and Race*. New York: Routledge.

Index